LATE MEDIEVAL IPSWICH
Trade and Industry

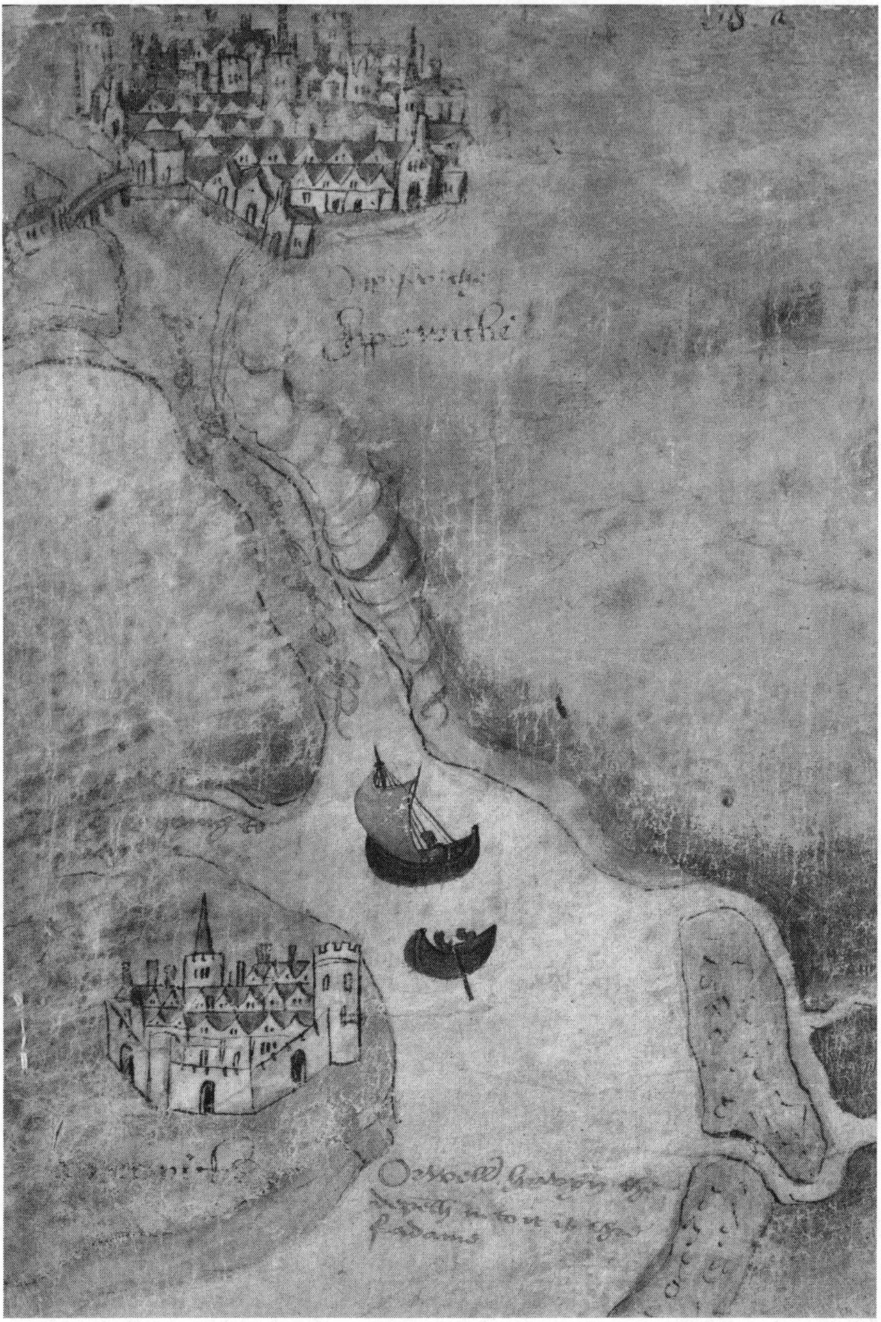

Henry VIII's Survey of the Coast, Yarmouth to Orwell 1539
© British Library Board (Cotton Augustus I.i.58)

LATE MEDIEVAL IPSWICH
Trade and Industry

Nicholas R. Amor

THE BOYDELL PRESS

First published 2011
The Boydell Press, Woodbridge

ISBN 978 1 84383 673 5

The Boydell Press is an imprint of Boydell & Brewer Ltd
PO Box 9, Woodbridge, Suffolk IP12 3DF, UK
and of Boydell & Brewer Inc.
668 Mount Hope Ave, Rochester, NY 14620, USA
website: www.boydellandbrewer.com

A catalogue record for this book is available
from the British Library

Printed and bound by
CPI Group (UK) Ltd, Croydon, CR0 4YY

Contents

List of Illustrations

TABLES

Dedication

To my brave and beautiful daughter Rosalind
and her ever loyal friend Amy

Acknowledgements

This book is the culmination of twenty happy years spent studying late medieval Suffolk. I am deeply indebted to many friends who have offered me assistance and shown me kindness in the various projects that I have undertaken over that time.

Professor Carole Rawcliffe has been a source of constant encouragement to me in writing this volume. Her enthusiasm for history is infectious, and her eye for the best turn of phrase is unmatched. Professor Mark Bailey and David Dymond have been my guides and mentors through all these years. Stumbling across their extra-mural course at the local college changed my life. My parents and my school teacher Ann James had already blessed me with an interest in history, but Mark and David turned this into a serious pursuit. John Blatchly has provided enormous support and shared with me his unrivalled knowledge of Ipswich.

David Allen, Professor Caroline Barron, Helen Bradley, Anthony Breen, James Davies, Rob Liddiard, the late Ray Lock, the late Professor Geoffrey Martin, Charles Moreton of the History of Parliament Trust, Olwen Myhill of the Centre for Metropolitan History, Clive Paine, John Ridgard and Anne Sutton all deserve mention for the assistance that they have given me. The staff of the Suffolk Record Office, both at its Bury St Edmunds and Ipswich offices, and of the Suffolk Archaeology Service have invariably been courteous and helpful.

Outside the world of history, Philip Judge has helped me with the maps, Paul Knights has advised me on the perils of sailing, and Graham Portlock has lent me his professional expertise in taking the photographs shown in Plates 3 to 6. My partners at Gross & Co have encouraged me in my endeavours, and Abby and Mark have held the fort in my absence.

Without the generous support of Caroline Palmer, Rohais Haughton and their colleagues at Boydell & Brewer this volume would never have appeared.

Last, but certainly not least, my family – Julia, Benjamin and Rosalind – have supported me throughout and endured stoically my long absences in the study. It is a great joy that all three of them can now gently tease me about my ‘obsession’ with the Middle Ages.

The Ann Ashard Webb bequest

This volume has been published with the support of the Centre of East Anglian Studies and the School of History of the University of East Anglia, and with the aid of a grant from the Ann Ashard Webb bequest. Ann Ashard Webb (1902–1996) made her bequest to the School with the express purpose of funding an accessible series of works on the history of Suffolk which would appeal to a wide readership. In addition to the main volumes in the series, it is intended to produce a number of more specialised titles, of which *Late Medieval Ipswich* is one. Others which have already appeared with support from the bequest are:

JUDITH MIDDLETON-STEWART *Inward Purity and Outward Splendour: Death and Remembrance in the Deanery of Dunwich, Suffolk, 1370–1547*

CHRISTOPHER HARPER-BILL, CAROLE RAWCLIFFE, R. G. WILSON (eds) *East Anglia's History: Studies in Honour of Norman Scarfe*

CHRISTOPHER HARPER-BILL (ed.) *Medieval East Anglia*

DAVID BUTCHER *Lowestoft, 1550–1750: Development and Change in a Suffolk Coastal Town*

MARK BAILEY *Medieval Suffolk: An Economic and Social History, 1200–1500*

RICHARD HOGGETT *The Archaeology of the East Anglian Conversion*

LUCY MARTEN *Late Anglo-Saxon Suffolk* (forthcoming)

Abbreviations

Annals	*The Annals of Ipswiche ... by Nathaniel Bacon serving as Recorder and Town Clerk ... 1654*
BL	British Library
CChR	*Calendar of Charter Rolls*
CCR	*Calendar of Close Rolls*
CFR	*Calendar of Fine Rolls*
CPR	*Calendar of Patent Rolls*
CUH	*The Cambridge Urban History of Britain: Volume I 600–1540*
Econ. Hist. Rev.	*Economic History Review*
HoP	*The History of Parliament: The House of Commons 1386–1421*
NCC	Norwich Consistory Court
NRO	Norfolk Record Office, Norwich
NRS	The Norfolk Records Society
PCC	Prerogative Court of Canterbury
PRO	Public Record Office, London (The National Archives)
PSIA	*Proceedings of the Suffolk Institute of Archaeology and History*
Rot. Parl.	*Rotuli Parliamentorum ut et Petiones et Placita in Parliamento*
SROB	Suffolk Record Office, Bury St Edmunds
SROI	Suffolk Record Office, Ipswich
SRS	The Suffolk Records Society
TRHS	*Transactions of the Royal Historical Society*

Introduction

This history of Ipswich examines the fortunes of the town in the late Middle Ages, and in particular the fifteenth century, a period that has long fascinated economic historians. Writing in 1933, Power and Postan describe it as one of 'great transformation from mediaeval England, isolated and intensely local, to the England of the Tudor and Stuart age, with its world wide connections and imperial designs'.[1] Some Marxist historians regard these years as the age of transition from feudalism to capitalism. Although not unreservedly adopting this line, Hilton points to the rise of the yeoman farmer and the small industrial towns of the cloth making regions as evidence that 'during the course of the relatively unfettered commodity production in the 15th century, the necessary pre-conditions were created for later capitalist development'.[2] Even those who reject overtly Marxist interpretations still attach importance to the fifteenth century as a key period of transition. Britnell accepts that 'the experience of the fifteenth century meant that opportunities for entrepreneurship were more widespread and less constrained by large families, high taxes or seigniorial exactions than in the past'.[3] Christopher Dyer stresses 'similarities between the economic and social history of the middle ages and that of the centuries after 1500', and recognises that 'particularly in the fifteenth century, the structures of society and economy were changing in ways that make them appear more "modern"'.[4] This, then, was a time when the modern town of Ipswich was first taking shape and, in order properly to understand the economic and social forces at work, a brief look at urban development in late medieval England is essential.

The fifteenth century may no longer be, as it seemed to Postan and Power, 'the

[1] Eileen Power and M.M. Postan (eds), *Studies in English Trade in the Fifteenth Century* (London: Routledge, 1933), p. xvii.
[2] Rodney Hilton, 'Introduction' in *The Transition from Feudalism to Capitalism* ed. by Rodney Hilton (London: Verso, 1978), pp. 9–30 (pp. 25–6).
[3] Richard H. Britnell, *The Commercialisation of English Society* (Cambridge: Cambridge University Press, 1993; repr. Manchester: Manchester University Press, 1996), p. 202.
[4] Christopher Dyer, *An Age of Transition? Economy and Society in England in the Later Middle Ages* (Oxford: Oxford University Press, 2005), pp. 7, 173.

most neglected century in English history', but shedding light on this period has been no easy task.[5] By 1400 the Black Death and successive epidemics of plague had caused a demographic collapse without parallel in recorded English history, and unleashed economic forces quite different to those that had prevailed before. Wages went up and rents and prices went down. Serfdom withered. The ordinary folk of England may have enjoyed 'a golden age in the history of standards of living', but in general the upper ranks of society did not fare so well.[6] They were troubled by declining yields from land, perquisites and rents which reduced their income, while facing higher labour costs in running their estates and households. From the final quarter of the fourteenth century they suffered recurrent financial difficulties, and many shifted from the direct exploitation of their estates to rentier management, in order to stabilise their incomes and avert risk. In Suffolk, great landowners, such as the monks of Bury St Edmunds, were among the first to do so, abandoning more remote manors such as Woolpit. Some lords with more modest holdings, as, for example, the Hotot family of Columbine Hall in Stowupland, persevered longer with direct exploitation, but even they eventually bowed to the inevitable and became rentiers in the third quarter of the fifteenth century.[7] As a result, lords abandoned much of the detailed record keeping that had characterised the high Middle Ages. Historians of the thirteenth and fourteenth centuries can draw on a wealth of manorial documents. In the fifteenth century surveys and accounts were often no longer needed and manor courts lost power and functions. Consequently, students of the period must accept that 'many manorial records become less detailed and informative'.[8]

Fortunately, as the flow of evidence from the countryside diminished, that from other sources, such as customs accounts, household accounts and wills, began to swell. Some historians have turned their attention to overseas trade, while others have focused on towns. Their combined efforts have addressed questions of particular relevance to this volume.

In recent years the historiography of late medieval towns has been characterised by heated debate over their economic and social fortunes which has developed into a 'fully blown Historical Controversy'.[9] Pessimists have argued that declining rent

[5] Power and Postan (1933), p. xvii.

[6] R.H. Britnell, *Growth and Decline in Colchester, 1300–1525* (Cambridge: Cambridge University Press, 1986), p. 1; Christopher Dyer, *Standards of Living in the Later Middle Ages: Social Change in England c. 1200–1520* (Cambridge: Cambridge University Press, 1989), p. 276.

[7] Nicholas R. Amor, 'Riding out Recession: Ixworth and Woolpit in the late Middle Ages' *PSIA*, 40 (2002) 127–44 (pp. 137–8); idem, 'Late Medieval Enclosure – A Study of Thorney, near Stowmarket, Suffolk' *PSIA*, 41 (2006) 175–97 (pp. 192 and 194).

[8] Mark Bailey, *The English Manor* (Manchester: Manchester University Press, 2002), p. 17; C. Dyer (2005), p. 6.

[9] Alan Dyer, *Decline and Growth in English Towns 1400–1640* (Basingstoke: Macmillan, 1991; repr. Cambridge: Cambridge University Press, 1995), p. 1.

rolls, reduced populations, decaying tenements and a flight from urban office are symptomatic of a severe decline in the quality and prosperity of urban life. In contrast, optimists point to rising levels of personal wealth in towns, the construction of handsome, if fewer, buildings, burgeoning urban culture and greater social mobility. Towns remained an 'indispensable and flourishing part of the economic system', facilitating the marketing and exchange of agricultural produce for finished goods, and the development of industry.[10] They argue that most towns fared relatively, and in some cases absolutely, better than the countryside around them. Alan Dyer points out that, between 1377 and 1524/5, the total population of England fell by 18 per cent, while the urban population fell by only 8 per cent, leading him to conclude that there was 'very modest urbanisation' during the period as the proportion of people living in towns actually grew.[11]

Bridbury offers the most stridently optimistic interpretation, asserting that the late Middle Ages was a 'period of tremendous advance … in social and economic affairs'.[12] The essence of his case is that the Black Death, by reversing previous trends in prices and wages, left ordinary people much better off and created a mass market for manufactured goods. With the possible exception of the middle decades, trade and industry remained buoyant during the fifteenth century, the cloth industry in particular flourished, and English merchants took control of foreign trade. Towns enjoyed their fair share of this economic growth. Although urban populations fell, civic authorities worked hard to continue attracting immigrants by making themselves more democratic and accountable, admitting a higher percentage of residents to the privileges of burgess status, and relaxing restrictive practices. Fewer people inevitably meant lower rents, falling property values, declining civic revenues and regular pleas of hardship by magistrates to the Crown. Civic poverty did not, however, equate with personal poverty on the part of individual townsfolk. In one of his most controversial arguments, Bridbury compares the tax assessments of 1334 and 1524 to show that urban wealth, as a percentage of total national wealth, had actually grown. The clear evidence for tax remission, between these dates, is interpreted as a political ruse, not a result of economic reality, as Parliament flexed its muscles and withheld from Henry VI the trust and deference shown to earlier monarchs. Merchants gave way to non-resident lawyers and rural gentry in late fifteenth-century Parliamentary elections, only because by then the burgesses who returned them had secured their charters and achieved their political objectives.

[10] J.L. Bolton, *The Medieval English Economy 1150–1500* (London: Dent, 1980), p. 247.

[11] Alan Dyer, '"Urban Decline" in England' in *Towns in Decline AD 100–1600* ed. by T.R. Slater (Aldershot: Ashgate, 2000), pp. 266–288 (p. 281). Rigby, however, seeks to rebut his analysis: Stephen H. Rigby, 'Urban Population in Late Medieval England' *Econ. Hist. Rev.*, 2nd ser., 63 (2010), 391–417.

[12] A.R. Bridbury, *Economic Growth: England in the Later Middle Ages* (London: Allen and Unwin, 1962; repr. Brighton: Harvester Press, 1975), p. 108.

'Their business was trade and industry, and politics mattered to them only when they thought that local interests were at stake.'[13]

In his contention that urban standards of living improved in the later Middle Ages, Bridbury enjoys a powerful ally in Christopher Dyer, who argues that 'the evidence for incomes, diet, housing, possessions and the environment suggests a degree of material improvement for many sections of urban society'.[14] White bread was preferred to brown; meat to fish; beef and mutton to bacon. The quality of domestic property improved. Wills and inventories reveal that more was being spent on clothing, textiles, pewter ware and better quality wooden furniture. This is not to deny the existence of deep pockets of urban poverty. In 1524 as many as half the taxpaying residents of many towns were assessed on the minimum of one pound.[15]

Christopher Dyer shares Bridbury's cynicism about the repeated pleas of poverty that flowed from nearly every franchised corporation to the Crown over their struggle to pay the annual fee farm, observing that 'their consciousness of civic poverty was at variance with their experience as individuals'.[16] Rigby also warns historians to distrust exaggerated claims of decay made by civic leaders with vested interests. Since the latter confronted the same economic problems as landowners in the countryside, their rental income must have declined, but such revenues were only a small fraction of total urban wealth.[17]

Bridbury's comparison between the 1334 and 1524 tax assessments has sparked the most intense debate. The reliability of these sources as evidence of urban growth has been challenged on the basis that they paint far too rosy a picture of towns such as Grimsby, Boston and Lincoln, where close study has shown obvious signs of decay. Such a challenge leads critics to conclude that either the 1524 taxation return 'greatly exaggerates the growth of the proportion of urban wealth' – a conclusion expressly addressed and rejected by Bridbury – or that the evidence simply cannot be relied upon in this context.[18]

There were undoubtedly success stories. On the back of the worsted cloth industry, Norwich grew to become, after London, the largest town in the country. Enterprising Norwich cloth-makers switched from the finishing of broadcloth to the manufacture of worsted within the city itself. Production costs were reduced by cutting out the processes of fulling and often dyeing too. The result was a versatile fabric that could be used for luxury wear or for relatively inexpensive clothing. Norwich became the distribution centre of the region. Fortunes were made in this

[13] Bridbury (1975), pp. 96–8, 101–2.
[14] C. Dyer (1989), p. 210; C. Dyer (2005), p. 155.
[15] S.H. Rigby, *Medieval Grimsby: Growth and Decline* (Hull: University of Hull Press, 1993), p. 132.
[16] C. Dyer (1989), p. 210.
[17] Rigby (1993), p. 118; Richard Britnell, 'The Economy of British Towns 1300–1540' in *CUH*, pp. 313–333 (p. 331).
[18] Rigby refers to and summarises a substantial body of academic literature on the topic: (1993), pp. 141–4.

way and were spent in buying the freedom of the city, building better quality housing and lavishly improving local churches.[19] Exeter too benefited from the cloth and fishing industries and its western location, becoming in the words of Phythian-Adams 'the only unambiguous example of urban success'.[20]

Nevertheless, although not quite a lone voice, Bridbury's view that urban trade and industry enjoyed 'an astonishing record of resurgent vitality and enterprise' is probably a minority one. Of those historians who have addressed the issues, the majority have concluded that most major provincial towns struggled for much of the fifteenth century. According to Kowaleski, 'to one degree or another, falling or stagnating populations, widespread epidemics, dwindling urban revenues, difficulties meeting payments on the city farm, petitions from townspeople claiming poverty, reduced urban building programs, and a weak property market characterized English towns in the fifteenth century'.[21]

In many respects, these were troubled times. As the timeline in Appendix 1 shows, more often than not England was at war either with itself or with a foreign foe. From 1455 the Wars of the Roses were waged intermittently between Lancastrians and Yorkists, until they finally ended thirty years later with Henry VII's victory at Bosworth Field. The sporadic breakdown in law and order precipitated by these hostilities is illuminated by the letters of the Paston family, which tell of the difficulties in carrying on normal economic life.[22] The flame of the Hundred Years' War, which had been ignited again so brightly with Henry V's victory at Agincourt in 1415, smouldered on under his inept son Henry VI and was finally extinguished by Edward IV at the Treaty of Picquigny in 1475. In between, England not only suffered a disruption of trade with northern France, following the inevitable end of its short-lived conquest of Normandy, but also lost Gascony and with it Bordeaux, the key port for the wine trade. On another front, the English capture of the Bay Fleet in 1449, and similar incidents thereafter, undermined relations with the Hanseatic League, caused a naval war between 1468 and 1474, and ultimately led to English merchants abandoning the Baltic. Even during periods of truce, merchants had to cope with state-sponsored piracy, confiscation and trade embargoes. The need to sail in convoy for mutual protection entailed additional

[19] Penelope Dunn, 'Trade', pp. 213–234 (pp. 215–17) and Jonathan Finch, 'The Churches', pp. 49–72 (pp. 61–71), both in *Medieval Norwich* ed. by Carole Rawcliffe and Richard Wilson (London: Hambledon Press, 2004).

[20] Charles Phythian-Adams, *Desolation of a City: Coventry and the Urban Crisis of the Late Middle Ages* (Cambridge: Cambridge University Press, 1979), p. 18; Maryanne Kowaleski, *Local Markets and Regional Trade in Medieval Exeter* (Cambridge: Cambridge University Press, 1995), pp. 91–5.

[21] Kowaleski (1995), p. 90.

[22] Colin Richmond, 'East Anglian Politics and Society in the Fifteenth Century: Reflections 1956–2003' in *Medieval East Anglia* ed. by Christopher Harper-Bill (Woodbridge: Boydell, 2005), pp. 183–208; Helen Castor, *Blood and Roses: The Paston Family in the Fifteenth Century* (London: Faber and Faber, 2004).

freight costs and delays. Although the North Sea had ceased by 1400 to be the front line in the naval war between England and France, the east coast continued to suffer attack. In 1452 Harwich, the neighbouring port town to Ipswich, was sacked by the French.[23] Pirates were also a constant threat. In 1456, for example, certain Hamburg merchants petitioned the king for assistance in recovering their linen cloth that had been seized by pirates *en route* from Ipswich to London and sold in Harwich. As late as 1484 a royal sergeant at arms was commissioned 'to arrest and imprison certain pirates who have committed depredations at sea near the port of Ipswich'.[24] The net result of all this maritime lawlessness was that, by the end of the century, although overseas trade was beginning to recover, English merchants were largely dependent on markets in the Low Countries and the declining wool staple town of Calais.[25]

England's trading partners had their own woes. A severe bullion shortage at the beginning of the fifteenth century triggered depression throughout western Europe: the so-called 'economic depression of the Renaissance'.[26] At the same time, the defeat of the Teutonic Knights at Tannenburg in 1410 damaged English trade in Eastern Europe. Even before Gascony fell to the French, its economy had been undermined by depopulation, wartime depression and monetary crisis. The latter years of the century saw widespread civil disorder in the Low Countries.[27]

Foreign wars destroyed or disrupted overseas markets for English goods, thereby depressing demand and prices. Factors closer to home had a similar effect. In the 1430s a series of poor harvests and high livestock mortality led to agricultural recession which reduced rural demand for urban goods. Peasant agriculturalists were left with little choice but to rely on their own resources of food and manpower, and keep to a minimum their visits to market. Towns then faced the spectre of a vicious cycle of economic decline. Falling demand for goods and services affected employment, discouraged immigration, and resulted in depopulation and recession. Such factors then inhibited any subsequent recovery of demand, since reductions in the urban workforce inevitably caused higher wages and prices, which gave rural industry a competitive advantage.[28]

In particular regions of the country, towns were beset by their own local

[23] *CPR 1446–52*, pp. 528–9.

[24] *CPR 1452–61*, p. 311; *CPR 1476–85*, p. 493.

[25] G.V. 3ell, 'English Mercantile Shipping at the End of the Middle Ages: Some East Coast Evidence' *Econ. Hist. Rev.*, 2nd ser., 36 (1961), 327–41 (p. 328).

[26] Peter Spufford, *Power and Profit: The Merchant in Medieval Europe* (London: Thames and Hudson, 2002), p. 12.

[27] Nelly Johanna Martina Kerling, *Commercial Relations of Holland and Zeeland with England from the Late 13th Century to the Close of the Middle Ages* (Leiden: E.J. Brill, 1954), p. 208.

[28] John Hatcher, 'The Great Slump of the Mid-fifteenth Century' in *Progress and Problems in Medieval England: Essays in Honour of Edward Miller* ed. by Richard Britnell and John Hatcher (Cambridge: Cambridge University Press, 1996), pp. 237–272 (pp. 266–70); A. Dyer (1995), pp. 8–10, 51; Britnell (2000), pp. 321–2.

problems. East coast ports such as Boston and Lynn encountered the phenomenal growth of London and its increasing domination of foreign trade, while watching their own harbours silt up. Exported wool that had once made them wealthy was no longer in such demand, and neither of them had built a thriving textile industry to take its place. If ships were not leaving with wool and cloth, they were not returning with wine and other imports to generate trade with the hinterlands.[29] Yarmouth had additional troubles of its own, which meant that long before 1400 its best days were over. In the words of Saul, 'reduced population, renewed war, a silting harbour and declining herring landings impoverished the town'.[30] The residents were, moreover, obliged to dig deep into their pockets to maintain the walls that made their town, on the military front line, a far costlier place in which to live than Ipswich, which was less exposed to attack.

Economic problems that had surfaced during the first two quarters of the fifteenth century reached crisis point during what has been described as the 'Great Slump', between the 1440s and the 1470s. Towns throughout England confronted, in Hatcher's words, 'an extraordinary range of powerful depressive forces', and most displayed a 'plethora of incontrovertibly inauspicious signs' of suffering.[31] Even those such as Colchester and Norwich, which had previously enjoyed prosperity, fell into decline, and it is difficult to identify any success stories at this time.[32] As Hatcher observes, there is a 'suspiciously close correlation' between those towns which are said to have prospered and those which have to date evaded detailed modern study.[33]

From the 1470s onwards the sky began to brighten. Peace at home and abroad heralded an export-led recovery, particularly in cloth and minerals. Those towns with their own community of international merchants, or their own cloth industry or other commercial specialism, were most likely to experience growth. In Thaxted, Essex, the production of cutlery became a successful enterprise, while Birmingham developed a niche in the production of scythe-blades, and Walsall one in horse-bits.[34] At some stage in the half century straddling 1500, England's population began once again to expand, albeit slowly at first, providing more workers for urban industries, reducing labour costs, and stoking demand for urban goods and services. Nevertheless, in the closing years of the fifteenth and the opening years of the sixteenth century, exports provided only a mild stimulus

[29] Maryanne Kowaleski, 'Port Towns: England and Wales 1300–1540' in *CUH*, pp. 467–494 (pp. 485–6); A. Dyer (1995), pp. 8, 15, 18, 32.

[30] A. Saul, 'Great Yarmouth in the Fourteenth Century: A Study in Trade, Politics and Society' (Unpublished doctoral thesis, University of Oxford, 1975), p. 210.

[31] Hatcher (1996), pp. 240, 269.

[32] Britnell (1986), pp. 266–8; Dunn (2004), p. 234.

[33] Hatcher (1996), p. 267.

[34] Britnell (2000), p. 315; C. Dyer (2005), p. 130.

to the home market. Any recovery was still 'patchy and localised' and it is unlikely that there was any growth in GDP.[35]

The debate over urban decay has generated much heat, but generalisations shed only limited light on the issues. No consensus has yet been reached on the meaning of the terms used to frame the debate. Simple words such as 'decay' and 'decline', and even 'town', are ambiguous. One part of a town might have been in decay while another part was flourishing. Residential use might have given way to successful industrial activity – is this a sign of decay or growth?[36] When does an industrialising textile village actually become a town? Judgements about the fortunes of any particular town might depend upon the specific aspects of urban life under scrutiny, and the period selected for study. An analysis of its economic fortunes might indicate decay between two particular dates, but growth between two others.

No town was immune from broader economic forces and events, but each responded in its own way. For example, Coventry and York are often cited as examples of failure, yet both 'enjoyed intervals of vigorous economic growth between 1350 and 1500'.[37] Colchester is usually regarded as a medieval success story, yet Britnell reckons that the townsfolk enjoyed growth to higher levels of output in just a quarter of the 190 years between 1334 and 1524.[38] According to Hatcher, 'the fortunes of each town changed over time, as did those of the multitude of external influences which played upon them from the broader economic contexts within which they existed'.[39] Some recent urban studies have avoided the traps set by wide generalisations and imprecise definitions. Instead, they have concentrated upon detailed reconstructions of specific elements of urban life and set them firmly within that town's local context. Studies of medieval Exeter, London and Norwich provide perhaps the best examples of such work. Reliance on general theories, however tempting, is no substitute for the careful study of urban archives and the drawing of tentative conclusions on the basis of the evidence they offer. Only by focusing on the fortunes of individual towns and their residents can a true and complete picture of urban life in the fifteenth century begin to emerge. Happily, as Britnell points out, 'that increasing variety of urban experience is one of the most rewarding features of urban history'.[40]

[35] A. Dyer (1995), p. 43. R.H. Britnell is circumspect about economic and national population growth before the 1520s: *The Closing of the Middle Ages?: England 1471–1529* (Oxford: Blackwell, 1997), pp. 236–247.

[36] Keith D. Lilley is quite optimistic: 'Decline or Decay? Urban Landscapes in Late-Medieval England' in *Towns in Decline AD 100–1600* ed. by T.R. Slater (Aldershot: Ashgate, 2000) pp. 235–265 (pp. 253–7).

[37] Bolton (1980), pp. 248–9, 251; Britnell (1996), pp. 170–1.

[38] Britnell (1986), p. 266.

[39] Hatcher (1996), p. 239.

[40] Richard H. Britnell, 'England: Towns, Trade and Industry' in *A Companion to Britain in the Later Middle Ages* ed. by S.H. Rigby (Oxford: Blackwell, 2003), pp. 47–64 (p. 50).

Ipswich provides an excellent subject for an economic history of a town in the final century of the Middle Ages. Although often mentioned in generalisations about fifteenth-century towns, its economic history has not previously been systematically researched. What now follows in this chapter is a description of the medieval town, a summary of the evolution and functions of the borough, a precis of its medieval trading history, and finally an analysis of the sources to be considered in the subsequent chapters which will examine its economy in more detail.

The Urban Landscape of Late Medieval Ipswich

Nestled in a valley, eleven miles from the sea, where the fresh water of the river Gipping meets the salt water of the river Orwell, lies the Suffolk town of Ipswich. Ipswich's jurisdiction over the port of Orwell extended as far as Polles Head (now Landguard Point) and was jealously guarded against incursion by the men of nearby Harwich. As an outward show of the town's authority, in 1433 every trade craft was called upon to provide a boat to sail the liberties and this custom continued into the nineteenth century.[41] The liberties of the borough itself extended to 8450 acres (3421 hectares), measuring five miles north to south and four miles east to west.[42] By the fifteenth century they included four wards, eleven parishes and the hamlets of Stoke, Brookes Hall, Wicks Ufford and Wicks Bishop.[43] The medieval core of Ipswich was surrounded by ramparts and, in short stretches, by walls. Part of the wall west of Northgate, then known as Bargate, still survives, but that in the parish of St Mary Quay has long gone and may have been demolished as early as the 1430s.[44] The parochial organisation within this core changed during the course of the Middle Ages, with the 1227 tallage rolls painting a quite different picture to that which emerges from the fifteenth-century records, and referring to the old parishes of St Mildred, Holy Trinity, St George, St Mary del Delfe and St Augustine.[45] Although the demarcation shown in Map 1 is based on later documents, it is probably a fair reflection of the wards and parishes that had evolved by 1400. Of the eleven parishes, that of St Margaret remained the most populous throughout

[41] BL, Ms Add. 30,158, f. 47r; *The Annals of Ipswiche … by Nathaniel Bacon serving as Recorder and Town Clerk … 1654,* ed. by W.H. Richardson (Ipswich: Cowell, 1884), p. 96; J. Wodderspoon, *Memorials of the Ancient Town of Ipswich* (Ipswich: Pawsey/Longman, Brown, Green and Longmans, 1850), p. 60.

[42] Wodderspoon (1850), p. 1.

[43] *Annals*, p. 1.

[44] Two grants of common soil in St Mary Quay were made to prominent burgesses in 1434 and 1439, the earlier refers to 'parcel of town walls' and the latter to 'late parcel of town walls': SROI C/3/8/6/3–4.

[45] Anthony M. Breen and John Ridgard, 'Ipswich Tallage Rolls 1227' The Suffolk Review, New Series, 54 (Spring 2010), pp. 12–26; Geoffrey Martin, 'The Borough and the Merchant Community of Ipswich, 1317–1422' (unpublished doctoral thesis, University of Oxford, 1955), pp. 158–9.

the fifteenth century, needing three burgesses, rather than the usual two, to collect royal taxes in the 1480s.[46] Moving west, the homes of many late fifteenth-century bailiffs, as well as the new hall of the archdeacon of Suffolk, must have given the parish of St Mary Tower an air of gentility. Conversely, the parish of St Helen, in the eastern suburbs, was the most sparsely populated and generated the lowest tax yield of all.[47] The residents of the riverside parish of St Mary Quay included many of the town's leading late fifteenth-century merchants, such as Henry Bolle, Richard Gosse and Thomas Harford, and, on the basis of testamentary evidence, may well have enjoyed the highest per capita wealth in Ipswich.[48]

The extent and location of industry is not always easy to identify. As we shall see, beer brewing was concentrated near the docks, while brick and tile making relied on the clay soils to the east of the town. But where did the dyers, tanners and pewterers, whose activities were so important to the local economy, ply their trades? Dyers may have gravitated to the north of the town. In 1424 Thomas Roberd and Thomas Smyth were both fined by the leet court of north ward for polluting a well in Brook Street in which they washed their dyed cloth.[49] John Halle was penalised by the same court for constructing a dye pit called 'Adam' in the town ditch in 1466.[50] Both he and his contemporary, Thomas Bunt, another dyer, lived in the parish of St Margaret.[51] Legend has it that Halle carried on his trade in what is now Soane Street. When he died, in 1503, he left his son a 'woodehows' where, no doubt, he stored his woad. A rather ambiguous reference, in a deed of grant of 1479, to 'Deyerylane', in the neighbouring parish of St Mary Tower, may provide evidence for the presence of other dyers there.[52] Many tanners carried on their noxious trade outside the town, but, needing a ready supply of water, those who stayed congregated close to the river, probably where it runs south-east from Friars Bridge. In the closing years of the fifteenth century the leet court of south ward, which had jurisdiction over this stretch of riverbank, imposed more than half the total number of fines it levied on tanners. Part of the town ditch in south ward was known as the 'Tann'.[53] The Winter family, who were so prominent in the pewter trade, enjoyed close connections with the parish of St Peter, with Edmund and his son Nicholas both being buried in the local church, and Edmund's brother William owning property and serving as tax collector there.[54]

[46] *Annals*, pp. 82, 122, 185; BL, Ms Add. 30,158, f. 37v; SROI C/2/10/3/1 f. 122.
[47] *Annals*, pp. 122, 122, 185; Rev C.H. Eleyn White, 'The Ipswich Domesday Books' *PSIA*, 6 (1888) 195–219 (p. 218).
[48] The mean bequest to the church of St Mary Quay for tithes forgotten, at 5s. 8½d., was significantly higher than that to any other Ipswich church.
[49] SROI C/2/8/1/7.
[50] SROI C/2/10/1/3 m. 10 (north ward).
[51] NRO NCC, Reg. Popy, f. 275; SROI R7/23.
[52] SROI C/3/8/7/1.
[53] SROI C/2/8/1/14 (south ward).
[54] PCC 32 Milles, f. 254v (PROB 11/8); SROI R2/293; BL, Ms Add. 30,158, f. 18v.

Visitors arriving in Ipswich by water might be guided upriver by a pilot before dropping anchor in Orwell Haven and completing their journey by small boat.[55] The well-to-do would dock at a private quay, of which there were many, and others at the common quay.[56] 'Every stranger' was required to weigh his merchandise at the common crane.[57] All would pay their dues at the customs house and porters would then carry their goods up the hill. Anyone arriving overland in medieval Ipswich would first pass through one of the town gates which interrupted the continuity of its ramparts, or over one of the bridges.[58] Once inside, the medieval visitor would have found the gridiron street plan, dating from Anglo-Saxon times, and even street names, still familiar to those who know Ipswich today. Notwithstanding its errors, John Speed's early seventeenth-century plan is the earliest extant one of the town and the nearest in time to the late medieval period (Plate 1).[59] Two other reconstructed maps of the medieval town show the ward and parish boundaries, and other topographical features referred to in this volume (Maps 1 and 2).

Those coming on official business would head for Cornhill where the Toll House, otherwise known as the Moothall, was the seat of local government.[60] Anyone seeking spiritual comfort in the town was spoilt for choice. In addition to eleven parish churches, there were three chapels, three friaries, two priories and, firmly outside the ramparts, three hospitals.[61] None of these held the sway and importance that the abbey commanded in Bury St Edmunds, but, as suppliers and consumers, the friaries and priories played an important part in the economic life of the town. A little further east of Cornhill, trades people would be drawn to the hustle and bustle of the markets and taverns between what we now know as Tavern Street and Buttermarket.[62] In September they might visit the annual three-day Holy Trinity fair.[63] Along with the inviting smells emanating from local breweries, bakeries, shops and stalls in and around these markets, the medieval visitor could not have helped but notice a much less pleasant odour. Despite the vigilance of the

[55] SROI C/3/3/1/1; *Annals*, p. 115; G.H. Martin, 'Shipments of Wool from Ipswich to Calais' *Journal of Transport History*, 2 (1956), 177–81 (p. 180).
[56] Wodderspoon (1850), pp. 225–6.
[57] *Annals*, p. 112.
[58] Keith Wade says there were three gates: 'Anglo-Saxon and Medieval Ipswich' in *An Historical Atlas of Suffolk* ed. by David Dymond and Edward Martin (Ipswich: Suffolk County Council, 1988; repr. 1989 and 1999), pp. 158–9. Lilian Redstone says four: *Ipswich through the Ages* (Ipswich: East Anglian Magazine, 1948; repr., 1969), p. 76.
[59] SROI MC5/50. Speed's principal errors were to misplace the Black Friars (Dominicans) who should be at *W/Z*, the White Friars (Carmelites) who should be at *V*, and Handford Mill which should be at *Y*.
[60] Martin (1955), p. 157.
[61] Wade (1999), pp. 158–9.
[62] Martin (1955), pp. 164–7; Redstone (1969), pp. 29–30.
[63] Redstone (1969), p. 76.

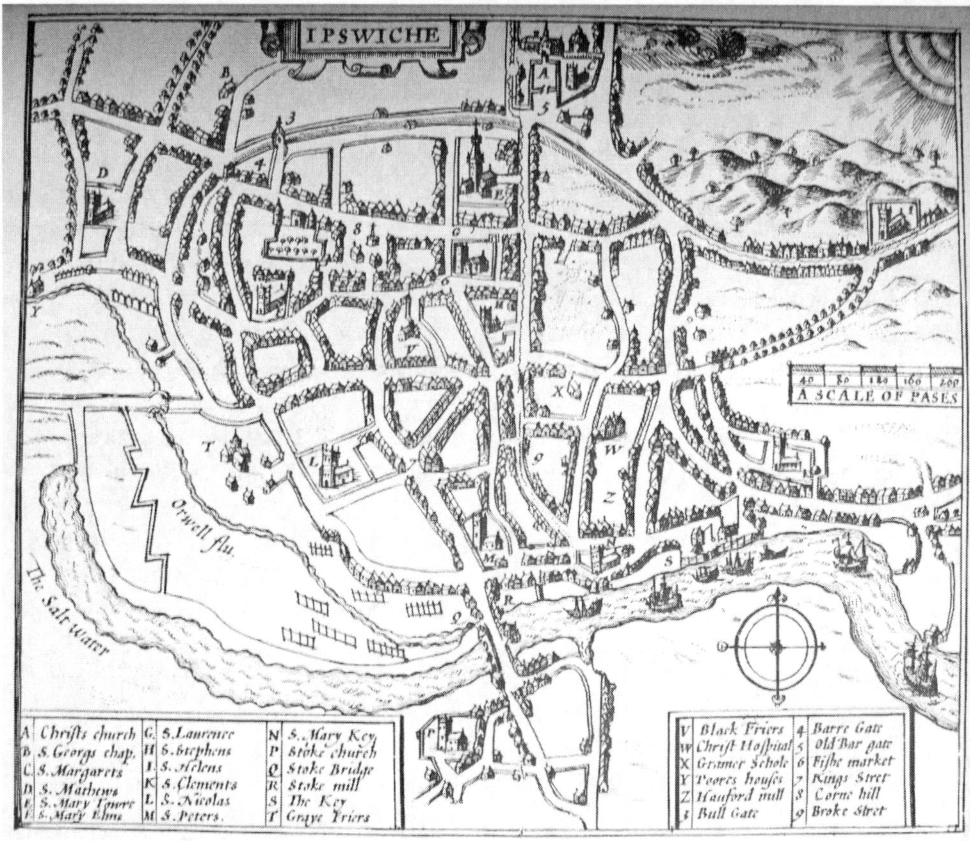

Plate 1: *John Speed's Map of Ipswich, published 1610*

borough authorities, open drains and the unlicensed public dumping of household rubbish including animal, perhaps even human, excrement remained a recurrent problem. Colehill, in the parish of St Nicholas, was a particularly popular tipping spot and in 1468 twenty residents of north ward alone were fined for leaving waste there.[64] Some townsfolk could seek refuge from the foul atmosphere in their own gardens, of which twenty-five are mentioned in local wills, including Roger Tymperley's herb garden.[65] A parcel of land on Shirehouse Hill, acquired by John Osberne in 1477, was surrounded on three sides by the gardens of the well-to-do.[66] The countryside was never far away and, notwithstanding the ramparts, there was no clear demarcation as town merged into country. Despite the fines regularly meted out by the leet court, many residents allowed their pigs to roam through the streets

[64] SROI C/2/10/1/6, m. 5r (north ward).
[65] NRO NCC, Reg. Sayve, ff. 11, 12.
[66] BL, Ms Add. 30,158, f. 34v.

and grazed their cattle on the ramparts themselves, while Robert and Joan Hill unlawfully took away bees that were swarming there.[67]

The Borough, its Burgesses and Officers

By 1400, when this volume begins, Ipswich had been a self-governing borough for two hundred years and an important trading port for six hundred more. A community of some importance long before the Conquest, it may even have been a 'burh' of the West Saxon kings and certainly it was home to a mint.[68] According to Domesday Book, the arrival of the Normans had a devastating effect on the town's infrastructure, population and wealth: 'But now there are ... 110 poor burgesses who cannot render anything to the king's geld ... And 328 dwellings have been laid waste in the borough.'[69] Whether this was due to Viking raids, the construction of the castle, or reprisals following Earl Ralph's rebellion, or had some other cause, is impossible to tell.[70] What is certain is that it took a long time for the town to recover. The documentary evidence is supported by recent archaeology, which has identified the burning of buildings in the years immediately after the Conquest, followed by prolonged contraction.[71] More than a hundred years were to pass before King John's borough charter was read to the townsfolk in the churchyard of St Mary Tower in 1200.[72]

The chief beneficiaries of those liberties, first bestowed by King John, were the burgesses of the town. In Martin's words, they enjoyed 'trading privileges, freedom from toll and a market for their produce' not only in Ipswich, but also in many of the nation's other boroughs.[73] This clearly gave them a competitive advantage in the market places of Ipswich. Among other rights, burgesses could not be sued in courts outside Ipswich in respect of tenements held or debts incurred in the town. In 1455 the bailiffs threatened William Ridout and William Heede with disenfranchisement for suing John Caldwell in an external court.[74] As in most other English towns and

[67] SROI C/2/8/1/13 (west ward).

[68] J. Newman describes the excavation on the outskirts of Ipswich of a wealthy Anglo-Saxon grave dating back to the seventh century: 'Boss Hall' *Current Archaeology*, 130 (1992), pp. 424–5. Geoffrey Martin appears to suggest that Ipswich was a burh: 'The Governance of Ipswich: From its origins to c. 1550' in *Ipswich Borough Archives 1255–1835* ed. by David Allen, (Woodbridge: Boydell for SRS, 43, 2000), pp. xvii–xxix (p. xviii). While the town is not included in Alan Dyer's list of burhs, it is ranked fourteenth in his list of towns with mints: 'Appendix: Ranking Lists of English Medieval Towns' in *CUH*, pp. 747–770 (pp. 748–50).

[69] *Domesday Book*, ed. by Ann Williams and G.H. Martin (London: Penguin Books, 2002), ii, f. 290r.

[70] Lucy Marten, 'The Rebellion of 1075 and its Impact in East Anglia' in *Medieval East Anglia* ed. by Christopher Harper-Bill (Woodbridge: Boydell, 2005), pp. 168–182.

[71] T. Loader, 'The Anglo-Saxon Buildings', presentation to 'Ipswich Unearthed' Conference, 27 October 2007 (unpublished).

[72] Martin (2000), pp. xix–xx.

[73] Martin (1955), p. 91; Martin (2000) p. xx; Colin Platt *Medieval Southampton: The port and trading community, AD 1000–1600* (London: Routledge and Kegan Paul, 1973), p. 78.

[74] *Annals*, p. 113.

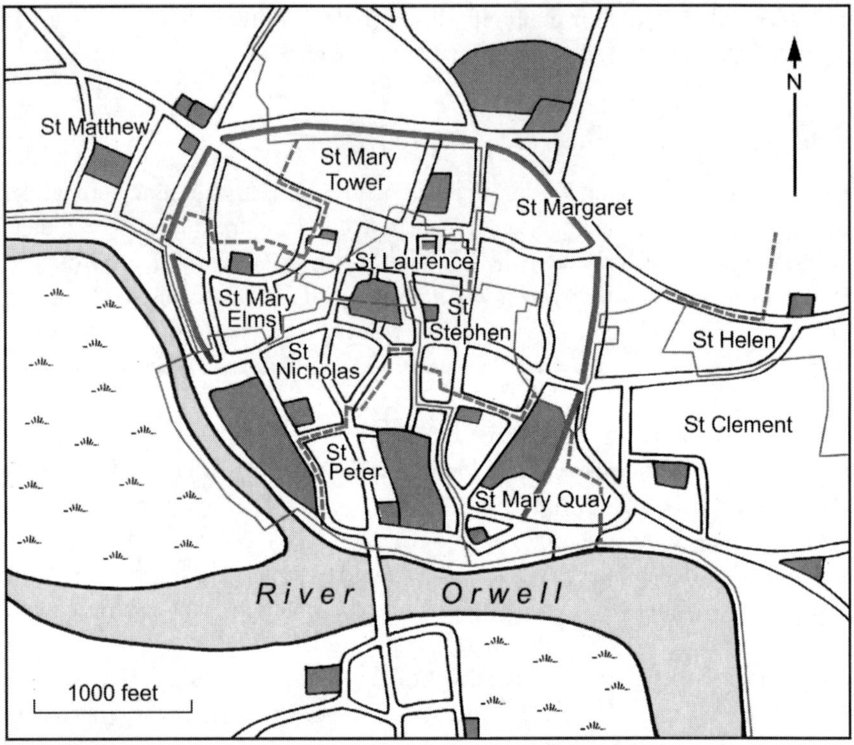

Map 1: *Medieval Ipswich, showing ward and parish boundaries*

Notes to Maps 1 and 2

The ward boundaries are marked by unbroken lines, and the parish boundaries by broken lines. Each ward comprised a number of parishes so the ward boundaries were also parish boundaries. The parishes in each of the wards were as follows:

Ward	Parishes
East	St Clement, St Mary Quay and St Stephen
West	St Matthew, St Mary Tower and St Mary Elms
North	St Margaret, St Helen and St Laurence (now spelt Lawrence)
South	St Peter and St Nicholas

Topographical features are numbered and shown in Map 2. The information is drawn from: Speed's map; L.J. Redstone (1969), plate 4; Wade (1999), p. 159; and Stephen Alsford's website *History of Medieval Ipswich: Ipswich and Suburbs at the Close of the Middle Ages* (2009), p. 1 (html//users.trytel.com/~tristan/towns/ipswmap1). Anthony Breen, Deirdre Heavens of SROI and Clive Paine have also been very helpful in providing additional information. Philip Judge and Julia Smith have helped with the design and drawing of the maps.

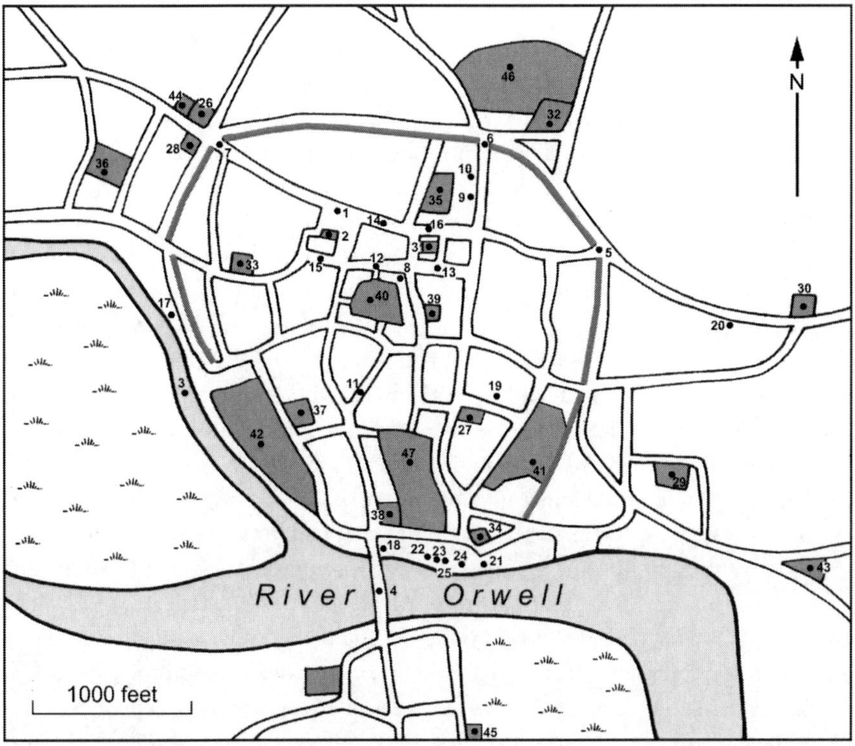

Map 2: *Medieval Ipswich, showing main topographical features mentioned in the text.*

Borough
1 Cornhill
2 Toll House/ Moothall inc. Fulling House

Bridges
3 Friars Bridge
4 Stoke Bridge

Gates
5 East ('Osterbolt')
6 Bargate
7 West (inc town gaol)

Houses/Halls
8 Ancient House
9 Oak House
10 Pykenham's Hall and Gateway
11 Silent Street

Markets
12 Butter and Cheese
13 Fish
14 Flesh
15 Timber
16 Vintry

Mills
17 Horsewade Mill
18 Two New Mills (inc. fulling mill)

Other
19 Felawe's Grammar School
20 Tile kiln

Quayside
21 Berthlotiscay
22 Bigod's Quay
23 Common Quay
24 Town Crane
25 Wool House

Religious
Chapels
26 All Saints
27 St Edmund de Pountenay
28 Our Lady

Churches
29 St Clement
30 St Helen
31 St Laurence
32 St Margaret
33 St Mary Elms
34 St Mary Quay
35 St Mary Tower
36 St Matthew
37 St Nicholas
38 St Peter
39 St Stephen

Friaries
40 Carmelite
41 Dominican
42 Franciscan

Hospitals
43 St James
44 St John
45 St Leonard

Priories
46 Holy Trinity
47 St Peter and St Paul

Legend for Map 2

cities, the freedom enjoyed by burgesses could be acquired by purchase, patrimony or apprenticeship. The standard rate of purchase was forty shillings, although this was not invariably the price paid. In the mid-fifteenth century Thomas Bishop, who served as recorder, was admitted in return for a payment of two sheep and six flagons of wine, and John Causton in return for a promise to maintain for seven years the ornaments and stages of the Corpus Christi pageant.[75] Non-residents who were English nationals could acquire 'foreign' burgess status, although within a year and a day they had to buy freehold property within the town or risk forfeiture.[76] The honour could also be bestowed as a way of currying favour with the great and the good. In 1491 the Earl of Oxford, by then the leading magnate in Suffolk, was given the freedom of the borough.[77] In 1483, and again in 1485, it was ordained that those born outside England, known as aliens, could not acquire burgess status. In view of the size and wealth of the Dutch community in late fifteenth- and early sixteenth-century Ipswich, this bar was not always enforced.[78]

A person could only acquire freedom by patrimony or apprenticeship if he was born or first apprenticed after his father or master had himself become a burgess.[79] Anyone wanting to become a burgess by patrimony was supposed to attend the general court with his father's sword in his hand. In 1419 John, son of Thomas Wade, did just that and was duly admitted.[80] The records suggest that seven years' service as an apprentice was required, although in practice the term could be longer. William Burre was indentured for seven years in 1446, to the Ipswich grocer John Wytton, and was finally admitted in 1455, nine years later. Robert Payn was admitted in 1488, after serving Thomas Drayll, again for nine years, rather than the eight initially stipulated.[81] Such freedom was far from being a universal right. Kowaleski estimates that only 21 per cent of Exeter householders belonged to the freedom of the medieval borough.[82] In the late fourteenth century about a third of adult males in London, Norwich and York were freemen.[83] Britnell reckons that

[75] *Annals*, pp. 100, 103.
[76] *Annals*, p. 80.
[77] *Annals*, p. 162.
[78] *Annals*, pp. 147, 151; BL, Ms Add. 30,158, f. 41v.
[79] *Annals*, p. ii.
[80] BL, Ms Add. 30,158, f. 2v.
[81] BL, Ms Add. 30,158, f. 19r; SROI C/2/10/3/1 f. 139. Many apprentices never completed their training. According to Elspeth M. Veale, in London, half of those apprenticed as grocers and two-thirds of those apprenticed as skinners failed to do so, and only the ablest and best connected ever became freemen: *The English Fur Trade in the Later Middle Ages* (Oxford: Oxford University Press, 1966; repr. London: London Record Society, 38, 2003), pp. 95, 100.
[82] Kowaleski (1995), p. 196.
[83] Caroline M. Barron, 'The Child in Medieval London: The Legal Evidence', in *Essays on Medieval Childhood* ed. by Joel T. Rosenthal (Donnington: Shaun Tyas, 2007), pp. 40–53 (p. 45); Penny Dunn 'After the Black Death: Society and Economy in Late Fourteenth-Century Norwich' (unpublished doctoral thesis, University of East Anglia, 2003), p. 88.

more than half the householders in Colchester may have been burgesses in 1488.[84] In fifteenth-century Ipswich, as we shall see, no more than a third of adult men were ever enfranchised, probably fewer. Although the town customs provide for the admission of widows, the extant fifteenth-century records include only one passing reference to a female freeman, namely Isabelle Smyth in 1476.[85] Whatever the proportion may have been, without doubt, for many of Ipswich residents, the prospect of acquiring King John's liberties remained an impossible dream.

Initially, Ipswich was ruled by twelve chief portmen from whose ranks were elected two bailiffs, four coroners, and, to enforce the judgments of borough courts, two sergeants. In theory they were democratically accountable to the burgesses, but in practice they formed a self-perpetuating elite. The bailiffs were elected each year by the portmen, and the latter in turn were elected by a body nominated by the bailiffs and coroners. Burgesses were simply expected to give public assent.[86] Only sixty-two men held the office of bailiff in the fifteenth century. Their biographical details are set out briefly in Appendix 2 and, for some of them, more fully in Appendix 3. No less than half of them were wealthy merchants, another eight were lawyers, at least three were members of the local gentry, and the remainder were prominent in the domestic wine trade, or the production of dyed cloth, pewter and tanned leather. Although significantly more appear to have lived in the parish of St Mary Tower than in any other single parish, the evidence does not suggest that they all huddled together in their own quarter of the town. If you wanted to be a bailiff, then it paid to be well born, since at least nine sons followed their fathers into office. Those who were not related were, as might be expected, often closely connected by friendship, entrusting each other with the administration of their estates. For instance, John Caldwell appointed John Drayll as the supervisor of his will in 1461, who, in turn, appointed Robert Wymbyll as his executor in 1465, while requesting to be buried in the Carmelite Friary next to William Debenham.[87] Nearly forty years later the dyer John Halle appointed two fellow former bailiffs as his executors, namely the mercer Thomas Baldry and the tanner William Ropkyn.[88]

As time went by, civic organisation became more sophisticated, the number of officers grew and their rights and obligations increased. Chamberlains were first appointed in 1319 to collect and account for the income of the town and to keep proper records. They did not enjoy the same status as the bailiffs and portmen, but

[84] R. Britnell, 'Town Life' in *A Social History of England 1200–1500* ed. by R. Horrox and W.M. Ormrod (Cambridge: Cambridge University Press, 2006) pp. 134–178 (p. 163).

[85] BL, Ms Add. 30,158, f. 33v; Sir Thomas Twiss (ed.) *The Black Book of the Admiralty, Appendix, Part II, Volume II,* 4 volumes (London: Longman for the Rolls Series, 55, 1873), p. 139.

[86] J. Tait, *Medieval English Boroughs* (Manchester: Manchester University Press, 1936; repr.1968) pp. 270–1; Martin (2000), pp. xx–xxi.

[87] SROI R2/87, C/2/10/1/2.

[88] NRO NCC, Reg. Popy, f. 275

were required to be 'sufficient persons of the inferiour sort of people'.[89] By 1470 the twelve were joined by a council of twenty-four, and even more burgesses attended the irregular meetings of the general court. In addition to those officers previously mentioned, there were two escheators, six justices of the peace, four clavigers, a clerk of the peace, a common clerk, an additional two sergeants, a master and six sub-porters with ill defined responsibility for the port, and four wardens of the Corpus Christi guild.[90] The office of claviger may have ultimately evolved into that of treasurer, but, as four clavigers and four treasurers were elected in 1487, at least for a time the two offices co-existed.[91] Residents served as assessors and collectors of the taxes that were raised periodically on behalf of the Crown or the borough, as jurors and valuers at sessions of the petty court, and as chief pledges, tithingmen and affeerers at those of the leet court. The twelve chief pledges were appointed as constables in 1484.[92] Four officials were appointed to oversee each of the markets and three served as wine drawers. In total, by the late fifteenth century, well over a hundred people had some part to play in the running of the town.

Borough officers exercised their powers first through the Portmanmoot, which came to be known as the great court, and later as the general court.[93] The bailiffs also sat in judgment in the petty court and in the leet courts of each of the four wards. They were expected to 'govern and maintain the borough, to render its judgements and to ordain and execute all things which behove to be done for its status and honour'.[94] Swift civil justice was expected both by resident traders and by foreigners bringing to the town's markets much needed supplies and contributing tolls to the borough purse. The governing elite shouldered diverse and sometimes conflicting responsibilities. They had to ensure the constant availability of an adequate supply of food and drink of satisfactory quality, properly measured and at a just price.[95] This meant preventing, or at least controlling, re-grating, forestalling, the illicit hosting of foreign merchants and other restrictive practices. The sale of perishable produce, such as meat and fish, merited particularly close supervision because of the threat posed to public health. Maintaining public order and punishing offenders was essential. In 1489 John Moyse was admitted as a freeman of Ipswich on condition that he constructed a pair of stocks at the quayside which could be used for the public humiliation of malefactors.[96] The needs of the propertied classes also had to be addressed by facilitating and safeguarding the transfer

[89] *Annals*, p. 55.

[90] BL, Ms Add. 30,158, ff. 29r–v, 32v; SROI C/2/10/1/3, m. 8r; C/2/10/3/1 f. 48; *Annals*, p. 97.

[91] John Webb (ed.) *The Town Finances of Elizabethan Ipswich* (Woodbridge: Boydell for SRS, 38, 1996), p. 1; *Annals*, p. 156; C/2/10/3/1 f. 58.

[92] *Annals*, p. 151.

[93] Martin (2000), pp. xxv–xxvi.

[94] Tait (1968), p. 270.

[95] Bolton (1980), pp. 335–6.

[96] SROI C/2/10/3/1, f. 185.

of land. Burgesses were granted privileges sufficient to make it worthwhile acquiring the freedom of the borough, but not so great as to undermine other objectives and stir up the unenfranchised majority. For instance, they alone were entitled to act as hosts to foreign merchants, but they were only allowed to buy a quarter of those merchants' goods.[97] The governors of the town sought to achieve all these goals by promulgating ordinances or 'customs', which have survived in various 'Domesdays'.

Although not obliged to share power with any ecclesiastical or baronial rival within the town, they had to work with local magnates and with the king. During the fifteenth century, the burgesses contended with the dukes of Suffolk and Norfolk and the earl of Oxford, who successively held sway in the region.[98] This was, however, a two-way process, since any successful magnate clearly wished to establish good relations with local townspeople. Through the person of Sir John Howard the town adhered to the Yorkist faction, particularly close links being established between Howard and his commercial agent Richard Felawe, one of the leading burgesses of mid-fifteenth-century Ipswich.[99] Dealings with the monarch were more distant, but potentially even more important. In 1446, in 1463 and yet again in 1488, the town petitioned a king – the first Lancastrian, the second Yorkist and the third Tudor – for charters to renew and extend its privileges.[100] The English coastline was divided into different customs jurisdictions, each managed from its own headport. Ipswich was the headport of a jurisdiction that stretched from Orford Haven to Brightlingsea and included the harbours of Colchester (via its outport of Hythe), Harwich and Maldon.[101] Therefore, many of the leading burgesses were servants of the Crown, collecting customs from the port's merchants, some of whom would have been their friends and neighbours. They provided the king with an inexpensive civil service, but not always an efficient or impartial one.[102]

The borough may well have been at a low ebb in the third quarter of the fourteenth century. Like all towns, Ipswich was badly shaken by successive outbreaks of plague which dramatically reduced its taxable population. Quite probably, many leading families were wiped out and fewer men of the right sort were available to fill borough offices. This was a common phenomenon, apparent, for example, in the nearby port of Yarmouth. In any event, there was a 'serious crisis in the borough's

[97] Twiss (1883), pp. 243–8; The Ipswich merchant William Wethereld was host to and exercised his influence on behalf of the Dutchman Herman Rollestorp in the 1420s: PRO C1/1500/3 (Reference courtesy Helen Bradley).

[98] J.C. Wedgewood and A. Holt, *History of Parliament 1439–1509 Register* (London: HMSO, 1938), p. 685; Richmond (2005), pp. 183–208.

[99] Wodderspoon (1850), p. 207; Anne Crawford (ed.) *The Household Books of John Howard, Duke of Norfolk* (Stroud: Sutton, 1992).

[100] *CChR (1427–1516)*, pp. liv–v, cxcvii–ix; SROI C/2/10/3/1 f. 93.

[101] Kowaleski (2000), pp. 472–3.

[102] Martin (1956), p. 178; Saul (1975), pp. 104–7.

affairs'.[103] In the closing years of the fourteenth century the town came closer than at any subsequent time during the Middle Ages to being dominated by members of one family, namely the Starlings, with two Geoffreys, the elder and the younger, between them serving as bailiff fifteen times between 1375 and 1399 and MP on ten occasions.[104] Perhaps strong characters were needed to lead the borough out of the malaise. In this respect, the town's history was not unique. Lynn's politics were dominated by John Brunham for much of the final quarter of the fourteenth century.[105] Fifteenth-century Ipswich saw no such concentration of power and 'was not again faced with a crisis that threatened to outmatch its powers'.[106]

England's Oldest Port

Ipswich is perhaps the oldest of all English ports, with an almost continuous record of maritime trading activity since about the year 600. It was one of only three emporia in Middle Saxon England, along with London and Southampton, which were 'fully urban … something altogether different from anything that had gone before: not only are they larger and richer, but they are positioned at key points in a much larger network of settlement, trade and communication'.[107] The town produced the first wheel-made pottery in post-Roman Britain, probably inspired by the expatriate Frisian community living there at that time.[108] This Ipswich Ware pottery can be found as far away as Kent and Yorkshire, while finds of imported seventh-century pottery bear witness to trading links with the Merovingian Empire. From the ninth century Ipswich Ware gave way to Thetford Ware pottery which was manufactured until the mid-twelfth century in the area of Carr Street.[109] Ipswich's international trade waxed and waned during the high Middle Ages, not least because the Normans deliberately promoted Dunwich as a rival.[110] By the time King John granted his charter, less than one per cent of England's overseas trade passed through the headport of Ipswich, and Ipswich's contribution to the subsidy

[103] Martin (1955), pp. 106, 129; Saul (1975), p. 232.

[104] J.S. Roskell, Linda Clark and Carole Rawcliffe (eds) *The History of Parliament: The House of Commons 1386–1421,* 4 volumes (Stroud: Sutton, 1992/3), I, p. 621.

[105] Kate Parker, 'A Little Local Difficulty' in *Medieval East Anglia* ed. by Christopher Harper-Bill (Woodbridge: Boydell, 2005), pp. 115–129 (p. 122).

[106] Martin (1955), p. 129.

[107] Francis Pryour, *Britain in the Middle Ages – An Archaeological History* (London: Harper Collins, 2006) pp. 42, 47–8; Richard Hodges, *The Anglo Saxon Achievement* (London: Gerald Duckworth, 1989) pp. 55–6, 97–101, 104.

[108] Barbel Brodt, 'East Anglia' in *CUH*, pp. 639–656 (p. 641); P. Blinkhorn, 'The Ipswich Ware Pottery Industry' presentation to 'Ipswich Unearthed' Conference 27 October 2007 (unpublished).

[109] Wade (1999), pp. 158–9; Peter Warner, *The Origins of Suffolk* (Manchester: Manchester University Press, 1996) pp. 168–9.

[110] Mark Bailey, *Medieval Suffolk: An Economic and Social History 1200–1500* (Woodbridge: Boydell, 2007), p.116.

of 1203/4 was lower than that of Colchester or even Orford.[111] Less than a hundred years later the town's fortunes may, once more, have been picking up. This is certainly the view adopted by Masschaele in his analysis of the 1283 subsidy roll. He describes Ipswich as 'a thriving port and prosperous town', whose householders had a 'remarkably high assessed wealth', and which appears to have enjoyed a significant lead in cloth production over neighbouring Colchester.[112]

Other scholars have painted the same picture of a successful late medieval port, whose leading burgesses were busily engaged in overseas trade, mingling on the quayside with fellow merchants from London, other parts of England, the Low Countries, Cologne, the Baltic and Spain. The geographical extent of their trade, and the nature of the principal commodities carried in their ships, are illustrated in Map 3. Having studied the wool trade that flourished there at the beginning of the fifteenth century, Martin had no cause to be despondent, describing a 'prosperous place', and concluding that 'Ipswich, with ... its ocean voyages, would serve as the very type of its time'.[113] Later, between the 1460s and the 1500s, the total number of sailings (arrivals and departures) would increase twelve-fold, while the number of sailings by English vessels would increase twenty-fold.[114] John Webb depicts a thriving late fifteenth-century merchant community, benefiting from the safest anchorage on the east coast between the Humber and the Thames. He notes that, between 1464 and 1518, only in Ipswich and Hull 'did shipping increase at all substantially in east coast ports north of the Thames'.[115] Most recently, Mark Bailey has remarked on the dramatic growth in Ipswich's share of foreign trade, and on its success in comparison with other east coast ports, but more ominously on its loss of prominence in the shadow of London during the fifteenth century.[116]

Closer to home, the emergence near Ipswich of the Orwell and the rivers Deben and Stour facilitated river borne transport into Suffolk and north Essex, and, as we shall see, the rivers served as arteries for the inland flow of wine.[117] Cereals and dairy products were shipped down to the Thames and London and up the coast to the northeast, and coal was being brought back from Newcastle.[118] Chancery records provide numerous examples of this busy east coast trade during the fifteenth

[111] Kowaleski (2000), p. 477; T.H. Lloyd, *The English Wool Trade in the Middle Ages* (Cambridge: Cambridge University Press, 1977), p. 12.

[112] E. Powell, 'The Taxation of Ipswich for the Welsh War in 1282' *PSIA*, 12 (1906) 137–157; James Masschaele, *Peasants, Merchants, and Markets* (Basingstoke: Macmillan, 1997), pp. 20–1, 28.

[113] Martin (2000), p. xxvii.

[114] Scammell (1961), pp. 334–5.

[115] John Webb, *Great Tooley of Ipswich: Portrait of an Early Tudor Merchant* (Ipswich: Cowdell, 1962) p. 5.

[116] Bailey (2007), p. 269.

[117] Brodt (2000), p. 639; Redstone (1969), p. 104; Webb (1962), p. 102.

[118] C.M. Fraser (ed.), *The Accounts of the Chamberlains of Newcastle-upon-Tyne 1508–11* (Newcastle: Society of Antiquaries of Newcastle-upon-Tyne, 38, 1986), pp. 30, 33, 57, 102, 110, 170, 215, 235, 237.

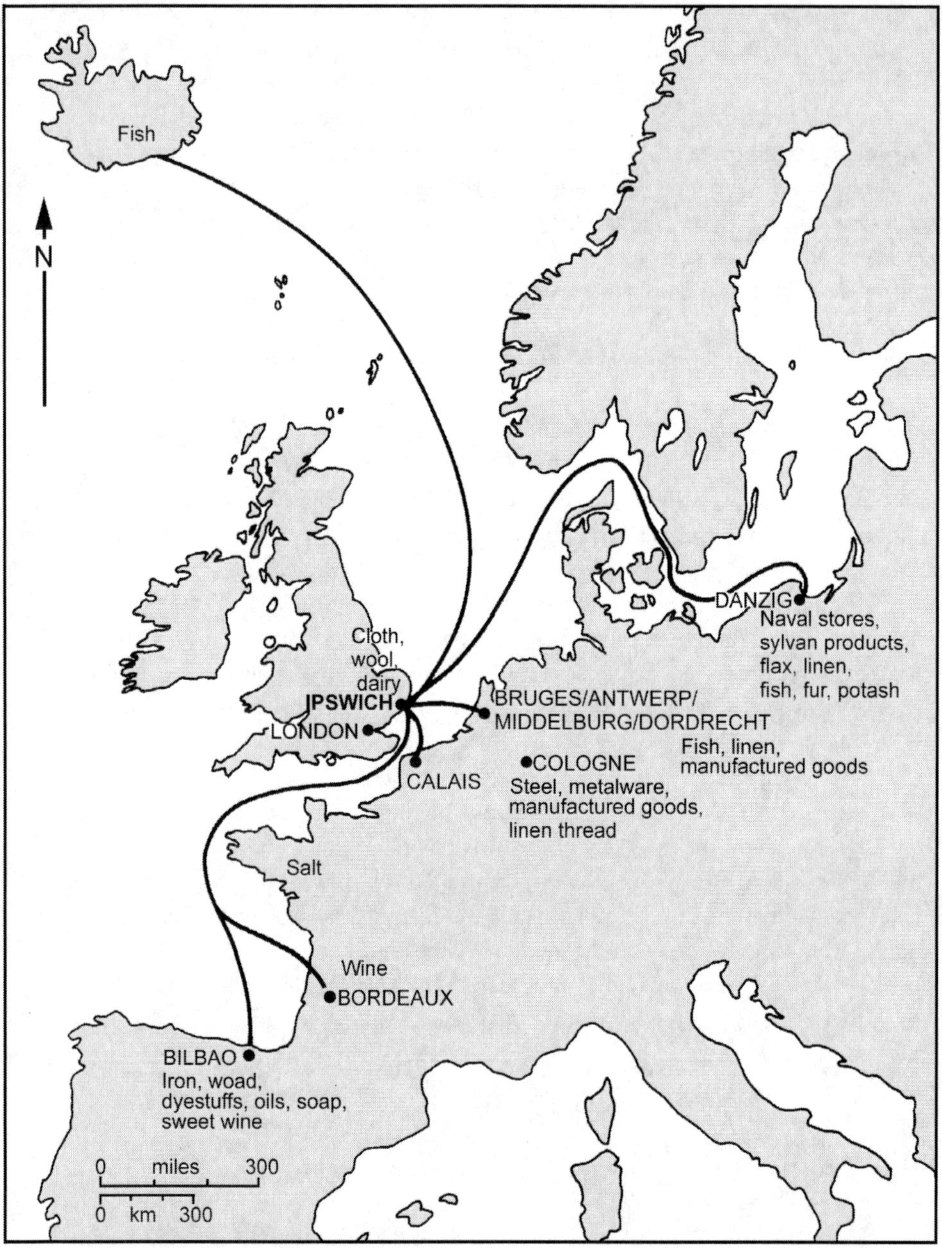

Map 3: *The principal trading partners, commodities and routes of the overseas trade of Ipswich in the fifteenth century*

century. A ship called *Laurence* of Ipswich was arrested in Hull in 1408. Richard Gouty of Ipswich, master of the ship *Nicholas* of Ipswich, became embroiled in a dispute with William Johanson of Newcastle in 1424. Some forty years later the bailiffs of Ipswich were ordered to seize the Tyneside ship *le Valentyne*. Thomas Ash of Stowmarket and John Forde of Ipswich were authorised to take East Anglian wheat from Ipswich to London, in 1429 and 1438 respectively, while Robert Wode was licensed to bring Norfolk barley from Yarmouth to Ipswich in 1440.[119]

One of the essential attributes of any medieval town was the wide range of non-agricultural occupations followed by its residents.[120] In their respective studies of Southampton, Exeter and Norwich, Platt, Kowaleski and Dunn have stressed the importance of regional and local trade and industry to resident burgesses. In Southampton they were left with no real option, being squeezed out of overseas trade by alien, notably Italian, merchants. The economic buoyancy of Norwich depended on 'the city's industry, and the trade it generated'.[121] In Ipswich the practitioners of some forty-nine different trades and crafts followed their banners, both starting and finishing at the church of St Laurence, in the annual procession of the town's Corpus Christi gild.[122] Among them were the tradesmen and craftsmen who figure prominently in this volume: victuallers such as bakers and butchers; building workers such as carpenters, glaziers and tilers; textile workers such as dyers and shearmen; metal workers such as pewterers and smiths; and leather workers such as shoemakers and tanners. Following the demise of the earlier gild merchant, there is no surviving record of craft gilds, but a degree of coherence within each of the various trades and crafts is evident in the organisation and funding of the Corpus Christi celebrations, which became an important focus of commercial and social life in late fifteenth-century Ipswich. The procession was living proof of the vitality and diversity of domestic trade and industry in the town.

On the back of the cloth industry, the taxable wealth of Suffolk grew during the late Middle Ages.[123] As the county town of Suffolk and its principal port, Ipswich could have expected to capitalise on such wealth. Indeed, Martin speaks of its 'consistently important landward trade'.[124] Nevertheless, in addition to the troubles that faced all towns in the fifteenth century, Ipswich's traders had particular problems of their own. They faced competition from Bury St Edmunds, other growing Suffolk towns, and, above all, from London, whose merchants dominated the trade in

[119] *CPR 1405–1408*, pp. 378–9; *CPR 1422–29*, p. 239; *CPR 1461–7*, p. 553; *CPR 1436–41*, p. 163; *CCR 1422–29*, p. 434; *CPR 1436–41*, p. 362.

[120] Susan Reynolds, *An Introduction to the History of English Towns* (Oxford: Clarendon Press, 1977), p. ix.

[121] Platt (1973), pp. 152–64; Kowaleski (1995), pp. 41–77, 279–324; Dunn (2000), p. 214.

[122] SROI C/4/1/2 ff. 72 r-v.

[123] A. Dyer (1995), p. 14.

[124] Martin (1955), p. 166.

luxuries and had an increasingly firm grip on the cloth industry.[125] Lilian Redstone suggests that, because the town was tucked away in the corner of the county, its location posed a serious disadvantage. She argues that, as well as being divorced from direct routes through the eastern counties from London, Ipswich did not enjoy the benefits of a network of radiating roads to the surrounding villages, as was the case with Norwich.[126] Certainly, the main road running from London to Norwich, which is marked in red on the fourteenth-century Gough Map, passed Ipswich by, and no by-road is shown connecting with the town.[127] Even so, a contemporary extent of the franchises of the town mentions highways radiating in various directions.[128] Other Ipswich records refer to highways linking the town to Hadleigh in the west, and south-east, across the heath and parallel with the Orwell, towards Nacton.[129] Roads also ran, as they do on Speed's map, from the various town gates and across Stoke Bridge towards Bury St Edmunds, Woodbridge and Colchester (Plate 1).

On balance, notwithstanding Redstone's *caveat*, historians have written positively about Ipswich's fifteenth-century fortunes. Speaking of the early sixteenth century, Alan Dyer groups Ipswich with Hadleigh and Lavenham as one of East Anglia's rising cloth towns, which was known 'to have been prosperous at that time'. According to his ranking of provincial towns, between 1334 and 1524/5 it moved up from seventeenth to seventh place in terms of taxable wealth, and between 1377 and 1524/5 from twenty-sixth to twentieth place in terms of its taxpaying population.[130] Webb observes that 'Ipswich enjoyed a period of particular prosperity in the last years of Henry VII's reign', although, on a gloomier note, he adds that 'the boom appears to have been short lived' and was over by 1520.[131] Even Phythian-Adams, while being generally pessimistic about the fortunes of late medieval towns, acknowledges that 'perhaps Ipswich sustained or even improved [its] *relative* ranking position'.[132] An important purpose of this volume is to test, by much closer examination of the sources outlined below, whether their optimism is well founded.

[125] Webb (1962), pp. 100–1; Nicholas R. Amor, 'Merchant Adventurer or Jack of All Trades: The Suffolk Clothier in the 1460s' *PSIA*, 40 (2004) 414–436 (pp. 426–7).

[126] Redstone (1969), pp. 103–4.

[127] Nick Millea (ed.), *The Gough Map: The Earliest Road Map of Great Britain* (Oxford: The Bodleian Library, 2007), pp. 70–1.

[128] While undated and written in English, the extent refers to fifteenth-century burgesses and to property belonging to the priors of St Peter and Holy Trinity: BL, Ms Add. 30,158, f. 44v.

[129] SROI C/2/10/1/5, m. 1r; C/4/1/4, f. 144r.

[130] A. Dyer (1995), pp. 26, 58, 62. His revised rankings in Dyer, 'Ranking Lists of English Medieval Towns' (2000), pp. 755–67, are different and slightly less favourable to Ipswich, showing perhaps what a difficult and imperfect exercise this is.

[131] Webb (1962), p. 9.

[132] Phythian-Adams (1979), p. 18.

A Rich Archive

Two early modern recorders of Ipswich, Richard Percyvale, editor of *Great Domesday* (1520), and Nathaniel Bacon, editor of *The Annals of Ipswiche* (1654), must take credit for much of what we know of medieval Ipswich. They made transcripts of the early customs and proceedings of the borough that have served historians well ever since. Bacon is perhaps the town's most notable historian. A scion of one of the leading families of late Tudor and early Jacobean England, he became a staunch supporter of the Parliamentary side in the Civil War. His life began in Coddenham in 1593; he graduated from Cambridge and was called to the bar; he became recorder of Ipswich in 1643 and subsequently served as MP first for Cambridge University and later for Ipswich.[133] In part thanks to them Ipswich possesses as fine a set of borough archives as any in the country.[134] There is a wealth of other primary sources to study, including customs records, national tax assessments and other central government records, household accounts and wills. These records are analysed in more detail below in those chapters in which they are cited.

Among the town's records, the surviving leet and petty court rolls are particularly full and span much of the fifteenth century. So many of the offences penalised in the leet court were of an economic nature that they cast a spotlight on trades such as baking, brewing, the selling of meat and fish, innkeeping and tanning. Martin rightly believes that, 'as the pleas heard in the petty court touched almost every aspect of life in the town, their details make these rolls the most varied and interesting of the medieval records'.[135] The petty court records are augmented by those of the very occasional sittings of the piepowder and maritime courts, which heard disputes involving foreigners and alien merchants.[136] Other borough documents include two chamberlains' accounts, one being a particularly detailed account for the year 1446/7, and the other shorter and undated, but probably for the year 1463/4. As we have seen, borough customs were recorded in various 'Domesdays' dating from the reign of Edward I.[137] Miscellaneous documents include grants, transfers, leases and a rental of land, four apprenticeship indentures and a fragment of a locally prepared taxation assessment for the town's east ward.

Accounts of both secular and religious households become an increasingly

[133] Janelle Greenberg, 'Bacon, Nathaniel' in *The Dictionary of National Biography* ed. by H.C.G. Matthew and B. Harrison, 60 vols. (Oxford: Oxford University Press, 2004), III, pp. 162–3.

[134] John Blatchly, 'Preface' in *Ipswich Borough Archives 1255–1835* ed. by David Allen (Woodbridge: Boydell for The Suffolk Records Society, 43, 2000), p. xi.

[135] Martin (1955), p. 132.

[136] The earlier petty court rolls lack pagination, with the result that references cite the date of the court. Later references cite the membrane or folio number.

[137] SROI C/4/1/1–7.

important source as the Middle Ages draw to a close.[138] Those of the Keeper of the Hospice of Framlingham Castle record the expenses of Margaret, countess of Norfolk, for 1385/6, including purchases from Ipswich, while those of Lady Alice de Bryene of Acton Hall for 1412/13 provide lists of guests at her table.[139] A number of unnamed men of Ipswich are mentioned among those guests, as well as a John Joye, who served four times as town bailiff. Later in the century the household accounts of Sir John Howard, who became duke of Norfolk (Shakespeare's 'Jockey of Norfolk'), of nearby Tendring Hall, Stoke by Nayland, provide many references to the town and its leading burgesses. In times of peace he looked to Ipswich merchants for Spanish wine and the pewter goblets from which to drink it. In times of war he needed from them rope and provisions for his ships. David Dymond's edition of the Thetford Priory accounts likewise records early sixteenth-century purchases from Ipswich of fish, cloth, tar, frankincense and hops.[140]

Among central government records now housed in The National Archives, as well as enrolled customs accounts (which record the trade of all ports under the jurisdiction of the headport of Ipswich), there is a valuable collection of more detailed particular accounts which were the working ledgers of local customs officials and list who shipped what, and in which vessels. A selection of the rolls of the royal court of Common Pleas, which had jurisdiction to hear claims worth not less than forty shillings, has been studied. The charter, close, fine and patent rolls, which are available in published calendars and register royal writs issued through Chancery, relate to many aspects of town life, for example, identifying merchants who traded out of the port of Ipswich, both denizen and alien. Tax assessments from the late fourteenth and early sixteenth century, as well as two fifteenth-century assessments of aliens, allow some estimate of population and of the number and status of aliens within the community. Alnage accounts, particularly those for the years 1396/7 and 1465/6 to 1468/9, tell us who were the clothiers and how important Ipswich was as a centre of cloth making. The rolls of medieval Parliaments have been referred to when relevant.

The former Ipswich archivist, Vincent Redstone, once remarked that 'few records are of so great a value and interest to the local historian as early wills'.[141] During the fifteenth century, over three hundred Ipswich residents proved their wills in either the petty court of Ipswich, the court of the archdeacon of Suffolk, the

[138] Sadly, no accounts of Ipswich religious houses are known to have survived, and certainly none is recorded in the organisations index of The National Archives.

[139] J. Ridgard (ed.), *Medieval Framlingham* (Woodbridge: Boydell for SRS, 27, 1985), pp. 86–128; V.B. Redstone (ed.), *The Household Book of Dame Alice de Bryene of Acton Hall, Suffolk, September 1412 to September 1413* (Ipswich: Suffolk Institute of Archaeology and Natural History, 1931).

[140] D. Dymond (ed.), *The Register of Thetford Priory* (Oxford: Oxford University Press for NRS, 59 and 60, 1994 and 1995/6).

[141] Vincent B. Redstone, 'Early Suffolk Wills' *PSIA*, 15 (1915), 291–304 (p. 291).

Norwich Consistory Court, or the Prerogative Court of Canterbury, providing the historian with an invaluable insight into their lives. Richard Felawe's testamentary provision of a school house and an endowment for Ipswich's renowned grammar school in 1482, makes his the best known of the town's medieval wills. Others shed light on the preoccupations of more humble souls as they approached their final hour. The spinster Katherine Tyndale bequeathed her best gown to help raise funds for building work on St Nicholas church, as well as itemising the other contents of her bedchamber and wardrobe in gifts to friends.[142]

The wealth of evidence that survives to document the town's commercial fortunes at such a crucial time certainly demands close analysis. This volume is, therefore, an economic study concerned primarily with the trade and industry of Ipswich, both overseas and domestic, during the fifteenth century. Although they are touched upon, such important topics as gender, government, law and order, leisure and culture, religion and social structure do not receive the detailed treatment they deserve, but which the constraints of space do not permit. The next chapter addresses some general economic themes, as illustrated by the Ipswich records, thereby setting the scene for a more detailed chronological survey. The bulk of this volume comprises six chapters which divide the century into three parts, exploring its opening, middle and closing years, and in each case focusing first on overseas trade and then on domestic trade and industry. The opening years span the period from 1400 to 1439, the middle years from 1440 to 1469, and the closing years from 1470 to 1500. The residents of Ipswich did not experience any defining events to justify such an artificial division, and they would certainly not have been conscious that they were moving from one period to another. As a result, no hard and fast demarcation can be made between the three periods, and some of the records referred to fall outside all of them. Nevertheless, this division offers a useful way of studying the sources in detail and considering the various factors that influenced the economic fortunes of the town. To quote the words of Susan Reynolds in her seminal work on English towns, it is sometimes necessary 'to tear the seamless web of history'.[143]

[142] SROI C/4/1/4, ff. 144r–145r; R1/119b.
[143] Reynolds (1977), p. 141.

– 1 –

Economic Context

The next six chapters trace the chronological course of Ipswich's trade and industry, both at home and abroad, during the fifteenth century. But first it is necessary to consider more general factors that influenced the economic well being of the town. In order to provide an appropriate sense of context, this chapter examines, in turn, the five basic topics of population, supply and demand, business organisation, investment and innovation, and regulation and competition.

Population

Medieval population levels have long fascinated urban historians because they are so important as an indicator of relative prosperity, and yet they can prove so elusive. As Hatcher observes, 'historical demography, a difficult pursuit in any age, is especially daunting in the English Middle Ages'.[1] Two fixed points punctuate the history of Ipswich's late medieval and early Tudor population. In 1377, 1507 townspeople paid Richard II's first poll tax, and, in 1524/5, 484 were taxed on Henry VIII's subsidy.[2] In attempting to convert such raw figures into population levels, historians have engaged in lively debate and used many different multipliers.[3] This chapter relies on Bailey's recent study of late medieval Suffolk to reflect current thinking in suggesting a multiplier of 1.9 for the former (1377), and between 4 and 6 for the latter (1524/5) figure.[4] It thus appears that at both dates the population of Ipswich was about 2900.

The application of the highest multiplier to the 1524/5 figure is justified by ref-

[1] J. Hatcher, *Plague, Population and the English Economy, 1348–1530* (London: Macmillan, 1977), p. 21.

[2] A. Dyer, 'Ranking Lists of English Medieval Towns' (2000), pp. 758, 761. Owing to the loss of relevant records, Dyer's figures for Ipswich are estimates. Nathaniel Bacon, in *Annals*, refers to a town roll, now lost, recording the names of 1340 persons who paid the third poll tax of 1381. As it is generally recognised that significant numbers of those liable in 1381 evaded payment, this lower figure is consistent with Dyer's estimate for 1377: *Annals*, p. 82; Rigby (2010), p. 398.

[3] Rigby provides the most recent summary of this debate: Rigby (2010), pp. 398–401.

[4] Bailey (2007), p. 183.

erence to Britnell's analysis of the population of nearby Colchester. He contends that the correlation between the number of taxpayers and the total amount of tax paid in any town is indicative of the proportion of householders there who evaded the subsidy.[5] In Colchester the mean tax bill was 5s. 10d., while in Ipswich it was double that amount, at 11s. 8d.[6] Almost certainly Ipswich was doing better than Colchester in the closing years of the Middle Ages, but such a dramatic difference suggests some serious under-counting by those tax collectors working in Ipswich.

Few late medieval towns maintained their earlier population levels, which means that, if these figures are correct, Ipswich was one of the success stories of the time. On any measure, the populations of other east coast port towns such as Boston, Lynn, Hull and Yarmouth fell sharply. Ipswich's population in 1377 was smaller than any of theirs, but by 1524/5 it had probably outgrown them all.[7] Despite the expansion of cloth-making towns such as Lavenham, over the same period the population of Suffolk probably fell by about 20 per cent, which only serves to underline Ipswich's impressive performance.[8]

Of course, the population almost certainly did not remain stable throughout the period. In seeking to identify fluctuations between these two dates, two possible sources are leet court rolls and wills. The courts of the 1480s record a far greater number of people being admitted to tithings than those of previous decades, indicating either their coming of age at twelve years, or their arriving to live within the jurisdiction of a leet court.[9] This phenomenon is consistent with the sharp rise in the number of wills proved in and after 1500 (Table 1), and with the upturn in the town's economy that appears to begin in the final decade of the fifteenth century. Considered together, this evidence may point to the beginning of a recovery in Ipswich's population at that time.

Late medieval towns faced enormous challenges in maintaining, let alone increasing, population levels and few managed to do so. Mortality remained much higher in towns than in the country, turning them into 'lethal "death traps"'.[10] Although the most virulent epidemics were probably over by 1400, plague was endemic and periodically erupted on a local or regional scale.[11] The dates of proof

[5] Britnell (1986), p. 201.

[6] A. Dyer, 'Ranking Lists of English Medieval Towns' (2000), pp. 761, 765.

[7] A. Dyer, 'Ranking Lists of English Medieval Towns' (2000), pp. 758–62. By 1662 Ipswich was almost certainly more populous than any of these towns: W.G. Hoskins, *Local History in England* (Harlow: Longman, 1984), pp. 278–9.

[8] Bailey (2007), p. 183.

[9] SROI C/2/8/1/17–22.

[10] J.M.W. Bean, 'Plague, Population and Economic Decline in England in the Later Middle Ages' *Econ. Hist. Rev.*, 2nd ser., 15 (1963) 423–437 (p. 430); Hatcher (1977), p. 24–5; Barrie Dobson 'General Survey 1300–1540', in *CUH*, pp. 273–290 (p. 276).

[11] Hatcher (1977), p. 17.

TABLE 1: IPSWICH WILLS PROVED IN EACH DECADE, 1440s to 1520s

Decade of death	*No. of wills*	*Average per year*	*Years with over twice the average*
1440s	42	4.2	None
1450s	48	4.8	1456 (17)
1460s	60	6.0	1465 (16)
1470s	57	5.7	None
1480s	47	4.7	None
1490s	45	4.5	None
1500s	69	6.9	1503 (17)
1510s	92	9.2	None
1520s	99	9.9	1526 (20)

Note

Table 1, and the following Tables 2 and 3, refer to all known extant wills made by residents for the relevant period and proved in the Ipswich petty court (up to 1499), the court of the archdeacon of Suffolk, the Consistory Court of the bishop of Norwich and the Prerogative Court of Canterbury (see Bibliography for sources). The increase in the number of wills from 1500 may be due to a greater tendency to make them, or to a higher rate of survival, particularly if executors increasingly chose to prove wills in the court of the archdeacon of Suffolk, rather than the Ipswich petty court. Nevertheless, there was no corresponding increase from 1500 in the number of wills proved in the court of the archdeacon of Sudbury by residents of Ixworth, Lavenham, Woolpit or other parishes within the hundred of Thedwastre (Amor (2002), p. 141).

of Ipswich wills point to outbreaks of plague in 1456 and 1465, and possibly to an attack of sweating sickness or some other epidemic in 1503 and 1526, as the death rate in each of these years was more than double the norm.[12] Owing to changes in attitudes to marriage and procreation, low fertility levels may possibly have reinforced these high mortality rates in keeping population levels down.[13] For example, as apprentices in the 1440s, William Burre and John Frere were prohibited from marrying or even becoming betrothed without the consent of their master, which would have reduced the likelihood of their begetting children until at least their early to mid-twenties.[14] It is impossible to establish if all apprentices were subject to the same prohibition, but only three of those who were eventually admitted as

[12] Bean refers to an outbreak of plague in Norwich in 1465: (1963) p. 429. Webb mentions sweating sickness in Ipswich: (1962), p. 152.

[13] Hatcher (1977), pp. 55–6. Mark Bailey considers late medieval fertility issues in detai in 'Demographic Decline in Late Medieval England: Some Thoughts on Recent Research' *Econ. Hist. Rev.*, 2nd ser., 49 (1996), 1–19.

[14] SROI C/2/10/1/1, m. 2r; C/6/11/1.

freemen of Ipswich in the fifteenth century were recorded as already being fathers.[15] In the absence of modern maternity care and medicine, infant mortality was high and the proportion of children who reached maturity was low by modern standards. As evidence of the number of sons who survived their fathers, the value of wills is debateable, but Thrupp has shown that they offer one of the few possible ways of estimating male replacement rates.[16] Her study of the wills of medieval London merchants showed these rates to be very low, probably misleadingly so. Fifteenth-century Ipswich wills tell a similar tale, with the replacement rate apparently never approaching parity. Even those who survived the dangers of childhood, became adults and escaped the plague could, on average, not expect to live much beyond the age of fifty.[17] There were, therefore, comparatively few elderly people in Ipswich, although evidence of rising standards of living and the foundation of almshouses may suggest that their numbers were growing.[18]

In the face of all these demographic challenges, medieval towns relied on a continuous flow of immigrants to maintain numbers. The more successful a town was economically, the greater its attraction to those seeking fame and fortune. Galloway points out that, of fifteen Ipswich residents making depositions before the Norwich Consistory Court in around 1500, none had been born in the town.[19] Many immigrants, such as Thomas Alvard of Woodbridge, arrived from nearby towns and villages which were trading partners of Ipswich. Others revealed their roots in testamentary bequests to churches that they remembered, and of property that they owned, outside the town (Table 2).[20] For example, in the mid-fifteenth century two well-heeled widows, Margery Wode and Alice Grenehood, shrugged off the loss of their first husbands and moved from the country to marry into the upper echelons of Ipswich society, without abandoning their old allegiances or properties. Margery owned land in at least thirteen different parishes, most of them in the Stowmarket area, while Alice paid for the installation of pews in Ashfield church and for pilgrimages from Mickfield to Walsingham and several other local shrines.[21]

Many of these churches and much of this property lay within 10 miles of

[15] BL, Ms Add. 30,158; SROI C/2/10/3/1–5 ff. 6r, 7v, 22v.

[16] S.L. Thrupp, *The Merchant Class of Medieval London* (Chicago, 1948; repr. Ann Arbor: University of Michigan Press, 1962), pp. 199–200; Hatcher (1977), pp. 28–9. Peter Coss suggests that 'fifteenth-century fathers were not above cutting grown-up sons and daughters out of their wills': 'An Age of Deference', in *A Social History of England 1200–1500* ed. by R. Horrox and W.M. Ormrod (Cambridge: Cambridge University Press, 2006), pp. 31–73 (p. 50).

[17] Thrupp (1962), p. 194; Britnell (1986), p. 130.

[18] SROI C/2/8/1/21 (east ward); C/4/1/4, f. 145r.

[19] James A. Galloway, 'Urban Hinterlands in Later Medieval England', in *Town and Country in the Middle Ages: Contrasts, Contacts and Interconnections 1100–1500* ed. by K. Giles and C. Dyer (Leeds: Maney, 2003) pp. 111–130 (p. 118).

[20] *Ibid.*

[21] NRO NCC, Reg. Wylbey, f. 154; Aleyn, ff. 17 to 19.

TABLE 2: BEQUESTS IN FIFTEENTH-CENTURY IPSWICH WILLS

	Bequest to Church		*Bequest of Property*	
Distance from Ipswich	*Total no. of churches*	*Percentage of total*	*Total no. of properties*	*Percentage of of total*
< 6 miles	28	34.1	22	28.2
6 < 10 miles	21	25.6	23	29.5
10 < 20 miles	19	23.2	24	30.8
> 20 miles	14	17.1	9	11.5
Total	82	100	78	100

Note

Table 2 enumerates bequests to churches and bequests of property in each case outside Ipswich. Only one bequest to a particular parish church by any single testator has been counted, but, if a testator made bequests to several different parish churches, each church has been counted. The same principle applies in enumerating bequests of property (see Bibliography for sources).

Ipswich, but some newcomers came from much further away. In the early fifteenth century Dutch merchants and sailors were arriving in substantial numbers in the port of Ipswich. Some stayed when their ships returned to the Low Countries. They spoke a language which, with a little effort, the English could understand and they sought opportunities to better themselves.[22] In 1407 Roger Bungey was suing the Dutchman Adrian Petirssone for reimbursement of the 15s. 4d. that he had loaned for Adrian's board, lodging and other necessaries in Ipswich.[23] At least twenty-one of the aliens who swore allegiance to the Crown in 1436 were living in Ipswich, of whom sixteen came from the Low Countries.[24] By 1440 the number of aliens had increased to at least sixty-three, and by 1483 increased again to at least eighty-four.[25] Of the latter, seventy came from the Low Countries, and the inflow of Dutch immi-

[22] Caroline Barron, 'Introduction: England and the Low Countries 1327–1477', in *England and the Low Countries in the Late Middle Ages* ed. by C. Barron and N. Saul (Stroud: Alan Sutton, 1995), pp. 1–28 (p. 20). J.L. Bolton refers to the technical *lingua franca* that exists between those who follow the same or similar trades or occupations: (ed.) *Alien Communities in London in the Fifteenth Century: The Subsidy Rolls of 1440 and 1483–4* (Stamford: Paul Watkins for the Richard III and Yorkist History Trust, 1998), p. 38.

[23] SROI C/2/3/1/41 (4 Oct. 1407).

[24] *CPR 1429–36*, pp. 539–87. They were recorded because they had sought letters of protection at the time of the siege of Calais: Bolton (1998), p. 29.

[25] PRO E 179/180/92, E 179/180/111. The latter figure is almost certainly an underestimate because French, Normans, Bretons and Channel Islanders, and Spanish, Italian, Breton and Hanseatic merchants, the Irish, regular clergy and children under twelve were all exempted from the aliens tax of 1483, although some in Ipswich paid it: Bolton (1998), p. 4.

grants continued during the course of the decade. The deaths of Duke Charles the Bold in 1477 and Duchess Mary of Burgundy in 1482 triggered a ferocious civil war which drove many into exile, with the flow of refugees peaking in 1482 and 1483.[26] Of the 177 individuals admitted to an Ipswich tithing in the ten years from 1479 to 1488, at least twenty-eight were Dutch.[27] By 1520 aliens may possibly have comprised more than 16 per cent of the population of east ward. Of the 171 taxpayers then identifiable from a partial subsidy assessment as either denizen or alien, twenty-eight were aliens. Aliens in Ipswich tended to live in east ward, which was closest to the docks. They congregated in a similar way in London, parts of Middlesex and Southwark where, in 1483, they comprised more than 6 per cent of the population.[28] Many of them supplied basic goods and services, but some in Ipswich, in 1520, were earning well above the average wage, which suggests that they were skilled artisans.[29] The contribution that they made to Ipswich's economy will be discussed below and touched upon again in later chapters. Many were transient, but others stayed longer and prospered.[30] Notwithstanding the decision to forbid aliens from becoming burgesses, a few, such as Giles Johnesone, were admitted as freemen.[31]

Supply and Demand

At the beginning of the fifteenth century England's economy was relatively undeveloped and unsophisticated, prompting comparison with today's 'Third World' in its dependence on the export of raw materials.[32] The range of goods available for supply to most English people was largely limited to the necessities of life: cloth, grain, leather, livestock and timber. The volume of consumer goods arriving in Ipswich from overseas was still small. Over the course of the century, testamentary bequests suggest that the supply side of the economy expanded dramatically (Table 3). The changing nature of imports will be considered in later chapters, as will the growing popularity of pewter.

The contemporary commentator, Sir John Fortescue, stressed that English people enjoyed 'abundant bedding', while, according to Hatcher, the bed became an

[26] SROI C/2/8/1/18–19. Barron (1995), p. 12; Bolton (1998), p. 34; A.F. Sutton *The Mercery of London: Trade, Goods and People, 1130–1578* (Aldershot: Ashgate Publishing, 2005), p. 272.

[27] SROI C/2/8/1/17–22.

[28] Bolton (1998), p. 8.

[29] Bolton (1998), p. 23; SROI C/1/9/1/1.

[30] Bolton considers that about 20 per cent of aliens in London were long term residents: (1998), p. 27.

[31] *Annals* (1884), pp. 147, 151; BL, Ms Add. 30,158, f. 41v; SROI C/2/10/3/1, f. 60.

[32] Barron (1995), p. 12; Richard Britnell, *Britain and Ireland 1050–1530* (Oxford: Oxford University Press, 2004), p. 331.

TABLE 3: CHATTELS BEQUEATHED BY IPSWICH RESIDENTS

	1400 to 1449	*1450 to 1469*	*1470 to 1499*
Total no. of wills	55	108	149
Bedding	4	11	26
Cloth	1	2	8
Clothing	11	16	35
Furniture	1	6	11
Jewellery	1	0	9
Kitchen and table (other than pewter and plate)	2	9	23
Pewter	0	4	10
Plate (gold and silver)	8	16	24
Trade goods	3	3	10
Washing utensils	1	5	12

Note
The figures in Table 3 exclude generic references to movables, stuff, utensils, etc. (see Bibliography for sources). Only one reference to any class of chattel in any single will has been counted.

'object of conspicuous expenditure' which demonstrated both economic and social success.[33] In 1472 John Martyn bequeathed to his daughter Margaret a mattress, a pair of sheets, a pair of blankets, two pillows, a canopy and bedding 'coloured red'.[34] Sixteen years later Thomas Goldwyn inherited from his father John a feather bed, a goose feather pillow, a coverlet of red and blue, a bolster and two pairs of sheets.[35] Clothing, jewellery and gold and silver plate are mentioned in wills with increasing frequency. More Ipswich residents owned better quality furniture in their living rooms and kitchens. Evidence of their greater interest in personal hygiene is provided by frequent references to wash basins, ewers, lavers and shaving dishes.

This supply side expansion was possible because many people were earning better wages and enjoying a much higher standard of living than their ancestors, or, indeed, their descendants for the next five hundred years.[36] By way of successive Statutes of Labourers the government had sought to hold back the tide of rising wages, but with very little success. In 1468, for example, the leet courts of the east

[33] Sir John Fortescue, *De Laudibus Legum Anglia* ed. by S.B. Chrimes (Cambridge: Cambridge University Press, 1942), p. 89; John Hatcher and T.C. Barker, *A History of British Pewter* (London: Longman for the Master Wardens and Commonalty of the Mystery of Pewterers of the City of London, 1974), p. 47.
[34] SROI R2/261.
[35] SROI R3/058.
[36] Hatcher (1977), pp. 50, 71; C. Dyer (2005), p. 129.

and west wards made token efforts to penalise carpenters who had demanded excessive wages.[37] The limited evidence of wage rates in the Ipswich records suggests, however, that it was not skilled craftsmen who were the worst offenders, but unskilled labourers. In the 1440s carpenters such as John Mancer and William Wrighte, working on the repair of market stalls and mills, might expect five pence a day, or perhaps four pence on shorter winter days. Labourers, whose job was simply to position the mill sail, could demand as much as four pence a day, and even Wrighte's apprentices earned him three pence each.[38]

Higher standards of living stimulated the market, but, in general, levels of demand in the English economy, and accordingly rates of industrial growth, were restricted by several factors. Most important was the impact of low population levels, which meant that, even if *per capita* demand was high, aggregate demand was not.[39] As we will see, the domestic markets available to most towns were geographically limited by the cost and the slow speed of transport and by the low level of market integration.[40] After the wine trade collapsed, nearly all Ipswich's inland trade was confined within a radius of 20 miles. The leading cloth towns of Suffolk appear to have lain largely outside its hinterland. Another factor was price deflation, caused largely, but not entirely, by a shortage of bullion, particularly silver. Prices were lower in 1480 than they had been in 1410.[41] As a result, even in a relatively buoyant market, manufacturers and tradesmen could not be confident of making a profit. This bullion shortage was alleviated, to some extent, by the use of credit. It was exacerbated, however, by the absence of a mature banking system, and by the tendency of the Crown and Parliament to restrict the flow of bullion and credit, and of wealthy individuals to hoard plate.[42]

English manufacturers and tradesmen faced a serious challenge from overseas competitors, many of whom were more highly skilled and better attuned to what consumers wanted. The woollen cloth finishers of the Low Countries offer a good example of this.[43] Furthermore, the export of wool and woollen cloth gave England a positive balance of trade and generated income that could be spent on overseas

[37] SROI C/2/10/1/5, m. 4v (west ward); C/2/10/1/6, m. 3v (east ward).

[38] SROI C/3/3/1/1; Bolton (1980), p. 274.

[39] Hatcher (1977), pp. 44–5; Britnell (1996), p. 157.

[40] Richard W. Unger, 'Market Integration', in *Money, Markets and Trade in Late Medieval Europe: Essays in Honour of John H. A. Munro* ed. by Lawrin Armstrong, Ivana Elbl and Martin M. Elbl (Leiden: Brill, 2007), pp. 349–380 (p. 350).

[41] Hatcher and Barker (1974), p. 276; D.L. Farmer, 'Prices and Wages, 1350–1500', in *The Agrarian History of England and Wales: 1348–1500* ed. by E. Miller, 8 vols (Cambridge: Cambridge University Press, 1991), III, pp. 431–525 (pp. 522–3).

[42] *Rot. Parl.*, iii, p. 468; iii, pp. 502, 509; iv, p. 126.

[43] John H. Munro, 'Medieval Woollens: The Western European Woollen Industries and their Struggle for International Markets', in *The Cambridge History of Western Textiles*, ed. by D. Jenkins, 2 vols (Cambridge: Cambridge University Press, 2003), I, pp. 228–324 (pp. 285–6).

luxuries.[44] Thanks to the expertise of immigrants, particularly the Dutch, the late Middle Ages witnessed some significant instances of import substitution. Beer brewing in Ipswich boomed. Bricks and tiles were made locally, rather than being imported. In Ipswich this nascent trade benefited from the expertise of Henry Herryson, 'brikemaker', who was born in Teutonic parts but resident in the town by 1436.[45] In 1483 James Anwyn from Flanders was established as a householder and employed three of his compatriots in the making of hats.[46] As if recognising that import substitution was not enough, protectionist measures were enacted in the second half of the fifteenth century, as we shall see with some local success, to discourage imports and promote domestic industries. Nevertheless, as the customs accounts show, many luxury items, such as linen and other mercery and haberdashery, continued to flow into Ipswich from the Continent. Nor was it possible to compensate by cultivating overseas markets, since efforts by English merchants in this respect during the fifteenth century generally proved unsuccessful.[47] They were ultimately driven from the Baltic and, for much of the century, lost ground in France. By 1500 Ipswich's merchants enjoyed some trade with Iceland and Spain, but, like their colleagues elsewhere in the country, their activities were largely concentrated on the Low Countries.

In Suffolk, as in England as a whole, woollen cloth was by far the most important manufacturing industry. Nationally exports grew strongly from about 1470, although in 1500 the domestic market still absorbed two-thirds of production.[48] Nevertheless, the alnage accounts for Suffolk, and the farm paid for the alnage, suggest that, during the fifteenth century, the country's most successful manufacturing industry, in its epicentre, grew by little more than one per cent per annum. That is less than half the rate of growth of national GDP during the Industrial Revolution.[49] In Ipswich the industry almost certainly shrank as the century wore on. These statistics speak volumes about the limitations of the late medieval economy.

Business Organisation

Low and unreliable aggregate demand, together with a shortage of labour, meant that few business organisations grew to any great size in England.[50] Indeed, local

[44] N. Ramsay, 'Introduction', in *English Medieval Industries* ed. by J. Blair and N. Ramsay (London: Hambledon Press, 1991), pp. xv–xxxiv (pp. xxxi–ii).
[45] *CPR 1429–36*, p. 566.
[46] PRO E 179/180/111.
[47] Britnell, *Britain and Ireland* (2004), pp. 333–5.
[48] Carus-Wilson and Coleman (1963), pp. 138–9; C. Dyer (2005), p. 150.
[49] P. Mathias, *The First Industrial Nation: An Economic History of England* (London: Methuen, 1969; repr. 1983) pp. 2, 3, 17, 222.
[50] Hatcher (1977), p. 48; C. Dyer (2005), pp. 213–14.

regulations often restricted the number of journeymen and apprentices that one person could employ.[51] While not unknown, notably in Italy, medieval joint stock companies were rare.[52] It was far more common for men, such as the late fifteenth-century Ipswich dyers Thomas Bunt and John Whetyngtone, to carry on business in partnership. Of all industries, it was clothmaking, with its extensive markets and specialist trades, that was best suited to big business. John Stanesby, the greatest clothier in Suffolk in the 1460s, who was responsible for over 10 per cent of the county's total production, employed eleven Italians in clothmaking at his premises in Bildeston.[53] Most of his contemporaries, and the clothiers who succeeded them, avoided such large payrolls by using self-employed contractors, remunerated on a piecemeal basis through a putting-out system.[54]

The largest establishments were often those engaged in metalworking or beer brewing.[55] The pewter workshops of the Winter family, for instance, employed a significant number of apprentices. Of the five alien beer brewers taxed in 1483, one retained four servants, two had three and another two kept two each.[56] In about 1520, twenty-eight households in Ipswich were recorded as containing servants and/or apprentices (Table 4).[57] The tanner John Forgon, for example, had five servants and three apprentices. The most impressive household, however, belonged to the alien John Vancleve. He was probably a merchant and was taxed on goods and chattels worth a remarkable £100. He paid five of his nine servants unusually high wages of at least forty shillings a year.

The household was the normal unit of production. In the subsidy assessment only one wage earner in five recorded in Ipswich appears to have been living independently.[58] The householder's wife and other family members were, moreover, often involved in his trade, as can be seen in the case of Thomas Lackford who was employed in the pewter workshop of his kinsman, Giles Lackford, in 1478.[59] Thomas Rodelond demanded twenty shillings compensation from Thomas Taylour in 1479 because Taylour had broken into his house, assaulted his wife and thereby deprived him, for seven days, of her essential services as his credit controller,

[51] As, for instance, in Bristol and Coventry: L.F. Salzmann *English Industries of the Middle Ages* (London: Constable and Company Ltd, 1913), p. 227; and in London: Thrupp (1962), p. 33.

[52] Spufford (2002), pp. 22–5.

[53] PRO E 179/180/111; Amor (2004), p. 426.

[54] A. Betterton and D. Dymond, *Lavenham Industrial Town* (Lavenham: Terence Dalton, 1989), pp. 26–7; Amor (2004), pp. 425, 427; C. Dyer (2005), pp. 168, 230–1.

[55] Thrupp (1962), pp. 8–9; H. Swanson *Medieval Artisans* (Oxford: Basil Blackwell, 1989), p. 73; Bolton (1998), pp. 19, 21; C. Dyer (2005), p. 230.

[56] PRO E 179/180/111.

[57] SROI C/1/9/1/1.

[58] SROI C/1/9/1/1.

[59] SROI C/2/10/1/7, m. 10r.

TABLE 4: NUMBER OF SERVANTS AND APPRENTICES IN IPSWICH HOUSEHOLDS c.1520

No. of households	*No. of servants and/or apprentices*
8	1
10	2
6	3
2	4
1	8
1	9

Note
Information from a fragment of a subsidy assessment of about 1520 (*source*: SROI C/1/9/1).

claiming and collecting his business debts.[60] Even in the case of those who were not kindred, the patriarchal relationship of master and servant was as much personal as contractual. Households had to be closely regulated to maintain public order.[61] Faithful servants were frequently remembered in their masters' wills. In 1448 Richard Rendelsham left to Isabel Tyler, for life, a messuage in the parish of St Mary Tower and made provision that, if she were ever in need, it might be sold and the proceeds used to support her.[62] Seventeen years later John Drayll instructed his executors to pay a salary to Margaret Copping, who had looked after him in his final illness.[63] In 1488 John Goldwyn left a blue gown and forty shillings to his servant Richard so long as he remained true and faithful to Goldwyn and his wife.[64]

In a manner reminiscent of feudal ties, servants were bound to their masters for fixed periods of time. The Statute of Labourers of 1349 actually threatened any 'workman or servant, of what estate or condition that he be' with imprisonment should he break his contract 'without reasonable cause or licence, before the term agreed'.[65] In an age of acute labour shortages this statute did not prevent servants from looking for better jobs elsewhere, nor other masters from seeking to entice them away. The Ipswich petty court frequently heard claims against runaway servants and their new masters. Estacia Stroop was a repeat offender. In October 1407 she fled the service of Semeine Osgot, in New Year 1408 that of Stephen Velvet,

[60] SROI C/2/10/1/7, m. 10v.

[61] P. Maddern, 'Order and Disorder', in *Medieval Norwich* ed. by Carole Rawcliffe and Richard Wilson (London: Hambledon, 2004), pp. 189–212 (p. 210).

[62] SROI R1/71.

[63] SROI C/2/10/1/2, mm. 14r, 14v.

[64] SROI R3/58.

[65] A. Luders and others (eds.) *The Statutes of the Realm (1101–1713),* 11 vols. (London: Rec. Comm., 1810–28), I, pp. 307–8.

and in early 1414 that of the new master of Ipswich grammar school, William Bury. He complained that Estacia had agreed to serve him and his wife as a maid, for a year from Christmas, at a fair wage, but had absconded after just a week without returning his money.[66] Masters were expected to treat their servants fairly and, if they did not, could not complain if they left. In 1401 one Loretta Thorp fled the service of William Snow and was recruited by James Cavendish. In her defence she said that she had been verbally abused by Snow, and feared worse. The petty court was not, however, convinced and both Loretta and Cavendish were fined.[67]

Apprentices usually lived under their master's roof. All four of the extant Ipswich indentures, two from the 1440s and two from the 1480s, bestowed on the apprentice a right to food, clothing, linen, wool, shoes and the use of a bed.[68] However well they progressed, they could not expect to be paid a regular wage.[69] Each of them was bound to serve, for a period that varied between seven and nine years, and was entitled to be fully and properly trained in their master's craft. In addition to training Thomas Heyward as a smith, on receipt of payment of ten shillings from his father, Geoffrey Osberne also sent the boy to school so that he could learn to read his primer.[70] If their master died they might well receive a generous bequest. For example, in 1445 the miller John Ladyesman bequeathed his tools to his apprentice and arranged for him to complete his training with a colleague, while in 1449 the prominent merchant John Deken left forty shillings to one apprentice and twenty shillings to three others.[71] The two late fifteenth-century indentures made provision for payment of money, in one case twenty shillings and in the other sixteen shillings and eight pence, by the master to his apprentice on completion of training, perhaps to provide some initial working capital.[72] The relationship between master and apprentice could be close, not unlike that of parent and child.[73] More than thirty years after he had completed his apprenticeship with Deken, John Drayll remembered him in a testamentary provision for the celebration of masses by the Carmelite friars.[74]

[66] SROI C/2/3/1/41 (25 Oct. 1407 and 16 Jan. 1408), C/2/3/1/48 (31 Jan. 1415); John Blatchly, *A Famous Antient Seed-Plot of Learning: A History of Ipswich School* (Ipswich: Ipswich School, 2003), p. 8.

[67] SROI C/2/3/1/36 (12 Apr. 1401, 21 Apr. 1401).

[68] SROI C/2/3/6/4 mm. 5r–v; C/2/10/1/1, m. 2r; C/6/11/1.

[69] The extant indentures make no reference to a wage, and none of the fourteen apprentices listed in the Ipswich subsidy of about 1520 received any wages: SROI C/1/9/1/1.

[70] SROI C/2/3/6/4 m. 5v.

[71] SROI R1/12–13; C/2/10/1/1, m. 5r.

[72] SROI C/2/3/6/4 mm. 5r–v.

[73] Caroline M. Barron, 'The Child in Medieval London: The Legal Evidence', in *Essays on Medieval Childhood* ed. by Joel T. Rosenthal (Donnington: Shaun Tyas, 2007), pp. 40–53 (p. 49).

[74] BL, Ms Add. 30,158, f. 4v; SROI C/2/10/1/2, mm. 14r, 14v.

Investment and Innovation

Robert Allen has argued that the high wage rates of the eighteenth century made capital investment in innovation worthwhile. They provided the stimulus for mechanisation in the textile industry, such as the development of the Spinning Jenny, which in turn paved the way for the Industrial Revolution.[75] In the fifteenth century real wage rates were even higher, and the textile industry was probably even more important to England's economy.[76] This prompts us to ask why, in Bailey's words, the Suffolk cloth industry was 'one of western Europe's prominent false starts along the road to industrial capitalism'.[77] Perhaps the most telling reason is to be found in weak aggregate demand. In the eighteenth century wages were forced up by British success in global markets, while in the fifteenth century the root cause was underpopulation. Despite the popularity of its woollen cloth on the Continent, England had yet to acquire an empire and the captive markets that went with it. James Hargreaves invested the capital equivalent of twenty years' wages in developing the Spinning Jenny. For John Stanesby of Bildeston and his contemporaries there were simply not enough buyers to justify the necessary investment in such expensive and risky research and development.[78]

The Middle Ages did, none the less, witness some innovation in textile manufacture. Most important, the horizontal treadle loom replaced the vertical loom, and was, in turn, to some extent, superseded by the broad loom. These changes not only improved the quality of the weave, but also achieved a threefold increase in productivity.[79] Carding instead of combing the wool, wheel spinning and mechanical fulling were other innovations. Indeed, Carus-Wilson famously described the introduction of the fulling mill as 'an Industrial Revolution of the thirteenth century'.[80] Like the new loom, these inventions enhanced productivity. Mechanical fulling may have cut costs by as much as 70 per cent, and increased productivity by up to 330 per cent.[81] They did not, however, catch on in the same

[75] Robert C. Allen, 'The Industrial Revolution in Miniature: the Spinning Jenny in Britain, France and India', Oxford University, Department of Economics Working Paper, 375 (2007) pp. 2, 3, 13, 14.

[76] Hatcher (1977), p. 71.

[77] Bailey (2007), p. 8.

[78] Bolton maintains the view that the limited supply of capital investment, rather than the lack of demand or new techniques, held back development in the cloth, shipping, mining and metal-working industries: (1980), pp. 282–3.

[79] John H. Munro, 'Medieval Woollens: Textiles, Textile Technology and Industrial Organisation', in *The Cambridge History of Western Textiles* ed. by D. Jenkins, 2 vols. (Cambridge: Cambridge University Press, 2003), I, pp. 181–227 (pp. 194–7).

[80] E.M. Carus-Wilson, *Medieval Merchant Venturers* (London, 1954; repr. London: Methuen, 1967), pp. 183–210.

[81] Munro (2003), p. 207.

way as the Spinning Jenny was later to do. In an industry in which quality was so important, these new inventions were simply not trusted to meet the required standards.[82] The use of fulling mills to make caps and hats was prohibited by statute in 1483 because it appeared that they were thereby 'broken and deceitfully wrought'.[83] The gig mill, which mechanised the napping process, and could reduce the work of hours to a few minutes, was banned by Parliament for the same reasons.[84] Fulling mills were dependent on water power, and, in a relatively flat county such as Suffolk, they had to compete for this precious resource with traditional grain mills. As we shall see, the Ipswich records make occasional reference to fulling mills, and Bailey has identified rather more in Suffolk than were once believed to have existed.[85] As the demand for corn fell, so fulling mills replaced some of the redundant grain mills. Even so, in fifteenth-century East Anglia, industrial mills never accounted for more than a quarter, and generally for far fewer, of the total number of mills.[86]

Another reason for the 'false start' was perhaps an unbridgeable technological gulf that still separated fifteenth-century manufacturers from the prospect of a real Industrial Revolution. The available resources of motor power were largely limited to human and equine muscle, water, wind and wood. The importance of horses to Ipswich people is attested by the care that innkeepers were expected to take in stabling them, by the frequency with which they were the object of dispute in the petty court, and by the number of people who were fined for dumping horse dung in public places. At one sitting in 1465 the leet court of south ward penalised ten people for this offence.[87] Watermills depended on a reliable flow of water. To make the most of the flow in the river Gipping, a new channel was dug above the flood plain to drive Handford and Horsewade Mills. It is named on John Speed's seventeenth-century map as 'Orwell Flu' (Plate 1).[88] Those who obstructed the flow of water with their own unlicensed weirs, such as John Bylys in 1467 and William Clovier in 1471, were penalised.[89] The existence of windmills in Ipswich is attested by an entry recording expenditure on the mill sail in the chamberlains' accounts

[82] Munro (2003), pp. 198–9, 201–2, 209–10.

[83] *Rot. Parl.*, vi, p. 223.

[84] Munro (2003), p. 210.

[85] Mark Bailey, 'Technology and the Growth of Textile Manufacture in Medieval Suffolk' *PSIA*, 42 (2009) 13–20.

[86] J. Langdon, *Mills in the Medieval Economy* (Oxford: Oxford University Press, 2004), pp. 43–4.

[87] SROI C/2/10/1/2, m. 12r (south ward). Since this was a plague year the authorities were especially vigilant to prevent and punish such common nuisances.

[88] Robert Malster, *A History of Ipswich* (Chichester: Phillimore, 2000), pp. 50–1; SROI MC5/50.

[89] SROI C/2/10/1/4, m. 1r (east ward); C/2/8/1/13 (west ward). Conversely, the general court granted to Stephen Withe a weir in the river 'over against Greenwich Cliff' for seven years at a rent of 6s. 8d. per annum, and he was not so fined: *Annals*, p. 125.

for 1446/7, and by references in the leet court in 1471 to 'Wyndemyllweye'.[90] The town had ready access to supplies of timber and its own timber market. Indeed, in 1410, the bishop of Norwich owned woodland in the Ipswich suburbs at Wicks Bishop.[91] John Waryn was an early fifteenth-century timber merchant who, no doubt, frequented this market and made a living by meeting the need for wood.[92] In 1479 Ralph Illingworth alleged that Robert Rous had removed one hundred oak, sixty elm and sixty ash trees from his close in nearby Sproughton and stripped from them bark, leaves and faggots.[93] Nevertheless, it was coal which powered the Industrial Revolution. While Ipswich maintained trading links with Newcastle throughout the fifteenth century, the level of that trade and, in particular, purchases of coal, appears to have been modest compared with some of Ipswich's east coast neighbours.[94] Although coal was increasingly important in the forging of iron and the firing of pottery, lime and possibly brick, it remained an underused source of energy, particularly in Ipswich.[95]

As so often in human affairs, it was war, in this case the Hundred Years' War, that spurred medieval people on to begin bridging the technological gulf. Cannon were first used in anger by English armies at the siege of Cambrai and the battle of Crecy in 1346. Building on the skills of bell founders, and using first bronze and later iron, guns evolved during the later Middle Ages.[96] Soon many large towns, Ipswich included, had their own gunsmiths.[97] The Dutch acquired a reputation for expert gun making, and a gunner known as Henry Ducheman was working in Ipswich in 1488.[98] Guns had to be made with precision; otherwise the consequences could be disastrous. Later centuries would witness the making of precision tools for use in other fields, which, unlike the inventions in the medieval textile industry, could be relied on to produce quality goods.

Ships probably represented the most valuable and sophisticated capital investment of the Middle Ages, which was likewise stimulated by the Hundred

[90] SROI C/3/3/1/1; C/2/8/1/13.

[91] PRO CP/40 596, m. 5r.

[92] SROI C/2/3/1/36 (16 Jun. 1401).

[93] SROI C/2/10/1/7, m. 14v.

[94] Fraser (1986) pp. 30, 33, 57, 102, 110, 170, 215, 235, 237.

[95] J. Geddes, 'Iron', pp. 167–188 (p. 171); John Cherry, 'Pottery and Tile', pp. 189–209 (p. 203) and 'Brick', pp. 211–236 (p. 223), all in *English Medieval Industries* ed. by J. Blair and N. Ramsay (London: Hambledon Press, 1991); Bolton (1980), p. 281.

[96] Salzmann (1913), pp. 107–13.

[97] Norwich had gunners and gunpowder by 1355 and fifty expensive guns by 1385: Maddern (2004), p. 193. A fifteenth-century bell founder of Bury St Edmunds used as his trademark a shield which bore not only a bell, but a cannon with a ball issuing from its mouth: Salzmann (1913), pp. 105, 107.

[98] SROI C/2/10/3/1, f. 109.

Years' War.[99] Ship design evolved during the fifteenth century. As we shall see, ships first grew to a size that enabled their crews to repel hostile mariners and pirates, and then shrank again in the more peaceful seas of the closing years of the century. The doggers that ventured to the fierce waters around Iceland also had to be well-constructed if they were to return safely. So did the carvels, which, by 1500, were undertaking the first European voyages of discovery, and thereby beginning the process of empire building that would one day make the invention of the Spinning Jenny worthwhile.[100]

Regulation and Competition

Free trade is, in theory, if not always in practice, one of the guiding principles of the modern economy. Such a concept was largely unknown in the medieval world, which worked on the basis that 'too much spontaneous interaction between individuals was a dangerous thing'.[101] True, there was some unfettered competition. The port of Ipswich witnessed a long and fluctuating campaign for control of its export trade, involving local merchants, members of various London companies, Hanseatic traders and other aliens. Unsuccessful businesses went to the wall. In Ipswich, as in York, tanners and tailors appear to have triumphed over cordwainers, skinners and pelterers in a battle for control of the supply and processing of raw leather.[102] Vintners suffered from the loss of the Gascon trade, while beer brewers took advantage of their discomfiture to promote their own product. Many petty independent traders, such as ale-wives and fish-wives, lost ground in the difficult years of the mid fifteenth century. Around the same time, local merchants found it increasingly difficult to engage in overseas trade. In both cases they lost out to those who were in a stronger position to exploit economies of scale, enjoyed more extensive trade networks and had better access to credit.

Nevertheless, for many reasons regulation trumped competition. As we have seen, municipal regulators often had the best of motives. One of their main concerns was to ensure that the town's food supply was cheap and wholesome. They sought to achieve this by regulating the time and place of sale, and the price and the quality of produce.[103] The gradual introduction of mechanical clocks made their task a little

[99] G.V. Scammell, 'Shipowning in England c. 1450–1550' *TRHS*, ser., 12 (1962), 105–122 (p. 114); Maryanne Kowaleski, 'Warfare, Shipping and Crown Patronage', in *Money, Markets and Trade in Late Medieval Europe: Essays in Honour of John H.A. Munro* ed. by L. Armstrong, I. Elbl and M.M. Elbl (Leiden: Brill, 2007), pp. 233–254 (pp. 235, 253).

[100] Power and Postan (1933), pp. 172–3.

[101] Britnell (1996), p. 237.

[102] Swanson (1989), pp. 60, 65, 151–2.

[103] Similar by-laws were enacted in most large towns: Britnell (1986), pp. 134, 137–8; C. Dyer (1989), p. 198; J. Kermode, 'The Greater Towns 1300–1540', in *CUH*, pp. 441–465 (pp. 454–6).

easier.[104] Local retailers could not sell fish before half way to prime (six in the morning), and non-resident pedlars could not do so before prime. To avoid all manner of subterfuge, merchandise brought by water to the town quay was not to be bought and sold by anyone between sunset and sunrise.[105] In theory, if not always in practice, the opportunity to pass off poor quality produce under cover of darkness was thereby reduced. Forestallers of fish and poultry, who set out to buy in bulk early in the day and sell later at inflated prices, were deterred by the threat of confiscation, fines, the pillory and, ultimately, exclusion from their trade for a year and a day.[106] Separate markets in discrete parts of the town were established from an early date for the sale of apples and bread, corn, dairy produce, fish, flesh and poultry.[107] Each was overseen by four 'good and honest' townsmen, knowledgeable in the merchandise on offer there. By keeping similar foodstuffs together, these overseers could more easily spot wrongdoing. To minimise the potential for disputes, all contracts for the future sale of goods brought to the town by water were supposed to be committed to writing, and the goods on display inspected by the overseers.[108] In order to avoid short measure, the borough authorities maintained specific standards and required victuallers to use measures that had been approved and impressed with the town seal.[109] The prices and quality of basic products, such as bread and ale, were set by central government through the assize, and enforced locally through the leet court of each ward.[110] Specific local customs prohibited the mixing of good corn with bad, and the sale of any poultry that was unfit for human consumption. Any fishmongers or butchers who sold spoiled produce, or any cooks who kept victuals beyond what we might call their sell-by date, faced, like forestallers, a series of escalating penalties for first and subsequent offences.[111]

Parliament also intervened in an attempt to regulate the trade of the nation. Sometimes it enacted protectionist measures to encourage domestic industry or

[104] M.E. Mate, 'Work and Leisure', in *A Social History of England 1200–1500* ed. by R. Horrox and W.M. Ormrod (Cambridge: Cambridge University Press, 2006), pp. 276–292 (pp. 290–1). The earliest known reference to a clock in Ipswich dates from 1594 and appears in the churchwardens' accounts of the church of St Clement: Arthur L. Haggar and Leonard F. Miller, *Suffolk Clocks and Clockmakers* (Wadhurst: The Antiquarian Horological Society, 1974), p. 19. However, more than a hundred years earlier, in 1487, Joos Clokmaker and his servant, who were probably both Dutch, were fined for not attending the leet court of east ward: SROI C/2/8/1/21 (east ward).

[105] Twiss (1873), pp. 103, 159–61.

[106] *Ibid.*, pp. 102–3.

[107] Martin (1955), pp. 164–5.

[108] Twiss (1873), pp. 119–21.

[109] *Ibid.*, p. 177.

[110] *Ibid.*, pp. 173–5; J. Davis, 'Baking for the Common Good: A Reassessment of the Assize of Bread in Medieval England' *Econ. Hist. Rev.*, 2nd ser., 57 (2004), 465–502 (p. 466).

[111] Twiss (1873), pp. 105, 145–7.

favour English shipping.[112] On other occasions, it tried to act as what we might call a competition authority, ensuring that certain trades were never practised together by the same person. In the leather industry, for example, statutes were enacted to protect consumers by keeping the crafts of tanner, currier and cordwainer/shoemaker in separate hands.[113] In an age that, by today's standards, understood little formal economic theory, the regulators, whether local or national, did not always know when to stop.[114] Consequently, many measures which restricted free trade in order to preserve social order served only to stifle entrepreneurialism.[115] We shall see how Ipswich's commercial disputes with several neighbouring towns damaged its economy, and how restrictive practices quite probably contributed to the loss of much of its share of the Suffolk textile industry.

The most glaring example of what, in retrospect, appears to have been unfair restriction was the limited franchise that Ipswich, like all other late medieval English towns, accorded to its residents. Only burgesses could trade freely in the town and only a minority of the male population was ever admitted to their ranks. Residents who were not admitted, known as 'strangers', were often worse off than English non-residents, known as 'foreigners'.[116] The extant borough records provide an incomplete list of admissions during the fifteenth century, covering sixty-six of the one hundred years.[117] They record a mere 424 names, giving an overall average of 6.4 admissions per annum. This average rose slightly during the course of the century, but only ever marginally exceeded seven. Very few of the named freemen were admitted by virtue of patrimony and there is no record of the admission of many leading burgesses, suggesting either that the admission of sons of freemen often went unrecorded, or that the relevant documents have been lost. Nevertheless, even if all the patrimonial admissions had been noted, it is difficult to conceive that they would have pushed the average above twelve admissions per annum.[118] In only five years did the annual recorded number of new burgesses rise above that figure.

Sons were only admitted on the deaths of their fathers, perhaps in their mid-twenties.[119] Former apprentices and non-residents are unlikely to have been admitted much younger. Even though freemen would generally have been richer than their neighbours and have enjoyed a better diet, it is unlikely that the majority

[112] *Rot. Parl.*, v, p. 507; vi, p. 263; vi, p. 403.
[113] *Rot. Parl.*, iii, p. 271; iv, p. 253; vi, p. 335.
[114] Bolton states that 'the whole concept of economic management as we know it today was alien to the Middle Ages': (1980), p. 327.
[115] Bailey (2007), p. 145.
[116] Kowaleski (1995), p. 221.
[117] BL, Ms Add. 30,158; SROI C/2/10/1/1, 2, 7; C/2/10/3/1–5.
[118] In late medieval Norwich and York the number of admissions by patrimony was relatively small, and, in Norwich, is unlikely to have exceeded 25 per cent of the total: Dunn (2003), pp. 83, 85.
[119] *Annals*, p. 32.

lived far beyond the age of fifty. Consequently, there seems to have been an average period in which a person could trade as a freeman of around twenty-five years. Multiplying twelve by twenty-five suggests that the total number of Ipswich freemen at any one time could not easily have exceeded 300, and might well have been fewer.[120] On the basis of these rather impressionistic calculations, between a quarter and a third of the adult male population enjoyed burgess status. In 1513 the wealthy merchant Thomas Drayll recognised the inequity of this situation, and perhaps the benefits of freer trade, in bequeathing a substantial sum to the borough on condition that those small traders, who were not freemen and whose premises were rated at less than twelve pence, should enjoy the right to open a shop and sell goods in the town free of toll.[121]

If, as seems likely, the population of Ipswich was sustained in the late Middle Ages, it is a sign of the relative economic buoyancy of the town. Indeed, thanks to immigration from the surrounding countryside and from overseas, particularly the Low Countries, numbers may even have begun to increase at the end of the fifteenth century. A significant proportion of those residents enjoyed unprecedented affluence and developed a taste for consumer goods, some of which by 1500 were made locally, rather than being imported. Even so, weak aggregate demand, the absence of large commercial organisations, and the lack of capital investment and innovation in anything but ships, together with restrictive practices, all imposed significant constraints on economic development in Ipswich, as elsewhere in England. The following chapters examine how, nevertheless, merchants, tradesmen and craftsmen carried on business in and from the town, often with notable success.

[120] I am grateful to Dr Charles Moreton of the History of Parliament Trust for providing me with material, including biographies, to be published in the forthcoming volume of the *HoP 1422–1461*. He considers that 'in 1429 the office-holders and their fellow burgesses would appear to have numbered just under 200'.

[121] Intriguingly, the figure differs significantly in the two surviving sources that refer to the bequest, Drayll's will giving a figure of £10 but Great Domesday recording £140: PCC Fetiplace, ff. 71r–72r (PROB 11/17); SROI C/4/1/4 f. 170r.

– 2 –

The Produce of Many Lands

Anyone setting sail from Ipswich to the Continent in 1400 could do so with confidence. 'The whole period was peaceful and international conditions conducive to trade.'[1] The perils of the sea did not, of course, all go away. In 1398 Ipswich merchants were ordered to assemble and man all available ships, barges and boats and proceed to attack, arrest and commit to prison pirates, robbers and other malefactors.[2] Nevertheless, the additional dangers to shipping posed by the Hundred Years' War had been temporarily lifted by the truce made by Richard II with the king of France in 1396. For a short while, Chaucer's merchant was granted his wish that 'the see were kept for any thyng / Betwixe Middelburgh and Orewelle'.[3]

Ipswich's overseas markets, like those of the nation as a whole, focused predominantly on the North Sea coast and the Low Countries from Picardy in the south-west, through Artois, Flanders and Zeeland to Holland in the north-east (Fig. 1). Middelburg was about 110 miles from the town. Calais was even closer, 82 miles away. The trip could, in theory, be completed in twenty-four hours, and was sometimes actually made in forty-eight. The need to wait for a convoy, tides and changes in the wind usually rendered the journey rather longer.[4] It is unlikely that anyone could have reached London much more quickly. Ipswich was, therefore, ideally positioned for North Sea trade.

Barron has stated that North Sea links were 'so close as to render the area a coherent region … England was truly a part of northern Europe, bound by language, religion and interdependent economies, into a single community and a common market'.[5] The trade between English merchants and their counterparts in the Low Countries was not, however, one of equals, since England possessed a 'comparatively

[1] T.H. Lloyd, *England and the German Hanse 1157–1611* (Cambridge: Cambridge University Press, 1991), p. 105.
[2] *CPR 1396–99*, p. 366.
[3] Geoffrey Chaucer, *The Canterbury Tales*, ed. by Jill Mann (London: Penguin Books, 2005), Prologue, lines 276–77 (p. 13).
[4] Martin (1956), p. 180.
[5] Barron (1995), p. 1.

undeveloped and unsophisticated economy', and 'in almost every manufacturing skill the men of the Low Countries led the way'.[6] This technological imbalance was reflected in the nature of the goods that crossed the sea in both directions.

The relationship with the Low Countries was of prime importance to English merchants, who were closely affected by political developments there. In 1400 Holland and Zeeland were ruled by Duke Albrecht of Bavaria. He kept out of the conflict between England and France, was anxious to foster trade and keen to attract English merchants.[7] Middelburg in Zeeland and Dordrecht in Holland became favoured destinations. Middelburg served as an outport for transhipment of goods to and from the markets of Bruges and Ghent and the great medieval fairs of Antwerp and Bergen op Zoom. These in turn provided a point of contact with the merchants of southern Europe. Dordrecht was the gateway to Cologne, other west German towns and the Baltic.[8] Flanders belonged to the dukes of Burgundy, whose sympathies were largely dictated by political expediency during the first three decades of the fifteenth century. Although they needed French grain, they were heavily and continuously dependent on revenue from the Flemish clothiers who had a desperate need for English wool. Conflicting political and economic considerations were reconciled, albeit temporarily, by the Anglo-French truce and the commercial agreement that Henry IV reached with Duke John in 1407.[9] The subsequent alliance maintained by Henry V and his younger brother John, duke of Bedford (as regent of France), with the Burgundians between 1419 and the late 1430s proved extremely beneficial for English merchants, although it was not destined to last.

In 1362 the wool staple was established at Calais where it stayed, subject to brief interruptions, for the remainder of the Middle Ages. As a result, virtually all the raw wool exported from England had to go through Calais. The government of the town was placed in the hands of a powerful new company of merchants, who became known as 'Staplers'. The costs of maintaining the garrison there during the Hundred Years' War had been crippling. The aim now was to encourage a thriving wool trade in Calais and make the town financially independent of the Crown. In addition to these fiscal considerations, there were good logistical reasons for locating the Staple in Calais, since the main buyers of English wool, the Flemish clothiers, did not have to travel far to make their purchases.[10]

Venturing further afield, long before 1400 Ipswich merchants had established markets in Iberia and in Gascony, which still belonged to the English Crown.[11] The truce with France reduced the risks of the long voyage, through the Channel, to

[6] *Ibid.*, pp. 12, 18.
[7] Kerling (1954), pp. 34, 209; Sutton (2005), p. 137.
[8] Kerling (1954), pp. 28–9, 132; Sutton (2005), p. 134.
[9] Barron (1995), pp. 5–7.
[10] Lloyd (1977), p. 211.
[11] Power and Postan (1933), p. xviii.

Bordeaux. With the right wind and weather, the trip could be completed in ten to fourteen days, but often took months.[12] Peace at least removed the need to run the gauntlet of the French fleet which guarded the Straits of Dover.[13] In northern Europe the main flow of trade was from east to west, carrying with it corn, furs, metals, hides and timber products. Ipswich merchants, like their counterparts in other east coast ports, were infiltrating the Baltic to sell woollen cloth and exploit what was, in the late fourteenth century, the 'principal growth area of English trade'.[14] They were even beginning to compete with the merchants of the German Hanse for a share of the spoils. Danzig, the principal port of Prussia, was the most convenient place for them to do so, and a colony was established there. The relationship between English and Hanseatic merchants during the fifteenth century was to be turbulent and there were early signs of the difficulties to come. In 1385 Robert Waleys of Ipswich, with seven others, complained to Parliament that his goods and merchandise had been seized in Prussia.[15] The mass arrest of English shipping in Danzig in 1396 was equally ominous.[16]

The good times of the 1390s did not last long. While the English ruling elite was happy to demand a share of the wealth generated by commerce, few were ready to heed the advice of the anonymous contemporary poet that "the trewe process of Englysh polycye" should be to "cheryshe marchandyse" above foreign conquest.[17] By 1400 storm clouds were gathering. As already mentioned, and as will become more apparent later, relations with Burgundy, France and the Hanse deteriorated in the fifteenth century and, before long, England was to find itself at war with all three (Appendix 1).

In addition to these looming political problems, there were serious economic difficulties. Late medieval western Europe was bedevilled by a lack of bullion, particularly silver, which caused monetary crisis and dampened the demand for English exports. This led to a depression which began in 1395 and lasted for twenty years.[18] Most rulers pursued a policy of bullionism, seeking to maintain and increase their country's stock of precious metal. Some, such as successive dukes of Burgundy, did so by regular debasements and recoinages. Edward III's attempt to do the same in 1352 was so unpopular that English kings turned to other means.[19] They tried to

[12] Webb (1962), p. 40; Margery Kirkbride James, *Studies in the Medieval Wine Trade,* ed. by Elspeth M. Veale (Oxford: Clarendon Press, 1971), p. 119.
[13] Platt (1973), p. 111.
[14] Lloyd (1991), pp. 82, 94–95, 107, 171.
[15] *CPR 1385–89,* p. 61.
[16] Lloyd (1991), p. 93.
[17] Sir George Warner (ed.) *The Libelle of Englyshe Polycye* (Oxford: Clarendon Press, 1926), lines 1, 6 (p. 1).
[18] Britnell (1996), p. 182; Martin Allen, 'The Volume of the English Currency, 1158–1470' *Econ. Hist. Rev.*, 2nd ser., 54 (2001), 595–611 (pp. 603–8).
[19] Bolton (1980), pp. 297–8.

prevent bullion leaving the country and thereby jeopardised the 'complex network of banking and credit' which spread out from its epicentre in Bruges for the benefit of English merchants, and those with whom they did business.[20] In 1397 Richard II insisted that merchants bring to the Royal Mint in the Tower of London one ounce of gold of foreign coin for every sack of wool, half last of hides and 240 woolfells leaving the country.[21] An immediate slump in exports was the inevitable result.[22] Matters were made even worse by the duke of Burgundy who, in retaliation, forbade the export of bullion from his dominions to Calais. The English bullion ordinance was rescinded in 1399, but by then the damage had already been done.[23] Further ordinances later in the fifteenth century, particularly that of 1429/30, were to play a major role in the long-term decline of the English wool trade.[24]

Having set the scene by describing the political and economic climate in which English merchants traded overseas in the opening years of the fifteenth century, we now turn our attention to Ipswich, and initially to the documentary sources surviving from that time. We will then proceed to discuss the goods that travelled to and from Ipswich, the merchants who bought and sold them and the ships in which they sailed.

John Bernard's Account

In 1401 John Bernard was at the peak of his career. One of about three dozen Ipswich burgesses who were active in overseas trade, he was engaged in shipping cloth, grain, herring and iron. In the 1390s he leased Bigod's quay from the countess of Norfolk and in 1399 bought, for £240, a parade of shops from his fellow burgess John Arnold. In tandem with these commercial interests, he had also climbed the ladder of preferment in the customs service. Starting out in the office of searcher of ships, he had been promoted to controller of the great and petty customs in the port of Ipswich by Richard II and confirmed in office by Henry IV.[25] Such a position brought him a modest but steady official income, as well as considerable opportunities for personal enrichment, and was much sought after.[26] In recognition of his status in the town, he had been appointed bailiff in 1396 and again in 1401. Good fortune is, however, a fickle mistress and Bernard's life was about to take a nasty turn.

[20] Barron (1995), p. 6.
[21] *CCR 1396–99*, p. 88.
[22] Sutton (2005), p. 145.
[23] Pamela Nightingale, *A Medieval Mercantile Community: The Grocer's Company and the Politics and Trade of London* 1000–1485 (London: Yale University Press, 1995), p. 343.
[24] Lloyd (1977), p. 257.
[25] K.N. Houghton, 'John Bernard', in *HoP*, II, p. 204.
[26] The controller in Boston was paid six pence a day: S.H. Rigby (ed.) *The Overseas Trade of Boston in the Reign of Richard II* (Woodbridge: Boydell for the Lincoln Record Society, 93, 2005), p. xvii. Thrupp comments on the value that medieval merchants attached to 'the temporary security of such appointments as the customs service … offered': (1962) p. 311.

In his role as controller, he was responsible for overseeing the collectors of customs. Normally, two collectors were appointed for both the great and petty customs and also for tonnage and poundage. To prevent fraud, it was the controller's job to check their work, ensure that their accounts were properly enrolled, keep an independent set of accounts ('counter roll'), witness their accounts before audit at the Exchequer, and keep secure half of the double-sided cocket seal. The office of collector changed hands regularly, but that of controller was more permanent and consequently entailed more trust. Bernard betrayed that trust. In 1401 he was charged with a conspiracy whereby he and two collectors had falsified the accounts and the counter roll with a view to defrauding the Crown of £525. Convicted of embezzlement, he was ordered to repay £120, his share of the ill-gotten gains, and fined a further £10. The episode may well have caused him acute financial embarrassment because, shortly after, he defaulted on payment for the shops that he had bought from John Arnold.[27] It certainly brought his civil service career to a premature end. Corruption was not uncommon in the medieval customs service and, at least once before, in 1315–17, Ipswich officials had been guilty of serious embezzlement.[28] John Bernard had, however, chosen both his time and his accomplices badly. Henry IV was under pressure from his first Parliament to crack down on fraud.[29] When one of the guilty collectors, the same John Arnold, confessed to the crime and implicated the others, the king took the opportunity to make an example.

Bernard's loss was posterity's gain. Almost certainly, in the course of investigation, the Crown demanded that his counter roll, hereafter described as Bernard's account, be produced at the Exchequer.[30] There it remained for centuries before being handed over to the Public Record Office. It provides a detailed record of 282 sailings between 1396 and 1398, not only from Ipswich, but also from Colchester, Harwich and Maldon. Dates of arrival and departure are given, as well as the name of each ship, its master, the name and occasionally the origin of each shipper, the nature of the cargo and the subsidy paid. Except in the case of wool and wine, the value of the cargo is also noted. Bernard's account does not say where cargoes had come from, nor where they were going, but 'it is frequently possible to determine roughly where a ship was laden by studying the mix of its cargoes and the names of the merchants who freighted in it'.[31] A few of the entries are illegible and sometimes mixed cargoes are valued in a way that makes it difficult to disentangle the separate items. Calculations are further complicated by variations in the value given to similar types of cargo, which may well reflect differences in quality and fluctuations in supply and demand. Nevertheless, most of the data can be retrieved (Table 5).

[27] Houghton, 'John Bernard', p. 204.
[28] Lloyd (1977), pp. 122–3; Rigby (2005), p. xxi.
[29] Rigby (2005), p. xxxvi.
[30] PRO E 122/193/33.
[31] Lloyd (1991), p. 81.

TABLE 5: SAILINGS, EXPORTS FROM AND IMPORTS TO THE HEADPORT OF IPSWICH 1396–98

Sailings	*Ipswich*	*Colchester*	*Harwich*	*Maldon*
Earliest date	Nov 1396	Feb 1397	Feb 1397	May 1397
Latest date	Oct 1398	Apr 1398	Sep 1398	Apr 1398
Months	24	15	20	12
Arrivals	75	35	45	10
Departures	51	11	37	18
Total	126	46	82	28
Exports				
Wool (897½ sacks or equivalent at £4 15s. a sack)	£4263	0	£1 (refuse)	0
Woollen cloth	£410	£418 10s.	£440	£105 10s.
Hides and skins (calf, cat, rabbit)	£38	£4	£25	0
Dairy products	£18 10s.	0	£2 10s.	£259
Other	£6 10s.	£12 10s.	£54 10s. (mostly fish)	0
Total	£4736	£435	£523	£364 10s.
Imports				
Wine	£4000	£1845	0	£280
Dyes, mordants, oils, teasels	£164	£42	£63 10s	£20
Iron	£110	£31 10s.	£1 10s.	£49
Salt	£80	£39	£60	£20 10s.
Grain	£35	£117	£69	0
Fish	£29	£153	£40 10s.	£4 10s.
Beer	£22	£9	£11 10s.	0
Stone	£19	£1	£7	£4
Soap	£9	0	0	0
Bricks/Tiles	£7	£1 10s.	£3	0
Woodland produce – ashes, bitumen, tar and timber	£2	£1 10s.	£7	£13
Other	£96 (e.g. mercery)	£154 (e.g. leather/ mercery)	£217 (e.g. furs)	£9 (e.g. canvas)
Total	£4573	£2394 10s.	£480	£400

Table 5 Note
Customs accounts tend to understate the true value of produce, as merchants were keen to minimise the amounts they had to pay. Unlike most commodities, which were charged at 5 per cent of value, wool, wine and woollen cloth were not subject to *ad valorem* customs duty. Therefore, with the exception of the woollen cloth valued in Bernard's account, they were not assessed in particular accounts. In Tables 5, 12 and 20, the values for wool and, in Tables 12 and 20, those for woollen cloth, are based respectively on the 'Mean price per sack for all wools' and the 'Mean values of cloth exports from all English ports' cited by Munro (2003), pp. 299–300; and idem, 'Spanish Merino Wools and the *nouvelles draperies*: An Industrial Transformation in the Late Medieval Low Countries' *Econ. Hist. Rev.*, 2nd ser., 58 (2005), 431–484 (pp. 444–5). The values for wine are likewise based on prices quoted in James (1971) and/or primary sources where available. All figures in Table 5 are rounded to the nearest ten shillings (*source*: PRO E 122/193/33).

Owing to its provenance and the circumstances of its production, the accuracy of John Bernard's account must be questioned. Close examination reveals a significant shortfall in the wool exports recorded by him for the year ending Michaelmas 1398 in comparison with those in the enrolled accounts for the same period (Table 6). Indeed, Bernard failed to record any wool exports by Ipswich's own merchants. Herein may lie his fraud. Nevertheless, despite its manifold shortcomings, his account remains of considerable value.[32]

Nothing else as comprehensive survives for Ipswich from this period, but other documents do cast more light on the town's overseas trade in the late fourteenth and early fifteenth century. The Staple system for the sale of wool generated records of its own, which were designed to prevent fraud and smuggling.[33] A certificate, sealed by the cocket, was issued to each master leaving Ipswich as evidence that customs duty had been paid. On arrival in Calais he presented it to the authorities for checking and return to London. It noted the date of sailing, the ship, the master, the shippers and the cargo. A cocket certificate was indented before issue and a duplicate sent to the Exchequer. If, in Calais, the information in the cocket certificate did not accord with the cargo in the ship, or if the Calais copy was different to the Exchequer copy, further investigation would be made. Some cocket certificates, as well as assorted particular accounts, survive from this time.[34]

Detailed particular accounts are now rare because once they had been audited by the Exchequer there was no need to preserve them. In contrast, central government ('enrolled') accounts are plentiful, but record only the total subsidy collected at the headport from each English ('denizen'), Hanse and other alien merchant, for each of the main categories of goods: cloth, wine, wool and other merchandise. Nor is

[32] Rigby (2005), xxxviii.
[33] Kerling (1954), p. 137; Martin (1956), 177–81 (p. 178); Lloyd (1977), p. 62.
[34] PRO E 122/50/41; E 122/51/2; E 122/51/10; E 122/51/28; E 122/51/39.

any detail provided about sailings from the various harbours within the headport's jurisdiction. Consequently, enrolled accounts paint a reasonably accurate picture of trends in trade, but they are of limited value in tracing the history of a specific port. Figures 1 to 3 below depict trends in the export of wool and woollen cloth, and the import of wine, from and to the headport of Ipswich during the fifteenth century.

The petty court rolls of Ipswich also shed light on overseas trade. Furnishing us with the names of twelve hundred litigants, the court rolls for each of the years 1400/1, 1407/8 and 1414/15 provide a much more comprehensive list of residents than any other contemporary record. As a result, it is generally possible to identify which of the merchants named in the customs accounts actually came from Ipswich. Although not all these litigants were residents, those from outside the town were generally identified as such. Moreover, some cases before the petty court provide evidence of overseas trade. Dyes, metals, salt, skins, spices and wine were all the subject of litigation. 'French' boots belonging to the merchant John Tot were, in 1408, seized as security for payment of a debt.[35] Two other useful local sources are later versions of the thirteenth-century custumal and of the customs of the quay and various markets, which set out the tolls to be charged on a wide variety of goods arriving in or leaving the port of Ipswich. Both have been published in the Rolls Series edition of *The Black Book of the Admiralty*.[36]

Finally, the records of the royal Chancery at Westminster serve many purposes. They tell us about Ipswich residents who were engaged in overseas trade; non-residents who were shipping goods in and out of Ipswich; cargoes that were leaving and arriving; customs officials of various ranks; and royal decrees that impacted on shipbuilding and the overseas trade of the town.

When Wool was England's Staple

Until the late fifteenth century, it was in wool that 'the real money was still to be made'.[37] For centuries, wool had been the country's principal export and one of its greatest sources of wealth. The Chancellor presided over the House of Lords seated on a wool sack. Sheep far outnumbered people, there being in excess of twenty million when the wool trade peaked in the early fourteenth century.[38] In the years

[35] SROI C/2/3/1/41 (27 Mar. 1408).

[36] Twiss (1873), pp. 179–207; Allen (2000), pp. 413–14; J. Masschaele, 'Toll and Trade in Medieval England', in *Money, Markets and Trade in Late Medieval Europe: Essays in Honour of John H. A. Munro* ed. by Lawrin Armstrong, Ivana Elbl and Martin M. Elbl (Leiden: Brill, 2007), pp. 146–183 (pp. 146–7).

[37] Sutton (2005), p. 102.

[38] Bruce M.S. Campbell, *English Seigniorial Agriculture* (Cambridge, Cambridge University Press, 2000), p. 158.

that followed, the trade declined as a result of royal interference. Nevertheless, wool remained, in 1400, more important than all other English exports added together.

Wool prices depended on quality, which varied from region to region, and also on supply and demand. The finer the wool and the shorter the staple, the higher the price. The best wool came from the Welsh Marches, but the nearby counties of the east Midlands and Lincolnshire also produced a high-quality product.[39] Suffolk wool was among the poorest in quality, because the county's climate was relatively warm and the grazing good, but also perhaps because flock management and breeding were amateurish compared with husbandry on the great Cistercian estates.[40] Before the Black Death, wool was produced everywhere in the county. Bailey has described the importance of sheep farming to the economy of the Breckland. As early as the Domesday Book, the Hundred of Lackford in north-east Suffolk had the highest concentration of sheep in East Anglia.[41] Nearer to Ipswich, the Hotot lords of Thorney, near Stowmarket, expected their serfs to wash and shear their flocks.[42] As a result of the demographic upheavals that followed the Black Death, sheep farming remained important but changed in significant respects. Sheep gave way to cattle on heavier soils and, on lighter soils, were increasingly reared by gentry rather than peasant farmers.[43] Although Suffolk wool was light and coarse ('slight'), it was still in demand both at home, for Suffolk's own cloth industry, and abroad. In the final quarter of the fourteenth century much cloth production in Flanders moved out of the towns into the countryside, where quality control was more relaxed and demand for top quality wools was less pervasive.[44]

As so much of the wool leaving the port of Ipswich was of better quality, from outside the county, a figure of £4 15s a sack does not seem unreasonable. On this basis, the wool subsidy was then payable at an extortionate rate of about 50 per cent, while the total value of the wool in Bernard's account came to £4263. This would account for 70 per cent of all the exports recorded there, and a remarkable 90 per cent of the value of all exports from Ipswich between 1396 and 1398.

Before the closing years of the fourteenth century, Ipswich had enjoyed no great prominence as a wool exporting port. It had not, for instance, been among those towns selected as a home staple in the middle years of the century, and for twelve years no wool apparently left the port at all.[45] After 1395 this all changed and Ipswich became very important indeed. In 1353 a Parliamentary petition requesting its

[39] Penelope Walton, 'Textiles', in *English Medieval Industries* ed. by J. Blair and N. Ramsay (London: Hambledon Press, 1991), pp. 319–354 (p. 321); Power and Postan (1933), p. 49.

[40] Munro (2003), pp. 187–8.

[41] M. Bailey, *A Marginal Economy? East-Anglian Breckland in the Later Middle Ages* (Cambridge: Cambridge University Press, 1989), p. 117.

[42] Amor (2006), p. 186.

[43] Bailey (2007), p. 217.

[44] Power and Postan (1933), p. 50; Lloyd (1977), p. 225.

[45] Carus-Wilson and Colman (1963), pp. 47–8.

inclusion on the list of home staples was rejected out of hand by Edward III. In 1404, however, a petition by the Commons and merchants of England against the diversion of its wool exports to Yarmouth, to assist the ailing economy there, was graciously granted by Henry IV. Meanwhile, the town had attracted allies with sufficient political muscle to protect its interests.[46] Why this sudden change of fortune? A reference in the 1404 petition to 'safe and secure shipping' from Ipswich may provide a clue. In comparison with Yarmouth, 'the Orwell was a safer and less conspicuous anchorage'.[47] Being further from the sea than many other east coast ports, it suffered less from storms, flooding, coastal erosion and the silting up of harbours, and was also less exposed to enemy raids.[48] On the other hand, since Ipswich was much closer to the sea than London, masters sailing from the port did not have to navigate a river as long as the Thames or risk the same coastal hazards. The modern yachtsman finds the trip to Middelburg or Calais easier from Ipswich than London, because of tides and the sandbanks off the Isles of Sheppey and Thanet.[49] In the Middle Ages merchants had to employ a special pilot to navigate the Thames.[50] Three merchants, who also exported from Ipswich, sent wool from London to Calais in 1417 in ships which were cast upon the rocks and lost off Ramsgate.[51] Commercial men have always been keen to spread their risk, and the port of Ipswich provided an opportunity to do so.

In her study of the Grocers' Company of London, Nightingale offers an intriguing explanation for the rise of Ipswich as a wool-exporting port. She considers that the bullion crisis undermined urban markets and encouraged a revival of regional fairs. Since less ready money and credit were available, these fairs provided the easiest means of exchange. The greatest of them was held each year, for up to three weeks from 14 September, at Stourbridge, just outside Cambridge. Nightingale suggests that, at Stourbridge, London merchants were selling their wares to provincial chapmen and using the proceeds to buy wool. Ipswich provided a convenient point of exit for the wool *en route* to Calais.[52] There is, no doubt, much force in her argument, but there are also certain weaknesses. As she herself notes, Lynn was an even more convenient and accessible port than Ipswich, and yet did not enjoy the same export boom. Furthermore, as we shall see, although London grocers were certainly shipping wool from Ipswich, they were outnumbered by

[46] *CPR 1401–05*, pp. 369, 475; *Rot. Parl.*, ii, p. 253; iii, p. 555. Lynn lost its wool trade to Yarmouth in 1404 and had to wait until 1406 for it to be restored: *CPR 1405–08*, p. 188.

[47] Saul (1975), p. 112.

[48] Kowaleski (2000), p. 468.

[49] Personal communication from Paul Knights, 15 November 2006.

[50] James (1971), pp. 136, 140.

[51] *CCR 1413–19*, p. 416.

[52] Nightingale (1995), pp. 368–9. Britnell also stresses the growing importance of Stourbridge Fair, from the late fourteenth century, as a national forum for the distribution of goods: *Britain and Ireland* (2004), p. 324.

London mercers and by merchants from the east Midlands (Appendix 5). Finally, whereas the revival of the fairs was relatively short lived, Ipswich retained a significant share of the wool trade throughout the fifteenth century.

Table 6 provides a breakdown of annual wool shipments from Ipswich at the turn of the century. Owing to the fragmentary nature of much of the data, any broad conclusions must be treated with caution. In the nine years between 1397 and 1411, for which information survives, relatively few sailings or shippers are recorded, never more than nineteen of one, or fourteen of the other. Undoubtedly, Ipswich wool fleets were smaller than those of London and sailed less often.[53] Over the entire period at least seventy-one different merchants dispatched wool from Ipswich, but few of them appear with any frequency in the records (Appendix 5).

TABLE 6: WOOL SHIPMENTS FROM IPSWICH, 1396–1411

	1396/7	*1397/8*	*1399/1400*	*1400/1*	*1401/2*	*1403/4*	*1406/7*	*1407/8*	*1410/11*
Sailings	9	13	11	11	19	3	2	1	14
Shippers	7	10	5	10	12	3	13	14	14
Cargoes	13	33	24	20	72	3	15	14	40
Sacks	349.25	548.07	446.45	429.02	823.03	5.30	156.29	84.10	581.30
Mean size of cargo	26.46	16.32	18.32	21.23	11.22	1.45	10.23	6.01	14.28
Enrolled wool	350	817	447	508	985	3387	1655	1585	529

Notes

The first five rows of data are taken from surviving particular accounts and cocket certificates. In some years, such as 1396/7, 1399/1400 and 1410/11, there is a fairly close correspondence with the figures in the enrolled accounts in the bottom row. The discrepancy in the year 1397/8 has already been commented on. In other years, omitted from the table, the data is incomplete or even fragmentary. Figures are given in sacks (364lbs) and cloves (7lbs). Woolfells, which were sheepskins, have been converted to sacks at a rate of 240 woolfells to the sack (Rigby (2005), pp. 260–2). One sack comprised the clip of about 260 sheep (Masschaele (2007), p. 163). A cargo is defined as the total volume of wool and woolfells belonging to any one merchant on any one ship.

Sources:

Particular accounts: 1396/7 and 1397/8, PRO E 122/193/33; 1399/1400–1401/2, PRO E 122/51/2; 1403/4, PRO E 122/51/10; 1406/7 and 1407/8, PRO E 122/50/41; 1410/11, PRO E 122/51/28.

Enrolled wool: Carus-Wilson and Colman (1962), pp. 54–6.

[53] Power and Postan (1933), p. 43.

The truce of 1396 between England and France did not hold, and state-sponsored piracy in the Channel became intense in the early years of the fifteenth century.[54] If one was going to lose a shipment to pirates, then better ten sacks than twenty. This meant that, in any one ship, the cargo as a whole generally belonged to a number of merchants, who spread their wool among various vessels. After 1401, the mean size of any single cargo laded by any given merchant on any given ship dropped dramatically, perhaps offering another example of the spreading of risk. On 4 April 1408, for example, the experienced master Andrew Johnessone sailed in his ship *Holyghost* with just over eighty-four sacks belonging to no fewer than fourteen merchants, from as far apart as Carlby in Lincolnshire, Ipswich, London, Scarborough and Northamptonshire.[55] None of their cargoes comprised more than eleven sacks. Three years later, on 29 April 1411, when five wool ships sailed from Ipswich, three merchants had wool on all of them.[56] Nevertheless, despite the constant danger, with a few fluctuations, the amount of wool exported from Ipswich continued to rise until the late 1420s.[57]

The First Manufactured Export

The growth of the woollen cloth trade is one of the enduring themes of fifteenth-century English history. Many years would pass before cloth overtook wool as England's main export, and the combined value of cloth shipments from Colchester, Harwich, Ipswich and Maldon recorded in Bernard's account was just over £1374, less than a third of the value of wool exports. Nevertheless, if we disregard wool, cloth accounted for more than 75 per cent of the value of all other exports. Ipswich's share of cloth exports in 1396–98 was worth about £410, just short of 30 per cent of the total from all four ports in Bernard's account. This percentage would almost certainly have been lower had the entries for the other harbours covered precisely the same period as those for Ipswich. Perhaps Suffolk cloth had yet to make the impact on export markets that was so apparent later in the fifteenth century, or perhaps some of the cloth laded across the county border in Harwich and Hythe had been made in Hadleigh and other Suffolk cloth towns.

Exports from the three Essex ports were predominantly of whole cloths, officially often described as 'cloths of assize', and also as 'broadcloths' (the term adopted here). They accounted in value for nearly two-thirds of all cloth exports from both Colchester and Harwich, and for all cloth shipped from Maldon. In Ipswich the

[54] C.J. Ford, 'Piracy or Policy. The Crisis in the Channel, 1400–1403' *TRHS*, 5th ser., 29 (1979), 63–78 (p. 63).
[55] PRO E 122/50/41.
[56] PRO E 122/51/28. This was common practice: Robin Ward, *The World of the Medieval Shipmaster: Law, Business and the Sea, c.1350–1450* (Woodbridge: Boydell, 2009), pp. 58–9, 74–5.
[57] Carus-Wilson and Colman (1963), pp. 55–9, 134–5.

position was quite different, with broadcloths accounting for only about an eighth of the value of such exports, and narrow *stricti* cloths, usually known as 'straits', for nearly two-thirds. The production of narrow cloths remained important in Suffolk until at least the third quarter of the fifteenth century.[58] Most of the rest are described as half whole cloths, otherwise known as broad dozens, which were probably the same width but half the length of a broadcloth. The customs of the Ipswich cloth market also refer to 'doubele werk [that they call tomennesette]' and 'longe webbe that they call omannessete'.[59] Worsted cloth, which provided the foundations for Norwich's late medieval wealth, was exported in small quantities from Colchester and Harwich, and possibly also from Ipswich.[60] We know that worsted was in circulation in Ipswich in 1415 because of a suit for debt in the petty court by Thomas Chirche, a draper of Hadleigh, against John Fryse, a Dutchman. In order to recover his money Chirche seized Fryse's goods, which included three pieces of worsted.[61]

In Bernard's account, straits are usually described as 'decenna', elsewhere they are called narrow dozens, both of which Britnell reckons measured 10 ells or about 12½ yards long, being significantly shorter than the 28-yard and 28-inch broadcloth.[62] They are likely to have been just under a yard wide, or half the width of a broadcloth. Values attributed to any given type of cloth vary, perhaps depending on whether it was finished, but broadcloths tended to be assessed in Bernard's account at one pound and straits at between five and seven shillings. This was probably less than their true market value, but perhaps a reasonable reflection of their relative worth.[63] In the alnage accounts, straits incurred a quarter of the subsidy imposed on broadcloths.

Of course, woollen cloth was not all of the same quality, and did not all fetch the same price. The particular account of 1413/14 makes several references to low-grade cloth, and also to cogware, matsales and says, which were all inferior styles.[64] In 1414 John Sutton shipped six hundred straits worth 6s. 8d. each and another five hundred worth 5s. 6d. each, two hundred cogware worth 4s. 10d. each, and two hundred matsales worth 4s. each, as well as twenty broadcloths worth 30s. each and

[58] Amor (2004), 414–36 (pp. 421–2).
[59] Twiss (1873), p. 197.
[60] Although Bernard's account records no worsted leaving Ipswich, it is mentioned in a later particular account of 1413/14: PRO E 122/51/39. The warfare and commercial contraction of late medieval Europe raised the price floor below which international trade ceased to be profitable and meant that the export of coarser, lighter and cheaper textiles, such as worsteds, was uneconomic: Munro (2003), pp. 244, 283–5.
[61] SROI C/2/3/1/48 (30 Jul. 1415).
[62] Britnell (1986), pp. 58–60; Betterton and Dymond (1989), p. 37.
[63] Higher values are given in Britnell (1986), p. 59, but the assessments offered by Power and Postan (1933, p. 7) for East Anglian cloths are not dissimilar to those in John Bernard's account.
[64] Britnell (1986), pp. 54, 173.

two hundred broad dozens worth 14s. each.[65] He was probably from London, but is known to have lodged, slightly later, with the Ipswich innkeeper John Bolle, so clearly frequented the town.[66] Thus, it is reasonably safe to assume that his enormous cargo was laded at the town's quay.

Suffolk cloth was famous for its bright colours, which stood the county in good stead in the battle for sales to the Baltic and Iberia in the fifteenth century.[67] In the Ipswich cloth market, customers could buy cloth the colours of Beverley (blue) and Lincoln (green), and no doubt many more.[68] In 1368 William Jonessone of Brouwershaven in Zeeland exported from Ipswich fourteen dozens of diverse colours in his ship the *Skenkewyn*.[69] Nevertheless, much of the exported cloth was despatched before being dyed, ready for finishing by the cloth workers of Holland and Zeeland.[70] This is perhaps symptomatic of the technology gap between England and the Low Countries to which Barron refers. It may also be that textile workers in the Low Countries were more highly skilled or, at least, had a better grasp of continental fashions and were more likely to finish the cloth in a way that appealed to the wider European market.[71] In 1415 Thomas Wysman sold two dozens, and Alice Wade twelve plain white dozens for £5 10s., both to Henry van Colen whose name suggests that he may have hailed from Cologne.[72] If so, he was a forerunner of the Cologne merchants who were to figure so prominently in Ipswich's overseas trade, and to export so much unfinished cloth to the Low Countries, in the middle years of the century.

Although Ipswich merchants had only the slightest of interests in the wool trade, in the closing years of the fourteenth century they dominated the local cloth trade. The largest single consignment left, in July 1398, in *The Trinity* of Ipswich with Robert Templeman as master. Assuming that *The Trinity* was headed for south-west Europe, this cloth was almost certainly finished. On board was a cargo worth £133 15s. belonging to several of the town's leading merchants. Henry Lomenour had the biggest stake, worth eighty-six pounds, including 160 straits, while John Parker shipped twenty-three broadcloths worth forty-one pounds. William Debenham and Thomas Lestyman transported much smaller cargoes of nineteen and eight straits respectively. Only a handful of Englishmen from outside Ipswich were using the

[65] PRO E 122/51/39.
[66] Sutton is described in the Ipswich petty court as a mercer, but this may have been a rather loose description and, as his fellow guest was the London grocer John Godston, he may have been a grocer too. For references to John Sutton: Nightingale (1995), p. 373; Sutton (2005), p. 227n; SROI C/2/3/1/48 (12 Mar. 1415, 30 Apr. 1415).
[67] George Unwin, 'Woollen Cloth – The Old Draperies', in *VCH, Suffolk*, ed. by William Page, 2 vols (London: Archibald Constable, 1907), II, pp. 254–66 (p. 255); Britnell (1986), p. 81; Bailey (2007), p. 299.
[68] Twiss (1873), p. 197; Salzmann (1913), p. 139.
[69] *CCR 1364–68*, p. 422.
[70] Webb (1962), p. 60.
[71] Walton (1991), p. 351; Munro (2003), pp. 285–6.
[72] SROI C/2/3/1/48 (24 Sep. 1415).

port for the export of cloth and there is no obvious London interest. The remaining shippers all bear names, such as those ending in -son or -ssone, that suggest they were Dutch.[73] Six of them were masters who carried modest cargoes of their own in their ships. Andrew Johnessone exported seven pieces of strait in December 1397 and a further five pieces in June 1398 in his ship, *Godbered* of Newhaven, which were worth in total just £2 4s.

Bernard's account does not tell us directly where all this cloth came from, nor where it was going, but there are clues both within the record itself and in other documents. The customs of the Ipswich quay refer to cloth of Coggeshall, Maldon, Colchester and Sudbury coming into the town and into the hands of merchants for shipment overseas.[74] John Parker's family came from Coggeshall in Essex, and he may well have sourced from there the broadcloths that he exported.[75] Bearing in mind the preponderance of straits in ships leaving the port, it is unlikely that its merchants relied heavily on the Essex cloth industry, which concentrated on broadcloths. Hadleigh was Suffolk's leading cloth-producing town at the time and, as several of its clothiers appeared before the Ipswich petty court, they were clearly doing business there. Ipswich had its own cloth industry which no doubt offered up for export any surplus that was not bought by residents.

To protect its own industry, Flanders was closed to English cloth, but during the fifteenth century Holland and Zeeland were to become the most important markets for English clothiers.[76] In 1389, after the wool Staple moved back from Middelburg to Calais, a select group of London merchants received a safe conduct from the lord of Holland and Zeeland to continue selling cloth. From these beginnings, was to grow the great Merchant Adventurers' Company.[77] The importance of this market to early fifteenth-century Ipswich is attested by the presence of masters and shippers with Dutch names, ships that came from the ports of Holland and Zeeland, and the 'Dutch' who appeared before the petty court. Not all such visitors were well behaved. In 1407 Henrichman Bury was convicted of burglary and banished for a year.[78] Nevertheless, the relationship between the town and the Dutch was to remain close.

An earlier generation of Ipswich merchants had been licensed by the Crown, in 1364, to take valuable cargoes of cloth to Brittany, Gascony and Spain and return with salt and wine.[79] *The Trinity* of Ipswich, which Henry Lomenour and his col-

[73] V. Harding, 'Cross-channel Trade and Cultural Contacts: London and the Low Countries in the Later Fourteenth Century', in *England and the Low Countries in the Late Middle Ages* ed. by C. Barron and N. Saul (Stroud: Alan Sutton Publishing, 1995), pp. 151–68 (p. 162).
[74] Twiss (1873), p. 187.
[75] PCC 1 Marche, ff 3v–4r (PROB 11/2A).
[76] Hanseatic and Genoese merchants were allowed to ship English cloth through Flanders: Harding (1995), p. 157.
[77] Kerling (1954), p. 141; Carus-Wilson (1967), p. xx.
[78] SROI C/2/3/1/41 (17, 22 Nov. 1407).
[79] *CPR 1361–64*, pp. 496–7, 507–8, 514.

leagues used to export cloth in 1398, is recorded in Bernard's account as returning to Ipswich four times, three times laden with wine and once with salt. The nature of this cargo suggests that the ship had come from south-west Europe and presumably was taking their cloth to the same destination. In just two voyages to the south-west, *The Trinity* carried on behalf of four merchants cloth worth well over one-third of the total cloth exports from Ipswich recorded in Bernard's account. It is, however, difficult to identify any other vessels that were so obviously employed on similar ventures. Far more appear to have been undertaking the shorter voyage to Holland and Zeeland with smaller cargoes. Twenty-two ships were needed to transport the rest of the cloth. This trade engaged a broader spectrum of merchants who were not in a position to risk the same capital as their wealthiest contemporaries. Nearly half of Ipswich cloth merchants apparently invested less than five pounds in the two year period covered by Bernard's account. Consequently, without being able to give exact figures, it can be said with some confidence that Holland and Zeeland, rather than France and Spain, were already Ipswich's largest market for cloth.

Exports of Raw Materials

The only other exports of any significance recorded in Bernard's account were skins and hides, and food and drink. The trade in skins and hides was limited almost entirely to Harwich and Ipswich, with Ipswich taking the greater share comprising exports worth about thirty-eight pounds between 1396 and 1398. The skins of lambs, badgers, rabbits, foxes and cats, and the hides of calves and horses, are mentioned in the Ipswich custumal, suggesting that they must all have been traded from time to time. The only skins and hides that are specifically recorded in Bernard's account were rabbit, cat and calf. Rabbit keeping and breeding had become big business by 1400.[80] Although the first reference to a rabbit warren in Ipswich itself is no earlier than 1466, the Prior of Ely already had one in neighbouring Stoke a century before.[81] The figures do not allow a calculation of total values, but nine cargoes of rabbit skins, eight of cat skins and eleven of calf hides were shipped from the town. Both cat and rabbit skins were valued at about one penny each and calf hides at about three pence, although these figures fluctuated quite significantly. Although at the close of the fifteenth century tanned hides were still being laded in the port of Ipswich, this trade may have peaked well before the century began.[82] Suffolk enjoyed the most intensive demesne cattle farming in England and one might have expected exports of hides from Ipswich to be higher. Rising standards

[80] Bailey (2007), pp. 227–30.
[81] SROI C/2/10/1/3, m. 1r (north ward); PRO CP 40/402, m. 106v.
[82] PRO E 122/53/1, E 122/53/9; Kerling (1954), p. 132.

of living had, however, fuelled growth in English leather retail trades which absorbed an increasing proportion of the raw material.[83]

John Bottold was one of two recognisably Ipswich merchants dealing in skins and hides. These included 500 cat and 650 rabbit skins, together with a cargo of cloth, that sailed on 20 March 1398 in the *Botolf* of Orwell. John Chapman was the other, exporting calf hides worth a total of five shillings. This aspect of the town's export trade was dominated by Dutch merchants, who accounted for over 70 per cent of the total value. Of the fourteen named shippers, ten had Dutch names, four of them also being masters. This state of affairs may well have continued, for James Dirrikssone was buying calf hides from Ipswich dealers in the year 1414/15, but not always paying for them promptly. He was sued in the petty court by Thomas Buntyng, Nicholas Kelle and Thomas Sherrene. Buntyng claimed to have sold Dirrikssone 106 calf hides for £1 3s. and Sherrene demanded payment from him for twenty-five worth 5s. 3d. Kelle and Sherrene settled their claims, but Buntyng's was found to be unjust and failed.[84]

Skins and hides were hardly ever shipped from Ipswich on their own and almost always accompanied cloth. This fact, coupled with the nationality of most of the shippers and ships, strongly suggests that they were carried to Holland and Zeeland. From there, calf hides were channelled through the fairs of Antwerp and Bergen op Zoom to the centres of continental parchment manufacture. Rabbit and cat skins provided one of the cheapest forms of fur for clothing.[85]

As for food and drink, the most important exports recorded in Bernard's account were dairy products. Forty-nine barrels of butter and 501 wey of cheese, together worth £259, comprised over 70 per cent of the total value of exports from Maldon. The Essex marshes were rich terrain for cattle. None of the other ports came close, and only 46 wey of cheese sailed in ships from Ipswich. The town's merchants had been active in the export of substantial cargoes of cheese earlier in the fourteenth century and would be again later in the fifteenth century. In the 1360s Richard Haverlond and John Holt had between them received Crown licences to ship 705 wey to Flanders and other parts beyond the seas, and in 1371 Hugh Walle had been licensed to carry 1000 wey to Flanders. Later, in 1389, Robert Fadinor was commissioned to buy 60 wey in Essex and Suffolk and transport them to the garrison at Calais.[86] This was fairly big business. It is, therefore, puzzling that Bernard's account records no exporter of cheese who can be unambiguously identified as a resident of the town, and that, in this respect, the later particular account of 1413/14 mentions only John Joye.[87] Possibly, dairy farmers were cutting out the

[83] Kowaleski (1995), p. 307; Bailey (2007), pp. 293, 296.
[84] SROI C/2/3/1/48 (9 Oct. 1414, 19 Mar. 1415).
[85] Kerling (1954), p. 130.
[86] *CPR 1364–67*, pp. 36, 248, 259; *CPR 1370–4*, p. 114; *CCR 1389–92*, p. 56.
[87] PRO E 122/51/39.

middleman and exporting direct. An earlier account of 1386 records that John Hyntlesham, John Arnold and Reginald of Needham were then exporting cheese.[88] Arnold was to become a successful merchant, if unreliable friend, in Ipswich, but he originated in Blaxhall.[89] According to Bernard's account, John Noreys of Culpho shipped six wey on 20 March 1397 in the *Botolf* of Orwell, mixed in with assorted cargoes of cloth, skins and mercery. Hintlesham, Needham Market, Blaxhall and Culpho were all well endowed with pasture.

The need to feed the English armies and garrisons in France meant that, on several occasions during the Hundred Years' War, wheat, malt, oats and even once two hundred bacons were shipped from Ipswich to Calais, Gascony or Harfleur.[90] At various other times in the fourteenth and fifteenth centuries grain was exported from the port.[91] England was not, however, a major exporter of such commodities.[92] As the European population contracted, demand diminished and prices fell, with the result that long distance transport of bulky foodstuffs became generally uneconomic, particularly in competition with the cheap and steady supply from eastern Europe. There is no record in Bernard's account of cereals or pulses being exported from any of the four ports.

Having examined the nature of the goods leaving Ipswich, we now turn to those arriving in the port.

Wine Flows Freely

Wine was far and away the most valuable commodity arriving in Ipswich, and, to only a slightly lesser extent, in Colchester and Maldon too. With a total worth of about four thousand pounds, it accounted for nearly 90 per cent of the value of all the town's imports. The customs duty on wine, like wool, was not charged *ad valorem*, but was fixed at a standard rate of three shillings a tun. Then, as now, the price reflected the quality and vintage. It also depended on the available supply and the port of entry.[93] Nevertheless, since Britnell reckons that in the late 1390s a tun was generally worth about five pounds, it appears that wine was relatively lightly taxed at a rate of 3 per cent.[94]

The Ipswich records refer to *caprike* wine; fortified wine, perhaps of Portugal; sweet wine, probably of Spain; white wine, perhaps of Chablis or Beaune; and wine

[88] PRO E 122/50/30.
[89] K.N. Houghton and L.S. Woodger, 'John Arnold', in *HoP*, II, pp. 54–6.
[90] *CCR 1349–54*, p. 293; *CPR 1350–54*, pp. 60, 196; *CPR 1416–22*, p. 11.
[91] Nils Hybel, 'The Grain Trade in Northern Europe before 1350' *Econ. Hist. Rev.*, 2nd ser. 55 (2002), 219–247 (p. 232).
[92] Kerling (1954), p. 104.
[93] James (1971), p. 7–8.
[94] Britnell (1986), p. 63n.

of Rochelle, north of Bordeaux, normally consumed in France and the Low Countries. The customs of the quay also mention 'eysel' (bitter) wine or wine vinegar.[95] Some of the town's taverns may even have served Rhenish wine from Germany, brought back in small quantities in wool ships, such as *Kogg John*, *Saint Maryship* and *The Trinity*, returning from Calais.[96] Nevertheless, nearly all the wine that arrived in the port was claret of Gascony shipped from Bordeaux.[97] Gascon wine was produced twice a year, the first ('vintage') in early autumn and the second ('reek') in winter after the feast of Candlemas (2 February).[98] Medieval wine did not keep for long, and among the town's customs was a rule that, during the period between the arrival of the old wine and the new, the bailiffs should search the town's taverns and cellars to sample what remained. If they found any that was unfit for consumption they should take it into the high street, condemn it in public and smash the vessel in which it was contained.[99] As 800 tuns (201,600 gallons) of wine arrived in two years, even though much of it was distributed beyond the town, it would have taken a lot of drinking to avoid wastage. Saturday night brawls, such as one in April 1415 in John Bolle's tavern, must have been commonplace.[100]

Wine-carrying ships arrived regularly in Ipswich during the months from November to May, and one even straggled home in July. Some ships arrived together, such as *The Trinity* and *Saint Maryship* on 2 November 1397, and some arrived in quick succession, such as the *Christopher*, *The Trinity* and *Saint Maryship*, which docked earlier that year between 7 and 9 May. This was, however, the exception rather than the rule. In times of war wine ships sailed in heavily and expensively guarded convoys. This convoy system tended to concentrate arrivals in a short span of time, rather than permitting the steady stream which emerges from Bernard's account.[101] Possibly ships were arriving in convoy elsewhere, before making the final leg of the journey to Ipswich. All wine merchants were ordered to gather in convoy off Sandwich in 1386 and off the Isle of Wight in 1387, to minimise the threat from the French navy.[102] More likely, during this temporary period of peace, convoys had been dispensed with, or at least relaxed. A dramatic fall in freight charges between 1381 and 1396, to less than a half their former rate, supports this view.[103]

[95] PRO E 122/193/33; SROI C/2/3/1/34 (26 Oct. 1400), C/2/3/1/37 (09 Jun. 1401); C/3/3/1/1; *Annals*, p. 66; Twiss (1873), p. 185; M. Postan 'The Trade of Medieval Europe: the North', in *The Cambridge Economic History of Europe, Trade and Industry in the Middle Ages* ed. by M. Postan and J. Habbakuk, 4 vols (Cambridge: Cambridge University Press 1952), II, pp. 119–256 (pp. 123–4).
[96] Harding (1995), p. 156.
[97] Postan (1952), pp. 123–4; E.M. Carus-Wilson 'Introduction', in *Studies in the Medieval Wine Trade* ed. by Elspeth M. Veale (Oxford: Clarendon Press, 1971), pp. xi–xiv (p. xii).
[98] Webb (1962), p. 40; Kowaleski (1995), p. 271.
[99] Twiss (1873), p. 177.
[100] SROI C/2/3/1/48 (30 Apr. 1415).
[101] James (1971), pp. 16–17, 25–6.
[102] *CCR 1385–89*, pp. 257, 435.
[103] James (1971), p. 152.

English merchants enjoyed the lion's share of the nation's wine trade in the 1390s, including that of Ipswich.[104] Ipswich merchants shipped at least 318 of these 800 tuns, which accounts for nearly 40 per cent of the total. In 1413/14 they shipped 142½ of the 182 tuns that arrived in the headport.[105] Only three of the thirteen named in Bernard's account invested in more than one voyage, namely Robert Templeman the above-mentioned master of *The Trinity*, his principal client John Parker and Roger Blast. Templeman sailed to collect both reek and vintage wines in 1397, but did not venture out again in 1398. Parker was the leading importer, with one cargo of fifty tuns and, together with John Wode, a half share in another of fifty-two tuns. Blast's investment was more limited, being four tuns from the 1397 vintage and a third share of eighteen tuns from the 1398 reek. Such joint ventures, where the reward and risk were shared not just on the voyage but in the specific cargo, were most common in the carriage of wine. Only two merchants in each of the wool and cloth trades entered into them, while eight did so in the wine trade. Among other denizens shipping wine into the town were William Thorp of Harwich and John Seburgh of Colchester who imported two cargoes of the autumn 1396 vintage in separate ships.

Although there is no sign of any Dutch interest in the wine trade, Gascon merchants had long enjoyed a privileged status in England, to encourage their allegiance to the Crown. The great charter of 1302 allowed them to live and carry on wholesale trade freely without staying with English hosts.[106] This measure is reflected in the customs of Ipswich, which exempted from local hosting regulations all sellers of wine and woad, another important import from Gascony.[107] The growing hostility of English merchants, jealous of such privileges, slowly pushed Gascons out of the home market.[108] As late as 1387, one Sodet, a merchant of Bordeaux, had shipped to Ipswich an enormous cargo of 110 tuns of vintage wine.[109] He may have been one of the last to trade on this scale. No Gascon merchants can be identified in Bernard's account, or in the particular account of 1413/14, as an importer of wine into the town, although they are mentioned in other contemporary records.[110] Janyn Shipman, a merchant of Bayonne, was sued, for example, in the petty court thrice in quick succession for debts, and on one occasion the claimants seized his dagger and lance as security for payment.[111] The sums involved make it unlikely that he was a humble sailor. If he was a merchant, he may have been disinclined to return.

[104] Lloyd (1991), pp. 106–7.
[105] PRO E 122/51/39.
[106] James (1971), pp. 71–3.
[107] Twiss (1873), pp. 147–9.
[108] James (1971), pp. 81–3; Bridbury (1975), p. 36.
[109] PRO E 122/50/30.
[110] James (1971), p, 191.
[111] SROI C/2/3/1/34 (21 Dec. 1400); C/2/3/1/35 (18 Jan. 1401, 1 Feb. 1401).

Dyes for Suffolk's Colourful Cloth

At a time when exports of English cloth were beginning to grow, the textile industry was dependant on imports for many of its raw materials, such as dye-producing plants, mordants, ashes, soap and teasels. Between 1396 and 1398 more dyes and dyestuffs arrived in Ipswich than in all three other ports in Bernard's account added together, with a value of £164. This evidence reinforces medieval Suffolk's reputation for coloured cloth. The principal cargoes were madder for reds and russets, and woad for blues. The customs of the quay mention weld, or dyer's rocket, which grows in England. When used alone, weld produced yellows, and, when combined with woad, greens and blacks.[112] Although indigo, which also produced blues, is not thought to have been employed in Europe as a dye before the mid-fifteenth century, two cargoes worth eight pounds arrived in Ipswich.[113] Dealing in woad appears to have required more investment than trading in madder. Bernard's account records the arrival of six cargoes of woad, two of which travelled together in the same ship, weighed 14 tons and were worth the impressive sum of seventy pounds. The larger of the two belonged to the Ipswich merchant Thomas Oston. Madder tended to come in more frequent but less valuable loads, and the total value of imports was still rather below the figure for woad. This difference is reflected in the petty court rolls. The 'woadman' Andrew Coke was in 1407 fighting off creditors, who seized his stock of woad worth an impressive £128 10s. 1d.[114] Madder appears in the court rolls, but in much smaller and cheaper quantities.

Alum was the principal mordant used in the medieval cloth industry, although copperas (ferrous sulphate) was also employed.[115] Mordants were necessary to fix most dyes, other than woad, into the fibre.[116] Alum was used with madder, and they appear together in the same disputes in the petty court rolls as,.[117] Copperas was required for darker shades. Both arrived by ship in Ipswich, although copperas came only in tiny quantities, and both are mentioned in the customs of the quay.[118] In the same ship as copperas, with the same shipper, came brimstone or sulphur ('*brenstone*') and '*tynsoyle*', which may also have been substances of the dyer's craft. Potash from wood ashes was necessary to make woad soluble. One small load of ashes arrived at Harwich, but, although they also appear in the customs of the quay,

[112] Twiss (1873) p. 195; Salzmann (1913), pp. 147–8; Postan (1952), p. 376–7; Walton (1991) p. 333–4.
[113] Walton (1991), p. 333.
[114] SROI C/2/3/1/41 (13 Dec. 1407, 16 Jan. 1408).
[115] Alum was also used in the tawing of leather, although usually in the Ipswich records the context suggests its employment in the cloth industry: John Cherry, 'Leather', in *English Medieval Industries* ed. by J. Blair and N. Ramsay (London: Hambledon Press, 1991), pp. 295–318 (p. 299).
[116] Walton (1991), pp. 335–6.
[117] SROI C/2/3/1/41 (16 Jan. 1408); C/2/3/1/48 (24 Sep. 1415).
[118] Twiss (1873), pp. 187, 189.

none was evidently imported into Ipswich. Quite probably they were readily available locally from men such as Richard Wagstaff, who claimed to have sold Richard Fyshere four barrels of wood ash in the summer of 1408.[119] Although old habits died hard, soap was beginning to replace fuller's earth and urine in the cleaning of cloth before finishing.[120] The best quality was white, but most of that used in dyeing was black. Thirteen barrels of soap, presumably black, valued at one mark (13s. 4d.) a barrel, arrived in Ipswich between 1396 and 1398, together with one chest of white soap worth the same. Teasels occur from time to time, being used primarily in the production of broadcloth to raise the nap after fulling.[121] One mixed cargo included teasels to the value of ten shillings, which must have been a substantial assignment. Thomas Peryman sued John Fuller for a more modest sum of three shillings over the sale of teasels in 1401.[122]

These raw materials came from various parts of Europe. Madder, for instance, was cultivated in Zeeland. Many of the ships carrying it to Ipswich were Dutch and sailed under the command of Dutch masters. Andrew Johnessone arrived with madder on five separate occasions, four times with cargoes of his own, entrusting a sixth load to Simon Wyssone in the *Skonausyt* of Zierikzee. On another occasion Johnessone shipped three cargoes of woad, including one of his own, in the same *Skonausyt*. Woad did not, however, grow in Holland or Zeeland, so this batch must have originated elsewhere, perhaps in the fields of Flanders or even Picardy, one of the markets temporarily opened by the truce with France.[123] Another small cargo of woad travelled with salt and wine in the *Botolf* of Orwell, presumably from southwest France or even Spain. The international trade in alum was dominated by Italians who sourced it from mines in Asia Minor and generally imported it into England through Southampton.[124] The trade into Ipswich appears, however, to have been appropriated by the ubiquitous Dutch, presumably as trans-shippers. Simon Wyssone arrived with three bales in August and Andrew Johnessone with fifteen in October 1398, both aboard the *Skonausyt*. Soap was another Italian import which caught the eye of these two intrepid Dutchmen, perhaps because some of it reached the Low Countries overland. Luxurious white soap was regarded as the cheapest product for its weight that could economically be carried over the Alps and on to the fairs of Brabant.[125]

[119] SROI C/2/3/1/41 (31 Jul. 1408).
[120] Postan (1952), p. 127; W.R. Childs, *Anglo-Castilian trade in the Later Middle Ages* (Manchester: Manchester University Press, 1978), pp. 109, 111; Spufford (2002), pp. 272–3.
[121] Postan (1952), p. 380.
[122] SROI C/2/3/1/36 (19 Apr. 1401).
[123] Kerling (1954), p. 125; Kowaleski (1995), p. 235; Spufford (2002), p. 333.
[124] Platt (1973), p. 157; Spufford (2002), p. 334.
[125] Spufford (2002), p. 273.

Essential Products from Overseas

Whether wielding swords or beating them into plough shares, medieval people needed iron. England always had an abundance of iron ore, but, such was the demand from nearly every trade and occupation, that significant quantities were still imported from abroad. Furthermore, Ipswich was a long way from the main English deposits.[126] Although overland transportation was not impossible, iron is heavy and the costs of carriage were high. It was almost certainly cheaper to bring it by sea from the continent. The arrival in Ipswich of about £110 worth of iron was recorded by John Bernard, this being more than in the other three harbours added together. One cargo is described as 'osmund', while two or three were 'iron of Spain'. The customs of the quay also mention 'bac' iron, old iron and iron of Normandy.[127] The term 'osmund' was originally used to describe superior quality iron from Sweden, but came to mean any similar iron sold in small bars or rods, by the barrel or sack, and not by weight.[128] The unworked iron of northern Spain was the most heavily traded in north and west Europe, often being laded with cargoes of wine and salt.[129] *La Katerine* of Ipswich, carrying all three products, ran aground on the sand at the mouth of the Thames near Queenborough in 1390. In the early 1400s one of the town's merchants, Roger Gosenold, sold Robert Waleys a consignment of iron, wine and salt for the not insubstantial sum of £31 13s. 4d., while iron and wine belonging to another local merchant, Thomas Lestyman, were seized by the petty court when he failed to pay for them.[130]

In the days before refrigeration, salt was essential both as a preservative and a seasoning in food. Like iron, it was produced in England, principally in Worcestershire. But this supply was not enough and, for Suffolk residents, not readily to hand. After 1350 England became a net importer.[131] Foreign salt came mainly either from Zeeland, or from the Bay of Bourgneuf in western France. The former variety ('white') was generally fine, and the latter ('Baysalt') much rougher, giving rise to the term '*sol gross*'.[132] Both feature in the customs of the quay.[133] The warm sun, shining on the sea coast of the Bay, evaporated water and produced salt without the need to burn fuel. As a result, French salt workers enjoyed a natural and increasingly important advantage over Zeelanders.[134] Between 1396 and 1398

[126] Geddes (1991), p. 167.
[127] Twiss (1873), p. 191.
[128] Rigby (2005), p. 274.
[129] Spufford (2002), p. 324.
[130] *CPR 1388–91*, p. 267; SROI C/2/3/1/36 (21 Apr. 1401); C/2/3/1/35 (27 Jan. 1401, 1, 22 Feb. 1401, 1 Mar. 1401).
[131] Saul (1975), p. 225.
[132] Kerling (1954), p. 100; Saul (1975), p. 225.
[133] Twiss (1873), p. 195.
[134] Kerling (1954), pp. 98–9.

twelve cargoes of salt arrived in Ipswich worth nearly eighty pounds. Only one arrived on a Dutch ship, carried on behalf of Peter Man, whose commercial interests lay solely in northern Europe. It is reasonable to assume that this came from Zeeland. Another was carried by a ship of Nantes, then the capital of Brittany, situated close to the coast of the bay of Bourgneuf. Six of the other eight cargoes were shipped by Ipswich merchants who traded in Gascony, and three arrived on board ship with wine. A generation earlier, in 1364, John Goldyng, Henry Starling and Geoffrey Starling had all imported salt from the Bay.[135] It seems safe to assume that most of the salt arriving in Ipswich was still coming, and would continue to come, from France.

An Early Taste for Beer

The value of Ipswich's recorded imports of grain between 1396 and 1398 came to just thirty-five pounds, significantly less than those of Colchester or Harwich. Colchester was a more populous town than Ipswich, with 2951 taxpayers in 1377, nearly twice the number recorded in Ipswich, and thus had more mouths to feed.[136] Much of the land surrounding Colchester was heath and wood, and was not suitable for arable farming. Local harvests were inadequate and the need to rely on grain from elsewhere was perennial.[137] Ipswich, however, was largely able to survive without foreign supplies. A consignment of 22 quarters of barley and 20 quarters of oats arrived by ship just before Christmas 1397, another of 150 quarters of oats two months later, and a third of 22 quarters and 10 tons (40 quarters) of wheat in the early spring of 1398. As 1½ quarters of wheat or barley provided no more than a subsistence diet for one person each year, and as, since the Black Death, Ipswich residents had become more demanding, foreign grain clearly supplied but a tiny proportion of their needs.[138] According to Unger, 'the land area required to supply a late medieval English town [with grain and fuel] was small by almost any measure' and, for one the size of Ipswich, would be about 36,000 hectares, or just under 140 square miles.[139] Except in exceptional circumstances, and at low points in the year, the town's rural hinterland apparently sufficed to keep people and animals fed.

Ipswich's consumption of fish from abroad was also very modest compared with that of Colchester, perhaps reflecting credit on its own fishing fleet. Nearly all the fish imported into Ipswich was herring, with just three small cargoes of lamprey and a tiny consignment of halibut. In Colchester they tucked into cod, haddock, herring, plaice, ray, salmon, *skepulwhite* and turbot. Three Ipswich merchants

[135] *CPR 1361–64*, pp. 507–8, 514.
[136] A. Dyer, 'Ranking Lists of English Medieval Towns' (2000), p. 758.
[137] Britnell (1986), pp. 42–5.
[138] C. Dyer (1989), pp. 152–3.
[139] Unger (2007), pp. 371–2.

shipped fish into Ipswich, as did Peter Man of Maldon, but most of it belonged to the Dutch masters of Dutch ships.

Conversely, Ipswich burgesses consumed imported beer at twice the rate of their contemporaries in Colchester, importing over 8000 gallons in two years. Hopped beer was not unknown in early medieval England. Hops have been found in a late Anglo-Saxon pit in Ipswich, and were quite possibly intended for use in brewing.[140] Archaeological remains of hops have also been unearthed in Norwich, Tamworth, Whitstable and York. In the late thirteenth century Richard Somer was selling 'Flemish ale', probably beer, in Norwich.[141] Hops may even have been cultivated in Kent by immigrant Flemish weavers before the Black Death.[142] In 1400 unhopped ale was still the principal drink for the vast majority who could not afford wine, helping them to avoid the wide range of enteric diseases lying in wait in most drinking water. Ale was exported regularly from east coast ports to the Low Countries throughout the first three quarters of the fourteenth century.[143] In 1364 John Heton, Robert Gatman, Richard Haverlond and John Holt were respectively licensed to ship 200 small barrels, 10 tons, 40 tons and 15 tons of ale from the port of Ipswich to Flanders or Brabant.[144] Ultimately, however, hopped beer, rather than unhopped ale, was to win the hearts and minds of English people. Suffolk's love affair with beer can be dated back at least to the days of John Bernard and quite possibly earlier. He recorded the arrival of nine cargoes of beer in the port, including 11 barrels of red beer and 24 barrels of white.[145] The ability to differentiate between beer *ordinaire*, red beer and white beer suggests that Ipswich had already become quite a sophisticated market for the product. Red and white beer sold at a premium. While the value of beer *ordinaire* fluctuated, it was never more than two shillings a barrel. The red and white were each worth about 2s. 7d. a barrel. A marketing executive of the time might have promoted it as 'reassuringly expensive'.

Beer was brewed in Holland and Prussia. Lloyd describes it as 'the new drink promoted aggressively by north-German merchants in the late fourteenth century'.[146] All the beer imported into Ipswich arrived on Dutch boats and all but one of the shippers had Dutch names. John Chapman was the only Ipswich importer; he paid customs on a cargo of eighteen barrels, comprising 648 gallons, in April 1398. Possibly the Dutchmen were importing German beer. They are

[140] P. Murphy, 'Palaeobotanical Evidence for the Agrarian Economy of the Anglo-Saxon town'. Lecture to 'Ipswich Unearthed' Conference, 27 October 2007 (unpublished).

[141] Judith M. Bennett, *Ale, Beer, and Brewsters in England: Women's Work in a Changing World* (Oxford: Oxford University Press, 1996), p. 79.

[142] Ian S. Hornsey, *A History of Beer and Brewing* (Cambridge: The Royal Society of Chemistry, 2003), p. 313.

[143] Kerling (1954), pp. 216–19.

[144] *CPR 1364–67*, p. 32.

[145] There were 36 gallons in a barrel and 12 barrels in a last: Rigby (2005), pp. 259, 261.

[146] Lloyd (1991), p. 81.

certainly known to have done so, but normally in ships of Amsterdam, of which none arrived in Ipswich. The largest consignment of 6 lasts, over 2500 gallons, came from Haarlem, an important centre of beer production in Holland. It is fair to assume that the rest came from Holland too. The golden days of beer brewing in Holland were soon to pass, as natural disasters and political crises deprived it of the necessary raw materials.[147] By 1413/14 imports of beer had fallen sharply with only one shipment, worth just fifty shillings, being recorded.[148] An enduring market for beer had, however, already been created in Ipswich and the subsequent history of brewing in the town is discussed below.

Building Materials

The importation of 41,000 paving tiles and 42,000 wall tiles between 1396 and 1398 bears witness to their growing popularity in Ipswich. No roof tiles appear to have been carried on incoming ships, probably because they had been manufactured locally for many years.[149] Paving tiles were used for interior flooring, which was becoming increasingly common in town houses, and wall tiles was another name for bricks.[150] Paving tiles were more expensive than wall tiles, twenty shillings purchasing 10,000 of the former, and between 12,000 and 15,000 of the latter. Many floor tiles were coloured and patterned, which would have added to their value.[151] The apparent scale of these numbers should not be overstated. One small fifteenth-century kiln in Hull was capable of producing between 47,000 and 48,000 bricks a year.[152] These Ipswich imports were, however, evidence of a trend and accounted for two-thirds in value of all the tiles recorded in Bernard's account. This suggests that bricks and tiles were more fashionable in Suffolk than across the county boundary. They had been used in England in Roman times, and in medieval Suffolk, which had little suitable stone, since the twelfth century. Polstead is the earliest of many Suffolk churches in which brick was employed, and Little Wenham Hall provides an example of its early use in vernacular architecture. The Hundred Years' War encouraged further interest in brick and tile-making among returning troops, who had admired brick built buildings in France and Flanders. Those tiles arriving in Ipswich could have come from any of the Low Countries or from Germany, it is difficult to tell which. Three of the ships carrying tiles were of Rotterdam and Schiedam in Holland, towns active in trans-shipment from north Germany; and

[147] Kerling (1954), p. 114–15.
[148] PRO E 122/51/39.
[149] Salzmann (1913), p. 119.
[150] Salzmann (1913), p. 125; Kerling (1954), pp. 128–9; Cherry (1991), pp. 197–8; Moore (1991), p. 226.
[151] Salzmann (1913), pp. 126–7.
[152] Moore (1991), p. 221.

two were from Brouwershaven in Zeeland. None of the shippers was local, although some were English. Wherever they came from, domestic manufacture meant that such imports would not be needed for much longer.

The paucity of stone in Suffolk may also explain why significantly more of it arrived in Ipswich than in the Essex towns. Since stone by its nature was heavy and expensive to carry, long distance transportation was to be avoided wherever possible. It was, however, far cheaper to send by sea than over land. Not all stone was used for building. Some may have served simply as ballast. Later in the century masters were fined twelve pence a ton for throwing ballast into the river Orwell.[153] Some, such as the pair of millstones and the quernstones that were shipped by Alexander Louf of Ipswich, were used in milling. The three pairs of 'hoenidstones' were perhaps employed as whetstones. Silkstone, freestone, black stone, ragstone and marble were all mentioned in the customs of the quay, but none appeared in Bernard's account. Most of the stone was transported in ships from Dordrecht, Rotterdam and Schiedam, and probably originating from northern Germany.

Nearly all the imported timber was German oak ('wainscot') boards used in building. Over five thousand of these boards were recorded by Bernard. As befitted its location on the edge of the treeless landscape of the Essex marshes, Maldon received most of them, while almost all the rest went to Harwich. Ipswich's share was only three hundred boards. While the county might have wanted for stone, as we have seen, there appears to have been no shortage of timber.

Wine, dyes, iron, salt, food, drink and building materials made up the lion's share, in value, of imports into Ipswich in the closing years of the fourteenth century. The list does not stop there, however. Mercery and household goods attest to greater consumer choice and rising standards of living. Pots and pans, plates, mats and even three mustard mills enhanced the home. Stoles, otter skin hoods, linen cloth, pouches, pins and Cologne thread beautified the figure. Altar cloths and crosses enlivened religious ceremony. Reams of paper facilitated administration and learning. In Colchester, where they were importing hampers of haberdashery, the consumer revolution may have gone even further. In the membranes of Bernard's account, it is possible to discern early signs of England's first consumer revolution.

Merchants and Masters from Far and Wide

Those merchants operating out of Ipswich at this time fell into several loosely defined groups, comprising wool merchants, local merchants (Appendix 6), merchants from other English towns and aliens, generally from the Low Countries.

At any one time, the number of merchants exporting wool from England probably did not exceed four hundred, of whom seventy-one were active in Ipswich

[153] *Annals*, p. 164.

between 1397 and 1413 (Appendix 5).[154] They can be sub-divided geographically. Among the four local men, John Rous, town bailiff between 1408 and 1410, was most prominent. Although neither he nor any other Ipswich merchant was recorded in Bernard's account as exporting wool, he did so throughout the first decade of the fifteenth century. He was a leading member of the Company of Staplers, in which capacity, like so many of his colleagues, he was expected to make loans to the king. Together with Thomas Broun, John Chirche and Richard Whittington, the most celebrated merchant of his day, Rous loaned the enormous sum of four thousand pounds to Henry IV to pay arrears of salary of the garrison at Calais. Repayment was often promised from the subsidy charged on the export of wool from a particular town, in this case Ipswich, which naturally encouraged merchants to continue trading there.[155] When Rous's house was burgled, among the documents alleged to have been stolen was a debenture. This was a semi-public document issued by the Staple of Calais in recognition of a debt, which could be circulated as a form of currency.[156] Rous had close contact with other prominent London merchants. In 1410 he was called upon to arbitrate on behalf of John Lardener, a wealthy citizen and mercer, who appears as a wool merchant in Bernard's account and who became captain of the castle of Oye in Picardy.[157]

Members of the most influential London livery companies competed for a controlling interest in the wool trade. Historically, the fishmongers and the grocers had secured the greatest share, but by 1400 the mercers were challenging strongly.[158] Of those London merchants known to have traded from Ipswich, three were grocers, one was a fishmonger and six were mercers. Perhaps the interest shown by mercers in this provincial town was a reaction against the restrictive practices operated by the longer established companies in the capital. The documented London contingent also included two drapers, a tailor/vintner, another vintner, and a woolman. Some of these men had achieved national eminence. John Woodcock and Nicholas Wotton both served as mayor of and MP for London.[159] Many of them had other far flung commercial interests. Geoffrey Brook was doing business with Italian merchants of Florence, Genoa and Piedmont, while Thomas Broun was one of several merchants who sent factors on an unsuccessful trade mission to Italy in 1412.[160] Neither Brook nor Wotton was above profiting by acts of piracy against Hanseatic shipping.[161]

Another sizeable body of merchants hailed from the east Midlands: from

[154] Power and Postan (1933), p. 41.
[155] *CPR 1405–08*, pp. 321, 414–15.
[156] SROI C/2/3/1/48 (23 Oct. 1414); Postan (1973), pp. 49–50.
[157] *CPR 1401–05*, p. 45; *CCR 1409–13*, p. 85.
[158] Lloyd (1977), p. 251; Sutton (2005), p. 125.
[159] C. Rawcliffe, 'John Woodcock' and 'Nicholas Wotton', in *HoP*, IV, pp. 896–9, 905–7.
[160] *CCR 1392–96*, p. 268; *CCR 1402–05*, p. 345; *CPR 1408–13*, pp. 461–2; Lloyd (1977), p. 284; Nightingale (1995), pp. 339, 381–2; Sutton (2005), p. 227.
[161] *CCR 1402–05*, pp. 345, 497; *CPR 1401–05*, pp. 508, 511.

Coventry in the west, through Leicester, Northampton and Oakham, to Carlby in the east. These were men of substance in their own communities. John Loudham and John Pykwell served as mayor and MP for Northampton and Leicester respectively.[162] Their wool was assembled in collection centres, such as Melton Mowbray in Leicestershire, ready for dispatch to the coast. For at least a hundred years the merchants of Northampton had been beating a path to Ipswich, and complaining about the tolls they had to pay when they arrived.[163] With the decline of Lynn, it became an even more convenient port from which to export their high quality wool. The attraction of the town as a destination may perhaps have been enhanced by the possibility of sale *en route* to Suffolk cloth-makers.[164] Of the remaining exporters, three came from the east coast ports of Yarmouth, Lynn and Scarborough. One, John Burton, whose 'mercantile interests were not geographically limited', may even have hailed from Bristol.[165]

By 1400 alien merchants had been largely driven out of the English wool trade by penal rates of export duty that made it impossible for them to compete with denizen sellers in Calais.[166] Italian merchants were allowed to export wool direct to the Mediterranean, but most of their vessels sailed from Southampton.[167] A hundred years before John Bernard's time Lucchese merchants had shipped wool out of Ipswich, and it appears that some Italians still retained a modest interest in the town.[168] In 1413, in response to an attack on English merchants in Italy, the Crown ordered an embargo on all trade with the Genoese. Normally, such an order would have been issued to the local authorities of all major port towns, but in this case it was only felt necessary to alert London, Southampton and Ipswich.[169] Of the three alien merchants named in one cocket certificate, Geoffrey Petressone was probably Dutch, Paul Meliane probably Italian, and John White, with his distinctly English name, one of the most intriguing figures in the records. Sutton tells of 'an itinerant mercer who went to Italy and stayed', with the name of John White. He acquired substantial property and used his wealth to endow an English hospice in Rome.[170] If this was the same man, then he may have been encouraged by fellow London mercers, with whom he probably maintained contacts, to join them in their Ipswich venture.

The involvement of local merchants in the export market seems to have been limited almost entirely to woollen cloth, in which they had established a majority

[162] C. Rawcliffe 'John Loudham', in *HoP*, III, pp. 628–9; C. Kightly 'John Pykwell', in *HoP*, IV, p. 151.
[163] Masschaele (1997), p. 141.
[164] C. Dyer, *Making a Living in the Middle Ages* (London: Yale University Press, 2002), pp. 302–3.
[165] J. Roskell and L.S. Woodger 'John Burton', in *HoP*, II, pp. 437–9.
[166] Carus-Wilson and Colman (1963), p. 196; Lloyd (1977), p. 284.
[167] Platt (1973), pp. 152–63.
[168] Lloyd (1977), p. 69.
[169] *CCR 1409–13*, p. 437.
[170] Sutton (2005), p. 227.

interest. Nineteen Ipswich merchants shipped over three-quarters of the cloth leaving the port. Of these, William Debenham, Henry Lomenour, John Michell, John Parker and John Roberd each invested more than twenty pounds, accounting for just under three-quarters of the Ipswich share of the trade. Ipswich merchants had control of half the salt trade, a stake of between 30 and 40 per cent in both wine and dyes, and a passing involvement in some other imports. Fourteen local merchants shipped wine. Gilbert Boulge, John Parker and John Roberd each brought back cargoes worth in aggregate at least two hundred pounds. Parker and Roberd despatched their woollen cloth on the same ships that brought back their wine. Bearing in mind the length, perils and cost of the voyage, it is not surprising that the trade with south-west France and Spain involved these men, Ipswich's more substantial merchants. Such a high level of risk and investment could only be justified by deep pockets and the prospect of large rewards. The majority limited themselves to the safer short-haul trade with the Low Countries.

Notwithstanding the hazards involved in owning, or at least sailing, one's own vessel, it bestowed distinct commercial advantages. Six of these Ipswich merchants, namely John Clerk, Robert Mersh, John Michell, John Roberd, Thomas Scot and Robert Templeman, were masters of ships. The most energetic of them were John Michell, who made six voyages in the *Kogg John*, and Robert Templeman, who made five in *The Trinity*. Both Michell and Templeman braved the long journey to Gascony. Roberd was not described as a master in Bernard's account, but he appeared as a mariner in the petty court when his small boat was seized as security for payment of a debt.[171] Generally, the relationship between merchant and master must have been a close one of trust and confidence, although it was subject to the occasional strain. In November 1407 John Rous and Andrew Johnessone were at loggerheads in the petty court, but, following a successful arbitration, Rous was happy to entrust a cargo of wool to Johnessone's care five months later.[172] The association must also normally have been profitable, although there were always failures. In March 1404 Thomas Wade, mariner and merchant of Ipswich, sought to avoid his creditors by obtaining royal immunity from prosecution in return for service in Ireland. By May he had clearly failed because he was kicking his heels in Newgate prison, detained 'for divers debts to divers of the king's lieges'.[173] Perhaps his ventures had fallen foul of the French pirates who, by then, so plagued English shipping.

The evidence of personal names suggests that about three dozen merchants from the Low Countries were trading with Ipswich; coincidentally a very similar number to that of resident Ipswich merchants. Twenty-one shipped cargoes to the town, twenty took cargoes away and only six did both. Seventeen mastered ships carrying

[171] SROI C/2/3/1/34 (7 Oct. 1400).
[172] SROI C/2/3/1/41 (29 Nov. 1407); PRO E 122/50/41.
[173] *CPR 1401–05*, pp. 376, 387.

goods both for themselves and for others. With few exceptions, they sailed vessels built in Holland and Zeeland. Table 7 shows their share of selected exports and imports. Among the cloth exporters, William Jacobissone stands out with a share worth £19 6s. 8d. No-one dominated the Dutch trade in hides to the same extent. The largest single cargo was six hundred calf hides, worth a little over seven pounds, exported by Cotkyn Whyte in the *Goodwill* of Brouwershaven in July 1398. The year before Whyte had exported 10 wey of cheese in the same vessel. Dutch imports into Ipswich were varied. The only products in which they did not trade were wine and salt. As merchant and master, Andrew Johnessone was the single most energetic individual recorded in Bernard's account. In just two years he undertook fifteen voyages in and out of Ipswich and Harwich, nearly all in his ship the *Godbered* of Newehaven. He would carry on his own behalf, on behalf of associates and on behalf of other shippers, almost anything that would turn a profit: cloth, hides, cheese, madder, woad, alum, soap, teasels, beer, onions, garlic and wainscot. In the process, he captured for himself nearly 60 per cent of the Dutch share of the market in dyes and other raw materials for the cloth industry. The value of the cargo he carried on each voyage was modest, suggesting that, like most ships of Holland and Zeeland, the *Godbered* was relatively small. In later years Johnessone would turn his hand to bigger challenges and sail wool ships such as the *Holyghost*.[174]

TABLE 7: DUTCH SHARE OF EXPORT/IMPORT OF SELECTED PRODUCTS IN IPSWICH 1396–98

Product	*Approx. per cent. share*	*Approx. value*
Woollen cloth (export)	11	£43 10s
Hides (export)	70	£26 10s
Dairy products (export)	40	£7 5s
Dyes etc (import)	38	£64 5s
Beer (import)	83	£18 5s

Source: PRO E 122/193/33.

Naturally, not all the money made by these merchants was invested locally. Much of it would have been repatriated to the cities, counties and countries from whence they came. The more illustrious among them may never even have set foot in the town. Nevertheless, whether or not they were resident in Ipswich, and wherever they spent their profits, they brought economic benefits to the town. Outgoing cargoes had to be collected and transported to the quayside. Incoming cargoes had

[174] PRO E 122/50/41.

to be weighed, stored and distributed to buyers in Ipswich and other towns and villages where the produce would ultimately be used. On occasions ships would remain in port serving as temporary warehouses for the cargo that they had delivered.[175] Each ship had to unload, reload and be made ready for the return voyage. Re-provisioning and perhaps repairs were required. Sometimes a ship would remain in port for only a few days, on average for about two weeks, but often for five weeks or more.[176] Since on-board accommodation for the master and crew was usually quite primitive, during that time many of them went ashore for food and shelter, rest and recreation.[177] It all generated activity in local shipyards, quays, shops, taverns and inns, and provided welcome employment for a variety of crafts and tradesmen.

A Multitude of Small Ships

One hundred and thirty-nine different ships feature in Bernard's account. Assuming that their names truly reflected their port of origin, of the 130 whose origin can be confidently identified, just fewer than half, fifty-eight, were built in England, and fifty-nine in the Low Countries. Of the remainder, eight came from northern France, two from western France and three from Germany. Although Parliament had enacted in 1381 that English merchants should only use ships whose masters were bound to the king's allegiance, the statute allowed an exception if none was available.[178] This proviso was interpreted so liberally that the law was effectively ignored.[179] Certainly, English overseas trade would have been severely restricted had it been enforced.

All but two of the wool ships recorded in Bernard's account were built locally in Gosford (now Woodbridge) Haven, at the mouth of the river Deben, or, in the case of the *Mary*, in Ipswich itself.[180] Save for the *Nicholas* of Nantes, all wine was carried in English-built ships. These came from as far away as Hull on the east coast and Plymouth on the south coast, with one even from Guernsey. Ships built in the Low Countries almost always carried less valuable cargoes. Although the value of a cargo did not necessarily correspond to its bulk, it is fair assumption that these bottoms were usually relatively small. They needed to be in order to sail the rivers and waterways of Holland and Zeeland. Their small size made them easier to load, quicker and more manoeuvrable, cheaper to build and then sail, and ideal for smuggling.[181]

Nine ships were built in Ipswich itself, another in the nearby Suffolk village of

[175] Ward (2009), p. 86.
[176] Warner (1926), lines 512–19; Childs (1978), p. 170; Ward (2009), pp. 87, 98.
[177] Ward (2009), pp.113–20.
[178] *Rot. Parl.*, iii, p. 120.
[179] Rigby (2005), p. xx.
[180] Kowaleski (2000), p. 473.
[181] Kerling (1954), pp. 174–5.

Levington and ten more in Gosford Haven. The town's shipyards and boat builders were kept busy, not just by its own merchants, but by the demands of the naval war waged intermittently against the French. The Crown required port authorities to build ships for the navy five times between 1294 and 1401.[182] In 1354 and again in 1372 local carpenters were ordered to complete the building of ships for the king's service, with the threat of arrest and imprisonment for any who proved contrary or rebellious.[183] Sailors were also needed. The number of crew depended, of course, on the size of the vessel, but a larger ship needed proportionately fewer men than a small one. In John Bernard's time, a ship of 120 tons needed perhaps thirty hands, while one of 80 tons might still need twenty-seven. Size was not, however, the only determinant. The type of vessel, the nature of its rigging and the conditions under which it sailed were also critical factors.[184] Naval vessels, or merchant vessels sailing in convoy, required larger crews. In 1372, for example, the crew of the *Magdalen* of Ipswich, *en route* from Gascony, was reinforced by twenty-eight fighting men.[185] Thirty years later no fewer than eighty mariners were summoned from Ipswich and neighbouring coastal villages to serve on *The Trinity* with its master John Mayhew.[186] Thomas Spaldyng was excused from appearing in the petty court to answer a debt claim because he was in the service of the king on the sea.[187] The demands of war boosted the local economy and provided employment, but they also strained urban resources and were not always welcome.[188] Following the English naval defeat at La Rochelle in 1372, the bailiffs of Colchester and Ipswich were ordered jointly to build a barge to defend the coast. By pleading poverty, they successfully persuaded the Crown that the cost should be shared with the up and coming town of Hadleigh. The barge was duly built, but the complaints did not stop. The Ipswich bailiffs were unable to raise the necessary funds from the burgesses and had to pay the town's contribution themselves.[189]

Summonses to assist the king's navy often stipulated the type of craft that was required and allow a glimpse of activity in the town's ship yards. In 1378 the bailiffs were ordered to repair and make ready the town barge; in 1379 to provide a balinger; and in 1382 to repair and make ready a crayer called the *Nicholas*.[190] Carus-Wilson describes all three as small vessels, and the crayer as a 'river boat'. Both barges and

[182] Kowaleski (2007), p. 237.
[183] *CPR 1354–58*, pp. 12, 18; *CPR 1370–74*, p. 219.
[184] Kerling (1954), pp. 175–6; Ward (2009), pp. 100–1.
[185] James (1971), p. 26.
[186] *CPR 1401–05*, p. 196.
[187] SROI C/2/3/1/34 (18 Nov. 1400).
[188] In his study of Yarmouth, Saul stresses the costs of war: (1975), pp. 3, 109, 143. Kowaleski is much more positive in her contention that 'central government was transferring more money to port towns than it was taking away in the form of taxes': (2007), pp. 253–4.
[189] Britnell (1986), p. 83; *CPR 1370–74*, p. 355.
[190] *CCR 1377–81*, pp. 51, 182; *CCR 1381–85*, p. 145.

balingers had started out only with oars, but had acquired sails by the fifteenth century.[191] Their oars made them fast and manoeuvrable and thus particularly suited for war at sea.[192] Crayers arriving in the port of London in the late fourteenth century were rather larger, capable of carrying over 40 tuns of wine. One of the many ships arriving in Ipswich was called *Hakebot*, which is more likely to be a description than a name. The *hakebot* was a vessel common in Flanders and had possibly evolved from a fishing boat.[193]

When he launched his expedition to Ireland in 1399, Richard II called up for naval service all vessels of 25 tons' burden and more.[194] If 25 tons was the minimum size necessary for naval service, it is unlikely that the ships he had commandeered in earlier years would have been any smaller. Nor are they likely to have been very much larger. Two-thirds of the ships hired by Henry IV and Henry V were below 100 tons.[195] The ships that took wool to Calais and brought wine from Gascony were the biggest. The *Christopher*, which was arrested in Sandwich in 1403 with wool belonging to John Rous, was of 80 tons burden.[196] The *Mary* was carrying a cargo of 110 tuns of wine when it arrived in Ipswich in October 1386, and *The Trinity* one of 62 tuns when it docked in May 1397.[197] These vessels were very probably cogs. Indeed, three of them were called *Kogg John*. The cog was a 'vessel frequently seen in northern waters and well adapted to the long hauls of the Anglo-Gascon trade. It was a sturdily-built craft, high sided and rounded at stem and stern; it was commonly very broad for its length.'.[198] The remains of a number of medieval cogs have been discovered, most famously those of the so-called *Bremen Cog* which sank in 1380 and was rediscovered, as a well preserved wreck, in the river Weser. It was 23.27 metres long, had a maximum beam of 7.62 metres, and a height amidships of 4.26 metres. A central mast carried a square rigged sail, and the rudder sat at the stern, behind the aftercastle which provided basic living accommodation. Weighing 55 tons, the *Bremen Cog* could carry up to 90 tons of freight in a hold with a capacity of 160 cubic metres. Although, 'tubby and ponderous looking', a full size replica 'demonstrated astonishing sailing and handling qualities'.[199] It could sail at 60 degrees to the wind and, in a fresh wind, theoretically reach a speed of 10 knots. Unladen its draft was only 1.25 metres, but fully laden it needed 2.25 metres of water in which to float. A ship of these proportions could not be sailed on to the shore at

[191] Carus-Wilson (1967), pp. 87–8.
[192] Kowaleski (2007), pp. 237, 248–9.
[193] Harding (1995), p. 161.
[194] *CPR 1396–99*, p. 511.
[195] Scammell (1961), 327–41 (p. 332).
[196] *CCR 1402–05*, p. 209.
[197] PRO E 122/50/30.
[198] Platt (1973), p. 71.
[199] Dirk Meier (translated by A. McGeoch), *Seafarers, Merchants and Pirates in the Middle Ages* (Woodbridge: Boydell, 2006), pp. 36–7.

high tide and unloaded when the tide went out. It needed to anchor in deep water. Thus arose a need for lighters, wharfs, gang planks, cranes and all the paraphernalia of the late medieval harbour, so frequently noted in the Ipswich records. The cog remained in use in north European trade from the early thirteenth to the mid-fifteenth century.[200] Its importance to the Ipswich economy is underscored by its becoming the centrepiece of the common seal of the town.

International relations in the 1390s were more conducive to overseas trade than probably at any time in the fifteenth century. Despite the long shadow of bullion shortage that fell over the economy of western Europe, those merchants trading from Ipswich were doing well. Wool and wine absorbed most of their capital, but cloth was of growing importance. Imports were much more varied than exports. Calais and Bordeaux were still the most important markets, especially for the bigger players. Nevertheless, the smaller ports of Holland and Zeeland were a growing attraction to those who wanted to limit their investment and risk to smaller cargoes. If not already, they were soon to become the main destinations for English cloth. The Baltic was and would remain a difficult market to penetrate. Although they had to share the spoils of trade with visitors from London, the east Midlands, east coast ports, the Low Countries and even Italy, Ipswich burgesses were enthusiastic participants in overseas trade. They had established a majority interest in the local export of cloth and a substantial minority interest in the import of wine. The likes of John Rous and John Parker stood comparison with some City merchants, but there were many others of more modest means.

The engines of overseas trade in 1400 were already ages old. A surplus of raw materials in one part of the world was matched by a shortage in another. Within the hinterland of Ipswich there were plenty of sheep, but no vines and precious little iron, salt or building stone. In addition, one nation might enjoy the benefit of a technological lead over another. The people of the Low Countries had developed ways of making beer and tiles that met a ready market in Ipswich. Those with capital were willing to risk it in foreign trade, even if they had the good sense to spread their risk. On the quayside at Ipswich the agents of great merchants, such as Nicholas Wotton, rubbed shoulders with locals, such as John Bernard, and Dutch masters of courage and adventure, such as Andrew Johnessone, who were willing to risk their lives and their own cargos, on small ships in dangerous seas, in carrying merchandise back and forth.

[200] Meir (2006), p. 34.

– 3 –

A Flourishing Town

Notwithstanding some encouraging trends in overseas trade, by 1400 many towns were beginning to feel the cold winds of recession. Declining population and monetary constraints meant less overall demand for goods which harmed networks and markets inland. Urban trade and industry were feeling the strain. How Ipswich coped with these pressures in the opening years of the century is the subject of this chapter. We begin with Ipswich's trading links with other English towns, particularly with London, the east coast ports and, nearer to home, the growing cloth town of Hadleigh. The extent of Ipswich's hinterland is examined through the distribution of its wine imports and the sources of its food supply. The remainder of the chapter focuses on Ipswich's own crafts and industries, in particular the manufacture of woollen cloth, leather goods and metal ware. But first we will look briefly at the main sources for this period.

Thomas, prior of the Benedictine house in Eye, was commissioned as a collector of the tenth granted by the clergy to Henry V in 1414. The money was needed to finance the expedition that culminated in English victory at Agincourt. Despite the glory to come, it was, no doubt, a thankless task, and many of his brethren would have been slow to pay. John, canon of the Gilbertine house of Fordham in Cambridgeshire, was one who allegedly refused to do so. Rather than appeal for royal or aristocratic assistance, Thomas took matters into his own hands and sued John for debt in the petty court of Ipswich.[1] As it happens, his claim was considered unjust and failed. Nevertheless, Thomas's confidence in the court reflects the reputation that it must have acquired for dispensing justice, not only in the town, but further afield. It had become a tribunal to which commercial men could turn for remedy. This story helps to explain why the petty court rolls are such a valuable source for understanding local trade and industry in the early fifteenth century.

Complete series of court rolls survive for eleven of the first fifteen years of the fifteenth century, and much of the material for this chapter comes from an analysis

[1] SROI C/2/3/1/48 (10 Sep. 1415).

of the rolls from three of those years.[2] In 1400/1 there were sixty-five court sessions, there were thirty-three in 1407/8 and forty-eight in the 1414/15. They generated a total of 1457 different cases, although most cases were brought to court more than once before being finally resolved. Indeed, many of these cases were not resolved by the petty court at all, but by arbitration, which was often regarded as a more economical, flexible and speedy route to justice. The petty court simply served as a means of getting the parties into the ring and allowing the arbitration to begin.[3] Several of these early fifteenth-century cases refer expressly to arbitration. In one, Richard Elmham and Geoffrey Balley agreed to the appointment of John Symond and Richard Belcham as arbiters of a dispute over the sum of 6s. 8d., and in another Stephen Benton and John Priour were chosen to calm the waters between Thomas Felde and Simon Butler who had fallen out badly through various disputes.[4]

Of these 1457 cases, three-quarters were the debt claims that are now of particular value to the economic historian. In the words of Kowaleski, 'debt litigation provides one of the clearest pictures of the commercial world of medieval towns and their hinterlands'.[5] For example, such cases give us the names of the litigants, and if the latter were non-resident, usually state from whence they came. Although the court rolls very often employ the generic occupational designation of 'mercer', at that time meaning, in the provinces, general trader, sometimes they provide more specific information about what litigants did for a living. It was not always considered necessary to note the amount in dispute, the precise nature of the quarrel or the goods that were seized as security for payment. One must, however, be grateful for the information that the clerk did record. Even at their fullest, these petty court rolls offer only a partial record. They tell us about the small proportion of transactions that went wrong, not about those that were satisfactorily completed without disagreement. The conclusions drawn in this chapter are, therefore, tentative and impressionistic.

Other Ipswich borough records shed further light on trade and industry. The register of the general court often recorded admissions to the freedom of the borough, the occupation of each apprentice admitted as a burgess, and the identity of his master. Unfortunately, the entries in the extant manuscript do not begin until 1415, and, even after that, many years are missing. Information about the various Ipswich markets may be found in the borough custumals and two chamberlains'

[2] The rolls for the years 1400/1, 1407/8 and 1414/15 were chosen as a sample: SROI C/2/3/1/34–37, 41, 48.
[3] C. Rawcliffe '"That Kindliness Should Be Cherished More, and Discord Driven Out": The Settlement of Commercial Disputes by Arbitration in Later Medieval England', in *Enterprise and Individuals in Fifteenth-Century England* ed. by Jennifer Kermode (Stroud: Alan Sutton, 1991), pp. 99–117 (pp. 99–100); Britnell (1996), p. 214.
[4] SROI C/2/3/1/35 (8 Mar. 1401); C/2/3/1/48 (14 Nov. 1414).
[5] Kowaleski (1995), p. 280.

accounts, although none of these documents is of an early fifteenth-century date.[6] A rental, probably dating from 1415, provides information about the use of the borough's commercial property.[7] There are fifty-five extant Ipswich wills from before 1450. Of the relevant central government records, the customs accounts have already been discussed in detail, but they make a contribution to this chapter too. Ipswich merchants occasionally caught the attention of the Court of Chancery or appeared before the Court of Common Pleas. Although they may be a controversial source, some alnage accounts are comparatively reliable, notably those for Suffolk in 1396/7.[8] The alnager was a Crown servant who collected alnage and subsidy on each cloth, stamped it with his seal of approval and kept a record in his accounts. Without his seal the cloth could not be sold.[9] These fourteenth-century accounts record who was producing cloth at that time and what type of cloth they were making, but not where individual clothiers came from. Nevertheless, by comparing the recorded names with those in the petty court rolls, it is possible to extrapolate information concerning which Ipswich residents were making cloth and what their contribution was to the county total.

Trading Networks and Hinterlands

Much has been written about the hierarchical networks of markets that evolved in the Middle Ages and the importance of towns within them. The so called 'central place theory', first conceived by the nineteenth-century German economist Johann von Thunen to explain the inter-relationship between these different hierarchies, has generated much recent debate.[10] Large towns inevitably had a wider hinterland than small ones. None could match the market dominance, range of specialist crafts and extensive trade links of London, which grew in importance and had ever greater influence on provincial towns as the Middle Ages wore on.[11] Many played a much more modest part, similar to that of the small town of Ixworth in Suffolk.[12] Nevertheless, within a spectrum that ranged from London to Ixworth, all towns performed common functions in the hinterlands that they served. They were channels for the inward flow of certain goods and the outward flow of others. They provided markets in which the produce of the countryside could be exchanged for the manufactures of the town. By regulating these markets and offering speedy

[6] SROI C/3/3/1/1; C/3/3/1/2; Twiss (1873).
[7] SROI C/2/1/1/3.
[8] PRO E 101/342/10; Richard Britnell, 'The Woollen Textile Industry of Suffolk in the Later Middle Ages' *The Ricardian* 13 (2003), pp. 86–99 (p. 97).
[9] *CFR 1399–1405*, pp. 36–7.
[10] Masschaele (1997) pp. 4–9; B. Campbell (2000); Unger (2007), pp. 363–9.
[11] Thrupp (1962); Caroline M. Barron, 'London 1300–1540', in *CUH*, pp. 395–440 (pp. 438–9).
[12] Amor (2002), 127–44.

justice, they reduced transaction costs. Some towns, such as Lynn and Yarmouth, concentrated far more on trade than manufacture.[13] Others, such as Norwich, were important centres of industry.[14]

For Ipswich's trade network we begin by considering the town's links with London. Although the journey would certainly have taken longer then than now, the capital was well within reach of Ipswich by ship and also overland by horse. By changing horses *en route*, an urgent messenger could just about complete the journey in a day, although two days would be more comfortable, and a fully laden cart might take three or four.[15] The town recorder, Thomas Bishop, was one of several men who rode to London on behalf of the borough authorities when they were negotiating a new charter from Henry VI in 1445–46.[16] Regular trade with the capital is evident from various sources. Of the six Londoners recorded as litigants in the petty court rolls here considered, all were claimants. Three were mercers, two were grocers and one was a fishmonger. Mercers, grocers and fishmongers belonged to the most powerful companies of the City, and all six were probably wealthy wholesale merchants.[17] As we have seen, members of the same companies were engaged in the export of wool from Ipswich. One of the six, John Aylesham, jointly with John Joye vintner of Ipswich, successfully sued Robert Breme for acknowledgement and payment of a letter of obligation in the sum of £5.[18] In the Michaelmas terms of 1384, 1403 and 1424, Ipswich residents appeared a total of eighteen times before the Court of Common Pleas in disputes with Londoners; including three grocers, two drapers, a mercer, a jeweller and a basket maker from the capital, for debts ranging from £2 13s. 4d. to £36.[19]

Trade took many forms, of which these disputes represent only a sample. London grocers enjoyed a near monopoly in the wholesale of pepper, ginger and other spices and luxury goods from the East, and were also very active in the dye trade.[20] London mercers commanded an increasingly dominant position in the wholesale of mercery, such as linens and silks.[21] Both companies, from time to time,

[13] Parker (2005), p. 119; Saul (1975), pp. 258–9.
[14] Dunn (2004), pp. 215–17.
[15] Masschaele (1997), p. 203–4; W. Childs, 'Moving Around', in *A Social History of England 1200–1500* ed. by R. Horrox and W.M. Ormrod (Cambridge: Cambridge University Press, 2006), pp. 260–275 (p. 262).
[16] SROI C/3/3/1/1.
[17] Thrupp (1962), p. 6.
[18] SROI C/2/3/1/48 (10 Sep. 1415).
[19] Derek Keene, 'Changes in London's Economic Hinterland as Indicated by Debt Cases in the Court of Common Pleas' in *Trade, Urban Hinterlands and Market Integration* ed. by James A. Galloway (London: Centre for Metropolitan History, Institute of Historical Research, University of London, 2000), pp. 59–81 (p. 60). Details of the Michaelmas term cases were kindly provided by Olwen Myhill of the Centre for Metropolitan History, University of London.
[20] Nightingale (1995), p. 1.
[21] Sutton (2005), p. 3; C. Dyer (2005), pp. 192–3.

operated what became known as an 'anti-fair' policy. This prohibited members from trading outside London, in provincial fairs and markets, and required their goods to be sold before they left the City.[22] The policy was motivated by avarice, pride and a determination to retain control of the distribution trade. Members were prevented from undercutting each other in the provinces, so that prices could be kept high. Travelling salesmen, known as chapmen, had to come to London to buy their goods, saving members from transaction costs and from tarnishing the reputation of their Companies in rustic wrangling.[23] Moreover, if merchandise was only available from London, these chapmen could not use their lower overheads and superior local knowledge to undercut the grocers and mercers. The success of the 'anti-fair' policy depended to an extent on the availability of coin. When coin was scarce and provincial fairs were flourishing, London merchants had no option but to visit them, or risk losing trade to the chapmen.[24] The grocer John Aylesham, a colleague of John Joye, fell out with the Cambridge University authorities while selling spices at Stourbridge Fair in 1419.[25] But once the early fifteenth-century bullion crisis was over its worst and the fairs were again on the wane, in the 1420s, the companies could enforce the anti-fair policy much more successfully, and, at the same time, recruit members in provincial towns such as Ipswich.[26]

Regional trade remained very important to Londoners and they developed an extensive distribution network through the chapmen, who continued to provide a direct link to the rural economy with its burgeoning demand for consumer goods.[27] The importance of Suffolk within this network is reflected in the number of fifteenth-century pardon cases. Debtors who persistently failed to appear before the royal courts to defend themselves were outlawed. By remedying their ways and appealing to Chancery, they could, however, be pardoned upon payment of a fine. Eighteen chapmen were pardoned in Suffolk for debts to London mercers, more than in any other county, and four of them came from Ipswich.[28] John Grene took this step early in the century, in respect of a debt of £17 13s. 4d. owed to John Chirche, mercer of London.[29] Ipswich grocers, such as Robert Hacon and Thomas Felde, and spicers, such as Robert Hall, would have obtained much of their merchandise via London. For example, Hacon and Felde contested, in the petty court, ownership of 72lbs of ginger worth £6 14s., which would almost certainly have been

[22] Power and Postan (1933), p. 274; Nightingale (1995), pp. 396, 472; Sutton (2005), pp. 118, 201.
[23] Caroline M. Barron, *London in the Later Middle Ages: Government and People 1200–1500* (Oxford: Oxford University Press, 2004), p. 81; Sutton (2005), p. 215.
[24] Nightingale (1995), pp. 383, 396.
[25] *Ibid.*, p. 387.
[26] *Ibid.*, pp. 395–6.
[27] *Ibid.*, pp. 365–7, 439–41.
[28] Sutton (2005), p. 217.
[29] *CPR 1422–29*, p. 308.

bought in the capital.[30] John Joye was facing a claim for 60s. by the London grocer Henry Otewy in 1410.[31] Not all the trade between London and Ipswich involved grocery and mercery, since Suffolk grain bound for London was laded in the port of Ipswich.[32] The number of London merchants who shipped wool from Ipswich, and of London drapers and mercers who appear in the records, suggests that wool or woollen cloth was also the subject of many transactions. In 1385 Robert Waleys, one of Ipswich's leading merchants in the second half of the fourteenth century, sued in the Guildhall of London for payment for wool and recovery of wool and money that, he claimed, William Malyn had received on his behalf.[33] In all relevant cases before the Ipswich petty court, and in most cases before the royal courts, Londoners were claimants rather than defendants. This suggests that the flow of trade was predominantly from London to Ipswich. It was not all one way, however, as the Waleys case shows.

Dealings between citizens of London and burgesses of Ipswich were not always litigious. We have already seen that John Rous arbitrated on behalf of John Lardener, and that John Aylesham and John Joye were working in some form of partnership when suing Robert Breme. Joye was sufficiently close to Alexander Reve, citizen and cheesemonger of London, to act as a trustee of his goods and chattels. Indeed, in 1419, he was himself described as a citizen of London and a member of the Company of Fishmongers, which suggests that he had dual residence.[34] Alice, daughter of Thomas le Mayster of Ipswich, married Simon de Wynchecombe, citizen and armourer of London, and went to live with him in the City, whilst continuing to hold property in Ipswich.[35] They were two of many East Anglians who felt the allure of the capital. London merchants were also moving the other way and taking up residence in the provinces.[36] John Snowe, a draper, dwelt in Ipswich and owned land in the parish of St Mary Quay. John Pollard, an embroiderer, was described as *alias* Harwich, Ipswich and York. John Chabbot, a vintner, also had a home in the town.[37]

Kowaleski has stressed the importance of coastal trade to the economy of medieval Exeter, where it accounted for 70 per cent of all maritime trade.[38] It is impossible to say what proportion of Ipswich's maritime trade was coastal, but evidence of commerce with the east coast ports of Harwich, Dunwich, Yarmouth, Lynn, Hull and Newcastle is plentiful. William Thorp of Harwich imported wine

[30] SROI C/2/3/1/48 (30 Oct. 1414).
[31] PRO CP 40/496 m. 371r.
[32] *CCR 1349–54*, p. 177; *CCR 1360–4*, p. 101.
[33] *CCR 1381–85*, p. 614.
[34] *CCR 1419–22*, pp. 50–1.
[35] *CCR 1399–1402*, p. 133.
[36] Thrupp (1962), pp. 226, 230–1.
[37] *CCR 1422–29*, p. 334; *CPR 1416–22*, pp. 291, 328.
[38] Kowaleski (1995), p. 4.

into Ipswich. His trading activity in the town led to four claims before the petty court in 1400/1, including one against Thomas Wolsey.[39] William Stirmyn, also of Harwich, was sued in the petty court in the same year.[40] William Southman of Yarmouth shipped stone into Ipswich.[41] His fellow burgesses John Hoberd and John Smyth appeared respectively in two separate suits as claimant and defendant in the petty court.[42] The Ipswich mariner John Gerard sought payment of twenty-five marks (£16 6s. 8d.) from John Norton, another Yarmouth merchant, in 1410.[43] Richard Thorp of Lynn exported wool from Ipswich in 1407, at a time when his own town was still recovering from the export ban that had been imposed three years earlier.[44]

Edmund Brook of Ipswich had a particular interest in trade with Hull, which served as the outport for York. He was sued by William de Burton of Hull in the court of Common Pleas in 1403, and five years later became involved in a protracted dispute, before the court of Admiralty, with a number of Hull merchants. Brook was awarded the enormous sum of £1466 13s. 4d, including general damages of £1000, after they seized his ship the *Laurence*.[45] John Shipman, a mariner of Hull, was being pursued by various creditors in the Ipswich petty court in 1414/15. One of them, William Walworth, took matters into his own hands. Presumably in order to prevent Shipman from fleeing the town without paying his dues, he seized the anchor of his ship and buried it in his own garden.[46] Richard Gouty, another Ipswich merchant, traded even further north. He was pardoned in respect of a debt of ten marks (£6 6s. 8d.) due to William Johanson of Newcastle. He was probably buying coal, which had already become the principal export of the north-east.[47] Coal is occasionally mentioned in the early fifteenth-century Ipswich records. For example, the mariner John Roberd owned a dozen chaldrons of sea coal which were seized in 1400 as security for the payment of a debt in the petty court.[48] Thomas Drury was possessed of eight chaldrons in 1408.[49]

Nearer to home, Hadleigh was emerging as Suffolk's leading cloth town and, after London, quite possibly Ipswich's most important domestic trading partner (Fig. 2). Early signs of its growth are evident from the accounts of Canterbury Cathedral priory. The priory's rental income from its manor in Hadleigh increased

[39] SROI C/2/3/1/34 (7 Oct. 1400).
[40] SROI C/2/3/1/34 (2 Dec. 1401).
[41] PRO E 122/193/33.
[42] SROI C/2/3/1/34 (4 Nov. 1400).
[43] PRO CP 40/596, m. 287r.
[44] PRO E 122/50/41.
[45] *CPR 1405–08*, pp. 378–9; *CPR 1408–13*, pp. 101, 139.
[46] SROI C/2/3/1/48 (25 Jun. 1415).
[47] Scammell (1961), p. 329).
[48] SROI C/2/3/1/34 (2 Dec. 1400).
[49] SROI C/2/3/1/41 (16 Jan. 1408).

significantly after the Black Death. In 1377 the fulling mill alone brought in a rent of five pounds a year.[50] The petition to the king in 1372, by the burgesses of Colchester and Ipswich, that Hadleigh should share their obligation to build a barge, has already been mentioned. Seven years later the king could raise a loan of fifty pounds from Hadleigh, but only forty pounds from Ipswich and fifty marks (£33 6s. 8d.) from Bury St Edmunds.[51] By this time Hadleigh had become the forty-third largest town in the country.[52] At least eleven cloth workers, seven fullers, six weavers, five cutters of cloth and three dyers were charged for poll tax in the town in 1381. No fewer than one in five of the adult male population was working in the textile industry, probably many more.[53] The age of the great Suffolk clothiers had yet to dawn, but already some very wealthy men were living in Hadleigh. John Kempston, a draper, had a running account with the London merchant Gilbert Maghfeld, buying his woad and iron and selling him cloth. Kempston appears to have overreached himself in the 1390s and was struggling to pay his debts to Maghfeld and other creditors.[54] Thomas Fulmarde stored 7 tons and 4 quarters of woad in his granary in Hadleigh in 1391. John atte Hulle was trading with the Baltic and John Seman with the Low Countries.[55] Britnell has noted that litigants from Hadleigh were appearing regularly in the Colchester borough court, often suing or being sued by fellow townsmen.[56] The same was happening in Ipswich.

Hadleigh residents appeared before the Ipswich petty court in each of the three years studied in this chapter. Out of a total of twelve litigants, at least three were drapers, namely Thomas Chirche, Thomas Greyne and John Kempston, while a fourth was probably a weaver. In three cases they were suing each other. They featured in equal numbers as claimants and defendants (Table 8). These figures are, however, somewhat distorted by the fact that Kempston had to defend five different claims in 1401, perhaps another sign of his financial woes.[57] The rate of resolution of cases involving Hadleigh litigants was unusually high, since eight of the twelve claims brought by them were successful. They had the clout and the determination to secure a result when so many other litigants appear to have lost patience and given up, or opted for arbitration and thus the prospect of making concessions over the final settlement. The median value of the Hadleigh claims was six times higher

[50] Mavis Mate, 'Agrarian Economy after the Black Death: The Manors of Canterbury Cathedral Priory, 1348–91' *Econ. Hist. Rev.*, 2nd ser., 37 (1984), 341–354 (p. 351).
[51] *CPR 1377–81*, p. 637.
[52] A. Dyer, 'Ranking Lists of English Medieval Towns' (2000), p. 759.
[53] The surviving tax list is incomplete: E. Powell, *A Suffolk Rising 1381* (Cambridge: Cambridge University Press, 1895), pp. 111–23; Unwin (1907), II, p. 255.
[54] *CPR 1388–91*, p. 283; *CPR 1391–6*, pp. 542, 675; PRO CP 40/556, m. 4v; James (1971), pp. 204–6.
[55] *CCR 1385–89*, pp. 564–5; PRO E 122/193/33.
[56] Britnell, 'Woollen Textile Industry of Suffolk' (2003), pp. 87, 98.
[57] SROI C/2/3/1/34 (4 Nov. 1400); C/2/3/1/35 (25 Jan. 1401, 8 Mar. 1401); C/2/3/1/36 (14 Apr. 1401); C/2/3/1/37 (21 Jul. 1401).

than that of claims by or against litigants living in the surrounding countryside. The two cases of which we have most detail involved commercial credit instruments, pointing to the growing sophistication of the Hadleigh economy.[58]

TABLE 8: ORIGINS OF NON-RESIDENT LITIGANTS IN THE PETTY COURT OF IPSWICH 1400/1, 1407/8 AND 1414/15

Origin	*No. of litigants*	*Percentage of litigants*	*No. of cases*	*Percentage of cases*	*Claimant less Defendant*	*Success rate*	*Median value of claim*
< 6 miles	38	27.3	87	32.7	5	-18	9s.
Hadleigh	12	8.6	24	9.0	0	2	£2 16s.
Other 6–9 miles	30	21.6	49	18.4	5	2	9s. 4d.
10–20 miles	25	18.0	54	20.3	-2	-3	£2 5s. 8d.
Bury St Edmunds	5	3.6	10	3.8	0	4	i.d.
London	6	4.3	7	2.6	7	1	i.d.
East coast ports	5	3.6	7	2.6	-1	-1	i.d.
Other > 20 miles	4	2.9	4	1.5	-2	1	i.d.
Overseas	12	8.6	21	7.9	-11	-11	15s. 2d.
Unidentifiable	2	1.4	3	1.1	-3	-1	n.d.
Total	139	99.9	266	99.9			

Notes to Table 8

All types of cases recorded in the petty court are included in this Table and also in Tables 16 and 23. (*Source*: SROI C/2/3/1/34–37, 41, 48)

'Claimant less Defendant' means the number of cases in which non-resident litigants were claimants *minus* the number in which non-resident litigants were defendants. In at least nine cases neither party was resident in Ipswich.

Success rate means the number of cases won or successfully defended *minus* the number unsuccessfully prosecuted or defended. Many cases, particularly in the earliest year, were inconclusive.

The median is used in this and subsequent tables, rather than the mean, because it is not distorted by isolated high value transactions. Its disadvantage is that it conceals just such transactions. Many trades, particularly in the retail sector, appear asymmetric in the sense that they involve many low value sales and a few high value purchases. In the victualling trades, sales transactions were often of such low value as to fall below the notice of the petty court. When there is an even number of cases the median has been calculated by taking the mean of the two middle figures. The claims made in cases concerned with assault, other crime or statute have been excluded from the calculation of median value. 'i.d.' means insufficient data available (fewer than 4 values) and 'n.d.' means no data available.

[58] SROI C/2/3/1/41 (26 Jun. 1408); C/2/3/1/48 (9 Jul. 1415).

Map 4: *Residents of Suffolk and North East Essex parishes appearing before the Ipswich petty court 1400/15*

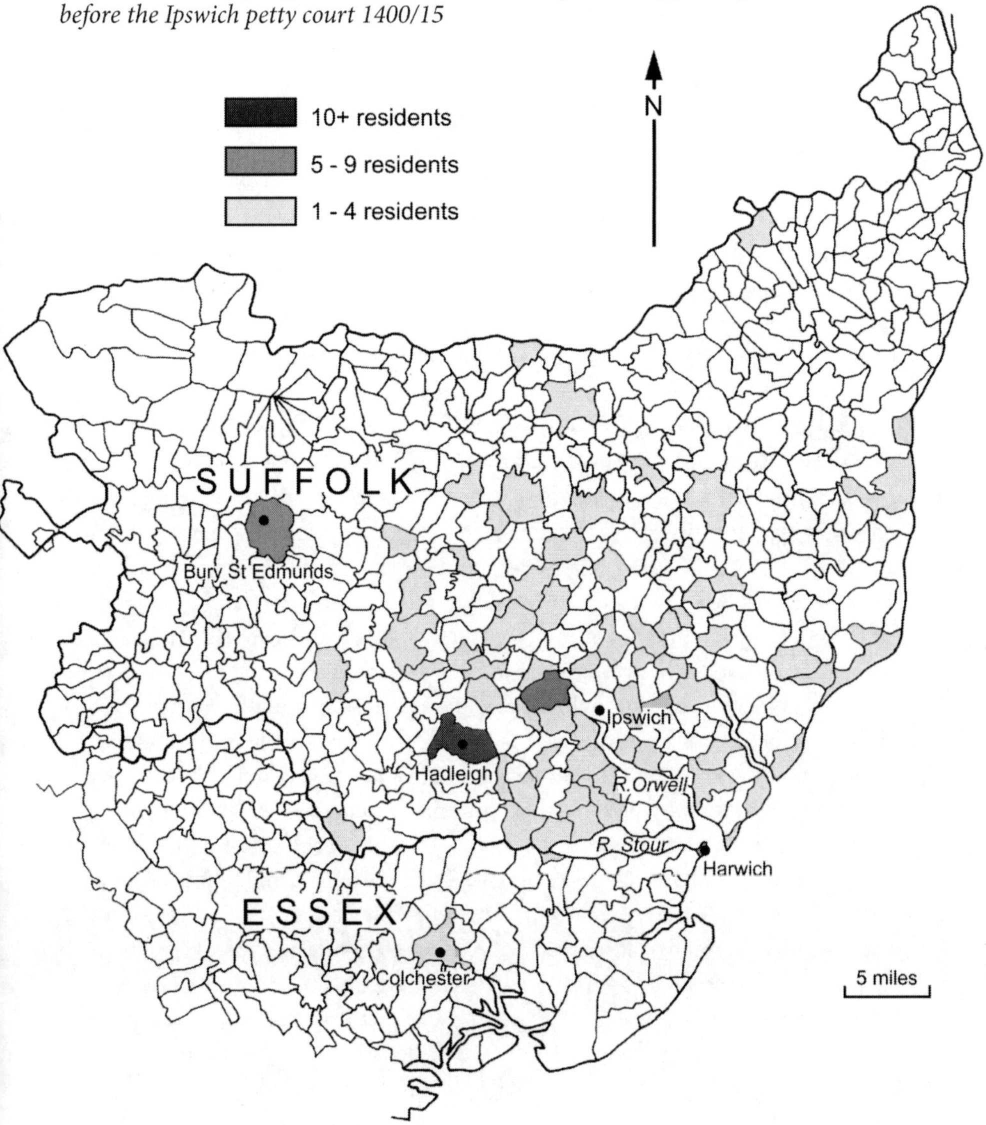

Notes to Map 4
This map, like maps 5 and 6, divides the two counties into parishes and is based on the format used by David Dymond and Edward Martin (eds) *An Historical Atlas of Suffolk* (1999). It draws on the records of those petty court cases which mention litigants' parish of origin in the three sample years, 1400/1, 1407/8 and 1414/15, that were analysed, and shows where those litigants came from in Suffolk and North Essex (*Sourc*e: SROI C/2/3/1/34–37, 41, 48).

The economic hinterland of Ipswich was concentrated within a radius of 20 miles of the town, a distance that 'marked the effective limit of a town's regional influence' (see Table 8).[59] In addition to those litigants already mentioned from London and the east coast ports, a few others came from further away: five from Bury St Edmunds and one each from Bungay and Norwich. Three-quarters of all non-resident litigants, however, lived within the 20-mile zone. The origins of those living in Suffolk and northern Essex are shown in Map 4. Trade with this hinterland involved an exchange of agricultural produce, in return for goods shipped through Ipswich and the manufactures of the town itself. In her study of the hinterland of Exeter, Kowaleski analysed debt litigation, drawing distinctions between short- and long-distance trade. She reached three significant conclusions: nearby residents were more likely to be defendants than claimants; the sums involved were likely to be larger in the cases of those living further away; and those who travelled furthest would more often be successful in their litigation than those trading at closer proximity.[60] Kowaleski's database was undoubtedly larger and more sophisticated than that used here. Nevertheless, it is worth asking whether her three conclusions match the data for Ipswich. It seems that the second and third do, but not the first.

Given that any dividing line is essentially artificial, the first step is to define short- and long-distance trade. Kowaleski drew her lines at 6, 12 and 25 miles. This study draws slightly different lines, at 6, 10 and 20 miles, and also focuses on certain towns. The difference between these two sets of criteria does not affect the results. The importance of the 6-mile line dates back to the thirteenth century at least. According to the legal treatise known as Bracton, markets should be 6⅔ miles apart, otherwise they would harm each other's trade,[61] as people would not normally travel on foot much beyond 6 miles in a day's round trip to market. A difference can certainly be discerned in the Ipswich data between what, for the sake of convenience, we may term 6- and 10-mile cases. Those living within a 6-mile radius appear to have had a more dismal experience in pursuing or defending claims. Many of them would have been small-scale peasant agriculturalists, lacking the status or acumen necessary for success in court. Nevertheless, significant similarities also exist between these cases because the disappearance of many of the smaller rural markets surrounding Ipswich meant that producers, who had once walked a short distance to their nearest village market, now made the longer journey to Ipswich.[62] Litigants were more often claimants than defendants, which suggests that they were bringing

[59] Masschaele (1997), p. 82.

[60] Kowaleski (1995), pp. 287–93.

[61] *Bracton on the Laws and Customs of England* ed. by S.E. Thorne (Cambridge, Mass: Belknap, 1977), III, pp. 198–9.

[62] Masschaele (1997), p. 185; N. Scarfe, 'Medieval and Later Markets', in *An Historical Atlas of Suffolk* ed. by David Dymond and Edward Martin (Ipswich: Suffolk County Council, 1988; repr. 1989 and 1999), pp.76–7.

more goods to Ipswich than they were taking away. They needed to sell some of their produce to pay rent, but perhaps many of them had neither the need, nor the means, to buy what Ipswich had to offer in return. They had yet to be touched by the consumer revolution. When the value of the claim was recorded, it was normally very modest. In only one exceptional case did it exceed two pounds, and in only seven cases was it more than twenty shillings. Litigants travelling between 10 and 20 miles to Ipswich were more often defendants than claimants. The value of the transactions they made was some five times higher than those of litigants living closer to the town. For their immediate needs, residents of small towns such as Debenham and Framlingham could still look to local markets, but only Ipswich had a ready supply of luxuries. Their mobility may have been a mark of greater social standing and financial means. They could afford spices in their food and wine in their goblets.[63] The ways in which Ipswich's trade network distributed the wine that arrived in the port and brought food into the town are considered next.

Wine Flows Inland

As we have seen, wine was by far the most important of Ipswich's imports in the opening years of the fifteenth century. The Vintry, where wine was sold from taverns, lay at the heart of the town. Wine was essential to civic entertaining and to retaining the friendship of Suffolk worthies.[64] Not surprisingly, vintners were among the leading burgesses. In the opening years of the fifteenth century they included in their number two William Debenhams, father and son, and John Joye, all of who served as bailiff and MP for the town (Appendix 2), as well as the portman John Wode.[65] The register of the general court records the admission of two dozen former apprentices as burgesses during this period, at least seven of whom had been apprenticed to these men.[66] Wine was frequently the subject of litigation in the petty court. Wode sold fortified wine for twenty shillings to John Catfield, made another sale to Robert Fadinor, and had to sue both for payment. He was fined twenty shillings in 1424 for selling, in his inn, 600 gallons of red wine at eight pence a gallon, when the maximum price fixed by statute and by the bailiffs was six pence.[67] Robert Crume faced three separate debt claims relating to the purchase of wine from John Clerk, Alan Deynes and John Lanas.[68] Lanas's claim was for the substantial sum of

[63] C. Dyer (1989), p. 197.
[64] SROI C/3/3/1/1, 2.
[65] BL, Ms Add. 30,158, f. 2r.
[66] BL, Ms Add. 30,158, ff. 3r, 6r. By the 1430s, in the records of admissions of apprentices, neither William Debenham nor John Joye was described as a vintner. This may reflect a change in occupation, or, as neither of them was ascribed any occupation, perhaps more likely, a failure in record keeping.
[67] SROI C/2/8/1/7 (west ward).
[68] SROI C/2/3/1/34 (7 Oct. 1400); C/2/3/1/35 (3 Mar. 1401); C/2/3/1/36 (31 May 1401).

£11 6s. 8d., which must have represented about 2 tuns of wine. John Waller sold wine to Thomas Spaldyng as part of a contract worth six pounds.[69] In June 1415 John Wolfard sued Robert Barbour for payment for the balance due for 3 pipes (1½ tuns), only to find, a month later, that his own stock was being seized by creditors.[70]

Wine was distributed in three ways: wholesale, retail and through direct importation by the consumer.[71] There might be a chain of wholesale transactions before it was finally put on retail sale. When the wine trade was controlled by Gascons, the first wholesale transaction was usually made at the port of arrival, as aliens rarely ventured inland.[72] In 1393/4 Peter del Bay and Peter de Pervyr, merchants of Bayonne, sold buret wine to John Outdreght a taverner of Ipswich. Peter Guilhamer was likewise doing business with Thomas Crust of Bury St Edmunds, who had presumably come to Ipswich to take delivery.[73] As the trade passed into English hands, the first sale might be made inland. In 1385 Margaret Marshall, countess of Norfolk, bought for her household at Framlingham castle 4377 gallons of wine, including Gascon red, St Emilion white and Rhenish wine. These purchases accounted for about 15 per cent of her household budget. Some wine arrived via the appropriately named Bigod's quay in Ipswich, and an Ipswich merchant, Gilbert Boulge, was one of her main suppliers.[74] On a less lavish scale, Lady Alice de Bryene of Acton Hall, near Sudbury, was another sufficiently important customer of Ipswich vintners to have received personal visits from John Joye. She bought 2 pipes and a hogshead of red, plus a hogshead of white, in 1418/19.[75] Residents of inland towns themselves became involved in the trade. Thus, for example, John Asty was licensed to import wine from Gascony, via Ipswich, to Bury St Edmunds.[76] Wine was usually sold retail by taverners, who also offered accommodation. Taverns were popular places with masters and their crews who had to endure abstemious lives at sea, and had nowhere else to stay when they arrived in port.[77] In the early 1400s, for example, John Deye, taverner of Ipswich, sought to recover payment in the petty court from the mariners John and Robert Smith.[78] Taverns could be unruly, and Deye also claimed compensation from one John Hopkyn for 'breaking' his house in what must have been a drunken brawl.[79] Wine merchants often kept their own taverns. Royal inquisitions

[69] SROI C/2/3/1/34 (26 Oct. 1400).
[70] SROI C/2/3/1/41 (9 Jan. 1408); C/2/3/1/48 (4 Jun. 1415, 16 Jul. 1415).
[71] James (1971), pp. 160–95.
[72] Kowaleski (1995), p. 262.
[73] James (1971), p. 191.
[74] Ridgard (1985), pp. 14, 15, 86, 95–6.
[75] James (1971), p. 65.
[76] *CPR 1364–67*, p. 17.
[77] Harding (1995), p. 163.
[78] SROI C/2/3/1/34 (16 Nov. 1400, 16 Dec. 1400).
[79] SROI C/2/3/1/34 (16 Dec. 1400).

of 1393/4, concerning the sale of ungauged wine, disclose that Alan Deynes had offered for sale in his tavern 1½ tuns of Rochelle, and 5½ tuns of Gascon wine, that he had imported himself. William atte Fen likewise sold 5 tuns of Gascon and 6 of Rochelle wine in his own premises.[80] As the price of wine rose, royal and aristocratic buyers increasingly imported wine themselves for consumption by their own households. In this way they cut out the middleman and avoided paying subsidy.[81]

The markets for wine that arrived in Ipswich were relatively far-flung. Inquisitions reveal that Gilbert Boulge and William atte Fen were selling to merchants of Bury St Edmunds, Sudbury and Norwich, and that William Strike had dealings with Stephen Chaunte of Bury St Edmunds. Innkeepers from as far apart as Newmarket and Beccles were indebted to Ipswich merchants, almost certainly for the supply of wine.[82] Earlier in the fourteenth century wine had also been dispatched from Ipswich to Thetford, and also probably to Bury St Edmunds, Colchester, Kersey, Melford and Sudbury.[83] Transporting wine to these destinations was no easy task. Ipswich porters had a lengthy list of two- and three-penny charges simply for unlading the wine and taking it up the hill into cellars in town.[84] Moreover, because medieval wine was perishable, it had to be shifted quickly. Carriage was costly and casks fragile. Transport by pack horse was impossible and a cart, probably with two horses, hauling up to a ton weight, was essential.[85] The tenants of the earl of Norfolk in the village of Earl Soham, known as 'Molmen', had once been required by custom to cart wine from Ipswich to Framlingham. The commutation of customary services meant that by 1385 the Countess Margaret had to rely on local boys.[86] Professional carters in Ipswich, such as William Eston and Robert Worsted, were also ready to help. They would know the roads well, many of which were much better than their reputation allows, and some of which were even metalled.[87]

The assize of wine, which fixed maximum retail prices, allowed a surcharge for overland transport which varied over time. In the fourteenth century the cost of carrying a tun of wine from Ipswich to Bury St Edmunds varied between 5s. and 6s. 8d., probably depending on season and weather, and carriage to Thetford involved a similar outlay of 6s. 8d.[88] Two men and a cart took victuals, no doubt

[80] James (1971), pp. 190–1.
[81] Kowaleski (1995), p. 260.
[82] *CPR 1399–1401*, p. 495; PRO CP 40/596, m. 404r.
[83] James (1971), p. 157. In 1370 the Ipswich merchant Robert Waleys made a series of high value claims in the Court of Common Pleas, probably for payment for wine: PRO CP 40/437, m. 5v.
[84] Twiss (1872), p. 179.
[85] Childs (2006), p. 261. The cost of road carriage has been variously estimated between 1.3d. per ton: Oliver Rackham, *The History of the Countryside* (London: Dent, 1986) pp. 263–4; and 3.5d. per ton: Bolton (1980), pp. 151–2.
[86] Ridgard (1985), pp. 14–15.
[87] C. Dyer (2005), p. 23.
[88] James (1971), pp. 22, 147, 157.

including wine, from Ipswich to Bury St Edmunds, for the Parliament which was due to be held there early in 1447, at a cost of 6s. 8d.[89] Nevertheless, if the price of a tun of wine was about £5, then expenditure on carriage cost represented a relatively modest percentage of its value. For valuable consignments such as wine, this was a price worth paying.

Although road transport was possible, rivers were preferred on account of both the lower outlay involved and the greater safety of the load. Opinions differ on quite how great the difference was, but, without doubt, carters charged significantly more than watermen for going the same distance. River transport was in fact better even if the route was longer and slower.[90] Riverine boats could be 30 feet long and were thus more capable of transporting larger cargoes than any cart.[91] It is a moot point how much the Gipping was used to transport wine and other goods into central Suffolk. The Ipswich custumal refers to merchants who did not intend to send their goods upriver into the region, implying that some would want to do so.[92] Evidence suggests that the Gipping was navigable as far as Stowmarket, or even Rattlesden. This may explain how the smiths of Stowmarket were able to gather together, on a Sunday late in November 1433, for a convivial evening, 'feasting and being entertained with unpressed wine'.[93]

Feeding the Town

Few victuallers enjoyed the status or wealth of vintners. Occasionally, a particularly enterprising soul would rise through the ranks. John Joye started his business life in Ipswich as a baker, before becoming a vintner.[94] His kinsman Richard Joye was another baker/miller who did well. He was a 'worthy burgess', and his apprentices, Thomas Bast and Thomas Periell, were admitted as burgesses too.[95] Richard's status is underlined by his role in attesting parliamentary elections in the borough in 1411, 1413 and 1414.[96] Some butchers, such as John Starling, who served the town four times as both bailiff and MP and the Crown as a customs official, were also men of

[89] SROI C/3/3/1/1.

[90] Rackham considers that road transport was five times more expensive than water transport: (1986) p. 264. Masschaele's pre-Black Death statistics suggest a much more modest differential, making road transport about three times costlier: (1997), pp. 209–10. Childs argues, however, that the differential was even greater, with road transport being as much as twelve times more expensive: (2006), p. 265. Unger suggests that improvements in the construction of smaller vessels may have reduced the cost of river transport in the late Middle Ages: (2007), pp. 373–4. The debate at least reveals how difficult it is to give precise answers to questions such as this.

[91] Masschaele (1997), p. 223.

[92] Twiss (1873), pp. 157–9.

[93] Amor (2006), 175–97 (pp. 189–90).

[94] SROI C/2/3/1/36 (26 Apr. 1401).

[95] BL, Ms Add. 30,158, ff. 1r, 3r.

[96] Information supplied by Dr Charles Moreton.

standing in the community.[97] At a more humble level, John Cook rose from pie baker to butcher. As Chaucer's *Miller's Tale* illustrates, victuallers were often suspected of dishonest practices and were carefully scrutinised by the borough authorities.[98] Nevertheless, they were essential to the well being of the town and they are well represented in the borough records (Table 9).

TABLE 9: LITIGANTS IN THE PETTY COURT OF IPSWICH KNOWN TO HAVE BEEN ENGAGED IN VICTUALLING TRADES, 1400/1, 1407/8 AND 1414/15

Trade	*No.*	*Median value of claim*	*Admissions 1415–39*
Baker (inc. miller)	3	7s. 3d.	3
Brewer	1	i.d.	
Butcher (inc. meat man)	12	8s.	1
Cheeseman	1	i.d.	
Dairyman	1	i.d.	
Fisherman/fishmonger	1	i.d.	4
Goose woman	1	i.d.	
Meat man (inc. butcher)	1	8s.	
Miller (inc. baker)	8	7s. 3d.	3
Mustarder	3	i.d.	
Pie baker	1	i.d.	
Spicer	0	n.d.	1
Vintner (including taverner)	12	£1 3s. 4d.	4–7
	45		13–16

Notes
Tables 9, 10, 18, 25 and 26 are not limited to Ipswich residents.
One butcher, John Waryn of Bramford, and two millers, John Deen of Melton and John Noreys of Culpho, were non-resident.
This list includes those litigants whose occupation is specified in the record, and others whose occupation can be ascertained from the context with reasonable confidence.
Details of admissions often omitted occupations.
(*Sources*: BL, Ms Add. 30,158; SROI C/2/3/1/34-37, 41, 48)

[97] K.N. Houghton, 'John Starling' in *HoP,* IV, pp. 466–7.
[98] Chaucer (2005), pp. 114–41.

As previously mentioned, in years of good harvests the rural hinterland of Ipswich could keep the townspeople fed, without reliance on imported grain. Because bakers and millers were notoriously litigious, the petty court records provide valuable glimpses of how they helped to provision the town. They also reveal what type of grain was most popular. Wheat was almost the only grain ever mentioned by name, which confirms that many consumers could now afford better quality white bread.[99] The sole exception involved a claim by John Soty against Thomas Drury for payment for supplying white, wholemeal and horse bread.[100] Drury was, however, probably a merchant, and his purchases may have sailed with him rather than being consumed in Ipswich. The records also note where the grain came from. John Ode, a baker, acquired his wheat from John Salle, abbot of Leiston. John Stampes, another baker, bought outside Ipswich from John Deen of Melton and John Noreys of Culpho. John Myles of Stowupland was supplying Ipswich with malt.[101] In the mid-fifteenth century grain arrived from Akenham, Ashbocking, Belstead, Cockfield, Crowfield, Dalehalle (in Whitton cum Thurleston[102]), Framsden, Gosbeck, Rushmere St Andrew and Witnesham, nearly all of which lay well within 10 miles of Ipswich.[103] Both William Austyn and John Stampes owned small boats, and perhaps used them to transport grain along the coast and down the river.[104] It was difficult to justify the cost of carting it overland for any distance. They may have employed the services of John and Thomas Catfield as watermen, since Stampes sued the two of them for breakages as they unloaded his boat in the port of Ipswich, and Austyn accused them of taking his boat without permission. Petty court litigation gives us some idea of the scale, as well as the distribution, of the grain business. Most disputes involving millers and bakers were over relatively small sums. Of the twenty-three relevant debt claims for which a value is given, seventeen were for less than twenty shillings, while the only two worth more than two pounds were made by Richard Joye.[105] For most litigants individual transactions were of modest value. This was to change quite dramatically by the end of the fifteenth century.

Few millers owned their own mills outright.[106] Sometimes they leased them and sometimes they simply operated them as salaried employees. Mill owners were usually men of much greater substance. In 1391 the bailiffs granted to John Arnold, Gilbert Boulge, William Gunneld and Henry Wall land near Stoke Bridge to build

[99] C. Dyer (1989), p. 197.
[100] SROI C/2/3/1/48 (20 Dec. 1414).
[101] SROI C/2/3/1/36 (26 Apr. 1401, 26 May 1401); C/2/3/1/37 (27 July 1401, 21 Aug. 1401); C/2/3/1/48 (21 Feb. 1415).
[102] W.A. Copinger, *Manors of Suffolk,* 7 vols (Manchester: Taylor, Garnett, Evans, 1905–11) II (1908), p. 374.
[103] SROI C/3/3/1/1.
[104] SROI C/2/3/1/37 (21 Jul. 1401); C/2/3/1/35 (8 Feb. 1401).
[105] SROI C/2/3/1/48 (22 Nov. 1414, 30 Jul. 1415, 10 Sep. 1415).
[106] Kowaleski (1995), p. 141.

two water mills.[107] The contract provided that, once the mills had been built, they should recoup their investment from the income, and then surrender them to the borough. The mills were duly built and eventually handed over, generating an income of £13 6s. 8d. for the town in 1446/7.[108] As these arrangements reveal, mills were expensive to build and maintain. A pair of mill stones was valued for the purpose of customs at three pounds, while a new sail for the grain mill cost twenty-six shillings and a new brace twenty shillings.[109] The erection of these two new mills, and the willingness of leading burgesses to invest capital in them, is a sign of the economic buoyancy of the time.[110] It is in stark contrast to William Ridout's resistance to paying rent on Horsewade mill in the more difficult economic climate of the 1450s.

Rising living standards generated more demand for meat and more business for butchers.[111] The erection of a new stall in the town's flesh market in 1378 was an early sign of this trend.[112] A rather later one was the juice dripping pan, with black metal mount, that Katherine Tyndale left in her will of 1442.[113] Twelve butchers can be identified with some confidence from the petty court rolls. Beef cattle, pigs and sheep were all the subject of litigation involving these men. William Cok bought bulls and sheep at market for £3 2s., John Cook heffers and cows, and Richard Deye pigs.[114] John Deve and William Grene acquired twenty-nine sheep from Walter Reynburgh for five pounds, but the transaction went sour when William Debenham claimed that nineteen of the animals belonged to him.[115] The best meat sold in the shops and stalls of Ipswich was destined for the dining tables of those affluent enough to afford it. The cheaper cuts were used then, as now, in pies for fast food.[116] Once the flesh had been stripped away, the hides and tallow were always in demand by Ipswich's leather workers and chandlers. Indeed, local butchers were prohibited from bringing skinned carcasses to town and were regularly fined in the leet courts for doing so.[117] Although butchers could make a handsome profit by supplying tanneries, it was not always easy to recover the money. George Feete bought a cow hide from John Aylston for 6s. 8d. and his failure to pay brought the case to court.[118]

[107] *CPR 1396–99*, p. 527; *CPR 1399–1401*, p. 159.
[108] SROI C/3/3/1/1.
[109] PRO E 122/193/33; SROI C/3/3/1/1.
[110] Kowaleski notes similar developments in Exeter: (1995), p. 89.
[111] C. Dyer (1989), p. 197.
[112] *Annals*, p. 80.
[113] SROI R1/119b.
[114] SROI C/2/3/1/48 (20 Aug. 1415); C/2/3/1/41 (23 Jan. 1408); C/2/3/1/34 (18 Nov. 1401).
[115] SROI C/2/3/1/48 (5 Feb. 1415).
[116] Martha Carlin, 'Fast Food and Urban Living Standards in Medieval England' in *Food and Eating in Medieval Europe* ed. by Martha Carlin and Joel T. Rosenthal (London: Hambledon Press, 1991) pp. 27–51 (pp. 40–1).
[117] Twiss (1873), cap. 57, pp. 143–5. The same applied in Bristol, Leicester and York: Swanson (1989), pp. 16, 138.
[118] SROI C/2/3/1/36 (21 Jun. 1401).

The wealthiest butchers, such as John Starling, owned or rented their own pasture. He was leasing land from Nicholas Smyth and, in 1415, was allegedly in arrears of rent to the tune of £7 4s. 8d.[119] Most butchers, however, bought fattened livestock from suppliers both in and out of the town. William Brook and Geoffrey Balley, for example, dealt respectively with the priors of the Augustinian canons of Holy Trinity and St Peter in Ipswich, who, like many members of the clergy, often sold surplus produce locally.[120] In the early fifteenth-century livestock also came from Hoo, Orford and Rushmere St Andrew, all parishes lying north-east of Ipswich.[121] By the middle of the century, however, the main source of red meat may already have switched to parishes lying to the north-west. Of the seven non-residents renting stalls in the Ipswich flesh house in 1446/7, four came from Needham Market, and two from Baylham and Coddenham respectively.[122] This reflects the growing importance of the wood pasture of High Suffolk in the fattening of cattle.[123]

Kowaleski found that butchers were the most affluent of all victuallers in Exeter.[124] In Ipswich the median value of debts in cases involving butchers, for which a value was given, was higher than in the litigation of bakers and millers, if not significantly so. Three of these twenty-two debts were, however, for significantly larger amounts. Geoffrey Balley was, for example, sued by the merchant John Clerk for the substantial sum of £28 13s. 11d., which suggests that at least some butchers clearly had the means, or the nerve, to commit themselves to high value transactions.[125] Furthermore, both John Ayston and Richard Deye had the means to employ servants.[126]

Fish, particularly herring, was a key element in the diet of medieval people, being a valuable source of protein and nutrition.[127] In religious houses and, indeed, among all observant Catholics, it was the only meat permitted on 150 holy days of the year.[128] Ipswich had its own fish market where the day's catch was set out on stalls for sale.[129] Fishermen were supposed to sell their catch themselves, but often left the task to others.[130] The customs of the fish market specified the tolls to be paid on the arrival of each cart of fish, specifically mentioning herring, porpoise, salmon, sturgeon and baleen whale.[131] References to oysters, mussels, flat fish and cask fish

[119] C/2/3/1/48 (8 Jan. 1415). K.N. Houghton refers to his land holdings: 'John Starling', *HoP*, IV, pp. 466–7.
[120] SROI C/2/3/1/34 (14 Dec. 1400); C/2/3/1/35 (15 Mar. 1401); PRO CP 40/596, m. 408r.
[121] SROI C/2/3/1/41 (23 Jan. 1408); C/2/3/1/36 (19 Apr. 1401); C/2/3/1/37 (29 Sep. 1401).
[122] SROI C/3/3/1/1.
[123] Amor (2002), pp. 134–5; Amor (2006), p. 188.
[124] Kowaleski (1995), p. 128.
[125] SROI C/2/3/1/36 (9 Jun. 1401).
[126] SROI C/2/3/1/36 (12 Apr. 1401, 14 Jun. 1401).
[127] Saul (1975), p. 1; C. Dyer (1989), p. 197.
[128] Kowaleski (1995), p. 307.
[129] *Annals*, pp. 71, 106.
[130] Twiss (1873), pp. 160–1.
[131] Twiss (1873), p. 199.

are also common. Some fish was imported from abroad, but most was probably caught locally. Fishermen dredged for shell fish in the oyster beds along the estuary of the river Orwell. Off shore, bottom- feeding flat fish, such as sole and plaice, came within reach thanks to new techniques of trammel fishing.[132] Despite being ordered by Henry V to keep away, the most intrepid souls ventured to Iceland in search of cod and other deep sea fish.[133] The petty and leet court records refer to a wide variety of fish being caught and sold in the town. For example, Thomas Catfield owned two barrels of white herring and a cask of red herring which John Peyton seized in 1401 as security for the payment of a debt.[134] His kinsman John Catfield was catching small fry to the detriment of local fish stocks in 1421, and three years later was forestalling mackerel, herring and oysters.[135] Fishing was a seasonal business and consequently, for the Catfields, like most fishermen, it was only a part-time activity. As we have seen, they found other employment by working as watermen. Similarly, Robert Fadinor had interests in other trades, but fishing was his regular occupation. He was fined in 1416 for forestalling porpoise, turbot and conger eel.[136] For most of those like them, fishing was a hard life which rarely led to riches or recognition.

In his study of the period before the Black Death, Masschaele used central place theory to stress the closeness of the ties between the rural and urban economy, and claimed to have identified networks of supply between large and small towns.[137] He argued that fifty of the country's largest towns, which included Ipswich, depended for their food on the markets of smaller towns within their particular network. These markets provided contact and collection points, and allowed merchants to source local agricultural produce without incurring inordinate costs.[138] A ring of small rural markets did, indeed, spring up around Ipswich, although, as we have seen, it is unlikely that many of them survived the Black Death. Britnell has sought to refute Masschaele's argument, notably by reference to Colchester, which showed 'no complex dependence upon external markets' for its foodstuffs. Furthermore, he argues that after the Black Death, 'as pressure on agricultural resources declined through reduced consumption, and as transport costs rose through scarcities of labour, supplies from the immediate locality became more preponderant'.[139] Nothing in this study suggests that, in the opening years of the fifteenth century, Ipswich relied on small town markets for grain or

[132] Mate, *Trade and Economic Developments* (2006), pp. 17, 45.
[133] *CCR 1413–1419*, p. 297; Redstone (1969), p. 32.
[134] SROI C/2/3/1/35 (22 Feb. 1401).
[135] SROI C/2/8/1/5 (south ward); C/2/8/1/7 (north ward).
[136] SROI C/2/8/1/3 (east ward). Porpoise was a 'royal' fish which belonged to the Crown, so Fadinor was breaking the law.
[137] Masschaele (1997), pp. 4–9.
[138] Masschaele (1997), p. 83.
[139] Britnell (2006), pp. 148–9.

fish, but there is some evidence that it looked to those, such as Needham Market, for some of its supply of meat. This does not, however, necessarily mean that livestock and deadstock reached the town in the manner envisaged by Masschaele, because the records suggest that many butchers were bringing their beasts to Ipswich themselves.

Having completed our examination of the victualling trades, we now turn to Ipswich's trades and industries.

Many Trades and Industries

Perhaps the most important distinguishing mark between a town and a village in the Middle Ages was the range of occupations followed by its residents.[140] Our survey of the principal industries of cloth, leather and metal-working by no means exhausts the list of occupations pursued by local townspeople and documented in the petty court rolls (Table 10). As well as the barbers, basket makers, blanket sellers, chandlers, coopers, potters, ropers and tailors who plied their trade in the shops and stalls of the town, the records reveal others following more unusual callings. John Leche, as his name suggests, practised medicine. He undertook to restore John Dalt's sight within eight days, so that he would have good and clear vision sufficient to discern colour with either eye. Not surprisingly, the treatment failed and, like many disappointed patients, Dalt sued for the return of the fifteen shilling fee. Thomas Goodlock was a less ambitious practitioner who charged sixteen pence for the treatment of a horse belonging to William Stephen. Unlike Leche, he failed to obtain his fee in advance and had to sue for his money.[141] The dramatic growth of literacy which took place in this period is reflected in the presence of the booksellers Robert Hegge and Hugh Wermouth.[142] Wermouth sold the clerk, Geoffrey Cersham, a missal for ten shillings, while John Jakelot of East Bergholt bought a primer, a psalter, a book containing the Office of the Dead and a grammar from Hegge for fifteen shillings. Thomas Bacon carried on business as a seller of the parchment which was in demand from a growing borough bureaucracy, and which has preserved so much valuable information for the historian.[143]

Although there is no sign of the frenetic construction work evident from late fifteenth-century wills and other documents, new buildings were appearing in Ipswich at the turn of the century, such as the mills referred to above, providing work for a variety of carpenters, daubers, and masons. A major contemporary development was a transition from dependence on imported bricks and tiles to their pro-

[140] Reynolds (1977), p. ix; C. Dyer, 'Small Towns 1270–1540', in *CUH*, pp. 505–37 (pp. 513–14).
[141] SROI C/2/3/1/48 (11 Apr. 1415, 7 May 1415).
[142] SROI C/2/3/1/34 (21 Oct. 1400); SROI C/2/3/1/48 (29 Sep. 1415).
[143] SROI C/2/3/1/36 (14 Jun. 1401).

TABLE 10: LITIGANTS IN THE PETTY COURT OF IPSWICH AND THEIR OCCUPATIONS, 1400/1, 1407/8 AND 1414/15

Occupation	*No. of litigants*	*Percentage of total*	*Median value of claim*	*Admissions 1415–39*
Building	5	1.9		1
Clothing	5	1.9		3
Leather	20	7.7	10s.	6
Merchant or mariner	26	10.0	15s. 2d.	4–7
Metal	16	6.2	12s.8d.	0
Other occupations	19	7.3		1
Religious	45	17.4		0
Servant/labourer	18	6.9		0
Textiles	47	18.1	24s.	4
Transport	5	1.9		0
Victuallers (including taverners and vintners)	45	17.4	See Table 9	13–16
Wood	8	3.1		2
Total	259	99.8		37

Notes
These categories are used by Christopher Dyer (2002), pp. 320–1, with the addition of 'Religious', which includes chaplains, clerks, rectors, vicars and members of religious houses. Seventeen such litigants came from outside the town.
Any litigants who are identified by rank rather than occupation have been excluded from this Table and also from Tables 22 and 31.
This data has been collated from cases where a litigant's occupation is given, or is reasonably clear from the context.
In many records of admissions, the occupation of a new freeman is not given and cannot be ascertained from other sources.
'Textiles' includes four litigants from Hadleigh and two from Colchester.
(*Sources*: BL, Ms Add. 30,158; SROI C/2/3/1/34-37, 41, 48)

duction within the town. The clay soils that had once been used to make Ipswich's renowned pottery now provided ample material for this new manufacture. Two tile kilns were then already in operation, in what is now Grimwade Street on the eastern side of Ipswich, and may well have produced glazed and decorated floor tiles (Plate 2).[144] Thomas Tholy owned a tile kiln close by in 1424, and John Snell

[144] Personal communication from Stuart Boulter of the Suffolk Archaeology Service, 6 March 2009, who kindly provided the photograph.

Plate 2: *Late medieval tile kilns excavated in Grimwade Street*

was carrying on trade as a tile maker by 1450.[145] Very soon there would be a thriving domestic industry in other Suffolk towns.[146]

Cloth Industry under Threat

The importance of the textile industry in Ipswich is apparent from the number of litigants who were involved in making or selling cloth, and the number of cases that concerned cloth. Linen is mentioned twice and worsted cloth once in the petty court rolls, but they were clearly far less important than fulled woollen cloth.[147] The various stages in the production of such cloth are illustrated by the records. Peter Codon of Dunwich, possibly the same man who was bailiff and MP there, was a

[145] SROI C/2/8/1/7 (east ward); PRO CP 40/756, m. 49r.

[146] C. Pankhurst, 'The Brick Making Industry', in *An Historical Atlas of Suffolk* ed. by David Dymond and Edward Martin (Ipswich: Suffolk County Council, 1988; repr. 1989 and 1999), pp. 146–7: H.E.J. Le Patourel, 'Rural Buildings in England and Wales', in *The Agrarian History of England and Wales: 1348–1500* ed. by E. Miller, 8 vols. (Cambridge: Cambridge University Press, 1991), III, pp. 820–919 (pp. 821–2); Barron (1995), p. 18; Amor (2002), p. 136.

[147] SROI C/2/3/1/34 (16 Nov. 1401); C/2/3/1/41 (25 Oct. 1407); C/2/3/1/48 (30 Jul. 1415).

supplier of fleeces, and sold 360 to William Golde at six pence each.[148] Thomas Wysman, was a wool carder whose job was to prepare the wool for spinning by brushing it between cards, teasing out the fibres to produce a smooth finish.[149] The two women, Celia Chelston and Agnes Brightyene, who sued the weaver John Cukhook, look suspiciously like spinners who might have prepared the wool for his loom.[150] He was one of four weavers who are mentioned in the early fifteenth-century petty court rolls, and also among that number was Adam Duchman who faced two claims for payment of debt in October 1400.[151] The fuller John Bette bought white cloth, perhaps to clean by fulling under foot in the old fashioned way, or in a fulling mill.[152] In 1415 Robert Saundres was leasing such a mill from Nicholas Stanwey, while thirty years later one was situated next to Stoke Bridge.[153] The Ipswich miller John George was suing the fuller William Andrew in 1400, and it is possibly that Andrew had been fulling his cloth in George's mill.[154] The process of fulling could shrink the cloth in size by more than half.[155] Once fulled, therefore, the cloth had to be stretched back into its proper shape between tenter hooks. A plot of land on the great embankment of the town was set aside in 1415 for a tenter-yard measuring in length 40 ells (about 45 metres).[156] A shearman, such as John Brewer, would then finish the cloth by the laborious, yet highly skilled, process of raising, with teasels, and cutting, with shears, the short fibres known as the nap, sometimes more than once, to produce a smooth velvety surface.[157] At any one or more of three stages in manufacture – in the wool, in the yarn or in the piece – the cloth could be dyed by a dyer such as John Brook, William Kent or Roger Norice, the last of whom, in 1415, rented a dye works from the borough, built up against the town wall in the parish of St Mary Elms.[158] Several Ipswich dyers, including Michael Dexter, John Dier and Thomas Smyth, were fined for allowing water polluted with dye to escape from their premises into the highways, common wells or river.[159]

Textiles provided a living for the largest occupational group in the town. How many people were involved? Forty-one residents can be identified, expressly or by implication, from the evidence of the petty court rolls alone. Despite the absence

[148] SROI C/2/3/1/41 (4 Oct. 1407); Mark Bailey (ed.), *The Bailiffs' Minute Book of Dunwich, 1404–1430* (Woodbridge: Boydell for SRS, 34, 1992), pp. 11–12, 26, 35, 68, 71.
[149] SROI C/2/10/1/2, m. 4v; Betterton and Dymond (1989), pp. 28–9, 36.
[150] SROI C/2/3/1/41 (8 Nov. 1407); C/2/3/1/48 (4 Oct. 1414).
[151] SROI C/2/3/1/34 (7 Oct. 1400, 21 Oct. 1400)).
[152] SROI C/2/3/1/37 (16 Jun. 1401).
[153] SROI C/2/3/1/48 (12 Mar. 1415); C/3/3/1/1.
[154] SROI C/2/3/1/34 (2 Dec. 1400).
[155] Munro (2003), p. 205.
[156] SROI C/2/1/1/3.
[157] SROI C/2/3/1/48 (14 Nov. 1414); Walton (1991), p. 332; Spufford (2002), p. 246; Munro (2003), pp. 209–10.
[158] SROI C/2/1/1/3; Munro (2003), p. 211.
[159] SROI C/2/8/1/3 (east ward); C/2/8/1/7 (north ward).

of any residential labels, at least twenty-four of the clothiers recorded in the alnage accounts of 1396/7 can be said, with reasonable confidence, to have come from Ipswich.[160] Some, such as William Debenham, were prominent burgesses who could be expected to have had an interest in an industry as important as cloth making. The total could be higher, but this is a cautious estimate.

The series of surviving alnage accounts for a period of four years in the late 1460s records a total of 577 Suffolk clothiers, 344 of whom appear only once. Only the earliest of the four accounts lists more than half the 577, and the latest names fewer than a third of them.[161] In other words, a single account provides only an incomplete, sometimes rather misleading, impression of the scale of the local textile industry. On this basis, four years' worth of alnage accounts in the 1390s might well have enabled us to identify fifty, rather than just twenty-four, Ipswich clothiers. In the 1460s many weavers, fullers and dyers were producing and selling their own cloth, but many were simply servicing clothiers.[162] Their names went unrecorded in the alnage accounts, which were never a complete record of all those working in textile manufacture. Consequently, if one assumes that there may have been about fifty Ipswich clothiers in the late 1390s, and doubles that figure to one hundred to include other cloth workers, the total may still underestimate the true scale of activity.

Estimating Ipswich's share of the county's cloth production is equally tricky. Table 11 provides a breakdown of the number of clothiers and cloths, and of the proportion of total subsidy paid in 1396/7. Nearly 10 per cent of Suffolk clothiers appear to have lived in Ipswich, although they were producing a rather lower percentage of Suffolk cloth.

TABLE 11: THE ALNAGE ACCOUNTS OF 1396/7

	Suffolk	*Ipswich*	*Ipswich (percentage)*
No. of clothiers	258	24	9.3
Broad 'dozens'	2059	151	7.3
Narrow 'dozens'	7673	607	7.9
Total subsidy	£49 2s. 2d.	£3 15s. 9d.	7.7

Source: PRO E 101/342/10

Cloth could be big business. The median value of claims in the petty court, at 24s., was the highest for any of the trades of Ipswich. There were, moreover, a few very substantial transactions indeed. The enormous debts of the woad merchant

160 PRO E 101/342/10.
161 PRO E 101/342/25; E 101/343/2; E 101/343/4; E 101/343/5.
162 Amor (2004), p. 422.

Andrew Coke have already been mentioned. After his death in 1414, the executors of Thomas Godewyn, a draper, were suing for recovery of a debt of £50.[163] Nevertheless, no single individual emerges from the alnage accounts as a major cloth maker. Richard Hunt paid the highest subsidy, of 11s., on sixty-six broad dozens. John Avelyne and John Dundale each produced eighty narrow dozens and paid subsidy of 6s. 8d., while William Debenham accounted for forty, and John Roberd a mere twenty-two.

The list of admissions to the freedom of the town includes the names of only three textile workers before 1440, all of whom were admitted following successful completion of an apprenticeship, namely: John Rolf with Thomas Smyth, dyer; John Bowyer with Thomas Roberd, woad dealer; and possibly John Boyton with Thomas Wysman.[164] In addition, Thomas Cowman was admitted as the former apprentice of William Markes, a draper.[165] Of the four, only Cowman made any mark on borough history, serving as treasurer in 1439/40 and 1451/2.[166] No fifteenth-century weaver or fuller is ever recorded as being enfranchised. Weavers in particular enjoyed very little status in the town, appearing only as defendants in petty court cases. In the Ipswich custumal they were even lumped together with spinners, seamstresses and other poor people of low degree, whose goods might not belong to them and were therefore not to be taken as security in legal disputes without the necessary precautions.[167]

Although the alnage accounts suggest that some wider cloths were woven in Ipswich, production concentrated on narrow cloths. These are mentioned fourteen times in the petty court rolls, whereas John Hacon's sale to Roger Austyn of one broad dozen is the only known reference to broad cloth.[168] Although much cloth for export and domestic consumption in Suffolk was coloured, it is surprising that dyed cloth is rarely mentioned in the fifteenth-century petty court cases. John Chaundler owned one russet cloth, while Thomas Wagstaf and Nicholas Smyth quarrelled over another.[169] Thomas Smyth sued John Brewys for three shillings in respect of cloth that he had dyed and sold to him.[170] These local records say nothing about the quality of the merchandise, but the alnage accounts specify that none of the Suffolk cloth presented was of the highest quality, that is cloth of scarlet. Made

[163] SROI C/2/3/1/48 (22 Nov. 1414).
[164] BL, Ms Add. 30,158, ff. 5v, 7v. In York and Exeter dyers, particularly those who traded in dyes, enjoyed the highest status of all textile workers: Swanson (1989), pp. 42–3; Kowaleski (1995), p. 155. Munro suggests that this was the general rule throughout later medieval north-west Europe: (2003), p. 221.
[165] BL, Ms Add. 30,158, f. 1r.
[166] *Annals*, p. 100.
[167] Twiss (1873), pp. 133–5.
[168] SROI C/2/3/1/48 (29 Jan. 1415).
[169] SROI C/2/3/1/34 (2 Dec. 1400); C/2/3/1/48 (14 Feb. 1415).
[170] SROI C/2/3/1/48 (22 Nov. 1414).

with the grain known as 'kermes', which was produced from shield-lice, sourced from Portugal and other Mediterranean countries, scarlet was produced almost exclusively in London.[171] In the days before the Black Death, urban clothiers had been accustomed to make a high quality product for an upper class market. The demographic changes of the fourteenth century had, however, created a demand for a more basic quality cloth for peasants and artisans who could now afford to buy.[172] Country towns, such as Hadleigh and Lavenham, developed their own less regulated cloth industries to meet this demand.[173] As we shall see, they would soon attract away much of Ipswich's remaining share of cloth production.

Leather was a Mucky Business

Leather provided a living for at least twenty named townsmen and their servants, and certainly many more. Although they were outnumbered by cloth workers and the median value of their transactions, as documented in the petty court records, was significantly less, they made essential goods, including harnesses and saddles for horses, sacks and bottles for the carrying of liquid, and military ware. They also met a growing demand for consumer goods such as boots, shoes, gloves, belts and small leather-bound caskets for the safe keeping of deeds, letters and other papers.[174] Some of them even worked on, and traded in, fur for the lining, edging and facing of clothes.[175]

Leather could be prepared in two main ways. Cattle hides were tanned by immersion in a decoction of oak bark, while the skins of various other animals were tawed with alum and oil. For example, John Brewys tawed the pelts of fox cubs for Nicholas Smyth.[176] Tanners could cheat in at least two ways. They could drastically shorten the period during which the leather was left to soak, from nine months or more to six weeks, by strengthening the concoction ('woozes') in which it was immersed, or by applying heat. This produced weakened and substandard leather.[177] Alternatively, they could dye 'counterfeit' leather and pass it off as being of better quality than it actually was.[178] In order to deter such fraud, tanners were expected to bring their wares to the Moothall for checking and marking and offenders were fined by the leet court.[179]

Tanning was a mucky business which used not only oak bark, but urine and

[171] PRO E 101/342/10; Childs (1978), pp. 58–9, 79; Spufford (2002), p. 333. Cloth of scarlet was not always red, as the colour took its name from the cloth not *vice versa*: Munro (2003), pp. 213–15.
[172] C. Dyer (1989), pp. 205–7.
[173] Bailey (2007), pp. 272–6.
[174] Cherry (1991), pp. 295, 314; SROI C/2/10/3/1, ff. 199, 210, 256, 265.
[175] Veale (2003), pp. 29, 148.
[176] SROI C/2/3/1/48 (13 Jun. 1415).
[177] Swanson (1989), p. 54.
[178] Salzmann (1913), p. 177.
[179] Webb (1962), p. 128.

other unpleasant materials, and as such was often a source of pollution. Even though it was not the case, as many believed, that the fumes spread disease, the smell was very unpleasant. William Knatte kept noxious pits called 'Barkputes', while Thomas Puntyng left bark vats to his wife which, in use, would have emitted very disagreeable odours, as well as polluting adjacent water supplies.[180] In 1419 Robert Parmasay faced a hefty fine of two shillings by the leet court for dumping the filth of his trade in the river next to Friars Bridge, and, two years later, William Keche and Edmund Gigehoo were penalised for similar offences.[181] As was the case in many other towns and cities, there may well have been increasing pressure for tanners to keep their operations out of town.[182] In this respect it may be significant that, after 1421, the extant Ipswich leet court rolls very rarely record any tanner being fined for causing pollution. As the century wore on an increasing number of them were non-resident. By the 1480s no fewer than nine of the twenty-two named tanners who were fined for selling defective leather, hailed from outside the town: one from Hitcham, two from Nacton, one from Nayland, three from Rattlesden, one from Stowe and another from Wetherden.[183] With the exception of Nacton and Nayland, these were High Suffolk villages, prospering on the strength of cattle rearing. It was, of course, the very same cattle which provided hides for tanning.

Eleven tanners were operating in Ipswich in 1283, but by the 1410s only six are cited in the extant leet court rolls.[184] Just one, Geoffrey Bury, was described as such in the petty court records.[185] William Keche and Robert Parmasay were the foremost tanners of their day, the former rising to become bailiff, and the latter serving first as town treasurer and later as chamberlain.[186] John Felaw, father of Richard, was working as a tanner between 1416 and 1421, being fined 12d. in 1419 for soaking leather in the town ditch in east ward and making pits there. He rose to become bailiff in 1439/40, but by then had probably abandoned tanning for wider trading interests.[187] Three tanners were admitted as burgesses in the 1430s, among them Edmund Gigehoo and Thomas Hammond, who became a freeman in 1438 and died in 1455.[188] Hammond's bequests of property and cash mark him out as a man of means. He may have used his two gardens for carrying on his work, and employed his servants in the trade.[189] Despite these notable successes, the evidence suggests

[180] C/2/8/1/13 (north ward); SROI R2/327.

[181] SROI C/2/8/1/4 (south ward) and C/2/8/1/5 (north ward).

[182] Tanners were driven out of late medieval London into the suburbs: Baron (2004), p. 68; and similarly out of Exeter: Kowaleski (1995), p. 302.

[183] SROI C/2/8/1/17–22.

[184] Powell (1906), pp.145–6, 149–53; SROI C/2/8/1/2–7.

[185] SROI C/2/3/1/35 (08 Mar. 1401).

[186] *Annals*, pp. 95, 103.

[187] *Ibid.*, p. 100.

[188] BL, Ms Add. 30,158, ff. 4v, 5r, 7v; SROI C/2/10/1/1, m. 9v.

[189] Thrupp (1962), pp. 130–1.

that, as a group, the early fifteenth-century tanners were not as active in the town as they were to become later.

Tanned leather was used by the likes of Robert Sadeler and John Nicoll, who both made saddles, and by cordwainers to meet the insatiable demand for shoes.[190] John Trewelove sold the better quality cordwain leather, both wholesale and retail.[191] He had built an extensive network of business contacts and, in 1400/1 alone, was driven to sue fifteen different suppliers and customers, among them the prominent cordwainer John Horkslee.[192] The glover William Gosse used tawed leather, as did a second glover, Thomas Newman, who became a burgess in 1434.[193] Gloves were frequently offered as gifts to oil the wheels of patronage in the late Middle Ages, and their popularity presents one more sign of improving standards of living.[194]

Changes in fashion during the second half of the fourteenth century, particularly the trend towards fuller sleeves and voluminous robes, called for the greater use of fur.[195] Widespread disregard for sumptuary laws, and higher personal incomes, meant that demand extended further down the social scale. As a Venetian envoy of the time observed, 'in England it is always windy, and however warm the weather the natives invariably wear furs'.[196] Katherine Tyndale kept out the cold North Sea winds that blew into Ipswich with a gown lined with the fur of Baltic squirrel.[197] References to skins in the petty court cases of this period outnumber references to hides. Seven of the named leather workers were described as skinners or pelterers, engaged in the buying, making up and selling of skins and furs. Nicholas Smyth was one of them, crossing swords in the petty court with a dozen different suppliers and customers over a fifteen-year period. He sold pelts to John Deye and '*ruskyn*' (poorer quality summer squirrel skins)[198] to Walter Drayll. As well as the fox skins mentioned above, he bought rabbit skins from John Brewys and hired him to sew various fur pelts for hoods. He also leased a store room from Thomas Page. His creditors seized furs and a hood of '*poleynwork*' (red or black Polish squirrel skins)[199] as security for the payment of his debts.[200]

Throughout the fifteenth century leather working was an occupation fit for leading members of the borough community. In the opening years John Horkslee

[190] C/2/3/1/41 (3 Nov 1407, 13 Dec. 1407); Swanson (1989), pp. 56–7.
[191] SROI C/2/3/1/35 (22 Feb. 1401).
[192] SROI C/2/3/1/35 (8 Mar. 1401); C/2/3/1/36 (7 Jun. 1401).
[193] SROI C/2/3/1/35 (8 Mar. 1401); BL, Ms Add. 30,158, f. 6v.
[194] Cherry (1991), p. 316; Swanson (1989), p. 60.
[195] Veale (2003), p. viii.
[196] Quoted in Veale (2003), p. 3.
[197] SROI R1/119b.
[198] Veale (2003), pp. 18, 228.
[199] Veale (2003), p. 225.
[200] SROI C/2/3/1/36 (23 Jun. 1401); C/2/3/1/37 (7 Aug. 1401); C/2/3/1/41 (4 Oct. 1407, 8 Nov 1407, 23 Jan. 1408,); C/2/3/1/48 (21 Feb. 1415, 23 May. 1415).

was bailiff eight times and John Knepping, a dealer in skins, was bailiff seven times and also served as MP. He invested in land, shops, a quay and a crane.[201] Both men engaged in overseas trade. Of the twenty-nine burgesses admitted between 1415 and 1439 whose occupation is given, six were leather workers.[202] Tanners and cordwainers engaged in continuous competition for control of the supply of raw leather, and for the profits that control earned, giving rise 'in many towns ... to a running battle for literally hundreds of years between' them.[203] Cordwainers appear to have had the better of this battle in early fifteenth-century Ipswich, but to have lost out later on. The nature of their trade meant that tanners were less welcome in polite society.[204] Even so, the success of William Keche, Robert Parmasay, Thomas Hammond, and other Ipswich tanners after them, supports the time honoured maxim that 'where there's muck, there's money'.

So Many Uses of Metal

Metal working provided employment for a wide variety of tradesmen, among them ironmongers, smiths, brasiers, founderers, cutlers and goldsmiths. As yet, there were no recorded pewterers in Ipswich.[205] The importation of foreign iron into Ipswich created welcome opportunities for ironmongers, such as the aptly-named Richard Irenmonger of Bury St Edmunds and his fellow townsman John Colbech. Irenmonger apparently supplied local craftsmen, for example selling iron worth 6s. 8d. to the smith John Gerard.[206] When Colbech was sued for the substantial sum of £32 13s. 4d., his creditor seized a barrel of steel as security for the debt.[207] Presumably, he rented storage facilities in town. The Londoner John Esgaston was another ironmonger who kept substantial stock in Ipswich.[208] In addition to Gerard, at least four other smiths are mentioned in the petty court rolls. John Smyth succeeded in recovering 7s. 10d. from the sale of ninety-four horse shoes.[209] Horses were the most commonly mentioned livestock in the petty court records, providing a ready market for the products of the smithy. In a town with so many churches and religious houses, bellmaking provided regular employment for founderers such as William Wodeward.[210] He would have used an alloy of copper and tin, close to

[201] *Annals*, pp. 88, 89, 91, 92; K.N. Houghton 'John Knepping', in *HoP*, III, p. 527.
[202] BL, Ms Add. 30,158, ff. 4v, 5r, 5v, 6v, 7r, 7v.
[203] Swanson (1989), pp. 55, 139, 152.
[204] *Ibid.*, pp. 3, 65, 139, 168.
[205] Ronald F. Homer, 'Tin, Lead and Pewter', in *English Medieval Industries* ed. by J. Blair and N. Ramsay (London: Hambledon Press, 1991), pp. 55–80 (p. 68).
[206] SROI C/2/3/1/36 (17 May 1401).
[207] SROI C/2/3/1/48 (11 Apr. 1415).
[208] PRO CP 40/596, m. 257r.
[209] SROI C/2/3/1/34 (16 Nov. 1400).
[210] BL, Ms Add. 30,158, f. 1v.

bronze.[211] When not casting bells, he could always rely on a significant domestic demand for metalware, using brass in the production of everyday utensils, such as pots and pans which were the household goods most commonly seized by creditors in petty court cases.[212] John Banbury and John Hill were described as cutlers, which came to mean makers of knives and similar table ware.[213]

Goldsmiths were forbidden from using iron, bronze, brass or other base metal, except in church plate, and worked almost exclusively with gold and silver.[214] Indirect, and thus largely circumstantial, evidence of their craft comes from those petty court cases in which burglars or creditors seized brooches, buckles, goblets, rings, spoons and mazers (maplewood drinking bowls mounted in gold or silver), all made of precious metals.[215] Among Ipswich testators who made wills before 1450, eight left silver spoons, belt buckles and mazers.[216] Silver spoons were particularly prized – 'being born with a silver spoon in one's mouth' remains a euphemism for being upper class.[217] The spoons were not only a 'symbol of status and wealth', but one of 'good breeding reflected in good table manners'.[218] Only John Mille was described as a goldsmith in the petty court records, although both Andrew and Frederick Goldsmyth may well have followed the same craft. Andrew was accused of illegally retaining a sapphire worth fifteen shillings, and one of Frederick's creditors had seized his mazer.[219]

The median value of claims made by metal workers was quite high, well above those made by leather workers, reflecting the relative scarcity of metals, particularly precious ones, and perhaps also the level of skill involved in the production of plate and jewellery. Nevertheless, provincial goldsmiths rarely owned such valuable materials themselves and more often worked with those of their clients.[220] In contrast to London, theirs was not one of the highest status trades. None of the burgesses known to have been admitted in the fifteenth century was described as a

[211] Claude Blair and John Blair, 'Copper Alloys', in *English Medieval Industries* ed. by J. Blair and N. Ramsay (London: Hambledon Press, 1991), pp. 81–106 (p. 89).

[212] Swanson (1989), p. 74.

[213] SROI C/2/3/1/48 (16 Oct. 1414).

[214] Marion Campbell, 'Gold, Silver and Precious Stones', in *English Medieval Industries* ed. by J. Blair and N. Ramsay (London: Hambledon Press, 1991), pp. 107–166 (p. 123).

[215] SROI C/2/3/1/35 (22 Feb. 1401, 1 Mar. 1401, 8 March 1401); C/2/3/1/41 (18 Oct. 1407, 25 Oct. 1407, 17 Nov. 1407).

[216] SROI R1/20; R1/28; R1/31; R1/60; R1/74; C/2/10/1/1, mm. 4v, 5r, 9v; NRO NCC, Reg. Aleyn ff. 17–19; PCC 1 Marche, ff. 3v–4r (PROB 11/2A).

[217] C. Dyer (2005), p. 141.

[218] P.J.P. Goldberg, 'The Fashioning of Bourgeois Domesticity in Later Medieval England: A Material Culture Perspective' in *Medieval Domesticity. Home, Housing and Household in Medieval England* ed. by Maryanne Kowaleski and P.J.P. Goldberg (Cambridge: Cambridge University Press, 2008) pp. 124–144 (pp. 134–5).

[219] SROI C/2/3/1/37 (28 Aug. 1401); C/2/3/1/35 (1 Mar. 1401); C/2/3/1/41 (6 Mar. 1408).

[220] M. Campbell (1991), p. 111.

goldsmith.[221] Edmund Page, an Ipswich goldsmith, died in 1445 leaving only modest assets and certainly no precious metal.[222]

The trading connections of Ipswich embraced London and the east coast ports, but landward, its hinterland was largely confined to a radius of 20 miles. Within that area, Hadleigh was the most important trading partner, and most of this activity revolved around the manufacture of cloth. Only the trade in wine extended further afield, laying the foundations of the wealth of the town and many of its leading burgesses. Such was its overwhelming importance in both overseas and domestic commerce that any interruption in the wine trade would be keenly felt. Townspeople obtained their grain, principally wheat, from the surrounding countryside within 10 miles of home, and looked increasingly to the wood pasture of High Suffolk for their meat. Butchers were enjoying the benefits of a growing demand for flesh and hides. Cloth was the leading industry, involving the largest single occupational group and generating the highest value transactions. Narrow cloths were far more popular than broad ones. Nevertheless, Ipswich clothiers were almost certainly losing ground to competitors in small towns, such as Hadleigh and Lavenham, who were producing inexpensive, basic quality cloth. Some leather was still made in Ipswich, but the manufacturing processes were unpleasant in an urban environment, and wholesale and retail leather trades had become of greater importance. Metal working provided a living for a wide variety of craftsmen, but not on the same scale as cloth and leather. With its busy port, Ipswich was a fairly prosperous town in the early 1400s, but the fault lines in its economy would be tested in the years to come. Its fortunes in these difficult mid-century years, blighted by the 'Great Slump', are considered in the next two chapters.

[221] BL, Ms Add. 30,158.
[222] SROI R1/35.

– 4 –

Merchants of Cologne

As we have seen, the closing years of the fourteenth century were favourable to English overseas trade in general and the merchants of Ipswich in particular. The good times were not, however, to last. One modern British Prime Minister reputedly described his greatest anxiety in office as 'Events dear boy, Events'.[1] The fifteenth century provided a superabundance of events which challenged the political leaders of the time and very often overwhelmed them. The middle years witnessed major developments in international relations with the Hanse, Burgundy, France and Spain, making this a roller-coaster period of hostilities interrupted by the occasional truce and treaty (Appendix 1). 'Recurrent warfare was the bane of international trade, obstructing its development and preventing its advantages from being realised'.[2] Such events significantly altered the environment in which merchants traded overseas, sometimes offering opportunities, but more often taking them away. Another layer of complexity and uncertainty was added to the pattern of their lives. In trading with continental Europe they had to contend with unpredictable political developments, in addition to underlying shifts in the supply and demand for their goods. As a result, English merchants faced mounting difficulties in all their overseas markets which reached a climax in the middle years of the century and resulted in a severe contraction in exports of wool and woollen cloth and imports of wine.

Despite early advances, English penetration of the Baltic was stalled and ultimately blocked. The Hanse, with whom they traded there, had long enjoyed privileges in England. They were allowed to form a corporate body, had their own community based on the Steelyard in London with satellites in major provincial ports, exercised freedom of trade and enjoyed exemptions from customs tariffs.[3] The desire of English merchants for reciprocal rights in Hanseatic territory, and the

[1] Harold Macmillan actually said 'The opposition of events': A. Jay (ed.) *Oxford Dictionary of Political Quotations* (Oxford: Oxford University Press, 3rd edition 2006), pp. 254, 272.
[2] Britnell, *Britain and Ireland* (2004), pp. 323–3.
[3] Power and Postan (1933), p. 98.

determination of the Hanse to deny them, was the root cause of all the friction between them, exemplified by the English capture of the Bay Fleet in 1449 and Lubeck fleet in 1458, the closure of the Baltic to English cloth in 1451–52, and the war with the Hanse between 1468 and 1474.

From 1419 to 1467 the Low Countries, which remained the most important overseas market for English merchants, were ruled by Philip the Good, duke of Burgundy. Needing both French grain and English wool for his people, Philip was torn in his allegiance between the two protagonists in the Hundred Years' War. His initial sympathy for England waned, particularly when confronted with the Calais Staple partition and bullion ordinances of the 1430s, which restricted the credit that could be made available to his merchants for their purchase of wool. His irritation was expressed in the intermittent banning of English cloth imports into Holland and Zeeland, which rarely lasted long because it proved so unpopular with many of his own subjects. Indeed, in the face of one such ban, in 1436, the Lowlanders swore allegiance to Henry VI in order to maintain the supply of cloth. Consequently, despite the difficult political situation, trade between England and Holland peaked in the third quarter of the fifteenth century.[4]

In France, English military fortunes went from bad to worse, leading to the loss first of Normandy, and ultimately of Gascony, causing irreparable damage to the wine trade. Only with Spain did relations steadily improve during this period. As early Spanish support for France in the Hundred Years' War dwindled, trade with England grew under the protection of a series of truces and safe conducts, culminating in a formal treaty with Castile. By the mid-fifteenth century the Spaniards had extended their operations to east coast ports and were beginning to take an interest in Ipswich. In 1463/4 the borough received a payment of twenty-five shillings as customs of the quay for the arrival and departure of a Spanish ship.[5]

Even so, only when Edward IV became king for the second time in 1471 did international trade really begin to pick up. Edward had the strength of character to impose peace on his own land, and, as 'the first merchant king', the good sense to mend fences with his neighbours through a series of treaties which provided the foundations for recovery in the final thirty years of the century.[6]

Ipswich did not, of course, escape the impact of these events. Some of the town's merchants were personally caught up in them, and the consequential litigation has left its mark in the records. In about 1450, for example, a Dutch ship, chartered in Prussia by William Baldry of Ipswich to carry merchandise back to England, was intercepted by French and Breton ships. It escaped, only to be captured on landfall by the inhabitants of Spurn Head in the East Riding of Yorkshire. Much later, in

[4] Barron (1995), p. 13; Kerling (1954), p. 208.
[5] SROI C/3/3/1/2.
[6] Nightingale (1995), p. 519; Sutton (2005), p. 271.

1467, Baldry laded a cargo of wine on five ships in Bordeaux but was forced by the 'submaire' of the town to pay further duties before being allowed on his way.[7] Gilbert Debenham esquire (the second of that name, and distinguishable from his son of the same name who became a knight) also traded with Prussia, where he employed Thomas Cadon as his factor. Labelled as a rascal and a rogue by historians, Debenham acted entirely in character by dealing harshly with Cadon. Having been imprisoned in Germany, on his release Cadon returned to England, no doubt in the hope of some home comforts. His expectations were dashed when, on arrival, he was re-imprisoned at the suit of Debenham, who claimed that he had failed properly to account with him.[8]

The aggravation was not all one way. Overseas merchants visiting Ipswich also found themselves embroiled in the troubles. In March 1451 local customs officers were ordered to protect visitors from Prussia or the Hanse from injury, while the conference at Utrecht continued between the king of England, the master of Prussia and the proconsuls of the Hanse. Six months later, perhaps once talks had broken down, the bailiffs and other town worthies were ordered to arrest Hanseatic ships and wares. In 1456 Hanseatic merchants complained to the king that, on sailing from Ipswich, they had been attacked by Englishmen in ships of war and prevented from leaving the port. At the same time, merchants of Hamburg sought compensation after English pirates intercepted them and seized seven packs of linen cloth from their ship *en route* from Ipswich to London.[9]

Despite all this conflict, as we shall see, it was the German Hanse and, in particular, the merchants of Cologne who dominated the overseas trade of Ipswich in the middle years of the fifteenth century.

Customs Accounts and Other Sources

In seeking more evidence about the goods that were shipped in and out of Ipswich during these difficult middle years, the value of those goods, the merchants who bought and sold them, and the ships that carried them, we need first to examine the surviving customs accounts. A continuous series of enrolled Exchequer accounts provides a snapshot of the state of trade in any given year, and the records for wool, woollen cloth and wine are readily available.[10] Graphs based on these accounts, illustrating rolling five-year averages, appear in Figures 1 to 3. They do not, however, offer much detail, and the information they provide generally relates to all the harbours within the jurisdiction of the Ipswich headport.

[7] *CPR 1446–52*, p. 389. Sutton comments on the Baldry family's 'multifarious' trade connections: (2005), p. 222.

[8] PRO C 1/16/469.

[9] *CPR 1446–52*, pp. 330, 431; *CPR 1452–61*, pp. 299, 311.

[10] Carus-Wilson and Coleman (1963), 55–70, 87–111; James (1971), pp. 108–16.

In contrast, a few particular accounts have survived for short periods, which provide much more detail and sometimes distinguish between the different harbours subject to the oversight of a headport. As we have already seen, Bernard's account of 1396–98 does this very clearly. The six particular accounts considered in this chapter, for the period 1459–65, are admittedly less specific.[11] Nevertheless, with careful study of the headings, dates, names of masters and merchants, and cargoes, it is possible to determine with reasonable confidence which entries relate to particular harbours.[12] They do not provide a continuous record, but when added together they cover an aggregate period of twenty-two and a half months, between 14 February 1459 and 7 March 1466, during which time fifty-seven ships arrived and seventy-six departed. The goods these ships carried and their values are shown in Table 12. Disconcertingly little data is provided for sailings in and out of Harwich and Maldon, raising a suspicion that such information may be hidden among entries for Colchester and Ipswich. There may, however, be a more pragmatic explanation that goes beyond the minutiae and layout of the accounts. Harwich was sacked by the French in the early 1450s and may not have recovered its full capacity to cater for ocean-going traffic.[13] Situated on the river Blackwater, Maldon possibly found it difficult to cater for the larger ships that sailed the mid-fourteenth-century seas.

In addition to these customs accounts, the borough records provide valuable insights into the overseas trade of the period, especially the petty court rolls and chamberlains' accounts. The wills of those who took part in overseas trade, or left among their possessions goods that had arrived from abroad, are another source. It is, therefore, possible to learn more about the goods that were carried to and from Ipswich in the mid-fifteenth century, the merchants who participated in overseas trade at that time and the ships that they used to carry their merchandise.

Fluctuations in the Woollen Cloth Trade

By 1460 woollen cloth had overtaken raw wool as the major export both of the nation and of Ipswich. The total value of cloth exports from Ipswich itemised in Bernard's account was £410, but according to the mid-century particular accounts it had risen to £3845 12s. 6d. Admittedly, an analysis of the enrolled accounts indicates that the few surviving particular accounts may not have been entirely representative of the entire 1460s, and, indeed, some may paint too rosy a picture. Even so, and even allowing for an increase in the valuations adopted by the customs

[11] PRO E 122/52/42; E 122/52/43; E 122/52/45; E 122/52/46; E 122/52/47; E 122/52/48.
[12] Britnell took the same view in his volume on Colchester, although he ascribes more of the woollen cloth trade to Colchester and less to Ipswich: (1986) pp.171–2.
[13] *CPR 1446–52*, p. 528.

TABLE 12: EXPORTS FROM AND IMPORTS TO IPSWICH 1459–66

	Total market value	*Share of denizens (%)*
EXPORTS		
Woollen cloth (2197½ broadcloths or equivalent at £1 15s per cloth)	£3845 12s. 6d.	12.2
Wool (Marginally less than 119 sacks at £4 per sack)	£475 19s. 2½d.	100
Dairy products	£367 1s. 4d.	92.1
Hides and skins (calf and rabbit)	£22 4s. 10d.	50.3
Firewood	£19 15s. 2d.	4.2
Grain	£7 16s. 8d.	0
Other	£33 16s. 8d.	53.2 (lead and tin)
Total	£4772 6s. 4½d.	27.5
IMPORTS		
Dyes, mordants, oils, teasels	£1095 0s. 10d.	7.9
Mercery and haberdashery	£935 15s. 2d.	5.8
Wine (£9 a tun)	£782 5s.	21.3
Fish	£333 9s. 6d.	11.1
Iron and ironwork	£346 17s. 6d.	16.1
Salt	£267 3s. 4d.	6.7
Wax	£129 13s. 1d.	15.0
Soap	£98 10s.	24.2
Woodland produce – ashes, bitumen, tar, wainscot	£80 12s.	20.5
Stone	£38 7s.	7.8
Furniture and furnishings	£32 12s. 6d.	20.2
Horticulture	£28 15s. 6d.	22.0
Furs	£8 10s.	0
Bricks/Tiles	£2 5s.	0
Other	£69 16s. 8d.	11.5
Total	£4256 13s. 1d.	11.8

Notes

(*Sources*: PRO E 122/52/42-48)

The market value of wine rose, particularly after the loss of Gascony. The figure of £9 per tun is taken from James (1971), p. 51, and from Ipswich petty court cases (SROI C/2/3/1/51 (6, 27 Jun. 1443).

Total imports include £3 8s. 4d. worth of goods the description of which is illegible.

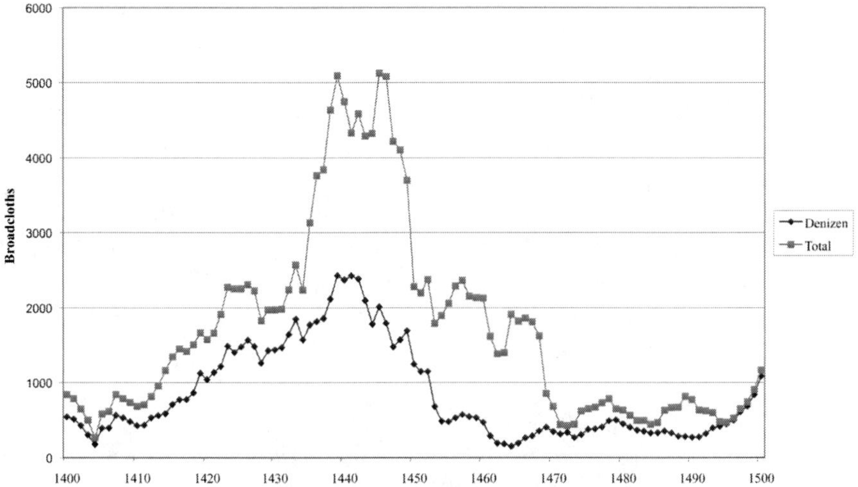

Figure 1: *Export of Woollen Cloth from the headport of Ipswich in the Fifteenth Century. Five-year rolling avergaes (after Carus-Wilson).*

officials, exports in the later period were still several times greater. The enrolled accounts, illustrated by the graph in Figure 1, confirm this growth, but, as they cover the intervening years as well, tell a rather more complex story. They show a very sharp rise in cloth exports to a peak in the 1440s, followed by an equally sharp fall in the 1450s and 1460s. Such fluctuations were magnified by the peregrinations of the Hanseatic merchants, first into the headport, and then out again when they returned to London. Indeed, the Hanseatic presence provided temporary insurance against the earlier downturn in the cloth trade and, for a while, their exports from the Ipswich headport were far in excess of their combined exports from all other English provincial ports.[14] Colchester enjoyed the bulk of this Hanseatic trade, and indeed hosted an adjunct to the London Steelyard, which suggests that Ipswich was probably less affected by these dramatic changes of fortune.[15]

By the 1460s Suffolk had become the leading cloth producing county in England, generating, according to alnage accounts, about 5000 broadcloths, or equivalent, a year in the second half of the decade.[16] Very nearly 2200 such cloths were exported through Ipswich in the twenty-two and a half months covered by the particular accounts, equivalent to about 1200 cloths each year. Assuming only one-third of the nation's cloth was sent abroad, a rudimentary calculation suggests that possibly

[14] Lloyd (1991), p. 229.
[15] Britnell (1986), pp. 171–2; Lloyd (1991), p. 229.
[16] Amor (2004), 414–36 (pp. 415, 417).

three-quarters of Suffolk's cloth exports were shipped through Ipswich. If, as may be the case, the particular accounts give too rosy a view of the volume of cloth exports, this may be an overestimate. Since Suffolk was the country's largest cloth producer, was situated relatively close to the main European markets, and produced cloth that was popular overseas, almost certainly a higher proportion than one-third of its output was being exported.[17] Moreover, some Ipswich exports may have originated beyond the county boundary, while some cloth that was produced in Suffolk, but for use within the cloth maker's own household, would have escaped the alnager's seal.[18] Nevertheless, even taking into account all these caveats, in the mid-fifteenth century quite possibly more Suffolk cloth was being shipped through Ipswich than was sent to London for export.

Whereas Bernard's account, and that of 1413/14, had listed a bewildering variety of cloths, the particular accounts for the early 1460s and later refer almost exclusively to 'woollen cloth curticus without grain', which equated to the broadcloth. This standardised nomenclature is likely to have been an administrative convenience rather than a reflection of reality. For customs purposes all cloths tended to be counted as broadcloths.[19] Suffolk clothiers continued, however, to make and export a range of cloths of different sizes and styles. Salzmann notes the continuing demand in eastern Europe for cheap, coarse Suffolk 'vesses or set cloths'.[20] Bailey refers to 'a wide variety of fashionable and colourful, but cheap and imitation, cloths for a new mass market'.[21]

The nature of the exported cloth depended to a degree on its destination. Suffolk cloth was popular in Prussia.[22] As the Baltic was a zone of flax and linen, rather than cloth production, the Prussians possessed little capacity for cloth finishing.[23] Consequently, they wanted coloured cloth. The Spaniards, at least in Castile, had the same requirement.[24] The Spanish merchants John Pevye and John Marteyn were shipping cloth, as well as a small quantity of worsted, from Ipswich in July 1464.[25] On the other hand, Holland and Zeeland had their own cloth finishing industry, so they wanted unfinished imports. London mercers, who enjoyed close relations with leading Suffolk clothiers such as William Forthe of Hadleigh and John Martin of Melford, were heavily involved in this trade, as were the merchants of Cologne who

[17] Bailey (2007), pp. 293, 299.
[18] *CFR 1399–1405*, p. 36; A.R. Bridbury, *Medieval Clothmaking: An Economic Survey* (London: Heinemann, 1982), p. 53.
[19] Childs (1978), pp. 78–9; Sutton (2005), p. 295.
[20] Salzmann (1913), p. 168.
[21] Bailey (2007), p. 299.
[22] Lloyd (1991), p. 221.
[23] Power and Postan (1933), p. 144.
[24] Childs (1976), p. 83.
[25] PRO E122/52/46. Pevye is described as a Spaniard in the accounts, and Marteyn as such in *CPR 1461–67*, p. 301.

were so prominent within the Hanseatic communities in Colchester and Ipswich.[26] The name of Johann 'van A' of Cologne appears in four of the six accounts, shipping a total of 665 cloths from Ipswich, while his colleague and compatriot Hermann Rinck shipped 149. Much of the cloth exported by the Cologners travelled as far as southern Germany.[27] Suffolk thus became a major supplier of both finished and unfinished cloth to the Continent. Markets were, however, both unpredictable and unstable. When relations with the Baltic states improved the demand for coloured cloth grew; but when those with Burgundy flourished there was more call for undyed cloth. The resumption of hostilities inevitably led to a dramatic, sometimes sudden, fall in demand.[28] These fluctuations kept Suffolk clothiers on their toes, conditioned them to be flexible and perhaps encouraged a keen interest in international relations.

Smuggling Wool

The divergent figures for wool exports provide perhaps the starkest contrast between the particular accounts for the late fourteenth and early fifteenth century and those for the years between 1459 and 1466. In the twenty-four months covered by Bernard's account nearly 900 sacks of wool, or the equivalent in wool-fells, were exported from Ipswich by thirteen different merchants in twenty-two sailings.[29] In a similar, if discontinuous, period some sixty years later, fewer than 120 sacks appear to have been exported by only five merchants in four sailings, all on the same day in August 1462.

The extant particular accounts are not entirely representative, as many of those recording wool exports have not survived. The enrolled accounts paint a slightly less dismal picture. Since all the headport's wool left through Ipswich, they tell us what was happening there over a longer period. The volume of wool exports from Ipswich continued to grow until the end of the first decade of the fifteenth century, then fell away sharply, before climbing again to a new and higher peak in the late 1420s (Figure 2). Exports remained fairly buoyant in the early 1430s, but after that, in many years, there were none recorded at all. Such shipments of wool as did leave the port may well have done so as an indirect consequence of Henry VI's financial woes, since he paid off loans from the Staplers by offering them an exemption from subsidy on their exports of wool from selected ports.[30] The decline ultimately bottomed out in the period covered by these later particular accounts.

[26] Britnell (1986), pp. 173–5; Sutton (2005), pp. 221–2, 278, 284.
[27] Nightingale (1995), p. 524.
[28] Power and Postan (1933), p. 153; Nightingale (1995), p. 547.
[29] PRO E 122/193/33.
[30] Power and Postan (1933), pp. 295–301; *CPR 1446–52*, pp. 315–6, 323, record just two examples in Ipswich.

Figure 2: *Export of Wool from Ipswich in the Fifteenth Century. Five-year rolling avergaes (after Carus-Wilson).*

Notwithstanding these local vicissitudes, the fifteenth century witnessed no more than a gentle decline in English exports of wool.[31] Ipswich's misfortunes were, therefore, more to do with its own particular circumstances than with the nation's fortunes. The Calais partition and bullion ordinances must take much of the blame. First introduced in 1429/30 and reintroduced on several subsequent occasions in amended form, they were a reaction to the European bullion shortage. In brief, they fixed the sale price of the wool at Calais, required payment up front in full in gold or silver, and provided for the division of the total proceeds among the Staplers in a manner similar to the dividend of a modern day company.[32] As a result, the carefully erected edifice of European credit linking England, Calais and the great fairs of the Low Countries began to crumble. These ordinances reduced the overall volume and value of sales, but they had a disproportionately adverse affect on smaller scale merchants who could no longer offer credit and then make a quick sale at a competitive price, but had to wait for their share of the proceeds.[33] Many of them had shipped their cargoes out of the provincial ports, with the result that when their trade declined, so did that of the provinces. Matters became even worse in 1436 with the declaration of war by Duke Philip of Burgundy. English wool was nevertheless still desperately needed by the clothiers of the Low Countries and the inevitable consequence was an upsurge in smuggling, in which Ipswich merchants

[31] Carus-Wilson and Coleman (1963), p. 123.
[32] Power and Postan (1933), pp. 82–3; Lloyd (1977), p. 261.
[33] Power and Postan (1933), p. 85; Lloyd (1977), p. 266.

were enthusiastically involved.[34] One such, Thomas Ingram, was implicated in the unsuccessful smuggling of wool and skins in 1438.[35] Gilbert Debenham was another, whose ship *le George* had almost certainly made many a clandestine voyage before it was caught in transit by the earl of Oxford in the early 1450s, 'with a large quantity of wool packed in a suspicious manner'.[36] So serious was the problem that, in 1449, Debenham's fellow townsmen John Andrew, John Bale, Thomas Denys, Thomas Caldwell and Richard Felawe were appointed to a royal commission to investigate smuggling in and out of Ipswich and other ports and places in Suffolk.[37]

Dairy Products and Other Exports

After cloth and wool, dairy products were now Ipswich's most valuable recorded export. In 1463/4 the borough received tolls worth 13s. 6d. for the use of the hambeam, which was employed for the weighing at the quay of various packets and barrels of cheese, this being more than twice the sum earned by use of the crane.[38] Over 1050 wey (235,200 lbs[39]) of cheese and a smaller quantity of butter then left the port for overseas markets in Holland, Zeeland and the Baltic, much of the cheese being of a high quality.[40] More still went to London.[41] This represents nearly twenty times the value of similar exports from Ipswich previously recorded in Bernard's account. Even allowing for the possibility that some entries actually relate to sailings from Maldon, growth in this sector was undoubtedly significant. Christopher Dyer suggests that a dairy cow might be expected to produce 80lb of cheese in a year.[42] On this assumption total exports would represent the annual output of 2940 beasts, or about 170 herds, spread over twenty-two and a half months' worth of accounts. As dairy farming was predominantly a small-scale tenant preserve in the fifteenth century, this level of export reveals an impressive organisation in getting all the

[34] Sutton (2005), p. 285.

[35] SROI C/2/6/2.

[36] PRO E 159/230 Mich. rot. 17; W. Haward, 'Gilbert Debenham: A Medieval Rascal in Real Life' *History*, n.s. vol 13 (1928–9), 300–314 (pp. 305–6).

[37] *CPR 1446–52*, p. 273.

[38] SROI C/3/3/1/2.

[39] It was enacted in 1431 that a wey should be 224 lbs: *Rot. Parl.*, iv, p. 381.

[40] As from 1431 the requirement to export all cheese and butter via Calais had been relaxed and was subsequently abolished, to avoid the merchandise being impaired by 'vermin and worms' on long journeys: *Rot. Parl.*, iv, p. 293; v, p. 24; Power and Postan (1933), p. 141; Kerling (1954), p. 118; C. Richmond *John Hopton: A Fifteenth Century Suffolk Gentleman* (Cambridge: Cambridge University Press, 1981), pp. 144–5.

[41] Scammell (1961), 327–41 (p. 329).

[42] Dyer does not mention butter. His figure pre-dates the Black Death and productivity may have improved afterwards: C. Dyer (1989), p. 114. Britnell gives a much higher annual figure per dairy cow, of 0.6 wey of cheese and 3.1 gallons of butter: 'Farming Practice and Techniques: Eastern England', in *The Agrarian History of England and Wales, 1348–1500*, ed. by E. Miller, 8 vols. (Cambridge: Cambridge University Press, 1991), III, pp. 194–210 (p. 207).

produce to the quay side.[43] The largest single recorded export was of 150 wey of cheese, credited to one Robert Coke in 1462.[44] If this was, in fact, Robert Cake – a successful draper, clothier and agriculturalist in Stowmarket – he may have been one of the enterprising souls who actually organized the exports. Several London merchants also appear to have shipped substantial quantities of cheese and butter from Ipswich.[45] At least some of them, such as the grocers John Clerk and John Kyng, also made cloth and had other trading interests in Suffolk. Perhaps they were using their contacts with rural textile workers, who were often also small-scale pastoralists, to source dairy products for export.[46]

The remaining exports are of far less importance. The level of the trade in hides, and skins which had been worth thirty-eight pounds in John Bernard's time, was in real terms largely unchanged. In the interim, however, the value of rabbit skins had fallen sharply because they had lost their scarcity value.[47] Small cargoes of firewood and of peas, oats, rye, wheat and mixed grain (probably rye and wheat) were exported, almost invariably by alien merchants, probably to Holland and Zeeland where foreign wood and corn were much in demand.[48] Relatively speaking, however, the quantities involved were modest; whereas 80,000 billets of firewood were shipped from Ipswich in the early 1460s, as many as 1,516,000 left the Sussex ports in 1489/90.[49]

Having considered exports, we now turn our attention to the imported goods that were unladed onto the Ipswich quayside in the mid-fifteenth century.

The Search for Alternative Supplies of Dyes

Nothing attests more clearly to the importance of cloth finishing in Suffolk than the remarkable volume of imported dyes and dyestuffs. As in John Bernard's time, madder and woad remained by far the most important, and, although individual cargoes of madder were more numerous, those of woad remained the most valuable. The loss of Gascony disrupted the flow of woad from one former source of supply and prompted a search for alternative sources and substitutes. Five cargoes were described as Hamburgh woad, suggesting that they had come from north Germany.[50] Although there is no evidence of direct importation to Ipswich from

[43] Bailey (2007), pp. 222–3, 240–1.
[44] PRO E 122/52/43.
[45] PRO E 122/52/42–3.
[46] Bridbury (1975), p. 46. Cloth making was combined with dairy farming in Wiltshire as well: Bolton (1980), pp. 269–70.
[47] Bailey (2007), p. 229.
[48] Kerling (1954), pp. 108–9, 112.
[49] Mavis E. Mate, *Trade and Economic Developments, 1450–1550; The Experience of Kent, Surrey and Sussex* (Woodbridge: Boydell, 2006), p. 83.
[50] Barron (2004), p. 88n.

Spain, another potential source, Spanish woad may have arrived on the second leg of the thriving triangular trade via Flanders.[51] Litmus was an alternative blue colouring matter made from various lichens, and at least ten cargoes, together worth £37 13s. 4d., reached Ipswich at this time.[52] An eleventh cargo was lost in transit because the ship was waylaid *en route* by pirates.[53] Without such dyes, the famous blue cloths of Lavenham could never have been made.[54] Two small loads of alum, which became difficult to obtain after the fall of Constantinople in 1453, and one tiny cargo of weld, are also recorded.[55] Some of the oil and soap brought to Ipswich was used in cloth making. Scoured wool fibres would be soaked in oil before carding or combing to prevent them from breaking and to bind them together both before and during spinning.

A Consumer Boom Well Underway

The rising living standards of ordinary people in the fifteenth century were a cause of concern, if not alarm, to social commentators of the time.[56] Writing in exile, Sir John Fortescue compared their level of material prosperity favourably with that of the French.[57] A Venetian visitor commented that 'everyone who makes a tour in the island will soon become aware of this great wealth [...] for there is no small innkeeper, however poor and humble he may be, who does not serve his table with silver dishes and drinking cups'.[58] Many of the material possessions that English people acquired were being imported from abroad, particularly from the more technologically advanced Low Countries, rather than being manufactured at home.[59] Indeed, as we have already seen, this phenomenon may well have held back the development of English consumer industries.[60] In the 1390s the value of mercery, haberdashery, furniture and furnishings arriving in Ipswich, as recorded in Bernard's account, had been relatively modest. In 1413/14 such goods still comprised less than 5 per cent, in value, of imports into the Ipswich headport.[61] In the 1460s particular accounts, however, they were assessed at just short of a thousand pounds.[62] Some of them would have

[51] Childs (1978), pp. 59, 108.
[52] Rigby (2005), p. 272.
[53] *CPR 1461–67*, p. 231.
[54] Betterton and Dymond (1989), p. 33.
[55] Spufford (2002), p. 334; Cherry 'Leather' (1991), p. 299.
[56] Bridbury (1975), p. 103; A. Briggs *A Social History of England* (London: Weidenfeld & Nicolson, 1983; repr. London: Penguin Books, 1987), p. 106; C. Dyer (1989), pp. 177, 271–2.
[57] Fortescue (1942), pp. 80–9.
[58] Britnell *Britain and Ireland* (2004), p. 523.
[59] Ramsay (1991), pp. xxxi–ii; Barron (1995), p. 11; Britnell (2006), p. 149.
[60] Ramsay (1991), p. xxxi.
[61] PRO E 122/51/39.
[62] Britnell notes the increase in imports of mercery, particularly linen, over the period from 1380 to 1480: *Britain and Ireland* (2004), p. 333.

been distributed further afield, but undoubtedly many of them found their way into the homes of Ipswich residents.[63] It is little wonder that some historians look on contemporary pleas of urban poverty with a degree of scepticism. One cargo included three feather beds; and another various different types of linen, including heysord, hoodbusk and streitbusk, indicating the breadth of choice available to consumers.[64] Eighteen separate loads of hats were needed to pander to regular changes in fashion for headgear.[65] Accessories such as pin cases, mirrors, clasps, buckles, beads, brushes, combs, trinket-like crosses and hair bands all found a ready market. Cupboards and chests showed off innovations in carpentry, while earthenware pots and pans used the new materials and glazes of the 'ceramic revolution'.[66] Some such goods subsequently figure in the wills of Ipswich residents. Thus, for example, Alice Pipho bequeathed a chest of Eastland board to her god-daughter in 1462, and John Drayle left Prussian chests to each of his sons in 1465.[67]

The Flow of Wine Almost Stops

Throughout the fourteenth century, and for much of the fifteenth, wine remained England's principal import. A fresh outbreak of the Hundred Years' War, followed by the English loss of Gascony in 1453, the drying up of licences and safe conducts for wine carrying ships, the imposition of the *tournois* by the French government and Edward IV's retaliatory prohibition on the import of Gascon wine, together caused a dramatic reduction in wine imports.[68] In decline from the mid 1440s, the Ipswich trade did not begin to recover until the end of the century (Figure 3). In John Bernard's time the 800 tuns that had arrived in the town accounted for very nearly 90 per cent in value of all current imports into Ipswich. The mid-century particular accounts record the import of just eighteen relatively small cargoes of wine from various sources (Table 13), which amounted in total to barely more than a tenth of the volume of the earlier period.

Some attempt was being made to find substitutes for Gascon wine, but at this early stage, at least in Ipswich, progress was limited.[69] Sixty-four gallons of Spanish wine, nearly three-quarters of all the recorded imports, arrived on 4 June 1464 in a

[63] David Sherlock discusses the import and distribution of chests into Suffolk: *Suffolk Church Chests* (Stowmarket: Mike Durrant for the Suffolk Institute of Archaeology and History, 2008), pp. 10–12.
[64] PRO E 122/52/42, 46.
[65] Maryanne Kowaleski, 'A Consumer Economy' in *A Social History of England 1200–1500* ed. by R. Horrox and W.M. Ormrod (Cambridge: Cambridge University Press, 2006), pp. 238–259 (p. 249).
[66] Dyer (1989), p. 207; Cherry, 'Pottery and Tile' (1991), p. 207; Kowaleski (2006), pp. 253–4.
[67] SROI R2/77; C/2/10/1/2, mm. 14r, 14v.
[68] James (1971), p. 44; Anne Crawford, *A History of the Vintners' Company* (London: Constable, 1977), p. 54; Britnell (1986), p. 176.
[69] James (1971), p. 84; Crawford (1977), p. 25.

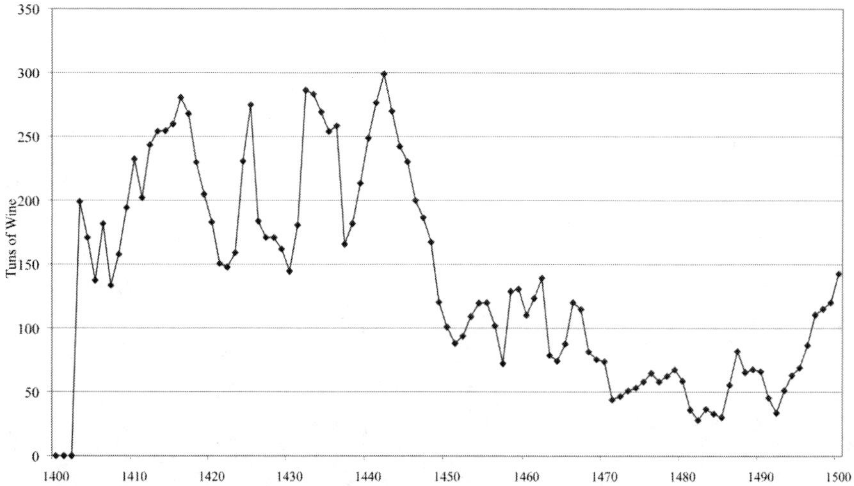

Figure 3: *Import of Wine to the headport of Ipswich in the Fifteenth Century. Five-year rolling avergaes (after James).*

TABLE 13: WINE IMPORTS TO IPSWICH 1459–66

Source	*Different cargoes*	*Volume (tuns)*
Gascony	5	18½
Malmsey	2	1
Nantes	4	< 2
Rhenish	3	about 1
Spain	3	64
Unspecified	1	½
Total	18	< 87

(*Sources*: PRO E 122/52/42–48)

ship under the command of John Pevye of Spain.[70] The strength of Spanish wine had been celebrated seventy-five years earlier by Chaucer in *The Pardoner's Tale*, so this must have been a red letter day for the burghers of Ipswich.[71] A tun of sweet Malmsey wine may also have come directly or indirectly from Spain.[72] The Rhenish wine imported by Dutch merchants probably arrived from Germany via Dordrecht. Although never particularly popular in England, it was better than nothing.[73]

[70] PRO E 122/52/46.
[71] Chaucer (2005), lines 562–72 (pp. 459–60).
[72] PRO E 122/52/47–8; Childs (1978), p. 128.
[73] Kerling (1954), p. 119.

The supply of wine never completely dried up. Indeed, in 1463/4 the borough authorities made eleven purchases of wine, seven more than in 1446/7, including a present worth five pounds for Sir John Howard.[74] Nevertheless, the sharp contraction in the flow of wine into Ipswich must have severely disrupted the extensive distribution network that had been built up earlier in the century. The vintners who had been so influential then must, like their contemporaries in London, have lost much of their sway.[75] Some may even have left the trade for more profitable occupations. When William Jamys was named as executor of the will of John Turtyvale, in 1456, he was described as a vintner. Seven years later, however, when his apprentice was admitted as a freeman, Jamys had apparently become a dyer.[76] Of all those admitted between 1441 and 1470, only William Wursop, in 1457, was actually named as a vintner.[77] Wursop never achieved office as bailiff, although he ranked as an esquire, was elected as the town's MP three times, and served as coroner and clerk of the peace on three successive occasions between 1480 and 1482.[78] He traded during the difficult years of the early 1460s. In 1463/4, for instance, he supplied white wine, red French and red Gascon wine to Sir John Howard, and made at least two separate sales to the borough, including one of sweet wine.[79] Even Wursop needed another source of income, earned by practising as an attorney in the Ipswich petty court in the 1470s.[80]

Nine different men were fined by the leet courts of the east and north wards in the late 1460s for selling wine at a price above the prescribed eight pence a gallon.[81] Robert Blomfeld was the most prominent, serving twice as bailiff and once as chamberlain. He also worked as clerk of the peace, in order perhaps to supplement his income as an innkeeper.[82] The name of a second, Pascall Tavener, suggests that he may have fled Gascony as a refugee after it fell to the French.[83] Among the others were the merchant Thomas Caldwell and the innkeeper John Myddlyton. Like Wursop, they supplied wine to the borough, but, unlike some members of Caldwell's illustrious family, neither of them achieved borough office. Of the remaining five, Richard Machet was chamberlain twice; and William Wattys was coroner, with just one year's break, continuously from 1466 to 1482, which suggests that it had become his principal occupation.[84] Few of them, it would seem, could rely solely on wine for their living.

[74] SROI C/3/3/1/1–2.

[75] Not one single vintner became an alderman of London between 1456 and 1516: Crawford (1977), p. 56.

[76] NRO NCC, Reg. Neve, f. 80; BL, Ms Add. 30,158, f. 25v.

[77] BL, Ms Add. 30, 158, f. 20r.

[78] *Annals*, pp. 144–6.

[79] Crawford (1992), I, pp. 219, 274; SROI C/3/3/1/2.

[80] SROI C/2/10/1/7.

[81] SROI C/2/10/1/2, m. 11v (east ward); C/2/10/1/3, m. 1r–v (north and east wards); C/2/10/1/4 (east ward).

[82] *Annals*, p. 128.

[83] James (1971), pp. 85–8.

[84] *Annals*, pp. 126–45.

Squirrels Keep their Skins

The nature of many other imports in the mid-fifteenth century remained much as it had been in the late fourteenth century. Fish, iron, salt, stone, timber and wax were, of course, all still in demand. Although herring remained the most common fish, the opening up of the Icelandic fishing grounds meant that cod ('stockfish') now represented a third in value of all fish imports recorded in the particular accounts.[85] In the 1390s John Bernard had recorded the arrival of 'iron of Spain', and in the 1460s John Pevye of Spain also brought iron in his ship in return for cloth.[86] The inward flow of squirrel skins slowed, as the supply from the forests of eastern Europe dried up and, paradoxically, squirrel came to be regarded as insufficiently exclusive. Instead, lighter and more expensive furs were popular with the well-to-do.[87] In 1442, the Norwich merchant Thomas Wath was storing in his warehouse in Ipswich thirty timbrels of ermine, twenty timbrels of snow weasel and six timbrels of marten.[88] In 1459 Laurence Johnesone imported two mantles of miniver.[89] Three timbrels of beaver skin arrived, perhaps from Spain, in 1462, but their value was in weather proofing, rather than as fashion.[90] As we shall see, beer was being produced commercially in Ipswich well before the mid-fifteenth century, and thus no longer needed to be imported. Hops were, however, arriving in sufficient quantities to suggest that, as yet, few, if any, were being cultivated in the region. They were often shipped with horticultural produce from Holland and Zeeland, such as cabbages, garlic and onions. The importation of bricks and tiles had all but dried up, since bricks were also now being produced locally and inlaid floor tiles were less in demand.[91]

Ipswich Merchants Crowded Out

At least fifty-six different Englishmen are named between 1459 and 1466 in the particular accounts, shipping in or out of Ipswich (Appendix 7).[92] Some were Ipswich merchants, others Suffolk clothiers. At least one was a senior member of the local gentry. A few came from London, one from Norwich and another from distant Bristol. Six were Staplers who, against the odds, continued to export wool from Ipswich. Their collective contribution to the town's international trade is apparent

[85] Power and Postan (1933), pp. 155–82.
[86] PRO E 122/52/46.
[87] Veale (2003) pp. 134–9; Kowaleski (2006), p. 250.
[88] SROI C/2/3/1/51 (8 Jan. 1443).
[89] PRO E 122/52/42.
[90] PRO E 122/52/43; Childs (1978), p. 139.
[91] Salzmann (1913), pp. 126–7.
[92] Since a few names are wholly or partly illegible, the total might be slightly higher.

from Table 14. Thanks to the contacts that many of them had made with Suffolk pastoralists, as explained above, they controlled the export of cheese and butter. They enjoyed a half share of the trade in hides, although by the mid-fifteenth century this was of little importance. Otherwise, they had less than a quarter share in the trade of any other commodity. They exported fewer than one in eight of all cloths leaving Ipswich and had an even smaller stake in the dyes and dyestuffs, mercery and haberdashery that were brought back. Had more wealthy London merchants used Ipswich for shipping their goods, and brought their capital with them, then the denizen share of trade could have been much greater. In their absence, English merchants in Ipswich had been largely eclipsed by foreigners and, in particular, by those of Cologne.

TABLE 14: SHARE BY NATIONALITY OF MAJOR TRADES IN IPSWICH 1459–66

Trade	*Denizen (%)*	*Hanse (%)*	*Alien (%)*
Woollen cloth	12.2	84.9	2.9
Wool	100	0	0
Dairy products	92	0	8
Dyes, mordants, oils, teasels	7.9	84.5	7.6
Mercery and haberdashery	5.8	89.9	4.3
Wine	21.3	0	78.7
Fish	11.1	33.9	55.0
Iron and ironwork	16.1	69.7	14.2
Salt	6.7	80.4	12.8

(*Sources*: PRO E 122/52/42–48)

Whereas in John Bernard's time many of the London merchants trading out of Ipswich had been mercers, in the mid-century particular accounts no such individuals can be identified. During this period both grocers and stockfishmongers made cloth and built distributive networks in East Anglia. It is therefore no surprise to find two members of each city company named in the particular accounts, and all four of them exporting dairy produce. The stockfishmonger James Wright also imported 100 wey of salt in 1464, which he may well have used to preserve his fish.[93] Ironmongers had not previously enjoyed a reputation for overseas trade, but they were beginning to flex their muscles. In 1463 they were granted corporate status by the Crown, with Robert Toke becoming one of the first two wardens.[94] In return for his share in a local ship, which he sold to the king, Toke was granted exemption from the payment of

[93] PRO E 122/52/46.
[94] *CPR 1461–67*, p. 297.

subsidy in the ports of Ipswich and London, to the tune of four hundred marks (£266 13s. 4d.) spread over four years from Michaelmas 1461.[95] Among his exports from Ipswich were lead and tin worth eighteen pounds.[96] Perhaps making use of contacts in the Spanish iron trade, another ironmonger, John Peek, imported five tuns of wine from Spain.[97] The seventh London merchant identifiable from the particular accounts is the draper John Stokker. He had left his mark on history back in 1450 by helping to fund and lead a team to negotiate with the Hanse in Utrecht, being imprisoned *en route* for several months in Lubeck, and, even when released, failing in his mission.[98]

In her study of the mercantile elite of London, Thrupp refers to medieval gentry 'poaching on the merchant's ground', in an attempt to supplement their failing incomes from land, and cites examples of 'lords with East Anglian estates' engaging in trade.[99] The most prominent member of the Suffolk merchant gentry was Sir John Howard, who was enobled in 1470 and became duke of Norfolk in 1483. He owned a house in Ipswich from which to carry on his business affairs, and, as we have seen, employed Richard Felawe as his commercial agent.[100] Howard presented cloth to the alnager, and, with a view to advancing his commercial interests, became an active member of the Grocers' Company in London.[101] Nor was he slow to use his exalted status to his own advantage, exploiting it to win a dispute with the Merchant Adventurers in 1472 over the charter of one of his ships.[102] He certainly did business as a merchant, and the particular accounts record him importing iron and timber in June 1462.[103] These commercial activities enabled Howard to acquire new estates, live in a style well above that of country knight and lend money to the impoverished duke of Norfolk. In doing so he laid the foundations of his family's fortunes for generations to come.[104]

Contrary to what Kowaleski found in Exeter, there is no evidence in Suffolk that the expansion of the cloth industry encouraged many inlanders to engage in international trade.[105] The names of only four of the 578 Suffolk clothiers recorded in the alnage accounts in the four years between 1465 and 1469 also appear in the particular accounts: namely, William Buntyng of Bury St Edmunds, Roger Crytote of Lavenham, who had become a freeman of Ipswich in 1449,[106] John Gosse of Ipswich

[95] *CPR 1461–67*, p. 229.
[96] PRO E 122/52/48.
[97] PRO E 122/52/46.
[98] Lloyd (1991), pp. 185–7, 189.
[99] Thrupp (1962), p. 243; Nightingale (1995), p. 511.
[100] Crawford (1992), p. xxii.
[101] PRO E 101/342/25; Nightingale (1995), pp. 535–6.
[102] Scammell (1962), pp. 119–21.
[103] PRO E 122/52/43.
[104] Crawford (1992), p. xxii.
[105] Kowaleski (1995), p. 277.
[106] BL, Ms Add. 30,158, f. 13r.

and John Hamond of Nayland. All but Gosse were major producers, presenting between them more than 1500 broadcloths, or their equivalent, to the alnager.[107] Yet, according to the particular accounts, they shipped only twenty-seven cloths, a tiny fraction of their output and little more than 1 per cent of total exports. Britnell found that less than 6 per cent of those appearing in the alnage accounts in late fourteenth-century Colchester were exporting cloth, and in Yorkshire, at the same time, Swanson estimates that the figure stood at 7 per cent.[108] If the Suffolk data is typical, then the demarcation between those who produced cloth and those who exported it grew even more marked during the fifteenth century. A similar division, between clothiers who organised the making of the cloth and merchants who traded it, is apparent in the late medieval Low Countries.[109] Munro suggests that the first group was subordinate to, and relied on credit from, the second. Although this may have been the case in mid-fifteenth-century Suffolk, there is no evidence for it. As we shall see, most outside capital came from wealthy Londoners.

In the late fourteenth century three dozen Ipswich merchants had dominated local exports of cloth, and enjoyed substantial shares in the importation of wine, dyes and dyestuffs and salt. In the years that followed there were always some with the capital and nerve necessary to risk such ventures. William Baldry and Gilbert Debenham have already been mentioned. John Deken was licensed in 1437 to take seven hundred cloths in his ship *Cristofre* to 'any parts at amity with the king'.[110] At least four Ipswich merchants appear to have been active in the Baltic in the years from 1438 to 1440 because they submitted claims for injuries suffered there.[111] John Caldwell may well have been one of them, as in the mid-1440s he sent his apprentice Thomas Bradde to trade on his behalf in Danzig, where Bradde fell into debt with local merchants including one Hans Stendell and was ultimately imprisoned in Ipswich gaol.[112] Later Caldwell sued William Baldry for the goods that Baldry had taken in exchange in Prussia for two hundred pounds worth of his cloth.[113] Richard Felawe and others were licensed in 1452 to ship two thousand cloths to unspecified foreign parts.[114] Admitted as a non-resident foreign burgess in 1435, John Motte was active in the trade with Spain, maintaining a factor in the Andalusian ports.[115] It is also worth noting that, in the fifteen years after 1450, John Gosse and William Winter both built their own private quays.[116]

[107] PRO E 101/342/25; E 101/343/2–4.
[108] Britnell (1986), p. 79; Swanson (1989) p. 141.
[109] Munro (2003), p. 219.
[110] *CPR 1436–41*, pp. 57, 59.
[111] Lloyd (1991), p. 222.
[112] PRO C 1/73/162; SROI C/2/5/2/1.
[113] PRO C 1/16/427.
[114] *CPR 1446–52*, p. 528.
[115] BL, Ms Add. 30,158, f. 7r; Childs (1978), pp. 187, 212.
[116] *Annals*, p. 119; SROI C/2/10/1/1, m. 9r.

Nevertheless, by the mid-fifteenth century only a small minority, even of the wealthier residents, participated in international trade. Britnell found evidence of similar retrenchment in Colchester.[117] The fate of the Ipswich common quay is symbolic of this decline. The income that it generated for the borough fell from seventeen pounds in 1344 to a mere 51s. 11d. in 1446/7, by which time, as a further measure of decay, just 3s. 4d. was spent on its upkeep.[118] By 1472 it had deteriorated into serious disrepair, and in the 1480s was to become an unlicensed rubbish tip and pig sty.[119] As we shall see, the subsequent restoration of the common quay in the closing years of the century marked an upturn in the fortunes of local merchants.

Various reasons for this loss of local interest suggest themselves. Since the high seas had become more dangerous, overseas ventures were now far riskier. Both Edmund Caldwell and William Keche encountered serious financial embarrassment during their careers, with Caldwell suffering imprisonment and Keche having to avoid his creditors in 1463 by obtaining royal immunity from prosecution in return for service in Calais.[120] The stop-start nature of trade with key foreign markets made it more difficult to develop long-term contacts and networks. Few could emulate John Caldwell and John Motte in affording to employ overseas factors. Moreover, local men faced stiff competition from powerful merchants of London and the Hanse with whom they found it difficult to contend. Markets in Holland and Zeeland were, for example, increasingly dominated by London mercers. Ipswich merchants were prominent among a provincial group who, in 1421 and again in 1432, had unsuccessfully resisted this trend by refusing to contribute to the salary of the Londoner John Wareyn as governor of the English merchants in the Low Countries.[121] This friction with London capitalists intensified when the Baltic was closed and east coast merchants were left with almost nowhere else to trade.[122] They faced a 'tightening of mercantile networks [...] and the freezing out of those who were not able to share them'.[123] A shortage of coin and credit caused particular problems for provincials, since larger ships, higher freight charges, and bigger, better paid, crews meant that overseas trade required more capital investment.[124] The adverse impact of the Calais Staple partition and bullion ordinances has already been discussed. When William Keche bought a load of salt in 1457 he had to put on the line all his lands and tenements, rents and services, and goods and chattels

[117] Britnell (1986), p. 176.
[118] *Annals*, p. 71; SROI C/3/3/1/1.
[119] *Annals*, p. 71; SROI C/2/8/1/21, 22 (east ward).
[120] SROI R2/87; *CPR 1461–67*, p. 262.
[121] Anne F. Sutton, 'London Mercers from Suffolk c.1200–1570: Benefactors, Pirates and Merchant Adventurers' *PSIA*, 42 (2009) 1–12 (p. 9).
[122] Kerling (1954) pp. 150–5.
[123] Britnell, *Britain and Ireland* (2004), p. 333.
[124] Wage rates for service in the navy were set by the Parliament of 1442: *Rot. Parl.*, v, p. 59. Britnell, *Britain and Ireland* (2004), pp. 323–4; Ward (2009), pp. 84, 109.

in Ipswich, by entering into a recognisance of debt with the shippers Burghard Wydoot and Hans Prise to pay them one hundred pounds within fifteen days of the ship's arrival.[125] We have seen that, even in the late fourteenth century, Ipswich merchants concentrated much of their investment in the wine trade, and, by 1413/14, wine comprised over 90 per cent, in value, of all their overseas trade,[126] so the loss of Gascony was a bitter blow. As a result of these powerful disincentives, the names of only six Ipswich residents can be identified with any confidence in the mid-century particular accounts.

Who were these six? We know their names: William Blake, Edmund Caldwell, John Gosse, William Keche, John Rever and John Smyth. The troubled careers of Caldwell and Keche have just been touched on. Although there is no record of Blake's admission as a burgess, he was one of those appointed to the office of porter in 1471.[127] Gosse and Keche both became freemen by patrimony in 1443, while John Rever was admitted four years later. John Smyth obtained the freedom in 1449 following an apprenticeship to John Deken, which may well have involved him in travel and even residence abroad on behalf of his master.[128] As might be expected, members of this group enjoyed considerable local influence. In a period between the mid-1450s and the mid-1480s three of them served as bailiff – Gosse five times, Keche once, and Rever twice – while Gosse, Keche and Rever held a variety of other borough offices. Gosse, Rever and Smyth were all clothiers;[129] Keche was a tanner and Rever a mercer. Smyth evidently maintained a number of commercial interests. He was described as a merchant, but was also being amerced as an innkeeper and brewer in the leet court. Yet, the total share of trade enjoyed by these Ipswich men was very modest. Gosse was the only exporter, shipping just one cloth.[130] The others imported a variety of merchandise, worth in total just under £184 10s., representing just 4.3 per cent in value of all the imports recorded in the particular accounts. By far the most valuable and welcome of these cargoes was Keche's twelve tuns of Gascon wine which arrived in 1459.[131]

Inevitably, we know far less about the foreign merchants who shipped their goods to and from Ipswich. The particular accounts do, however, distinguish between denizen, Hanse and other alien shippers. Their respective shares in the major trades, namely those worth more than two hundred pounds, are set out in Table 14. Alien merchants, whose names suggest that they were mostly Dutch, had acquired a majority share of the fish trade. From the early fifteenth century the

[125] SROI C/2/10/1/1, m. 10r.
[126] PRO E 122/51/39.
[127] BL, Ms Add. 30,158, f. 29v.
[128] BL, Ms Add. 30,158, ff. 8v, 10r, 12v.
[129] PRO E 101/342/25; E 101/343/2.
[130] PRO E 122/52/47.
[131] PRO E 122/52/42.

herring catch was gutted and cured on board ship and taken, so preserved, to Holland and Zeeland, rather than being landed fresh at Yarmouth and other east coast ports. As a result, for a short time, the Dutch fishing industry prospered, while the English declined.[132] Aliens also dominated the waning trade in wine, some hailing from the growing regions in Spain and western France. In 1443 both Peryn Maynard of Bordeaux and Peter Reymond of Toulouse were involved in litigation in the Ipswich petty court over the sale of wine.[133] Although alien merchants named in the particular accounts outnumber Hanseatic merchants by ninety-one to sixty-one, their collective investment in international trade was far less. No alien could match Hans Bowman, Henning Buryng, Henry Iserhode, Herman Rinck or Johann 'van A' who each shipped more than one hundred cloths, and together accounted for well over half of recorded cloth exports. All other major commodities, apart from wool, were controlled by the Hanseatic merchants. Those from Cologne valued their cloth trade with this country so highly that their city often remained on good terms with England when her relations with other members of the Hanse soured.[134]

Some overseas merchants stayed at home and relied on factors based in the port, while others resided, often in the homes of local hosts, in Colchester or Ipswich.[135] In 1465, for example, Hans Sandowe bought nine coloured broad cloths called 'Newegreyes', through his factor, Henry van Trye, from William Warner of Ipswich.[136] One Hanseatic merchant, John, *alias* Hans, Bonsthorp, was living in the riverside parish of St Mary Quay when he made his will in 1459. Feltman Lutkyn, presumably a fellow resident Hanseatic merchant, was named as his sole executor. He wistfully directed that he should be buried 'in the church tomb wheresoever I die'.[137] Members of the trading family of Garne also probably chose to live in Ipswich. Peter Garne, an alien, appears in the particular accounts in 1459 importing a wide range of products. In October 1464 he was being sued in the Ipswich petty court for payment of an account by the clerk Ralph Belaby. In the same month he acted as a pledge before the Ipswich maritime court for his kinsman Gerard Garne, in the latter's dispute with another merchant-mariner. Isabel Garne, perhaps Peter's wife, was brewing beer in east ward three years later, which suggests a protracted period of residence.[138]

Why did the merchants of Cologne show such interest in Ipswich in the mid-fifteenth century? Suffolk cloth was an obvious attraction, but there may have been

[132] Saul (1975), p. 176; Bolton (1980), p. 276; Rigby (1993), p. 138; Kowaleski (2000), pp. 485–6.
[133] SROI C/2/3/1/51 (4, 6, 27 Jun. 1443).
[134] Power and Postan (1933), p. 100; Lloyd (1991), pp. 183, 203–4.
[135] *Annals*, p. 35; Britnell (1986), pp. 174–5.
[136] SROI C/2/10/1/2, m. 5v.
[137] SROI R2/37.
[138] SROI C/2/10/1/2, mm. 1r, 11v (east ward); C/2/10/1/3, mm. 1v, 9r (east ward); C/2/10/1/4 (east ward).

subsidiary reasons. As already discussed, Ipswich's proximity to the Continent was one, and its proximity to Colchester perhaps another. Colchester lay within sufficiently easy travelling distance of London to serve almost as an outport of the Capital. Rifts between the various cities of the Hanseatic League in the 1460s, boiling over in 1468 to poison the relationship between their representatives in England, may have already encouraged the Cologners to leave London for a more conducive home at the Steelyard of Colchester.[139] As they were investing in unfinished cloth, they may also have been manoeuvring for advantage over the London mercers who increasingly dominated this trade, but were noticeably absent from Ipswich.

Ships of War

Seafaring had always been a hazardous occupation, but, as we have seen, fifteenth-century waters were rendered even more dangerous by naval wars, and by piracy that was tolerated, if not sponsored, by the contending nations. This had a profound effect on the design of merchant shipping and particularly on the well loved cog. Vessels were built bigger to resist attack. 'Until the widespread use of artillery a large ship was virtually unassailable by smaller ones'.[140] More masts were added to give extra speed, while a combination of square and lateen sails allowed greater manoeuvrability. Castles were erected fore and aft.[141] It is difficult to identify many ships visiting Ipswich in the late fourteenth century of more than 100 tons. By the mid-fifteenth century, however, some English ships had burdens of 300 or 400 tons. Although none as large as this is known to have docked in Ipswich, one of the town's ships was 140 tons, another 160 tons and a third ship, 'of Orwell', 240 tons.[142] Table 15 analyses the number of broadcloths or equivalent laded in those vessels in which the cargo was entirely, or almost entirely, cloth, and makes a comparison between these two periods. Converting the diverse descriptions of cloth in Bernard's account into broadcloths is far from an exact science. Furthermore, in his day the bigger ships rarely just carried cloth, and have thus been excluded from the present calculation. Even so, for all its limitations, a dramatic increase in the mean number of broadcloths carried in each ship is apparent.

Larger and more sophisticated ships were more expensive to build, maintain and operate. They represented the most valuable of all industrial investments in medieval England.[143] Ventures on this scale attracted money from the Crown and gentry, as well as London merchants, and also encouraged the acquisition of shares

[139] Lloyd (1991), pp. 203–5.
[140] Childs (1978), p. 161.
[141] Power and Postan (1933), pp. 159–60; Childs (2006), p. 267.
[142] M. Oppenheim, 'Maritime History' in *Victoria County History, Suffolk* ed. by William Page, 2 volumes (London: Archibald Constable, 1907), II, pp. 199–246 (p. 209).
[143] Kowaleski (2007), p. 235.

TABLE 15: NUMBER OF BROADCLOTHS EXPORTED PER SHIP

Dates	*Departures*	*Total no. of broadcloths or equivalent*	*Mean no. of broadcloths or equivalent*
1396–98	13	Approx 197.5	15.2
1459–66	29	1766	60.9
Increase			400%

Sources: PRO E 122/193/33, E 122/52/42–48

in ships to spread the cost and the risk. Such shares were a reasonably liquid form of capital which could be bought and sold, and even bequeathed by will.[144] Sir John Howard owned a dozen or more ships which sailed as far as Prussia and Spain. He shared ownership of one, the *Edward*, with the king, and sold another, the *Mary Howard*, of 500 tons, to the Crown in 1481 for five hundred marks.[145] A third, named after his wife, the *Margaret Howard*, was captained by William Parker, who himself appears as master and merchant in the particular accounts.[146] Howard's factor, Richard Felawe, established a partnership with Sir William Rider, jointly owning the *Gyles* of Hull, until Rider complained about the lack of profit from his investment.[147] The abovementioned Robert Toke acquired a lucrative quarter share in the ship *le Margarete* of Ipswich, which he sold to the king in 1462 in return for the exemption he enjoyed from subsidy.[148]

The political difficulties that bedeviled mid-fifteenth century Europe affected all England's major overseas markets and made international trade an even riskier business than before. Several Ipswich merchants were personally embroiled in these troubles. Those who could afford to do so resorted to bigger ships in order to provide greater protection against attack by hostile navies and pirates. The Low Countries remained their key first step to and from the continent and their most important trading partner. Trade with Normandy and Gascony was severely disrupted by the loss of these territories in war. Early ventures into the Baltic were ultimately frustrated, but contacts with Spain did gradually increase.

Customs officials monitoring the flow of goods through Ipswich from the late fourteenth century to the mid-fifteenthcentury would have noted both similarities and changes. Fish, iron, salt, stone, timber and wax remained essential commodities, but wool and wine had lost most of their earlier importance, owing to the Calais

[144] Scammell (1962) pp. 109, 114.
[145] Crawford (1992), p. xxii; Nightingale (1995), p. 535.
[146] PRO E 122/52/43; *CPR 1467–77*, p. 355.
[147] Scammell (1962), p. 115.
[148] *CPR 1461–67*, p. 229.

ordinances and the war with France. Woollen cloth had replaced raw wool as the principal export, reflecting the rapid growth of the Suffolk textile industry. Sustained imports of dyes and dyestuffs attest to the continuing significance of cloth finishing, despite a strong overseas demand for unfinished cloth. Dairy products, particularly cheese, had become almost as valuable an export as wool, with the greater share of the trade being in the hands of London merchants. The consumer revolution that was now peacefully gathering pace attracted mercery, haberdashery, furniture and furnishings to the town. Although the entries in the trade balance sheets changed between the two periods, the final totals were not dissimilar.

The provenance of the merchants shipping their wares through Ipswich was, however, very different. In the late fourteenth century local men and London mercers had been prominent. A few Ipswich burgesses maintained an interest in international trade, as did a handful of Suffolk clothiers and local gentry. Staplers retained control of the modest exports of wool. From London came grocers, stock-fishmongers, ironmongers and drapers. The Dutch and Spanish had significant stakes in the fish and wine trades. By the mid-fifteenth century, however, they had all been eclipsed by merchants of the Hanseatic League, particularly those of the city of Cologne, who had taken the lion's share of Ipswich trade. Despite all the troubles of the mid-fifteenth century, in Ipswich overseas trade held up well, but largely on the backs of these Hanse merchants. When they took their business away in the late 1460s the town faced a whole new set of challenges.

– 5 –

The Town in Troubled Times

That the middle years of the fifteenth century were particularly difficult for the English economy is now beyond doubt. Whatever side historians may take in the debate over urban decline, on this they all agree. Even Bridbury acknowledges that progress may not have been continuous during the later Middle Ages and warns against 'the enticing assumption of a steadily ascending curve of growth'.[1] Coining the phrase 'The Great Slump' in his 1996 essay, Hatcher summarised much of the research that had already been published on this period. On top of many other economic woes, he identified 'a sharp contraction in the number of markets and in the amount of trade which was carried on within them'.[2] The breakdown in normal political life during the Wars of the Roses created uncertainty and sapped confidence in a way that made the merchant's life more difficult.[3] Added to this, he had to cope with a chronic shortage of bullion, particularly lower value silver coinage, even more serious than in the opening years of the century. This chapter examines the impact of the Great Slump on the Ipswich economy, and its trade and industries.

A variety of sources: the proceedings of the general court, fragments of petty court rolls mainly for 1443, and two chamberlains' accounts, all from the borough archives, as well as wills, rolls of the Court of Common Pleas for Hilary term 1450, alnage accounts for the late 1460s, Howard household accounts and other national and local sources, tell us much about the town's fortunes during this difficult period. In seeking to build a picture of Ipswich in the middle years of the fifteenth century, however, the leet court rolls are perhaps our most important source. In order to understand these rolls we must first travel much further back in time. Long before King John granted the town its charter, the men and women of Ipswich had met together in the leet court. Its role in Ipswich, as in many other urban and rural communities, was to organise residents within tithings and enforce the frankpledge

[1] Bridbury (1975), p. 82.
[2] Hatcher (1996), pp. 245–6.
[3] Reynolds (1977), p. 147; Nightingale (1995), pp. 520–1; A.J. Pollard, *The Wars of the Roses* (Basingstoke: Palgrave, 2001), pp. 84–5.

which had, since Anglo-Saxon times, been the chief form of local control over petty crime.[4] Its jurisdiction extended over a wide range of offences. Infringements of trading regulations are considered in more detail below. From the presentation of 'common nuisances', such as pollution and wandering pigs, sprang the public health responsibilities of modern municipal authorities. Assaults, night-walking, prostitution and other outrages against public order and morality were all penalised.[5] On one occasion the borough authorities even sought to enforce religious orthodoxy, in 1467 fining Sayma Naylere six pence for following heretical beliefs contrary to the Catholic faith.[6] The modest level of her fine may reflect their reluctance to become involved in such matters and the fact that such cases lay within the remit of the ecclesiastical courts. They showed no such reluctance to exercise the jurisdiction of the leet court over other areas of town life.

In Ipswich a leet court met, in each of the four wards, once a year on Tuesday of Whit week, in the presence of the bailiffs and under the watchful eye of three local worthies who served as chief pledges. All residents of the ward over the age of twelve were expected to attend, and absentees were penalised. A long list of presentments made to the court of the various offences was compiled and the accused were fined, ordered to amend their behaviour, or, very occasionally, found innocent. It must have been one of the busiest days in any bailiff's year of office and a mere fraction of the records of the proceedings of these leet courts now survives.[7] Notwithstanding the many lacunae, the leet court rolls still offer the best series of extant Ipswich borough records from the middle years of the fifteenth century. The evidence they provide is analysed in detail in this chapter, after first considering the Great Slump and its impact on Ipswich's trading networks.

[4] Allen (2000), p. 85; Bailey (2002), pp. 178–84.

[5] The leet courts of Coventry and Norwich had very similar judicial responsibilities to those of Ipswich, although in Coventry the court also exercised legislative authority in framing by-laws that the Ipswich leet court does not appear to have had: M.D. Harris (ed.) *The Coventry Leet Book* III and IV (London: Kegan Paul, Trench and Trubner for The Early English Text Society, 138, 1913; repr. Cambridge: D.S Brewer, 2006), pp. xix, xx, xxviii; William Hudson (ed.) *Leet Jurisdiction in the City of Norwich* (London: Bernard Quaritch for The Seldon Society, 5, 1892), pp. xxxiv–vii.

[6] SROI C/2/10/1/4, m. 4r (south ward).

[7] Out of documentation for a possible forty courts in any decade, six rolls survive from the 1400s, ten from the 1420s, thirteen from the 1430s, only one from the period from 1440 to 1459, and twelve from the 1460s, making a total of forty-two. There is internal evidence to suggest that the single court surviving from the 1440s or 1450s was held in north ward in 1455, but it is impossible to be sure. Thomas Denys and John Caldwell are both named as bailiffs. Furthermore, the two bakers presented to the leet court for north ward in 1465 were also presented to the undated court. The roll of one court remains from the 14th century. The proceedings of another forty-four courts, held in the 1470s and 1480s, are considered in Chapter 7.

The Great Slump

The crisis of the mid-fifteenth century began, for Ipswich as elsewhere, with harvest failure. The absence of food imports from customs records suggest that the town could normally rely on its own hinterland for its food supply without much need for foreign grain. The late 1430s were, however, difficult years for farming; the weather was bad, harvests were poor and consequently the price of all grains rose sharply.[8] Wealthy landowners, who could sell their produce at inflated prices, did well, but in both town and country consumers suffered. The threat of famine stalked the land.[9] In Ipswich the townspeople rebelled. It was alleged that early in 1438 'a crowd of about three hundred persons arrayed in manner of war, forcibly carried off 52 quarters of wheat worth 104 marks' (£69 6s. 8d.).[10] Their leaders, John Blankpayn and William Taliser, were both respectable men. Blankpayn was a freeman, a barber and a brewer who had held office of treasurer in 1432/3, as well as being chief pledge in the leet court of north ward in the years 1436 to 1438.[11] Taliser was another barber and brewer. Although not recorded as a freemen, he had almost certainly been admitted as such, since he was a chief pledge in the leet court of west ward in 1424 and again in 1436.[12] Following the riot both men appear to have enjoyed a rapid rehabilitation, being appointed as two of the four clavigers in five of the following six years.[13] Nevertheless, the authorities must have been keen to quash such unrest as firmly as possible for fear of losing their privileges again, as they had done in both the thirteenth and fourteenth centuries.[14] At least one of the town's leading merchants responded positively to the discontent by importing grain from Norfolk. Early in 1440 Robert Wode was granted a royal licence to ship 160 quarters of barley from Yarmouth. Was it mere coincidence that in the following September he was elected as bailiff?[15]

A further blow to the economy was delivered by yet another monetary crisis. During the 1420s and 1430s the shortage of bullion had been alleviated by freshly-mined silver from Serbia and Bosnia.[16] Relief was, however, short lived. Production from these mines was declining even before they were overrun by the expanding Ottoman Empire. Their decline and eventual loss triggered the worst bullion

[8] Farmer (1991), p. 504; Hatcher (1996), p. 246; Dyer (2005), p. 244.
[9] Nightingale (1995), p. 445.
[10] *CPR 1436–41*, p. 199.
[11] BL, Ms Add. 30,158, f. 3v; *Annals*, p. 95; SROI C/2/8/1/9–11 (north ward).
[12] SROI C/2/8/1/7, 9 (west ward).
[13] Annals, pp. 100–3.
[14] Redstone (1969), pp. 55–6.
[15] *CPR 1436–41*, p. 362; *Annals*, p. 100.
[16] Spufford (2002), p. 360.

shortage of the Middle Ages.[17] The mint in the Tower of London was the only one in north-western Europe to stay open, but its output was negligible and England was not spared the consequences.[18] The total value of silver coin in the country fell from between 1.5 and 2 million pounds in 1331, to one-tenth of that amount by 1422. It may well have fallen further still before beginning to recover by 1470.[19] The supply of silver groats, by which most everyday trade was conducted, all but dried up.[20] This made the buying and selling of small quantities of merchandise very difficult and forced those tradesmen lucky enough to secure it to rely on expensive credit.[21] A large number of gold coins ('nobles'), worth 6s. 8d. each, came into circulation, but were of little use in low value trade, and the Ipswich petty court cases considered in this volume contain only a single reference to a noble.[22] No wonder that a the Parliament of February 1445 received a petition about:

> the great hurt that the poor commons of this noble realm of England bear and suffer at this time for lack of half pennies and silver farthings [...] and also the poor common retailers of victuals and other necessities for lack of such coin of half pennies and farthings, often are unable to sell their said victuals and items.[23]

The extent to which economic recession was caused by the bullion crisis has generated much debate. Hatcher and Bailey stand on one side of the argument in rejecting the proposition that it was the 'prime cause' of retrenchment and pointing to a 'wide range of adverse factors'. According to them, had the bullion crisis been the 'dominant problem ... then its first effect would have been to depress prices rather than economic activity, and its second effect would have been to make the remaining money work harder by circulating it more rapidly'.[24] Both Nightingale

[17] Wendy Childs, '"To oure losse and hindraunce": English Credit to Alien Merchants in the Mid-Fifteenth Century', in *Enterprise and Individuals in Fifteenth-Century England* ed. by Jennifer Kermode (Stroud: Alan Sutton, 1991), pp. 68–88 (pp. 68, 72). Allen suggests that, although English mines generally only produced modest volumes of silver, at this time of acute bullion shortage, those in Devon may have made a 'significant contribution to mint outputs': Martin Allen, 'Silver Production and the Money Supply in England and Wales, 1086–c.1500' *Econ. Hist. Rev.*, 2nd ser., 64 (2011), 114–131 (p. 127).
[18] Nightingale (1995), p. 463.
[19] M. Allen (2001), p. 607; R.H. Britnell, 'Uses of Money in Medieval England', in *Medieval Money Matters* ed. by Diana Wood (Oxford: Oxbow Books, 2004) pp. 16–30 (p. 25).
[20] Britnell (1996), pp. 181–2.
[21] Nightingale (1995), pp. 469, 477; J. Bolton, 'What is Money', in *Medieval Money Matters* ed. by Diana Wood (Oxford: Oxbow Books, 2004), pp. 1–15 (p. 11).
[22] C. Dyer (2005), p. 178. Pamela Nightingale makes the same point in 'Gold, credit, and mortality: distinguishing deflationary pressures on the late medieval English economy' *Econ. Hist. Rev.*, 2nd ser., 63 (2010), 1081–1104 (pp. 1084, 1094); SROI C/2/3/1/48 (28 May 1415).
[23] *Rot. Parl.*, v, pp. 108–9.
[24] Hatcher (1977), pp. 52–3; John Hatcher and Mark Bailey *Modelling the Middle Ages: The History and Theory of England's Economic Development* (Oxford: Oxford University Press, 2001), p. 190.

and Mayhew convincingly challenge the proposition that the circulation of money can be easily accelerated, since this 'usually amounts to a major economic contraction'.[25] Nevertheless, it cannot be denied that there were many other factors inimical to trade, and that these factors were interwoven with the supply of coin and credit. In several mid-century claims before the Ipswich petty court for payment under a letter of obligation (*scriptum obligatorium*) the debtor argued that he had been forced to sign by duress, coercion and false imprisonment.[26] At least five claims were brought by the notorious Gilbert Debenham esquire, who 'specialised in fraudulent actions over these obligations'.[27] In Ipswich this defence appears to have been invariably unsuccessful, but the fact that it was worth raising at all suggests that sometimes it may have been true and occasionally persuaded courts to find for the defendant. At a time when law and order seemed on the verge of breaking down, granting or taking credit could be a risky business.

In Ipswich, the petty court records document the provision of credit in three forms; by recognisance of debt, letter of obligation and account. Recognisances of debt could be enrolled in the petty court, and in the courts of many other towns, as a formal record of the amount due, and the creditor could thereby take security over the debtor's assets and call on borough officers to help him to make good his title. Such devices were often used when the risk of default was high.[28] Just one mid-fifteenth-century Ipswich court roll records no fewer than twenty recognisances of debt over a fifteen-year period. These were given and taken by the town's most prominent burgesses, in sums ranging from 6s. 8d. to one hundred pounds.[29]

The letter of obligation was often used to record credit transactions, evolving, in time, into a form of paper money.[30] It usually contained the full record of a transaction, including a summary of any conditions and stipulations, the names of parties, the date of sealing, the amount of debt and the date or dates of payment. Sometimes it also stipulated the place and actual mode of payment.[31] As mercantile law developed, debts became easier to recover. Letters of obligation could be enforced in any court, and could be bought and sold.[32] The great advantage that a letter of obligation enjoyed over a simple record of debt was that it left little scope for argument. The contents could not easily be challenged in court and the only

[25] P. Nightingale 'Money and Credit in the Economy of Late Medieval England', in *Medieval Money Matters*, pp. 51–71 (p. 64); N.J. Mayhew 'Coinage and money in England, 1086–c.1500', pp. 72–86 (p. 80), both in *Medieval Money Matters* ed. by Diana Wood (Oxford: Oxbow Books, 2004).

[26] SROI C/2/3/1/51 (17 Jan. 1443, 21 Mar. 1443, 16 May 1443, 19 Nov. 1444).

[27] SROI C/2/3/1/51 (26 Mar. 1443); C/2/10/1/2, m. 1v; C/2/10/1/3, m. 5v; Haward (1928–9), 300–314 (p. 304).

[28] Bolton (2004), p.12; Nightingale (2004), p.64.

[29] SROI C/2/10/1/1.

[30] Bolton (1980), pp. 304–5.

[31] M. Postan, *Medieval Trade and Finance* (Cambridge; Cambridge University Press, 1973), p. 30.

[32] Britnell (1986), p. 105; Kowaleski (1995), p. 202; Sutton (2005), p. 218.

defence was to produce a release ('acquittance'), or show that the letter had been entered under duress or was a forgery.[33] The number of disputes in the Ipswich petty court over letters of obligation increased as the century wore on, suggesting that they were gaining wider circulation. In the year 1400/1 just one case was determined, in 1407/8 two, in 1414/15 six, and, in only seven months of the year 1442/3, twelve.[34] A slightly later case shows the extent to which dependence on credit had pervaded even the rural economy. The carpenter John Kyng gave the sawyer Walter Goodale a letter of obligation for the sum of four pounds on 21 January 1460, which he failed to repay on the following 1 August. Although the obligation was contracted in Ipswich, with the result that the subsequent dispute fell within the jurisdiction of the court, both Kyng and Goodale came from sleepy Badwell Ash, 20 miles away in the heart of the Suffolk countryside.[35]

An account was a more general settling up, when, for instance, each party had been supplying goods to the other, or the debtor had received a series of supplies from the creditor, and the day of reckoning had arrived. William Debenham pursued William Wright in 1443 for the sum of 12s. 8d., this being the balance allegedly due following a reckoning of account for several sums between the two of them.[36]

Whichever of these three forms the credit took, it could only be recovered if the debtor had cash to pay, and, given the dearth of coin, this was far from guaranteed. To encourage debtors to try harder, creditors' coercive powers of enforcement were strengthened.[37] Consequently, John Sextayn, John Intebergh and Robert Crystyng were all serving time in Ipswich gaol in 1443/4 for non-payment of debt.[38] Even the most prestigious of families could fall foul of the law. John Caldwell was bailiff eight times, his son Benedict four. The father rebuilt, at his own expense, the town's west gate shortly after 1448 and its use continued as a gaol.[39] Yet, at the time of John's death in 1461, another son, Edmund, was languishing there, in debt for the considerable sum of £54 5s. 6d., and John's will made provision to secure his freedom.[40]

Whatever powers of coercion creditors might have had, prudent lenders were unlikely to advance funds to those who had little prospect of being able to repay. If they did, then notwithstanding medieval laws against usury, they demanded crippling rates of interest.[41] The mean value of the recognisances referred to above was £17 7s. 10d. and that of the letters of obligation in dispute in the petty court in 1443 was £10 13s. 8d., sums far beyond the means of most petty traders. Deprived

[33] Postan (1973), p. 33.
[34] SROI C/2/3/1/34–37, 41, 48, 51.
[35] SROI C/2/10/1/4, m. 5r.
[36] SROI 2/3/1/51 (17 Jan. 1443).
[37] Sutton (2005), p. 99.
[38] SROI 2/3/1/51 (23 Jul. 1443, 26 Mar. 1443, 19 Nov. 1444).
[39] *Annals*, p. 106; Elizabeth Owles, 'The West Gate of Ipswich' *PSIA*, 32 (1971), 164–67 (p. 165).
[40] SROI R2/87.
[41] Nightingale (1995), p. 469.

of both coin and credit, such people could not carry on in business; and as a result the bullion shortage seriously inhibited retail trade.[42] In the year 1400/1 the petty court had heard 639 discrete cases of debt and detinue. In seven months of 1443 it heard just ninety-seven, but the mean value of such claims had risen more than four-fold, from £1 12s. to £7 4s.[43] A decline in the volume of such litigation was already evident by 1407/8 and may have had other causes, such as administrative changes and a growing preference for informal arbitration. Nevertheless, even in the years 1407/8 and 1414/15 the court was considering about twenty such cases a month, whereas in 1443 it dealt with fewer than fourteen.[44] Without doubt, a decrease in litigation reflected a corresponding fall in trade. The petty trader was disappearing from the petty court. Although not quite as pronounced, the same pattern of higher value but fewer cases was also evident in the Colchester borough court which 'adds to the probability that Colchester's trade contracted during the fifteenth century'.[45] The Ipswich chamberlains' accounts for the year 1446/7 paint a similar picture.[46] Seven stalls in the flesh market were empty because no-one wanted to hire them. The draper John Marchant rented one under the Moothall, but he was on his own. So, in their markets, were the shoemaker John Sheyt, and the fish wife Beatrice Leme. Stalls were the place of business of the petty trader and they were lying empty.[47]

The economic downturn affected not only traders, but also landlords and tenants. As the former struggled to recover payment, and the latter declined to pay, rental values fell. Both William Debenham and John Gosenold were suing in the petty court in 1443, with little apparent success, for arrears of rent.[48] The town mills tell an even sorrier tale. In 1448 the general court ordered Peter Terry to pay arrears on his farm of the mill.[49] Seven years later William Ridout and William Heede, both members of the civic elite, were the culprits. Ridout had taken a lease of Horsewade mill for a term of thirteen years in October 1447 at a rent of twenty pounds per annum, only two-thirds of the amount that had been payable in 1345. On 26 September 1455 the general court first ordered him and Heede to give security for the settlement of arrears of thirty pounds within the week. The deadline passed without payment, and was extended to 1 November. On 9 April 1456 a fresh date was set for the surrender of twenty pounds of the arrears within the fortnight. A

[42] Nightingale (1995), p. 483.
[43] In the vast majority of cases in 1400/1 no specific sum was given. It seems likely that only the more significant claims were quantified, which means that the mean value of all cases may have been even lower.
[44] SROI C/2/3/1/34, 35, 36, 37, 40, 48, 51.
[45] Britnell (1986), pp. 206–8.
[46] SROI C/3/3/1/1.
[47] Nightingale (1995), p. 483.
[48] SROI C/2/3/1/51 (14 Mar. 1443, 4 April 1443).
[49] BL, Ms Add. 30,158, f. 11r.

day before this deadline, Ridout told the court that he refused to pay anything. The authorities appear to have accepted defeat and in the following January the mill was re-let to John Lackford for the same rent.[50] By 1463/4 it had been re-let again, this time to Robert Deye, at a lower rent of ten pounds per annum.[51]

The evidence of borough records is supported by other sources. In 1449 an allowance of £6 3s. 4d. was made upon the half-subsidy then payable by Ipswich to the king, equivalent to a reduction of 19.1 per cent from what had been paid in the lay subsidy of 1334. Ipswich's woes were far from unique. The hundreds of Carlford and Claydon, situated north and east of the borough, received above average reliefs, suggesting that any recession in the town was also affecting its hinterland. The struggling boroughs of Dunwich and Orford were both granted reductions of a third. In all, about four hundred settlements in Suffolk received concessions, amounting to a total reduction of 15.7 per cent in the county subsidy. These reliefs were allowed to places deemed 'devastated, wasted, destroyed, impoverished or otherwise burdened'.[52] Later, Ipswich's new charter of 1463 was granted by Edward IV in response to another plea of poverty.[53] As we have seen, Bridbury takes a somewhat cynical view of such pleas. His cynicism may not be entirely misplaced, but there is plenty of other evidence from Suffolk to show that times were hard. The average annual income from the market court in Newmarket collapsed between the 1420s and the 1470s from 49s. 11d. to 8s. 11d.; Blythburgh fair reached its lowest ebb; and in 1465 stalls in Mildenhall market were abandoned for want of business. The middle years of the fifteenth century were difficult for nearly everyone, but particularly so for the petty trader.[54] The impact of these difficulties on Ipswich's hinterland and trade networks is considered in greater detail next.

Contraction and Protection

An analysis of the origins of non-resident litigants in the petty court for the middle years of the century offers the best way of assessing those trade networks (Table 16). Table 8, which analysed similar data for the opening years of the century, was dominated by cases involving litigants from close to Ipswich, no fewer than 60 per cent of whom lived within ten miles of the borough. Table 16 draws on a much smaller database, but suggests that most litigants were now coming from further afield. Just as the resident petty trader was disappearing from the petty court, so was the local non-resident.

[50] BL, Ms Add. 30,158, f. 10v; *Annals*, pp. 71, 114–15.
[51] SROI C/3/3/1/2.
[52] D. Dymond and R. Virgoe, 'The Reduced Population and Wealth of Early Fifteenth-Century Suffolk' *PSIA*, 36 (1986) 73–100 (pp. 76, 78, 94–7).
[53] *CChR 1427–1516*, pp. 197–9.
[54] Bailey (2007), pp. 265, 287.

TABLE 16: ORIGINS OF NON-RESIDENT LITIGANTS IN THE PETTY COURT OF IPSWICH, 1443/4 AND 1464–67

Origin	*No. of litigants*	*Percentage of litigants*
< 6 miles	5	13.9
Hadleigh	2	5.6
Other 6–9 miles	3	8.3
10–20 miles	7	19.4
Bury St Edmunds	2	5.6
London	6	16.7
East coast ports	0	0
Other > 20 miles	5	13.9
Overseas	3	8.3
Unidentifiable	3	8.3
	36	100

Sources: SROI C/2/3/1/51, C/2/10/1/2–4

Ipswich had previously enjoyed a close trading relationship with London, which appears to have been maintained in the middle years of the century. Part of the church of St Laurence was called the London Gallery, perhaps being designated for use by visitors from the capital.[55] The great London merchants exercised an ever tighter hold on credit, and provincial traders, particularly in the textile industry, now looked to them for supplies. Among prominent Londoners taking a particular interest in Ipswich were three grocers, a mercer and three fishmongers. Nightingale suggests that the grocers' continued interest in the wool trade generated profits that enabled them to recapture the market in dyes and finance provincial cloth making.[56] Richard Lee served as alderman and mayor of London, as well as building up a distributive business in the provinces. With his fellow grocer Stephen Burgess, he traded in 1465 with the Ipswich dyer John Deye.[57] Early in his career John Wendey, a mercer, lent substantial sums to the chapman William Burre, probably the same man who was apprenticed to the Ipswich grocer John Wytton in 1446. Wendey went on to become governor of the Merchant Adventurers under Richard III.[58] Sons of Ipswich burgesses also moved to London to be apprenticed to mercers, such as Richard Bull, who was admitted to their Company in 1463.[59] One London fishmonger, Stephen Wolf, sought recovery in 1450 of the sum of three pounds from

[55] Mentioned in the will of Edmund Blake who died in 1444: SROI R1/20.
[56] Nightingale (1995), pp. 477, 485–6; Britnell (2000), pp. 324–5.
[57] Nightingale (1995), pp. 449, 514; SROI C/2/10/1/3, m. 6v.
[58] SROI C/2/10/1/1, m. 2r; SROI C/2/10/1/3, mm. 9r, 12r; Sutton (2005), p. 551.
[59] Sutton (2005), pp. 221–2.

the Ipswich merchant Henry Parker.[60] John Motte and John Stanesby were two more with strong local connections. As previously mentioned, Motte had been admitted as a foreign burgess in 1435. He kept an account with the innkeeper John Myddylton, who in 1466 owed him a balance of thirty shillings.[61] Both he and Stanysby created cloth-making empires, to which we will return below.[62]

The risk of default, illustrated above, made investment in trade very unpredictable in the mid-fifteenth century. Many Londoners preferred to put their money into property.[63] In 1452 John Kyng, a grocer, purchased a joint interest in a messuage with houses, buildings, curtilages and gardens in the parish of St Mary Quay, which he may have used for the purpose of overseas trade from the town. He clearly regarded Ipswich real estate as a worthwhile investment. Twelve years later, again jointly with others, he also acquired lands and tenements with houses, buildings, shops, cellars and solars in the parish of St Laurence.[64]

If London remained important, other trading partners appear to have mattered less at this time. Ipswich's east coast trade suffered. Although some coal continued to arrive from Newcastle, a toll of just ten pence was payable on the single cargo that arrived in 1446/7.[65] Sir John Howard bought a chaldron of coal in the town in 1465, and a ship called *Le Valentyne* of Newcastle-upon-Tyne was seized in the same year, by authority of a royal commission.[66] No merchant from any of the east coast ports appeared before the petty court, although the rolls of the Court of Common Pleas identify John Felaw's customers in Lowestoft and Yarmouth.[67] The same rolls suggest that Hadleigh remained the town's most important local trading partner. Among the four litigants, hailing from there and in dispute with Ipswich residents in Hilary term 1450, was William Hyllary, a gentleman of Hadleigh, who sued the Ipswich fullers Nicholas Fox and John Mundekyn for £12 3s. 4d. and £4 10s. respectively.[68] Yet, the textile workers of Hadleigh, who had been so prominent in the Ipswich records of the early fifteenth century, were far less so during this later period. Their complicity in a Yorkist rebellion of the late 1440s and in Cades's revolt in 1450 may be a sign of difficult times for that town in the middle years of the century.[69] John Munnyng, one of only four who made fleeting appearances in the Ipswich petty court, was a woad dealer who sought payment from John Deye, the

[60] PRO CP 40/756, m. 11v.
[61] SROI C/2/10/1/4, m. 5r.
[62] SROI C/2/10/1/3, m. 6r; Amor (2004), 414–36 (pp. 420, 426–7).
[63] Thrupp (1962), pp. 118, 128.
[64] SROI C/2/10/1/1, m. 4v; C/2/10/1/3, m. 4v.
[65] SROI C/3/3/1/1.
[66] SROI C/3/3/1/1; Crawford (1992), I, p. 479; *CPR 1461–67*, p. 553.
[67] PRO CP 40/756, mm. 49v, 184r.
[68] PRO CP 40/756, m. 185r.
[69] *CPR 1446–1452*, pp. 338, 343, 356, 359; Britnell, 'Woollen Textile Industry of Suffolk' (2003), 86–99 (p. 89); Bailey (2007), p. 192.

Ipswich dyer, of the balance of an account in the sum of £1 6s. 1½d.[70] Britnell notes a similar trend in Colchester. Litigants from Hadleigh and several other Suffolk towns, who had been very active in that borough court between 1390 and 1410, very rarely appeared there between 1445 and 1465.[71]

Instead of free trade, there are growing signs of protectionism. Whenever possible, Ipswich was trying to guard itself from competition. Borough charters often granted freemen two particular rights. One was a monopoly of free trade, which extended to merchandise but not basic provisions, within their own walls, and the other was a right to trade free of toll in other towns. For example, the bailiffs issued a certificate that John Yaxlee was a burgess of the town, coupled with a prayer that he be allowed to trade elsewhere free of toll.[72] Needless to say, these contradictory principles were a source of constant dispute between freemen of different towns, each claiming that their rights had priority over the others. The issue was further complicated by the award of charters and freedoms to ecclesiastical and lay lords which, so they claimed, benefited their tenants too. Disagreements were, in theory, resolved by giving priority to the beneficiaries of the earliest charter, so called 'priority of seisin' or 'priority of charter'. In practice it was not always so easy.[73] 'Priority of seisin was, in fact, less straightforward than legal theory might suggest' and led to many disputes.[74] In granting to local manorial lords the freedom of the borough, the burgesses of Ipswich had, in the early days, been cautious to limit the commercial rights that such freedom bestowed.[75] The difficulties of the mid-fifteenth century meant that, once more, they had to be careful. When enfranchising Sir Roger Chambyrleyn and John Tymperley esquire in 1454 they stipulated that the pair should be free from toll on all corn and other produce grown or raised on their manors and on all things bought for their own provisioning, but not otherwise.[76]

Such precautions might prevent the further erosion of the burgesses' privileges, but what could be done to claw back rights that might already have been given away? In such instances, the town was ready to go to court. Although details are sparse and the outcome unknown, in the 1450s taxes were being raised to fund litigation, and steps were being taken to secure the arbitration of disputes with Bury St Edmunds and Stowmarket, as well as the Prior of Ely, who held extensive manors within the liberty of St Ethelreda in the south-east around Woodbridge.[77] These

[70] SROI C/2/10/1/3, m. 6r.
[71] Britnell (1986), pp. 172–3.
[72] PRO E 210/625.
[73] Salzmann (1913), p. 224; Platt (1973), pp. 78–9; Masschaele (1997), pp. 112, 119, 131.
[74] Masscahaele (2007), p. 168.
[75] Masschaele (1997), pp. 150–1.
[76] BL, Ms Add. 30,158, f. 17v.
[77] *Annals* (1884), pp. 113, 116; David Dymond and Peter Northeast, *A History of Suffolk* (Chichester: Phillimore, 1985; repr. 1995), p. 36; Bailey (2007), p. 17. Masschaele refers to fifteenth-century disputes over priority of seisin; idem (2007), p. 171.

disputes are 'symptomatic of harsh competition in a contracting market'.[78] At the same time, the authorities were attempting to regulate trade within the town more tightly, undoubtedly to discourage unfair competition. They had always had to balance the interests of local craftsmen and victuallers in limiting competition and the interests of their residents in ensuring cheap supplies, but the plight of small traders inclined them in favour of their own producers.[79] Foreign butchers were forbidden from having stalls without the consent of the chamberlains. Fullers and clothiers were required to sell their cloth only on market day at the Moothall. The commercial operations of wool merchants and mercers were likewise confined to the Wool House. Merchants arriving by land or water had to weigh their merchandise at the common crane and thus to pay tolls.[80] Whether or not such protectionism brought short-term benefits, it may also have had adverse consequences which will be considered below, in an examination of the town's industry and, in particular, of its cloth making.

The impact on Ipswich of the Great Slump is now assessed, from two different angles. First, we will look at the victualling trades, using the generous information of the leet court rolls, and then at other domestic industries – particularly cloth, leather and metals.

Regulating the Supply of Food and Drink

As noted above, the rolls of the four annual Ipswich leet courts are an invaluable source for the mid-fifteenth-century. Table 17 seeks to illustrate changes in the Ipswich economy, by calculating the mean number of offences against various categories of trade regulation presented in each court. This type of evidence has been chosen because offenders appeared regularly before the court throughout the period, making it possible for meaningful comparisons to be made. The picture they present is, however, incomplete. All but one of these categories relate to victualling, the exception being presentments regarding the sale of leather, which are considered separately. Nevertheless, the supply of food and drink is the most fundamental of economic activities and, as such, constitutes a reasonable measure of prosperity. The relative number of offences that were recorded in each category can, therefore, be fairly considered as one indicator of the town's economic fortunes.

Owing to the fragmentary nature of the surviving rolls, the figures are not free of distortion. Rolls do not survive in equal numbers from each ward. Offences were probably penalised by the leet court of the ward in which the culprits lived, which was often also where they worked. For example, offences relating to the sale of meat

[78] Bailey (2007), p. 265.
[79] The Coventry authorities faced the same pressures: Harris (1913), pp. xxxii, xxxvii.
[80] SROI C/3/3/1/1; *Annals*, pp. 104, 105, 112.

TABLE 17: MEAN NUMBER OF OFFENCES PRESENTED TO EACH LEET COURT 1359–1468

	No. of courts	*Brewing ale*	*Selling ale*	*Brewing beer*	*Baking bread*	*Selling bread*
1359	1	11	9	0	2	13
Late 1410s	6	18.67	14.5	0.83	1.67	5.5
Early 1420s	10	19.6	12.7	0.5	2.1	5
Mid–late 1430s	13	19.2	17.61	0.46	1.67	5.76
1455?	1	15	19	1	2	2
Late 1460s	12	12.8	17.83	0.75	1.91	3.33
Total	43					

	Selling fish	*Selling meat*	*Inn-keepers*	*Selling leather*	*Plus*	*Minus*	*Balance*
1359	0	0	3	0			
Late 1410s	2.83	0.83	2	2			
Early 1420s	2.5	1.7	2.7	0.9	4	5	-1
Mid–late 1430s	2.92	0.23	3.23	1.92	6	3	3
1455?	2	0	2	0	3	6	-3
Late 1460s	4	3.17	5.4	2.75	5	4	1
1430s *v.* 1460s					7	2	5

Notes
The trends identified by these figures and in the commentary below may be the result of local administrative and bureaucratic changes rather than economic reality, but the identification of similar trends by historians of other towns makes it implausible that such changes offer a complete explanation.
The presentments to the leet court are not necessarily a complete record of Ipswich's victuallers. Some may never have sinned, or at least have never been caught. This seems improbable, certainly in the case of brewing and baking, since the assizes of ale, including beer, and of bread were generally regarded as a means of raising revenue from all those engaged in these trades (see: Thrupp (1962), p. 94; Britnell (1986), p. 89; Swanson (1989), p. 21; Bennett (1996), p. 163). Indeed, the town charter of 1446 assigned to the bailiffs all income from the assize of ale (*CChR 1427–1516*, pp. 54–5). The same cannot be said with equal certainty for other offences. Even so, since it is unlikely that traders in one decade were more virtuous than those in another, relative comparisons can be made with some confidence.
'Plus' means the number of offences for which the mean is greater than the mean in the previous decade and 'Minus' has the opposite meaning.
'Balance' means 'Plus' less 'Minus'.
The final line of 'Plus' and 'Minus' compares the 1460s with the 1430s.
Sources: SROI C/2/8/1/1–12, C/2/10/1/2–6.

were usually presented in the leet court of west ward, where the flesh market was situated; however, since it was furthest from the quay, presentments relating to the sale of fish were rarely, if ever, made there. As a result, our figures may inflate the mean number of presentments for sale of meat in the 1420s, and those of fish in the 1430s. In offering this type of analysis, such distortion is unavoidable, but nevertheless, after focusing on each category of victualling offence in turn, we will be in a stronger position to argue that some valid conclusions can be drawn.

In an age when most drinking water was not to be trusted and hopped beer was only beginning to seize the popular imagination, ale was the first choice of the vast majority of Englishmen and women. At the time, Sir John Fortescue opined that the people 'do not drink water, except ... by way of devotional or penitential zeal'.[81] They 'drank ale and beer much more mundanely – in the morning, as well as in the evening; as simple liquid refreshment; and for its salubrity, not just its intoxicating effects'.[82] The average working adult may have consumed up to a gallon a day, so that altogether more than a thousand gallons a day were drunk in a town the size of Ipswich.[83] Demand was, moreover, rising because, as *per capita* incomes rose after the Black Death, the consumption of ale by the lower orders increased. At the other end of the social spectrum, as the flow of wine into the country slowed, their betters also drank more ale.[84] Accordingly, in fifteenth-century Ipswich ale was big business, being brewed from malt, water and yeast in every ward, and penalised in every leet court.

The importance of maintaining good quality and fair prices in the brewing and sale of ale had long been reflected in national legislation and local custom.[85] The royal assize tied the cost of a gallon of ale to the price of grain, with a higher price being set for urban sales than rural ones. Accordingly, the customs of Ipswich required the bailiffs to announce each Michaelmas what such assize would be.[86] In 1465 they ordained that the best ale should be sold for 1½d. a quart, and the weakest for ½d. a quart.[87] The difference in quality was often reflected in the terms 'single' or 'small' ale, and 'double' ale. Double ale may have been brewed with twice the weight of malt, or alternatively the extracted sugars ('wort') may have been boiled for twice as long.[88] Presentments to the leet court frequently refer to ale being brewed and sold contrary to the assize and custom, by dish and cup rather than by lawful measure, or for excessive profit. In 1434 a cup was said to hold one-tenth of a gallon.[89] Although the price of ale was thus controlled, there were apparently no

[81] Fortescue (1942), p. 87.
[82] Bennett (1996), p. 9.
[83] C. Dyer (1989), p. 64; Bennett (1996), p. 17.
[84] Bennett (1996), pp. 43–4.
[85] *Ibid.*, pp. 99–100.
[86] Twiss (1873), pp. 174–5; Britnell (1986), p. 89; Swanson (1989), p. 21.
[87] *Annals*, p. 125.
[88] P.W. Hammond, *Food and Feast in Medieval England* (Stroud: Alan Sutton, 1993; repr 1995), p. 56.
[89] SROI C/2/8/1/8 (east ward).

presentments concerning poor quality. Nor was any mention made of the ale taster, whose role was to test the quality of the ale, and whose office was filled by annual election in many communities.[90] The commercialisation of brewing, particularly in towns, generally led to an improvement in quality, perhaps making the ale taster redundant.[91] The fines imposed were usually modest, often only four pence, rarely as much as two shillings, and only once more than that. In 1468, while serving as bailiff, William Style paid a fine of 3s. 4d.[92]

The number of individual brewers whose names are recorded rose from 86 in the 1410s to 97 in the 1420s, and 119 in the 1430s, before falling again to 66 in the 1460s.[93] Included within their ranks were several of town's leading burgesses, 16 of whom served as bailiff. Like so many brewers, they would have regarded brewing as a secondary occupation and, even if they themselves were named in the leet court, they very often left their wives to do, or at least supervise, the work. The decline, between the 1430s and the 1460s, in the mean number of brewing offences presented to the leet courts, and in the number of brewers, may indicate a down turn in the drink trade. It may be an early indicator of allegiances changing from ale to beer. Or it may be a sign of the growing commercialisation and concentration of brewing in fewer hands, and of a divorce between those brewing and those retailing ale ('tipplers').[94] Although the recorded numbers of both brewers and tipplers fell between the 1430s and the 1460s, the reduction in the number of tipplers was much less dramatic. The number of brewers fell to little more than half the earlier number, while the number of tipplers fell by less than a fifth from 136 to 110. In consequence, tipplers outnumbered brewers by a proportion of five to three. The number of individuals who were doing both fell from twenty-four to eight, suggesting perhaps that brewing was becoming a wholesale business, while tippling remained a retail trade.[95]

The commercialisation of brewing, and the growing divide between wholesale and retail business, had one momentous consequence for future generations: the emergence of separate alehouses as places to drink ale and beer with their familiar tables, trestles and benches.[96] Some ale was still peddled on a casual basis from

[90] For example, in the small west Suffolk town of Ixworth: Ixworth Priory Court Book 1467–83, Joseph Regenstein Library, University of Chicago, Bacon MS 912. In Exeter the borough authorities were not concerned with disputes over the quality of ale, which were normally addressed by personal pleas: Kowaleski (1995), p. 187.

[91] Peter Clark, *The English Alehouse: A Social History* (London: Longman, 1983), p. 31.

[92] SROI C/2/10/1/6, m. 2v (south ward).

[93] Those who simply brewed domestically for their own households were not subject to the assize. Generally, however, nearly all other brewers in any community were presented: Bennett (1996), pp. 160, 162.

[94] Mate, *Work and Leisure* (2006), p. 285.

[95] Clark (1983), p. 32; Bennett (1996), p. 46.

[96] Clark (1983), p. 34; Dyer (2005), p. 172. Mate suggests that, where the number of tipplers was double or triple the number of brewers, at least some brewing must have been carried out in separate establishments: *Trade and Economic Developments* (2006), pp. 73, 75.

doorsteps or in the streets, as Lettice Ganneker had done in south ward in the 1430s.[97] An increasing volume was, however, sold from cellars or basements, which later evolved into alehouses. There, patrons could not only drink, but also eat and play games such as dice and cards, which had recently arrived from the continent. Late medieval Ipswich was not a puritanical society, and at Christmas and other religious festivals games were encouraged. The authorities were, however, less tolerant when they were played 'at the wrong time, by the wrong people, and in the wrong place'.[98] Gaming by apprentices was particularly frowned upon and regarded as a threat to their masters' time and property, as well as to public order. When William Burre and John Frere were apprenticed respectively to the grocer John Wytton in 1446 and the barber John Sextayn in 1448, they both agreed not to participate in gaming in their master's house under penalty of 2s.[99] In 1448 the cordwainer John Lackford, who had been caught cheating at games called 'Whistilds, Prelleds, and Quarter spells' was fined the exemplary sum of 26s. 8d. by the general court and threatened with the pillory if he did the same again.[100]

At the beginning of the century beer was being imported from the Low Countries. By the 1410s it was being brewed in Ipswich. Events on both sides of the North Sea encouraged this transition to domestic production. First flooding, then difficulties in procuring supplies of foreign barley, undermined the industry in Holland, so that after 1403 the volume of beer shipped abroad dropped sharply.[101] In Ipswich the expatriate Dutch community, and a steady flow of Dutch sailors, provided a ready market. It may be significant that very soon beer brewing was concentrated in east ward near the docks.[102] The earliest known reference is to a Simon Bierbrewer who, in 1416, was fined four pence for throwing 'the filth of his trade' into the salt water. Eight years later Derek van Pape was penalised for a similar offence, dumping by the water gates the malt dregs of beer so that 'a very bad smell arose'.[103] The first recorded fines for brewing and selling beer were imposed in 1419 and, from the outset, were significantly more than those ever levied on brewers of ale, with Geoffrey Pape alone paying the remarkably large sum of 13s. 4d.[104] The size of these fines may reflect hostility to the aliens who dominated beer brewing at this time. It may also indicate hostility to the product itself, which was long held in suspicion. Norwich brewers were forbidden from using hops which were considered 'unholsome for mannes body', as were brewers

[97] SROI C/2/8/1/10–11 (south ward).
[98] Mate, *Trade and Economic Developments* (2006), p. 163.
[99] SROI C/2/10/1/1, m. 2r; C/6/11/1.
[100] *Annals*, p. 105.
[101] Kerling (1954), pp. 113–14.
[102] SROI C/2/8/1/2–3 (east ward).
[103] SROI C/2/8/1/3, 7 (east ward).
[104] SROI C/2/8/1/4 (south ward). Geoffrey Pape was still brewing beer in Ipswich in 1430: CP 40/676 m. 102r.

in Coventry and Oxford.[105] The most likely explanation is, however, that beer brewing was a much more substantial operation than ale brewing, generating higher profits.[106] Greater capital investment was required, since the necessary equipment and brewing vessels often cost more than twenty pounds.[107] This was not, however, an insurmountable obstacle, as beer was less perishable, which meant that it could be brewed in greater quantities and distributed over longer distances.[108] It was fined accordingly. There was no separate assize of beer, which appears to have been regulated in Ipswich in accordance with the assize of ale.[109] Once again, the authorities were concerned primarily with fair measure, rather than quality. Several beer brewers were charged with selling beer by the jug, rather than by an authorised measure.[110] As with ale, beer came in two different qualities, namely 'single' and 'double'.[111]

Until the middle of the century there were only ever three beer brewers at any one time recorded in the Ipswich leet court rolls. By the 1460s, however, six were carrying on business, all in east ward. Unusually, one was a woman, Isabel Garne.[112] Most of them had Dutch names, such as Beerbruer, Claysone and Willyamsone, and there is little evidence of the English yet becoming involved.[113] Nevertheless, beer was being drunk not only by the expatriate Dutch, but by the locals. Katherine Monk bought in supplies from Rumbald Herreyssone for Twelfth Night revels, and Sir John Howard procured beer regularly from Ipswich both for his household and his ships. In April 1467 his purchases for a feast included both single and double beer.[114] They were growing to like the more bitter taste of beer, as well as the price, as it was generally cheaper than ale.[115] Herreyssone, probably a native of Arneburgh in Saxony, was one of those who helped to popularise the drink. As the leading beer brewer in the town in the 1430s, he was the first to leave more than a fleeting mark on its history.[116] He may have started in a small way, being fined just 6d. in 1434, but during the years 1436 to 1438 he paid 6s. 8d., 10s. and then 6s. 8d again, which suggests considerable expansion. He was taxed as an alien householder in

[105] Swanson (1989), p. 22; Bennett (1996), p. 120.
[106] Britnell (1986), p. 197.
[107] Dyer (2002), p. 323.
[108] Hornsey (2003), p. 302; C. Dyer (2005), p. 172.
[109] Strictly speaking, beer should not have been regulated by the royal assize of ale: Bennett (1996), p. 106.
[110] SROI C/2/8/1/11 (east ward).
[111] Mate *Trade* (2006), p. 69.
[112] SROI C/2/10/1/3, m. 1v (east ward); C/2/10/1/4, m. 1r (east ward). With the exception of the occasional widow of a beer brewer, women were rarely involved in this trade: Bennett (1996), p. 78.
[113] SROI C/2/10/1/4, m. 1r; C/2/10/1/6, m. 3v (both east ward).
[114] SROI C/2/3/1/51 (26 Mar. 1443); Ronald Hutton, *The Rise and Fall of Merry England* (Oxford: Oxford University Press, 1994), pp. 15–16, 60; Crawford (1992), I, pp. 193–4, 270, 274, 399.
[115] Mate, *Trade and Economic Developments* (2006), p. 77.
[116] *CPR 1429–36*, p. 563.

1440, and established extensive trading interests in the years that followed.[117] He was a ship owner of *le Cogship* which was captured by pirates in 1440, and was involved with Simon Rankyn, a merchant of Cambridge. As well as brewing and selling beer, he had interests in grain and wood ash. One of his business associates was John Drayll, twice bailiff and one of the richest men in mid-fifteenth-century Ipswich. Herreyssone gave Drayll a letter of obligation for the sum of eighteen pounds, which he later dishonoured and, in consequence, spent a few days in Ipswich gaol.[118]

Baking and brewing were closely allied trades. Nearly half of all bakers were also brewers of ale. During the fermenting of ale the yeast content multiplies several-fold, providing a rich supply of raw material for baking. Swanson notes the close association of the two trades in York, and Ipswich provides many similar examples.[119] Bread, like ale, was regulated both nationally and locally. Indeed, because invariably there were fewer bakers than brewers, even tighter regulation was possible. The royal assize of bread dates from the late twelfth century and established a fixed relationship between the quality, price and weight of each loaf.[120] The local customs of Ipswich concentrate, in some detail, on protecting the quality of bread.[121] The leet court presentments refer to the sale of various types of unnamed bread, while the customs describe a range of wheaten breads running from the best quality 'wastel', through 'simnel', to 'first cocket' and 'second cocket' loaves. There were others, including the most expensive, known as 'manchet', and 'tourte' made from unbolted flour.[122] The earlier leet courts and the customs emphasise the importance of establishing the correct weight of each loaf, as well as the adequate sifting and relative fineness of the flour.[123] The fineness of the flour depended on the amount of bran that was allowed to pass through the sieve ('bolter'). The less the bran, the better the bread, both in terms of snobbery and contemporary medical opinion. The bolter itself had to comply with regulation, different types being used when making specific kinds of bread. Second cocket could be sieved with a bolter of 'beuquer', but the finer breads had to be made from flour that had passed though one from Rennes. Use of the wrong bolter was in theory punished by an escalating series of penalties. For the first and all succeeding offences, the bolter was to be burned beside the pillory. For the second offence, the baker was also to be fined. Next, he was to be pilloried. Finally, the miscreant had to give up his occupation

117 PRO E 179/180/92.
118 SROI C/2/10/1/1, m. 1v; C/2/8/1/8–11 (east ward); C/2/6/3; C/2/3/1/51 (21, 26 Mar. 1443, 23 Jul. 1443).
119 Swanson (1989), p. 21.
120 Swanson (1989), pp. 11–12; Kowaleski (1995), p. 187; Davis (2004), 465–502 (pp. 465–6).
121 Twiss (1873), pp. 172–3.
122 Hammond (1993), p. 48.
123 SROI C/2/8/1/2 (west ward); C/2/8/1/3 (north ward); C/2/8/1/5 (north ward).

for a year and a day. Other breaches of the assize met with a similar series of penalties. Bakers of certain types of bread were not allowed to bake others, and faced escalating fines for doing so. In practice, like the assize of ale, the assize of bread was used by the borough authorities as a form of licence fee or taxation, and differences in fines almost certainly reflect differences in the scale of operations.[124]

The baking of bread was concentrated in fewer hands than brewing. Twenty-six different bakers appear on the surviving Ipswich leet court rolls; seven in the 1410s, eleven in the 1420s, seven in the 1430s, two in the 1450s, and nine in the 1460s. Rarely were more than two bakers presented to any one court, suggesting that, at any given time, eight serviced the whole town. The fines imposed on them were often significantly higher than those levied upon brewers of ale, at least two-thirds being for two shillings or more. Among prominent bakers were the brothers John and Richard Joye.[125] As we have seen, John soon turned his attentions to the more lucrative wine trade, but Richard persevered. After his death, his widow Gudren continued their business, as Ipswich's only recorded female baker. She cannot have been particularly successful because, when she died in 1442, she left a very modest estate.[126] John Wode baked bread, brewed ale and kept an inn, but his primary occupation was also as a vintner.[127] While four mid-fifteenth-century bakers are known to have been freemen, none of them ever became bailiff. Indeed, two of them, Thomas Medewe and John Trotte, avoided the limelight by buying exemption from holding the office of chamberlain.[128] One is left with the impression that baking was generally a primary occupation and bigger business than brewing ale, but that few bakers joined the ranks of the urban elite. Like butchers and tanners, they were rarely welcome in the highest circles.[129]

Some bakeries appear to have been passed down from father to son. Bartholomew Trotte was baking in the 1420s and 1430s, and John Trotte from the 1460s to the 1480s. The Soty family business in south ward lasted even longer. Thomas was active in 1359, John in the 1410s and 1420s, another Thomas between the 1430s and 1460s, and Gregory in 1479.[130] The second Thomas fell out with one of his grain suppliers, John Sewall of Rushmere, in 1443 and was sued in the petty court on account of 3 quarters and 7 bushels of wheat, for which he failed to pay £2 4d.[131] He died in 1469 leaving an estate suggestive of comfortable prosperity, but

[124] Swanson (1989), p. 12.
[125] CP 40/596, m. 224r.
[126] SROI R1/15.
[127] BL, Ms Add. 30,158, f. 3r.
[128] BL, Ms Add. 30,158, ff. 30v, 33v.
[129] Kermode (2000), p. 455.
[130] SROI C/2/8/1/1, 4, 5, 8, 10, 11; C/2/10/1/3, m. 2r; C/2/10/1/4, m. 4r; C/2/10/1/6, m. 2v; C/2/10/1/7, m. 4r (all south ward).
[131] SROI C/2/3/1/51 (19 Mar. 1443).

no great affluence. He bequeathed two shillings to the church of St Nicholas for making a window in the vestry, and a tenement with garden to his widow Joan for life with a remainder to his son Gregory.[132]

Baking bread on a commercial scale required a capital investment that few could afford. For every baker, there were many more 'regrators' who bought bread ready-baked and sold it on to the public at a profit. The number of different regrators rose from twenty-five in the 1410s, to twenty-nine in the 1420s, and to a peak of fifty in the 1430s, before falling back to twenty-nine in the 1460s. Furthermore, having held fairly steady during the first three of these decades, the mean number of presentments per court declined quite sharply in the 1460s. This trend may be a sign of retrenchment in the consumption of bread and perhaps of a fall in population levels. Certainly, the extra-ordinarily high number of deaths in 1465, as recorded in extant wills, probably marks a visitation of plague. The decline in numbers of regrators may also mirror the move towards commercialisation that was apparent in the brewing of ale during the same period. Perhaps the difficult mid-century years had culled the small-scale, casual seller of bread and thus concentrated regrating in fewer hands. Certainly, between the 1430s and the 1460s, the number of female regrators, who tended to operate as streetsellers with a basket under their arm, fell even more sharply than the total number of regrators, from six to two.[133] Probably the best way to reconcile an increase in the number of bakers with a decrease in that of regrators, is by concluding that, by the 1460s, the bakers themselves had seized a greater share of the retail market.

Such was the importance of fish to the medieval diet that no fewer than six of the heads of the Ipswich customs were dedicated to regulating the fish trade.[134] It was, therefore, not difficult for local fishermen to fall foul of one or more of them. Their activity is reflected in the number of presentments to each court relating to the sale of fish. Having remained fairly steady in the 1410s, 1420s and 1430s at just under three, the mean increased to four in the 1460s. The number of different offenders rose from eleven in the 1410s, to fifteen in the 1420s, rose again to nineteen in the 1430s, and levelled off at twenty in the 1460s. During the years here under review, three-quarters of all presentments of offending fishermen were made to the leet court of east ward, and nearly all the remainder to that of north ward.

Whereas the fishmongers of London had once enjoyed considerable political power, no Ipswich fishmonger was ever appointed as bailiff.[135] Among them, however, were always a few freemen, for whom the fish trade appears to have been a primary occupation. Like many Londoners, Robert Kyrkehous combined his business as a fish-

[132] SROI R2/183.
[133] Hammond (1993), p. 48.
[134] Twiss (1873), pp. 100–5, 160–1.
[135] Thrupp (1962), p. 6. The fishmongers 'declined sharply in influence in the fifteenth century': Barron (2004), p. 230.

monger with an interest in the woollen cloth industry.[136] Although dogged by controversy, he ultimately became a councillor and, shortly before he died, chamberlain in 1485/6.[137] John Palmer was admitted specifically as a fisherman in 1447.[138] Fish wives also appear in the records, for forestalling, and in the 1430s and again in the 1460s they made up half of those presented to the leet courts. Alice Rolf was active as a fish wife in the 1430s, probably in succession to her late husband Robert, who disappears from the records after 1434, and when she remarried it was to another fishmonger, Thomas Pratt. She seems to have done quite well for herself, bequeathing eight silver spoons and two silk belts with silver ornamentation to her local church of St Laurence, as well as linen kerchiefs to her many friends, when she died in 1448.[139]

Butchers were the object of suspicion in medieval towns and often fell under the scrutiny of the local courts and borough authorities.[140] They could be fined for polluting roads, ditches and waterways with dung and the entrails of slain beasts.[141] When selling their meat, they could also fall foul of the law in a number of ways. Straightforward presentments were made for dealing in spoiled meat, or for offering any flesh for sale at inflated prices.[142] In a manner that would outrage modern day animal lovers, butchers were expected to slaughter bulls only after baiting them with dogs to soften the meat.[143] To avoid suspicion of cattle rustling, and to ensure a steady supply of leather to local tanners, they were also supposed to bring to town, with the carcass, the hides and skin of deadstock.[144] In each case fines were payable for non-compliance.

The mean number of offences relating to the sale of meat presented at each leet court rose sharply in the 1460s, hinting at rising demand for the flesh, not only of bulls, but also of sheep, pigs and calves.[145] Presentments were not limited to west ward, which had previously been the main forum for considering such cases, but were made in all other wards too. The number of individual butchers, however, remained, at eleven, the same as in the 1420s. Furthermore, three of those named in the 1460s came from outside Ipswich; two from Woodbridge and one from Baylham. Within the town, they maintained a fairly close circle. As suppliers of hides and tallow, as well as meat, they often enjoyed prosperity. John Sewale, for example, made a return of six shillings on the sale of tallow in the mid-1440s.[146]

136 PRO E 101/342/25.
137 BL, Ms Add. 30,158, f. 37r; *Annals*, p. 152.
138 BL, Ms Add. 30,158, f. 10r.
139 SROI C/2/8/1/8–11 (north ward); R1/74.
140 Swanson (1989), p. 25; Kermode (2000), p. 455.
141 SROI C/2/8/1/2 (west ward); C/2/8/1/4 (south ward); C/2/8/1/8 (south ward).
142 SROI C/2/8/1/5, 7 (west ward); C/2/10/1/2, m. 11v (east ward); Twiss (1873), pp. 144–7.
143 SROI C/2/8/1/11 (north ward); C/2/10/1/2–6 (all wards).
144 SROI C/2/10/1/2–6 (all wards); Twiss (1873), pp. 142–5.
145 SROI C/2/10/1/2–6 (all wards).
146 SROI C/2/3/1/51 (30 Jul. 1443).

Nevertheless, because of the social stigma attached to their trade, they found climbing the social ladder difficult.[147] No fifteenth-century butcher, after John Starling, is known to have become bailiff. John Sudbury rose to hold office as chamberlain in 1439 and coroner three times between 1440 and 1454, only to fall out of favour and suffer disenfranchisement in 1459.[148] John Deve was admitted as a freeman in 1418, but only on condition that he assumed the thankless task of collecting, for the borough, the butchers' tolls for the following seven years.[149] This may have given him a supervisory role over them. Just two butchers of the 1460s, John Broun and John Manser, were recorded as freemen.[150] Broun carried on a successful business for more than thirty years, leasing the butchery from the borough for twenty pounds per annum in 1463/4.[151]

Medieval merchants and pedlars were perpetually on the move, in need of accommodation for themselves and their horses. All large towns had many inns and guest houses, and an extraordinary number of beds. The stabling they provided was as important to commercial well being then as the car park is today, and the borough authorities were as sensitive to the cost of horse bread, oats and hay as they now are to car parking charges.[152] They needed to restrain the prices that innkeepers charged for food and fodder, and the additional services that they offered to their guests. There were regular presentments in the local leet courts for selling bread, ale, meat, fish, horse bread hay and oats to guests for excessive profit. Sometimes, the charge is more particular. In 1423, in west ward, Anthony Denys and William Wethereld were selling two pence worth of victuals for three pence, while in east ward William Langlonde and William Snow did even better, making a 100-per cent return by selling a penny's worth of victuals for two pence.[153] In some inns, prostitutes were available to provide night time entertainment. John Smyth, a Dutchman, kept an inn for many years 'at the quay', no doubt meeting the needs of visiting seamen. In 1468 he was fined two shillings for encouraging fornication and adultery within his house.[154]

Most of these inns were little more than private dwelling houses, or medieval B&Bs. In Ipswich, for every innkeeper who paid a fine of two shillings or more, five paid less. Some were, however, much grander.[155] A long list of furniture and fur-

[147] Swanson (1989), p. 14.
[148] *Annals*, p. 100; BL, Ms Add. 30,158, f. 22v.
[149] BL, Ms Add. 30,158, f. 2r.
[150] BL, Ms Add. 30,158, ff. 10r, 13r, 24r; *Annals*, p. 119.
[151] SROI C/3/3/1/2.
[152] Barron (2004), pp. 59–60. The quality, weight and price of these products were all subject to statutory assize: *Rot. Parl.*, iii, p. 269.
[153] SROI C/2/8/1/6 (east ward).
[154] SROI C/2/10/1/6, m. 3v (east ward).
[155] John Schofield and Geoffrey Stell, 'The built environment 1300–1450', in *CUH*, pp. 371–393 (p. 389).

nishings, prepared in 1467 for the creditors of the innkeeper John Myddylton, included eleven feather beds.[156] On a more modest scale, in 1446 Nicholas Lamb, another innkeeper, bequeathed a set of bed clothes to each of his children.[157] In Tudor York there were beds for 1035 people and stabling for 1711 horses.[158] As a busy port, Ipswich could have been expected to offer facilities for several hundred visitors at any one time. The demand for beds reflected the volume of traffic in and out of the town and, accordingly, serves as a barometer of the economic climate. Between the 1430s and the 1460s the mean number of innkeeping offences presented to each leet court rose by two-thirds and the number of offending innkeepers almost doubled, from eighteen to thirty-three. Like brewing, innkeeping was a business that could be delegated to wives and servants, while the head of the household continued to pursue his day job. When the husband died the wife might appear on the record, as did the widows of Richard Disse and John Hardyng.[159] Innkeeping could also be carried on in tandem with victualling and other trades, and, having a captive market, many Ipswich innkeepers did so. Two-thirds of them were brewers, one was a baker, five were fishmongers, including Robert Kyrkehous, and one, Robert Wulcy (alias Wolsey), was a butcher.[160] John Joye and John Wode, leading vintners, both kept inns. The level of fines imposed on the latter in the twenty-two years from 1415 to 1437 mark him out as the leading local innkeeper of his age. Among innkeepers, it was not only Robert Kyrkehous who had an interest in the cloth trade. John Depyng, Robert Deye and John Smyth also presented cloth to the alnager in the 1460s.[161] Remkyn Smyth was a tailor.[162] Earlier in the century, innkeepers included Thomas Cowman, a leading draper, and John Turner the dyer.[163] Although, as we have seen, Ipswich's civic leaders generally fought shy of personal involvement in the victualling trades, innkeeping was different. Not only for John Joye, but also for John Caldwell and William Wethereld, and, in the closing years of the century, Richard Haxwade, keeping an inn could run in tandem with their mercantile activities, and was no impediment to attaining high office as bailiff. For clothiers and other merchants, their yards served as private markets and provided an ideal forum for the buying and selling that was essential to their trade.[164]

Looking back to Table 17, in the light of this commentary, there is evidence of an upturn in some victualling trades in the late 1460s, especially when compared with the 1430s. The mean number of cases presented to each leet court rose in six

[156] SROI C/2/10/1/4, m. 1v.

[157] SROI R1/27.

[158] D.M. Palliser, *Tudor York* (Oxford: Oxford University Press, 1979), pp. 166, 171.

[159] SROI C/2/8/1/11 (north ward); C/2/10/1/5, m. 4v (west ward).

[160] In medieval Exeter fishmongers were often innkeepers: Kowaleski (1995), pp. 138–9.

[161] PRO E 101/342/25; E 101/343/2.

[162] SROI C/2/10/1/3, m. 1v (east ward).

[163] SROI C/2/8/1/7 (west ward); C/2/8/1/12 (probably north ward); C/2/3/1/51 (6 Jun. 1443).

[164] Nightingale (1995), p. 440.

trades; the selling of ale, fish and meat, the brewing of beer, the baking of bread and the keeping of inns. It fell in two; the brewing of ale and the selling of bread. As already noted, evidence from other towns points to a similar concentration of ale brewing in fewer hands, and a separation of those brewing ale from those selling it. When this evidence is viewed alongside the growing demand for beer, it seems unlikely that the total consumption of malt-based alcohol was less in the 1460s than it had been in the 1430s. The apparent decline in the sale of bread may conceal purchases from outside the town. In 1450 the executors of a Bury St Edmunds baker, John Joynour, were suing the executors of the Ipswich merchant John Deken for the substantial sum of £16 16s.[165] It may also reflect an opposite trend to that evident in the sale of ale. The divide between those baking bread and those selling it was disappearing. Bakers were taking a larger share of the market themselves and forcing out casual hucksters. The offence of baking bread against the ordinance had always included sales, but those sales were growing.

If we accept that there was an upturn in the victualling trades, it is tempting to leap to the conclusion that the economy of Ipswich was generally more buoyant by the late 1460s. Their apparent strength may, however, better reflect the fortunes of overseas trade, which was largely in the hands of aliens who needed food and accommodation while in port, than that of local trade and industry. In this respect it may be significant that, of all fines imposed on innkeepers, the proportion payable by those in east ward rose sharply in the middle years of the century and still stood at very nearly 50 per cent in the late 1460s. Before passing judgement, therefore, we must examine the fortunes of other sectors of the local economy such as textiles, leather and metals.

Trades and Industries in Recession

Cloth, leather and metal industries did not absorb more than a significant minority of townspeople. Rich and poor alike needed to be clothed, and tailoring always provided a living for those such as John Budd, who, in his will of 1465, bequeathed a shaping board, two pairs of scissors and a pressing iron.[166] John Hastyngs was the foremost of four known chandlers during this period, pursuing a long and successful career, and becoming a burgess in 1457, a portman in 1470, and bailiff four times between 1473 and 1490.[167] Starting out from a shop in the parish of St Mary Elms, he made his living supplying, among other items, candles, which were the only artificial form of light in his day.[168] He was fined the substantial sum of twenty

[165] PRO CP 40/756, m. 299r. Bailey cites bakers with 'a client base beyond their home town': (2007), p. 267.
[166] SROI R2/156.
[167] BL, Ms Add. 30,158, ff. 21r, 29r; *Annals*, pp. 133, 140, 145, 159.
[168] SROI C/2/10/1/2, mm. 14r, 14v.

shillings in 1468 for selling them at excessive prices.[169] The leet court rolls highlight the substantial number of labourers and servants who populated Ipswich and who rarely appear in other sources. Sadly, we usually only know about them because they were fined for not attending the court, and, even when they did, we learn far more about the fights in which they became involved than the more salubrious aspects of their lives. Table 18 provides some indication of the relative importance of each of the various crafts and industries in Ipswich at this difficult time in the town's history.

Cloth Industry in Decline

Just as they had done earlier in the century, the clothiers of Ipswich continued to produce cloth in a variety of types, colours and sizes. References to straits in court rolls still slightly outnumbered those to either broadcloths or dozens, with just one mention of a kersey.[170] Yet, by the late 1460s in Ipswich, as elsewhere in Suffolk, more cloth was being turned into broadcloths than into straits. Four years of alnage accounts, for the period from 1465 to 1469, record that in the town 189 broadcloths and 618 straits (equivalent to about 154½ broadcloths) were presented to the alnager, but no kerseys.[171] One broadcloth was described in the petty court as 'murregrey', while nine others were 'newegreyes'. When a colour was specified, dozens and straits generally appear to have been white, suggesting that they were not dyed, although one strait was blue. Other cloth was described as 'murrey', which was a dark red or purple-red colour, and as 'musterdevillers', which was usually of a mixed grey colour.[172] Similar fashions appear in bequests in contemporary wills. For instance, Margaret Fastolf owned a gown of murrey, and Joan Freborne a gown and tunic both of violet cloth, as well as a gown of musterdevillers. Alice Pipho left one black gown and another of musterdevillers.[173] This was an age in which the leaders of fashion favoured darker cloths.[174] The very rich, however, still treasured their top quality scarlets. Margaret Fastolf clearly had many gowns, but her 'best' was scarlet. So too was that most favoured by John Drayll, who died a very wealthy man.[175] Whether these expensive cloths were produced or purchased locally is doubtful. The Paston women complained about the poor choice available in the shops of Norwich as compared with London.[176] It is unlikely that Ipswich, a much smaller

[169] SROI C/2/10/1/6, m. 2v (south ward).
[170] SROI C/2/10/1/2, m. 4v.
[171] PRO E 101/342/25; E 101/343/2; E 101/343/4; E 101/343/5.
[172] SROI C/2/10/1/2, m. 3r; C/2/10/1/3, m. 6r; Peter Northeast (ed.) *Wills of the Archdeaconry of Sudbury, 1439–1474* (Woodbridge: Boydell for SRS, 44, 2001), p. xxvii.
[173] SROI R1/135; R2/5; R2/77.
[174] Veale (2003) pp. 140–1.
[175] SROI R1/135; C/2/10/1/2, mm. 14r, 14v.
[176] Dyer (2005), p. 146.

TABLE 18: STATED OCCUPATIONS IN THE IPSWICH PETTY, LEET AND GENERAL COURTS

Occupation	*(1) No. of litigants in the petty court 1443–67*	*Percentage of (1)*	*(2) No. of those amerced in the leet court 1415–68*	*Percentage of (2)*	*Admissions 1440–69*
Building	3	3.1	2	1.7	2
Clothing	5	5.2	6	5.1	1
Leather	3	3.1	8	6.8	13
Merchant or mariner	43	44.3	4	3.4	4
Metal	4	4.1	3	2.5	2 to 4
Other occupations	13	13.4	6	5.1	11
Religious	10	10.3	7	5.9	3
Servant/labourer	1	1.0	45	38.1	0
Textiles	6	6.2	16	13.6	7
Transport	0	0	1	0.8	0
Victuallers (including taverners and vintners)	5	5.2	11	9.3	22
Wood	4	4.1	9	7.6	0
Total	97	100	118	99.9	65 to 67

Notes

All but one of the petty court cases date from 1443/4 or 1464–67.

The leet court entries used in this Table include only those concerning individuals whose occupations are specifically stated in the roll. No-one has been added simply by reason of the activity for which he or she was presented to the court. This avoids the risk of including those, such as brewers, whose primary occupation was probably quite different. Those presented for selling badly tanned leather are only included if they were among the minority specifically described as tanners, which means that the number whose primary occupation was tanning may be understated.

The occupation of freemen was frequently omitted from the record of their admission during this period. Other sources have, therefore, been consulted in order to build as full a picture as possible. Such sources, particularly leet court records, are more likely to identify the practitioners of certain trades than others. Since victuallers and tanners are more readily recognised than textile workers, their numbers may be relatively exaggerated. The category Textiles includes drapers and mercers.

Sources: BL, Ms Add. 30,158; SROI C/2/3/1/51, C/2/8/1/1–12, C/2/10/1/1–6.

town, had more to offer. The gentry family of Hotot, just down the road in Thorney outside Stowmarket, were at this time looking to London for their clothes.[177]

Textile workers continued to operate in Ipswich. Those designated by occupation in the leet court records included six dyers and a woad dealer, six fullers, two weavers and a card maker. Thirteen fullers, not necessarily all resident in the town, leased stalls in the fulling house in the Moothall in 1446/7.[178] Of the six involved in textiles and named in the petty court rolls of the middle years of the century, one was the fuller John Wythie from Norwich, another was the draper William Recher of Bury St Edmunds and the remaining four came from Ipswich. Among them was Thomas Wysman, who combined the roles of wool carder and shearman. Wysman was clearly troubled by his customers. He fell out with the dyer John Deye in 1464 when Deye failed to pay him in full for supplying two kerseys, a dozen and 28 stones of flock.[179] Rather earlier, Ralph Reacher may have pursued a similar line of work. When his house was burgled in 1443, he alleged that the perpetrators had stolen a spinning wheel and a pair of teasels.[180]

However important their skills may have been to the town, textile workers rarely enjoyed high status. Among those recorded as being admitted as freemen in the middle years of the century, only three can be identified with confidence as such, namely the dyers Thomas Smyth, in 1454, and John Deye and Edmund Sewale, both in 1463.[181] None of them ever aspired to high borough office. The frequent mentions of Deye above suggest that he built a flourishing business. He presented a small quantity of cloth to the alnager in 1466, so his interest in the industry probably extended beyond his particular craft.[182]

Even if textile working was not a prestigious calling, trading in cloth certainly was. John Baldwyn, who was admitted in 1458, and had become a councillor by 1479, was engaged in the cloth trade, on a scale that was significant by Ipswich standards, as a draper and clothier.[183] He presented to the alnager six straits in 1466 and twelve broad cloths in 1468.[184] Many of the town's leading burgesses similarly presented cloth in the late 1460s. Indeed, among their number were seven men who held office as bailiff in the twenty years between 1460 and 1479, and who together during that period served no fewer than fifteen times. Another twelve freemen were clothiers; and a further three, though not admitted, appeared before the leet court as residents. Between them they produced, in four years, the equivalent of 171½

[177] Amor (2006), 175–97 (pp. 192–4).
[178] SROI C/3/3/1/1.
[179] SROI C/2/10/1/2, m. 4v.
[180] SROI C/2/3/1/51 (21 Mar. 1443).
[181] BL, Ms Add. 30,158, ff. 17r, 22r, 25v.
[182] PRO E 101/342/25.
[183] BL, Ms Add. 30,158, f. 22r; SROI C/2/10/1/7 m.
[184] BL, Ms Add. 30,158, f. 22r; PRO E 101/342/25, E 101/343/4.

broadcloths. These twenty-three comprised only half the number of individuals who presented cloth in Ipswich, and accounted for just half the cloth that was sealed there. Who were the others? Some of them may have been Ipswich townsfolk who simply escaped mention in other records, but, given the survival of a contemporaneous series of leet court rolls, this explanation does not satisfactorily account for all the missing names. Others were probably men of standing in the countryside around Ipswich who brought their cloth to town for sealing. A John Howard, possibly the future duke of Norfolk, presented twenty broadcloths at Easter 1467. On the same date Thomas Mannyng, who operated on a much humbler scale, presented two straits. A will of 1483 suggests that he may have hailed from Sudbourne, 17 miles north-east of Ipswich.[185] The alnage accounts themselves speak of 'various unknown strangers from towns close to Ipswich and Stowmarket'.[186]

Cloth production in Ipswich and Suffolk at the end of the fourteenth century has already been considered. How did output in the 1460s compare? Descriptions and sizes of medieval cloths varied from town to town and from period to period, making any precise answer to this question impossible. Nevertheless, if one assumes that a broad dozen of 1396/7 equated to half, and a narrow dozen to a quarter, of a broadcloth in the 1460s, then production in Suffolk at that earlier date totalled just short of 2950 broadcloths. Bridbury states that mean annual production in Suffolk in the years 1394–98 was 2797 broadcloths.[187] By contrast, in each year of the late 1460s county-wide production was the equivalent of about 5000 broadcloths.[188] This suggests an increase in output of between 70 and 80 per cent, raising Suffolk from sixth place to become the leading woollen cloth producing county in England.[189] The location and volume of cloth making in Suffolk, in the years 1465/6 to 1468/9, is illustrated by Map 5. This growth in cloth making had almost certainly not been steady, nor geographically evenly spread, and analysis of sums paid for the farm of the alnage provides some clues as to the rate and distribution of growth.

Collection of the alnage, in common with that of other royal taxes, was farmed out during the fifteenth century. The alnager in each area paid an annual sum to the Crown and in return enjoyed a share of what he collected. The office came up for renewal from time to time and appears to have been filled by competitive bidding.[190] A bidder would, no doubt, have been guided by what he thought he could recoup. As

[185] SROI R3/26.
[186] PRO E101/343/4.
[187] Bridbury (1982), p. 114.
[188] Amor (2004), p. 417.
[189] Munro (2003), p. 274. Britnell suggests that the annual number of sealings in Suffolk had doubled over this period, and, if one allows for the fact that a broadcloth was slightly longer than two dozens end on end, he may not be far wrong: (1986), p. 188.
[190] In 1445 Henry Kyng was granted the alnage of Norfolk and Norwich for thirty-two pounds, subject to the proviso that he would match any higher offer that might subsequently be made: *CFR 1445–52*, p. 6.

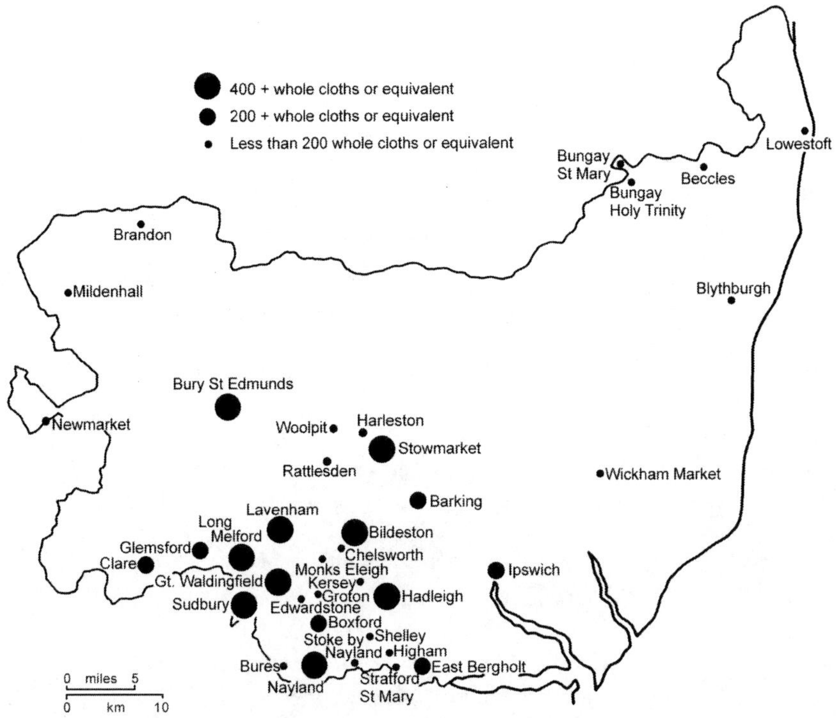

Map 5: *Cloth making in Suffolk 1465/6 to 1468/9*

the amount that the alnager raised was proportionate to the level of cloth making activity in a given area, the value of his bid must have borne some relationship to that activity. Using as a measure the relative value of the bids that were made at different times, it is possible to estimate the rate of growth of the cloth industry. The task is, however, made more difficult in East Anglia by the fact that the alnager's territory did not remain the same. That said, the total farm paid for Essex, Hertford, Norfolk, Norwich and Suffolk increased at the rates set out in Table 19.[191]

If these figures do indeed offer an accurate reflection of the state of the textile industry, they suggest a steady growth in the opening years of the fifteenth century, which appears to have stalled in the last six years of the first quarter, before beginning again in the middle, and finally slowing down in the penultimate decade of the century.[192] This apparent mid-century spurt may, however, have been concentrated in the Hundred of Babergh. For a time, the towns of Lavenham, Great

[191] *CFR 1399–1405*, p. 184; *CFR 1413–22*, p. 432; *CFR 1471–85*, p. 181; *CFR 1485–1509*, p. 201.
[192] Britnell is of the view that 'the Suffolk industry was to revive vigorously in the later decades of the fifteenth century': 'The Woollen Textile Industry of Suffolk' (2003), p. 89.

TABLE 19: INCREASE IN FARM PAID FOR ALNAGE OF ESSEX, HERTFORD, NORFOLK, NORWICH AND SUFFOLK

Period	*Total percentage increase*	*Annual percentage increase (uncompounded)*
Easter 1403 to Easter 1423	5.0	0.25
Easter 1423 to Michaelmas 1479	17.6	0.31
Michaelmas 1479 to Michaelmas 1493	1.7	0.12

Notes
In 1479 the alnage payable for Suffolk was just short of 60 per cent of the total for the entire territory, which means that the fortunes of cloth making in the county clearly had a significant influence on the amount of each bid. From this date Cambridgeshire and Huntingdonshire were also included, but, as the alnage payable for them both was less than 1 per cent of the total, their inclusion has no significant impact on the figures.
Sources: see footnote 191.

and Little Waldingfield, Brent Eleigh and Acton comprised a discrete area for the farming of the alnage, perhaps in itself marking the importance of cloth making there and its value as a source of royal revenue. Between Michaelmas 1425 and Easter 1457 the amount payable for that farm rose by a striking 34.2 per cent, constituting an increase (uncompounded) of 1.08 per cent per annum, more than three times the growth rate in Essex, Hertford, Norfolk, Norwich and Suffolk as a whole.[193] Outside Babergh, the fortunes of the Suffolk cloth towns in the mid-fifteenth century may not have been so rosy. As previously mentioned, the involvement of textile workers, particularly those from Hadleigh, in civil unrest in the late 1440s and again in 1450, hints at malaise within the industry at that time.

Expansion was certainly not driven by Ipswich's clothiers. In 1396/7, the town's share of county production had been between 7 and 10 per cent. In the late 1460s, even counting those non-residents who presented cloth in Ipswich, that share had sunk to less than 2 per cent. Furthermore, the number of broadcloths or their equivalent had fallen from about 227 a year to about 86. In the league table of Suffolk's cloth making towns, Ipswich had slipped to tenth place, and none of its clothiers ranked among the top one hundred in the county.[194] John Mersh was the most active, presenting just forty straits in 1466/7 and thirty broadcloths in 1468/9. Compared with many in Babergh and Cosford, his output was very modest. Elsewhere in Suffolk great clothiers left bequests to teams of spinners, fullers and

[193] *CFR 1422–30*, p. 114; *CFR 1452–61*, p. 174.
[194] Amor (2004), p. 419.

weavers working for them under a putting-out system.[195] No-one in mid-fifteenth-century Ipswich seems to have made any such provision. In some Suffolk towns the proportion of the economically active population involved in the cloth trade was one-third or more, but in Ipswich it was less than one-tenth.

In seventy years cloth making in Ipswich had suffered a serious reverse. Why had this happened? The flight of the textile industry from town to country was a common phenomenon in medieval Europe. It happened in Flanders in the fourteenth century, and in England in the fifteenth century in Coventry, Leicester and Winchester, and in counties as far apart as Kent, Wiltshire, Yorkshire and, of course, Suffolk.[196] Late medieval cloth making was acquiring many of the characteristics of a capitalist business. Investment capital was needed to pay for looms and other equipment, and working capital was essential to fund cash flow until the cloth could ultimately be sold.[197] In Suffolk, as in Yorkshire, there were two main sources of capital, which combined to push cloth production out of towns and into the country. One was the enterprising local people who had grown rich by engrossing and enclosing agricultural land and were looking for ways to invest their money. In Suffolk, the draper Robert Cake of Stowmarket, who successfully combined husbandry and cloth making, provides a good example. Cake was that town's leading clothier, presenting 56 broadcloths and 112 straits, both in Stowmarket and in Bury St Edmunds, in the four years between 1465 and 1469. He was also farming in Thorney, outside Stowmarket, at a time when the land there was being enclosed; and, in his will, he left a virgate of land.[198] Other Suffolk clothiers, operating on a far more modest scale than Cake, still produced the majority of cloths in the county in the 1460s.[199] The second source of capital was to be found in London. As noted above, London merchants provided credit to provincial traders, and increasingly invested directly in the Suffolk cloth trade.[200] Two such were John Stanesby and John Motte. They both based their cloth making in the small town of Bildeston, and were major players by the late 1460s. Stanesby had connections with Italians and employed eleven, who were presumably expert weavers, on his own premises to make cloth. Motte, on the other hand, relied on a team of local outworkers.[201]

[195] Betterton and Dymond (1989), pp. 26–7; Amor (2004), 414–36 (p. 427); Dyer (2005), p. 230.
[196] Lloyd (1977), p. 225; Phythian-Adams (1979) pp. 48-50; Swanson (1989), pp. 142-3, 149; J.N. Hare, 'Growth and Recession in the Fifteenth-Century Economy: The Wiltshire Textile Industry and the Countryside' *Econ. Hist. Rev.*, 2nd ser., 13 (1999), 1–26 (pp. 11–2); Munro (2003), pp. 249–55, 296; Mate *Trade and Developments* (2006), p. 12.
[197] Until 1463 clothiers had reduced their need for working capital by paying workers in 'pins, girdles and other unprofitable merchandise', but such practice was then made unlawful: *Rot. Parl.*, v, p. 502.
[198] Amor (2004), p. 422; Amor (2006), p. 190; SROB R2/11/212.
[199] Amor (2004), pp. 417, 419, 431.
[200] Leading German and Italian mercantile firms made similar investments in the *nouvelles draperies* of rural Flanders: Munro (2003), p. 260.
[201] Motte remembered his outworkers in his will: PCC 11 Wattys (PROB 11/6).

Together they presented 538 broadcloths and 7940 straits in the four years covered by the alnage accounts, and were responsible for about 12.5 per cent of the total county production, which represents considerably more than the total output of Ipswich.[202] While Stanesby had by far the largest individual output in Suffolk, William Forthe (alias Ford) of Hadleigh came second. He was a native of that town and chose to be buried there, but also maintained close links with the London mercers.[203]

London merchants were clearly familiar with Ipswich and knew its leading burgesses well. They were happy to export goods through the port and buy property in the town, but showed no significant interest in making cloth there. As we have seen, the London grocer John Kyng bought property in Ipswich in the 1450s, but when he turned his attentions to the Suffolk textile industry he based his operations in the village of Shelley.[204] There were good reasons for him to do so. Bailey traces the roots of the rural cloth industry to the high population density, emphasis on pastoral farming, secure tenancies of small holdings and underemployed labour force which characterised Suffolk before the Black Death. To make ends meet, free peasants had to acquire skills beyond those of husbandry. These preconditions for industrialisation enabled a rapid growth of textile production to occur afterwards. The clothiers of new boom towns could exploit the pool of expertise that had already developed in earlier urban centres of production, as well as a skilled rural workforce, to make their fortunes.[205] Furthermore, in the fifteenth century, the engrossment and enclosure of the fields in places such as Thorney pushed peasants off the land.[206] Consequently, even in an era of low population, people were looking for employment.

Proficient textile workers were, of course, available in Ipswich as well. There is no evidence that they were subject to the strict regulation of gilds which might have made it difficult for outsiders to use their services. They may, however, have been more expensive. Although there is no record of the wages demanded by textile workers there, in 1468 the carpenters William Sextayn, Simon Bole and John Terry were fined by the leet court for receiving excessively high wages.[207] If by then the town's economy was beginning to grow again, skilled textile workers, as well as carpenters, may have been able to name their own price. Wage costs, however, only constituted a fraction of the cost of cloth production, and thus provide only part of the explanation.[208] As we have seen, the difficult years of the mid-fifteenth century had persuaded the Ipswich authorities to adopt protectionist measures at precisely the wrong time. As the economy began to recover, such measures proved to be a

[202] Amor (2004), pp. 426–7.
[203] Amor (2004), pp. 426–7; Sutton (2005), p. 222.
[204] Amor (2004), p. 427.
[205] Bailey (2007), pp. 297–9
[206] Amor (2006), p. 190.
[207] SROI C/2/10/1/5, m. 4v (west ward); C/2/10/1/6, m. 3v (east ward).
[208] Munro (2003), pp. 217, 259–60.

significant disincentive to non-residents venturing into cloth making. They would be reluctant to pay tolls on the raw materials that they brought into town, and on the cloth that they sold there. Nor would they wish to sell it only on market day at the Moothall, especially if they could operate with little restraint elsewhere in Suffolk.

At least one more reason for Ipswich's woes suggests itself. Historically towns had been able to offer a better type of cloth than the countryside, which guaranteed many of them a share of the quality market. Ipswich may have lost ground in this respect, not only to London, which offered so much more choice to wealthy customers, but, closer to home, to Bury St Edmunds where the cloth industry remained more buoyant. William Recher was a Bury draper, who supplied at least two tailors in Ipswich in the 1440s, namely William Dalton and John Reed. Both were freemen, and Dalton attended meetings of the general court, so presumably he ran a fairly prestigious business.[209] It is difficult to understand why these men would buy cloth from Bury if the same quality was available locally. In conclusion, in the late 1460s, the cloth industry in Ipswich appears to have been squeezed on two sides. Proto-capitalists were funding a rural industry to produce basic quality cloth for wide distribution both at home and abroad, while Bury St Edmunds may have been more successful at catering for the affluent.

Tanners Prevail

As already noted, in the early years of the fifteenth century tanners kept a low profile. Only six appeared before the leet courts in the late 1410s, and the same number in the early 1420s. By the late 1430s there were ten, and in the late 1460s twenty-three. Their fines were as likely to represent licence fees or taxes, similar to those imposed on bakers and brewers, as penalties for shoddy workmanship. If, as seems likely, this reflects an expansion of Ipswich's tanning industry, quite possibly tanners were moving into an industrial vacuum created by the decline of the town's textile industry. Skilled workers who had once found employment making woollen cloth were now tanning leather instead. Tanners appear to have overtaken cordwainers in terms of prosperity and social rank, which suggests that they had taken back control of the lucrative trade in leather. Among cordwainers, apparently only John Lackford became a freeman, and despite his fondness for gaming, he went on to become a member of the town council.[210]

As the town's leading tanner in the first half of the fifteenth century, William Keche's first recorded appearance before the leet court occurred in 1415 and his last in 1438. During this period he incurred more than half of the larger fines of 12d. or more imposed on tanners by the court, and twice paid the unusually high penalty

[209] SROI C/2/3/1/51 (10 Jan. 1443, 2 Jul. 1443); BL, Ms Add. 30,158, ff. 4v, 17v.
[210] BL, Ms Add. 30,158, ff 20v, 29r.

of 3s. 4d. Keche was clearly a freeman and, following his death, his son, also a William, was admitted in 1443.[211] The father was bailiff in 1437/8 and the son in 1453/4.[212] As previously mentioned, William junior was active in overseas trade, being described as a 'merchant alias tanner' in 1463, by which time he was suffering financial embarrassment. By October of the following year he was dead. His executor, John Hyll, was then unsuccessfully defending a petty court claim by one of those creditors, the ubiquitous Gilbert Debenham, for payment of £14 1s. 8d. under a letter of obligation.[213]

Gradually the status of these men was improving, and by the 1460s tanning had become an almost respectable trade. Of the twenty-three tanners active at this time, at least seven were freemen, although only one ever held borough office, William Knatte, who was chamberlain in 1472/3. Such was the demand for leather that three tanners came from out of town, from Combs, Dedham and Rattlesden. Henry Jude of Dedham suffered the largest fine of all, paying five shillings in 1468, a sum indicative of operations on a fairly large scale.[214] Three, perhaps four, others were Dutch. Two of them paid heavy fines too, which could have reflected the scale of their business, or, just as probably, prejudice against their nationality.

If tanners were doing better, the outlook in the mid-fifteenth century was not so bright for tawyers and skinners. We have already seen that the supply of alum, a vital raw material for tawyers, was interrupted by the fall of Constantinople and was not properly restored until the discovery in 1462 of deposits in the papal states of Italy. The tawying of leather no doubt continued in Ipswich, but there is little trace of it in the extant records. With the exception of John Sharp, admitted in 1454, there is no mention of any glovers, who were major users of tawed leather, becoming freemen, nor of a single glover appearing before the petty court or leet court.[215] Skinners were losing work for several reasons. Changes in fashion, particularly the introduction of new sombre fabrics and styles, meant that 'fuller and darker furs of marten and sable' were now preferred to squirrel. But they were suitable for use only as facings, not as linings, and were far beyond the pocket of most people. Furthermore, they were larger skins than squirrel, and therefore required less stitching. Consequently, in York and other provincial cities there was a sharp fall in the number of skinners admitted as freemen.[216] Three skinners were presented to the Ipswich leet court in 1438 for miscellaneous offences, but none had any significant impact on the town's history.[217] John Warde was the only person described

[211] BL, Ms Add. 30,158, f. 8v.
[212] *Annals*, pp. 99, 110.
[213] SROI C/2/10/1/2, m. 1v.
[214] SROI C/2/10/1/6, m. 2v (south ward).
[215] BL, Ms Add. 30,158, f. 17r; SROI C/3/8/5/2.
[216] Veale (2003), pp. 138–41, 148–151; Swanson (1989), pp. 60–2.
[217] SROI C/2/8/1/9 (west ward); C/2/8/1/11 (north ward).

as a skinner to become a freeman between 1440 and 1469. Although he was elected as an assessor of tax in 1453, and attended the general court in 1454, where he was described as worthy, he never achieved higher office within the town.[218] Indeed, skinners appear to have lost the high profile that they had enjoyed in the early years of the century. Even so, furs continued to arrive in Ipswich and to be worn by the town's wealthiest residents. The same ladies who led Ipswich fashion with their fine clothes also wore fur. Margaret Fastolf's gown of murrey was faced with the fur of polecat, while Joan Freborne's gowns of violet cloth and musterdevillers were both lined with winter squirrel. Alice Pipho owned a russet tunic trimmed with fur. Among the men, John Drayll left no fewer than three fur-lined gowns.[219]

The Clash of Arms

Metal working was stimulated by the demand for arms during the wars that plagued the middle years of the fifteenth century. Following the resumption of hostilities with France, burgesses were urged in 1452 to arm themselves with 'jacks, sallets, bowes, arrows, swords, targetts, poleaxes and other weapons of warre'.[220] Later, Sir John Howard, one of the strongest supporters of the Yorkist cause in the civil war, looked to Ipswich in the 1460s for supplies of arms. He paid John Gonner 2s. 6d. for six days' work, in a forge making chambers for guns. He hired the armourers William Boteler and Robyn, the latter of whom worked for twelve days in furbishing his equipment, and paid an unnamed smith twenty pence for 'semewys' and 'koferys' to be used in making bows and arrows. His commercial agent Richard Felawe traded in iron on his behalf, procuring 20 hundred weight for four pounds.[221] Of course, arms that went away to war bright and shiny often came back as scrap metal. When William Boteler fell out with his landlord Thomas Wath, the court seized ten swords worth 20d., fifty-nine pieces of armour with steel caps worth 2s., a shield worth 4d., five dagger blades worth 7d., a throat protector worth 2d. and a pole-axe worth a 1d..[222] Given the low valuation, each of these items must have sustained considerable wear and tear.

The unremitting belligerency of these years provided a golden opportunity for smiths, the arms manufacturers of their day. It is a measure of their importance that one was actually depicted hard at work on the front of Oak House in Northgate Street (Plate 3). John Osberne, was admitted as a freeman in 1458, and later presented his apprentice Robert Lynkolne for admission. He served as chief pledge in

[218] BL, Ms Add. 30,158, ff. 10r, 16v; SROI C/2/10/1/1 mm. 2r, 9r.
[219] SROI R1/135; R2/5; R2/77; C/2/10/1/2, m. 14r–v.
[220] *Annals*, p. 109.
[221] Crawford (1992), I, pp. 219, 225, 226, 260, 309.
[222] SROI C/2/10/1/3, m. 1r.

Plate 3: *Carving of a smith on corner post of Oak House, Northgate Street*

east ward between 1467 and 1475, and was a member of the council by 1470.[223] Henry Basse was admitted as a burgess in 1457 and, such was his success, two of his apprentices followed in his path, namely his kinsman Robert and Edmund Bladsmyth.[224] Even before his admission Henry had proved his worth to the borough, in 1455, by helping to collect funds for its litigation with Bury St Edmunds, and afterwards he eventually became chamberlain in 1466/7.[225] Robert Basse continued the family business. In the more settled years, at the end of the century, he counted barrel hoops among his prosaic, yet essential products, and numbered local coopers among his customers, suing one of them, Thomas Barker, for £1 15s. 6d.[226] He also, no doubt, looked to merchants for his supplies of iron which, in turn, may explain why he was himself sued by Edmund Daundy in 1500 for four pounds.[227] By far the most prominent, however, of these men of iron was Edmund Winter who is first seen supplying ironwork in the 1440s for the town's mills.[228] His later career was built on a quite different metal, namely pewter, which became increasingly popular as the century wore on, and is considered in chapter 8.

There are various references to precious metals in Ipswich's mid-century records. At a time when investment in trade was likely to generate losses, and investment in property rent arrears, there was a strong temptation for the wealthy to hoard their plate.[229] This reinforced a natural desire to use precious metals to broadcast their wealth and entrench their standing in local society, while also creating a portable resource that could be melted down in emergencies.[230] William Grygge accused Margaret Sohorde of breaking into his house in May 1464 and stealing four marks of silver in money, a flat piece of silver plate, three silver spoons, four rings of silver and gilt, and a gold ring.[231] Sixteen of the 108 extant Ipswich wills proved between 1450 and 1469 mention belongings made of gold or silver. Most of these were silver spoons, but the wealthiest residents could do better. Robert Drye owned two covered silver bowls ornamented respectively with vines and an upright eagle. The cover of John Drayll's best silver bowl was topped with two gold crowns.[232] It seems unlikely, however, that the intricate work on these precious objects was undertaken locally. Although several people bear the name goldsmith, within the extant Ipswich records of the period there is not a single reference to anyone practising the craft.

[223] BL, Ms Add. 30,158, ff. 21v, 38r; SROI C/2/10/1/4, m. 1r; C/2/10/1/6, m. 3v (both east ward).
[224] BL, Ms Add. 30,158, ff. 21r, 35r, 38v.
[225] BL, Ms Add. 30,158, f. 18v; *Annals*, p. 126.
[226] SROI C/2/10/3/1, f. 116.
[227] SROI C/2/10/3/5, f. 211.
[228] SROI C/3/3/1/1.
[229] Nightingale (1995), p. 469.
[230] Dyer (2005), p. 141.
[231] SROI C/2/10/1/2, m. 8r.
[232] SROI R1/90; C/2/10/1/1, m. 4v; C/2/10/1/2, m. 14r–v.

The evidence set out in this chapter supports the view that the country and, in particular, Ipswich suffered the effects of a Great Slump in the middle years of the fifteenth century. Exact dating is impossible, but the storm clouds were gathering by the late 1430s and beginning to clear by the late 1460s. Although the surviving evidence does not allow precise statistical assessment, as was the case in many other English towns, Ipswich's economic fortunes probably reached a nadir around 1450. Agricultural depression and bullion shortage combined with civil disorder to make life difficult for most townspeople. In the late 1430s the town's food supply ran so low as to provoke riot. During the recession that followed petty traders were particularly badly hit. The civic authorities responded with protectionist measures which may have provided short-term relief, but had longer term adverse consequences. Merchants from traditional trading partners, such as Hadleigh and the east coast ports, became far less visible. Conversely, as London merchants tightened their grip on the country's cash and credit, their profile within the town, already quite high in the early years of the century, was further enhanced. Fortunes were still to be made and some men, such as John Drayll, died very wealthy with impressive collections of plate. They were, however, in a minority.

By the late 1460s the Ipswich economy was beginning to recover. Notwithstanding some contra-indications, this recovery was particularly evident in the victualling trades. The brewing of ale was becoming concentrated in fewer hands, the divide between brewers and tipplers was growing and, in consequence, specialist alehouses were opening for business. The brewing of hopped beer was still largely an expatriate Dutch preserve, but its consumption was growing in popularity among the locals. More people were keeping inns and providing room and board for a burgeoning flow of visitors. Tanners were flourishing and enjoying higher status within the town's hierarchy. If they had been losing out to the cordwainers and skinners earlier in the century, by the 1460s the economic tide within the leather industry had turned in their favour. Smiths benefited from the enhanced demand for weapons of war.

Nevertheless, all was not well. Set against these positive signs, the decline of the Ipswich cloth industry stands in even starker contrast. Many of the town's leading burgesses presented cloth to the alnager, but they did so in relatively modest amounts. Textile workers commanded very little status in the town, with the exception of a few successful dyers who were admitted as burgesses. Protectionist measures adopted in the depths of recession repelled the capital investment that was becoming increasingly necessary in cloth making. The success of rural entrepreneurs and London proto-capitalists moved the centre of gravity for textiles to the Hundred of Babergh, causing the town's share of county production to shrink dramatically. Even at the top end of the market, Ipswich appears to have been losing out to Bury St Edmunds. In Suffolk the cloth industry was growing ever more important. How would Ipswich seek to make up lost ground in the final years of the fifteenth century?

– 6 –

Calmer Waters

The closing thirty years of the fifteenth century are generally considered to have been propitious for overseas trade. Edward IV pursued a foreign policy that was more sympathetic to merchants, mending fences with the rulers of some of England's most important overseas markets (Appendix 1). The wine trade with Gascony began to recover in the 1480s, while trade with Spain continued to grow, and that with Iceland was formally reopened by a treaty that Henry VII negotiated with the king of Denmark in 1490.[1] Henry also encouraged English shipping with early Navigation Acts, requiring the wine of Gascony and the woad of Toulouse to be imported in English bottoms with English crews, and exports by English merchants to be carried in English vessels if available.[2] Overseas sales of cloth grew steadily from the 1470s.[3] The Merchant Adventurers of London dominated this commerce and 'their trade and wealth was reaching a zenith'.[4] A combination of events, including the discovery of new deposits of silver ore in central Europe and the response of Philip the Good of Burgundy, who was willing to pay a good price for it, drove German bullion north and English cloth south in a way that made Antwerp the focus of Merchant Adventurer activities.[5] Munro has referred to 'the rise of the Antwerp market and the final victory of the English cloth trade'.[6]

It was not, however, all plain sailing. English merchants were almost entirely excluded from the Baltic, not so much by the Hanse as by the decision of the king of Denmark to close the Sound against them.[7] Nor did Henry VII always favour the Merchant Adventurers. He was suspicious of the rulers of the Low Countries, who remained sympathetic to the defeated Yorkist regime and harboured the various

[1] James (1971), pp. 46-50; Barron (2004), p. 62; Childs (1978), pp. 57–8; Webb (1962), p. 71.
[2] *Rot. Parl.*, vi, pp. 407, 437.
[3] Carus-Wilson and Colman (1963), p. 139.
[4] Sutton (2005), p. 318.
[5] Bolton (1980), p. 297; Spufford (2002), p. 361; J.L. Bolton and F.G. Bruscoli, 'When did Antwerp Replace Bruges as the Commercial and Financial Centre of North-Western Europe? The Evidence of the Borromei Ledger for 1438' *Econ. Hist. Rev.*, 2nd ser., 61 (2008), 360–79 (pp. 364–5).
[6] Munro (2003), pp. 292–5.
[7] Lloyd (1991), pp. 284–5.

pretenders who threatened his crown.[8] These suspicions resulted in periodic trade reprisals and embargoes which even the *Intercursus Magnus*, agreed with the duke of Burgundy in 1496, did not bring to a complete end.[9] Furthermore, both the Yorkist kings and Henry VII interfered with trade by imposing bans on the import of many manufactured goods, and on the export of unfinished cloth.[10] This latter measure was particularly irksome to the Merchant Adventurers, who thrived on such trade, but its effectiveness is doubtful. Certainly, in defiance of the prohibition, exports 'continued to flourish'.[11]

Whereas London merchants at this time were generally prospering, the fortunes of provincials were mixed. 'Bristol, Southampton, and some of the other southern ports still enjoyed a decent overseas trade'.[12] East coast ports, such as Hull, Boston and Lynn, were certainly not doing so well.[13] Colchester's overseas enterprise had dwindled to a very low level, and 'only one or two Colchester merchants continued to trade abroad'.[14] How did the port of Ipswich fare?

The sources surviving from the closing years of the fifteenth century are not as rich as those for earlier decades. Two particular accounts are discussed in this chapter, one for a brief period from October 1483 to February 1484, and the other for the whole of the year 1491/2.[15] The latter provides a summary of Ipswich's exports and imports during this year (see Table 20). At certain points in the late fourteenth and fifteenth centuries it has proved possible, with reasonable confidence, to extract from particular accounts those entries that relate to Ipswich, as distinct from the other harbours within its jurisdiction. This cannot be done here, except in the case of wool, which continued to be shipped solely from Ipswich itself. Nevertheless, the evidence contained in these two accounts does allow some tentative conclusions to be drawn about the town's overseas commerce. Furthermore, in conjunction with the contemporary borough records, which are plentiful, we can identify those Ipswich burgesses who were trading abroad, as well as the goods that they were exporting and importing.

The importance of many of these commodities has already been discussed. We now consider the more significant developments in the closing years of the century in the nature of goods freighted, the location of overseas markets to and from which they were carried, the identity of the merchants who bought and sold them, and the design of their ships.

[8] Sutton (2005), p. 317.
[9] Britnell (1997), p. 230; Sutton (2005), pp. 327–34.
[10] *Rot. Parl.*, v, p. 507; v, pp. 621–2; vi, p. 263; vi, p. 403.
[11] Lloyd (1991), pp. 236–7; Sutton (2005), p. 336.
[12] Barron (2004), p. 116. Platt is also very positive about Southampton's trade: (1973), p. 169.
[13] Kowaleski (2000), p. 485; Barron (2004), p. 116.
[14] Britnell (1986), p.176.
[15] PRO E 122/53/1; E 122/53/9.

TABLE 20: EXPORTS FROM AND IMPORTS TO THE HEADPORT OF IPSWICH 1491/2

	Total	*Share of Ipswich merchants (%)*
EXPORTS		
Woollen cloth (561+ broadcloths or equivalent at £2 15s. per cloth)	£1543 8s. 4d.	19.6
Wool (408 sacks or equivalent at £3 5s. a sack)	£1326	0
Dairy products	£422 11s. 8d.	22.2
Grain	£201 10s. 4d.	20.6
Worsted	£75	76
Beer	£24 18s. 4d.	15.4
Hides (tanned calf)	£18 13s .4d.	25
Firewood	£7	0
Other	£169 18s. 4d.	29.1
Total	£3789 0s. 4d.	14.8
IMPORTS		
Mercery and haberdashery	£517 11s. 8d.	8.4
Fish	£401 3s. 4d.	0.8
Salt	£341 10s.	0.9
Dyes, mordants, oils, teasels	£312 10s.	27.2
Iron and ironwork	£165 13s. 4d.	6.2
Wine (£5 a tun)	£107 10s.	76.7
Horticulture	£62 3s. 4d.	0
Wax	£43 1s. 8d.	0
Woodland produce – ashes, bitumen, tar, wainscot	£23 6s. 8d.	0
Furs	£16	0
Stone	£15 3s. 4d.	59.3
Furniture and furnishings	£13 14s. 8d.	14.6
Soap	£4 13s. 8d.	0
Bricks/Tiles	£2	0
Other	£48 6s. 8d.	15.4
Total	£2074 8s. 4d.	11.9

Note

Merchants have been regarded as Ipswich residents if they appear fairly regularly in the borough records without being described as coming from anywhere else.

Source: PRO E 122/53/9.

Exports Old and New

Cloth remained the town's most valuable export. After twenty very lean years, the 1490s witnessed some recovery in local trade (Figure 1). The Treaty of Utrecht in 1474 had ended hostilities with the Hanse, but isolated the merchants of Cologne, once so prominent in Ipswich, who had broken ranks by maintaining good relations with England during the war years. This fact may help to explain why Hanseatic exports from the town fell so sharply and, with odd exceptional years, remained so low. In 1491/2 Hanse merchants exported 209 broadcloths, which still comprised more than one-third of the total, but their 'trade then came to an abrupt halt' and their annual shipments never again approached even a hundred broadcloths.[16] By the same token, denizen exports started to rise from the mid 1490s, and Ipswich merchants shared in this growth. Already by 1491/2 seven of them were exporting cloth, shipping nearly one broadcloth in every five that left the headport. In the middle years of the century, as we have seen, John Gosse was the only recorded Ipswich merchant exporting cloth; and even he shipped just one broadcloth. A quarter of a century later Roger Wentworth dispatched forty, and Thomas Alvard seventeen. In addition, John Cutler exported thirty-eight double worsteds. This type of cloth had not previously figured significantly in the customs accounts of Ipswich, or indeed any other English port.[17] Their relatively low value meant that, for many years, it had not been cost effective to send such coarse lighter textiles abroad.[18] The more peaceful seas of the 1490s reduced transit costs and appear to have made overseas trade in worsteds once again worthwhile.

The export of wool from Ipswich enjoyed something of an Indian summer in the late 1480s and early 1490s, peaking at 2251 sacks in 1495/6, before declining once more.[19] In 1491/2 wool was, after cloth, the town's most important export. The enrolled customs accounts record the shipment of 592 sacks or their equivalent, and the particular accounts very nearly 600. All of them left in a convoy of eight ships on 28 September 1492. To spread the risk of losing cargo, each merchant divided his wool between the various vessels. Christopher Broun used all eight to despatch just over a hundred sacks or their equivalent. The sixteen shippers were denizens and Staplers, but none appears to have been a burgess of Ipswich. Of those whose place of residence can be identified, four came from London, two from Lincolnshire, and possibly one from Norwich.[20] Of the Londoners, Thomas Burgoyne was a prominent mercer, William Welbek a haberdasher, and Richard

[16] Lloyd (1991), p. 278; Carus-Wilson and Coleman (1963), pp. 110–19.

[17] Power and Postan (1933), p. 4.

[18] Munro (2003), pp. 239, 244.

[19] Carus-Wilson and Coleman (1963), pp. 68–74.

[20] *CPR 1476–85*, pp. 24, 84, 243; *CPR 1485–94*, pp. 40, 377, 446; *CPR 1494–1509*, pp. 204, 308, 309, 527; *CCR 1485–1500*, p. 365.

Drakes a fishmonger. Christopher Broun and Thomas Robertson both served as mayor of the merchant staple organisation in Boston. It is, perhaps, surprising that only one London mercer emerges from this account. A hundred years earlier no fewer than six London mercers had been shipping wool from Ipswich (Appendix 2). Indeed, only ten years previously a similar number had been responsible for 43 per cent of the wool and 35 per cent of the fells leaving the town.[21] Perhaps some of the nine named Staplers in the 1491/2 particular account, who cannot be traced in other records, were London mercers, but none of them is mentioned as such in Sutton's history of the Company.[22] Although no Ipswich merchants figure as exporters, they certainly had an interest in the wool trade. For example, in his will of 1499 the merchant Richard Haxwade refers to the wool which was stored in his solar.[23]

Dairy products remained a key export, as they had been in the middle years of the century. Ipswich burgesses enjoyed a substantial share of this trade, shipping nearly a quarter of the total. William Harlewyn laded 100 wey of cheese onto one ship, mastered by John Yolistoke, in October 1491. Its continuing importance to the town's economy is reflected in a measure, introduced by the borough authorities in 1488, requiring all those who bought cheese within the liberties to pay for the privilege of weighing it on the common beam, or to forfeit two pence to customs.[24]

Exports of grain, insignificant in earlier years, were also substantial. Between mid-July and early September 1492 alone, 432 quarters of wheat, worth £108, were despatched. Some grain went to feed the garrison in Calais. More was undoubtedly exported to Holland and Zeeland, whose people were suffering a serious shortage that year and were prepared to pay high prices.[25] The balance perhaps was sold in Iceland where English merchants were now free to trade.[26]

Beer, which had been an import at the beginning of the century, was now being exported, albeit still in relatively small quantities. Troops stationed at Calais were long standing and no doubt grateful customers.[27] English beer was also being carried back to its metaphorical homeland in Holland and Zeeland from Ipswich, and also from Boston, Lynn and Yarmouth.[28] We may assume that it was beginning to develop as a distinctive and attractive local product in its own right. Horticultural products, mostly from Holland and Zeeland, had long figured in customs accounts, but the value of this trade was significantly enhanced by the growth of beer brewing in

[21] Sutton (2005), p. 288.
[22] Anne Sutton has confirmed in personal communication, 4 January 2009, that none of the nine are known to her as mercers.
[23] SROI C/2/10/3/5, ff. 206–7.
[24] *Annals*, p. 157. A pre-existing by-law may have imposed this penalty because Peter Powle was fined ten pence in 1472 for not paying custom on 5 wey of cheese: SROI C/2/8/1/14 (west ward).
[25] Kerling (1954), p. 108.
[26] Power and Postan (1933), p. 175; Webb (1962), p. 71.
[27] Bennett (1996), p. 93.
[28] Kerling (1954), pp. 116–17.

England. Hops were one of the principal ingredients in beer, but were not cultivated in this country to any significant extent until the late sixteenth century.[29] Accordingly, they had to be brought from abroad.[30] The 23½ sacks of hops that arrived in 1491/2 accounted for three-quarters of the total value of imported horticultural products.[31]

Hides were another minor trade although, in contrast with earlier particular accounts, they are now specifically described as being tanned. The significant share of these exports enjoyed by Ipswich merchants underlines the importance of tanning in the town, a subject discussed in more detail elsewhere. Many of the items included under the general heading of 'Other' may reflect a transit trade whereby overseas goods, such as linen and osmond iron, were brought first to England before being transported elsewhere. An example of this, Thomas Harford's ventures to Iceland are discussed later.

Winds of Change

Despite the introduction of import controls, mercery and haberdashery, along with household utensils, remained the most valuable class of goods arriving in Ipswich. English people's appetite for overseas luxuries could not easily be sated. Even so, nearly all these imports comprised different types of linen and cloth, rather than prohibited trinkets and other manufactured goods. As distinct from the middle years of the century, no basins, buckles, candlesticks, clasps, cupboards, ewers, lavers or shears apparently entered Ipswich from abroad in 1491/2. Perhaps government measures were more effective than has sometimes been thought. Although they are not mentioned in the particular account, among the textiles then being shipped into England were exotic 'cloth indies', possibly silk, which the Ipswich chandler William Guybone had in his store in 1498.[32] This was the year that Vasco de Gama first arrived in India, so direct trade routes to the East had not yet been established. Guybone's cloth had probably travelled with spices up the Red Sea, before being carried in Italian bottoms from Alexandria to Southampton or London, and ending its long voyage in his shop.[33]

Fish were the next most valuable import in 1491/2. In the middle years of the century herring had still predominated, but in the 1491/2 particular account less than 3 per cent of the catch was explicitly described as herring, a sign perhaps of its

[29] Bennett (1996), p. 90.

[30] Hops were imported not only into Ipswich, but also into Kent. Between the 1480s and the 1520s the consignment of hops arriving at the Kent ports increased six-fold: Mate, *Trade and Economic Developments* (2006), p. 87.

[31] Since a sack probably contained about 280lbs, imports in 1491/2 amounted to about 6440lbs.

[32] SROI C/2/10/3/5, f. 51.

[33] G. Barraclough (ed.) *The Times Atlas of Word History* (London: Times Books 1979), pp. 146–7; Spufford (2002), pp. 386–7.

declining popularity and the new taste for marine fish.[34] This growing demand encouraged fishermen to exploit the rich grounds of the North Sea around Iceland. Henry Gotkens was one of many who braved the cold weather and rough waters. In September 1487 he returned to Ipswich for the last time and prepared himself for death by making his will:

> I Henry Gotkens desire that Henry Withtenbek have his share of those fish which we carried together from Naudia, just as is written in our charter, and, whatever share he has, then the said Henry shall have of my part 300 fish, just as we agreed in Iceland.[35]

A comparison between Tables 12 and 20 suggests that the quantity of dyes and dyestuffs arriving in Ipswich had also fallen quite dramatically since the 1460s. As we shall see, the domestic market for finished cloth remained sufficiently buoyant to support some successful dyers in Ipswich. Furthermore, cloth merchants clung tenaciously to certain overseas markets, such as Spain, where they could exchange finished cloth for wine, beaver skins and other Iberian products.[36] Although Ipswich was not a major port of call for Spaniards in the closing years of the century, it was not unknown to them.[37] In 1474, for example, Henry Bolle paid customs on the sale of eight quarters of grain to a Spaniard.[38] John Martyn took delivery of six rolls of beaver skins in 1478, allegedly to safeguard on behalf of Thomas Chylde.[39] Ten years later Martyn, by then a vintner, brought a claim against Juan, the master of a Spanish ship which had docked at the town's quay, which suggests a long standing commercial connection.[40] Nevertheless, at a time when most continental demand was for unfinished cloth, the need for dyes and dyestuffs in England was much reduced. Imports into Ipswich may have been further depressed by sales by London grocers to local dyers of dyes and dyestuffs that had been shipped into the capital.

In 1491/2 wine imports into Ipswich were still very modest compared with those of a hundred years before. The leet courts of the 1470s and 1480s fined just six people, including John Martyn, for selling wine at excessive profit, all of them being recorded in the latest extant rolls of 1487 and 1488.[41] As we have seen, the loss of Gascony had seriously disrupted the trade there, while at the same time creating modest opportunities for those dealing in wines from other areas. In 1489, for example, John Hewett and John Hapet contested ownership, in the Ipswich petty

[34] Kowaleski (2006), pp. 243–4.
[35] SROI R3/44.
[36] Childs (1978), p. 83; Barron (2004), p. 114; Britnell *Britain and Ireland* (2004), p. 322.
[37] Childs (1978), p. 179.
[38] BL, Ms Add. 30,158, f. 32r.
[39] SROI C/2/10/1/8, m. 7v.
[40] SROI C/2/10/3/1, f. 127.
[41] SROI C/2/8/1/21, 22 (east ward).

court, of three butts of romeney, a sweet wine which originated in the Ionian islands.[42] Nevertheless, the signs of resurgence were encouraging, and Ipswich merchants were turning their attention once more to the produce of the vineyards of south-west France (Figure 3). As early as September 1481 Thomas Caldwell and John Martyn, with others, had chartered from Lord John Howard *The Barbara* which set sail to Bordeaux, presumably to bring back wine.[43] Later, in 1488, Thomas Oake made his will before setting out, with some trepidation, on a voyage to the same destination, leaving instructions that he should be buried 'where God disposes for me that I die'.[44] In September 1491 Hewett and Martyn were quarrelling over unspecified chattels worth twenty-five pounds which, bearing in mind their common interest in the trade, may well have been wine.[45] The 1491/2 particular account records that the same John Hewett imported sixteen tons of Gascon wine. As this commercial recovery progressed, Bretons won a significant share of the carrying trade. In 1495 two of them, Gronundus Guyseney and Arnold Gylham, were embroiled in litigation in the Ipswich petty court over three consignments of Gascon wine, two of which were described as red and claret.[46] Five years later Guyseney was being sued by the executors of Roger Wentworth for more than thirty-five pounds.[47] It was this Breton dominance that Henry VII had set out to challenge in his Navigation Act of 1489.[48]

The next generation of Ipswich merchants, such as Henry Tooley, would not only prosper from the wine trade, but also rebuild the extensive inland networks that, as we have already seen, had been so important in the early fifteenth century, but had been largely destroyed by later troubles. Tooley would sell wine in Chelmsford, Bury St Edmunds and Thetford.[49] The revival of the wine trade was not solely a matter of commercial profit, it evidently had a more romantic side. In 1509 we hear of Elizabeth, daughter of Robert Buxton late of Ipswich, living as the wife of Helyot Sorby, merchant of Bordeaux.[50]

Ipswich Merchants Win Back Markets

In any consideration of the fortunes of those late fifteenth-century merchants who shipped their goods in and out of Ipswich, the most remarkable feature is surely the success of local men. Bearing in mind that the town was just one of four harbours

[42] SROI C2/10/3/1, f. 198; Crawford (1977), p. 25.
[43] Crawford (1992), II, p. 112.
[44] SROI R3/89.
[45] SROI C2/10/3/1, f. 298.
[46] James (1971), p. 46; SROI C2/10/3/3, ff. 72, 73, 79.
[47] SROI C2/10/3/5, f. 205.
[48] *Rot. Parl.*, vi, p. 437.
[49] Webb (1962), p. 99.
[50] *CCR 1485–1500*, p. 254.

within the headport, we can see that Table 20 sheds a very positive light upon their activities. Ipswich burgesses enjoyed a significant share of the export trade in cloth, including worsteds, as well as dairy products, grain and hides. They almost monopolised the import of wine and held their own in the import trade of dyes and dyestuffs. The total value of their exports and imports was divided in the proportions shown in Table 21. Given their miserable performance in the 1460s, they had clearly recovered an enormous amount of ground.

TABLE 21: IPSWICH MERCHANTS' EXPORTS AND IMPORTS 1491/2

	Percentage in value of all exports/imports made by Ipswich merchants
EXPORTS	
Woollen cloth	54
Dairy products	16.7
Grain	7.4
Worsted	10.1
Hides (tanned calf)	0.8
IMPORTS	
Mercery and haberdashery	17.8
Dyes, mordants, oils, teasels	34.8
Wine	33.8

(*Source*: PRO E 122/53/9)

A hundred years before, three dozen Ipswich residents appear in the extant records as participants in overseas trade, but by the mid-fifteenth century their number had dwindled to a mere six. The two late fifteenth-century particular accounts record the names of thirteen, but we know of others, such as Edmund Daundy and Thomas Waltrot, who were similarly engaged at this time. Some, including Thomas Drayll who exported lead, are mentioned just once. For others, there is evidence of much more extensive trading interests. Thus, for example, William Harlewyn, John Hewett and Roger Wentworth each exported and imported goods whose aggregate value in 1491/2 alone exceeded £125, putting them on par with all but the greatest of the Ipswich merchants of the late fourteenth century. They had diverse interests. Harlewyn imported a wide variety of goods, including linen and stone, but limited his exports to dairy products. On 1 April 1492 Hewett took delivery not only of wine, but of woad valued at sixty-six pounds from a ship which Thomas Decham had sailed from south-west France. As well as the forty broadcloths, Roger

Wentworth exported fifty-four quarters of grain in early September 1492. He is described in the petty court records as a 'gentleman', was admitted as a foreign burgess in 1482, served as a collector of customs and MP for Ipswich, and was a cousin of the Howards.[51] On a slightly more modest scale, Thomas Alvard exported cloth, dairy products grain and hides, while his imports included glass, salt and wine, valued in total at nearly eighty pounds.

By the closing years of the century some twenty-seven Ipswich residents were described as merchants in the Ipswich petty court proceedings (Table 26). The median value of their disputes was higher than was the case for any other category of occupation. They were also prominent in borough affairs, holding the office of bailiff between them eighteen times in the final twenty years of the century. Of course, not all the leading figures in the town were merchants, some were lawyers and others pewterers. Nevertheless, merchants were once again in the ascendancy. What were the reasons for this turn of fortune?

The Ipswich economy at the close of the century was more buoyant than it had been in the middle years. Leading merchants still maintained their own private quays. In 1500 Richard Haxwade's widow Agnes disposed of his half interest in one called 'Berthlotiscay' in the parish of St Mary Quay.[52] Furthermore, the borough authorities became more proactive. They appointed a master porter with subordinates to take responsibility for the port facilities.[53] They invested in the repair of the dilapidated town quay, in the building of a new crane and in work on the common house.[54] Although it is impossible to quantify the amount, the records suggest that their outlay was significant. In 1476 the portmen and burgesses contributed cash and carts of broom wood towards the repair of the quay, and the then chamberlain John Baldwyn was authorised to spend money received from admissions to the freedom of the borough on the repair of the quay and crane.[55] Contributions for the common quay were collected from impositions on both the parishes and individuals. Several burgesses, such as Thomas Medewe in 1472 and John Trotte in 1476, were excused from holding office in return for their contribution.[56] In 1509 Edmund Daundy bought a similar exemption, from holding office as bailiff for six years, in return for a payment of thirty-three pounds and a consignment of brick and lime so that 20,000 bricks could be laid upon the common quay.[57] These facilities may have been improved in response to a growing demand, or alternatively in the hope of stimu-

[51] BL, Ms Add. 30,158, f. 38v; SROI C2/10/3/1, f. 35; C2/10/3/2, f. 99; Wedgewood and Holt (1938), p. 540.
[52] SROI C/2/10/3/5, ff. 207–8.
[53] BL, Ms Add. 30,158, ff. 30v, 32v.
[54] *Annals*, pp. 132, 133, 139, 141–4.
[55] *Annals*, p. 139; BL, Ms Add. 30,158, ff. 33v–34r.
[56] BL, Ms Add. 30,158, ff. 30v, 33v.
[57] *Annals*, p. 181.

lating recovery, at the behest of influential merchants who were happy to see public money spent in this way. It is not easy to disentangle cause and effect. Whatever the reason, as we have seen, they were well used.

Other factors encouraged Ipswich merchants to turn again to overseas trade. The exodus of Hanseatic merchants from the town from the mid 1470s, the declining share of trade in the hands of other aliens, and the increasing tendency of Londoners to concentrate their trade in and out of the capital, created space into which local men could step. Hanseatic and alien merchants had a much reduced share of exports and imports (Table 22). Hanseatic interest was now limited almost entirely to the export of cloth and the import of linen. The volume of alien trade, albeit more diverse, was far smaller. In the middle years of the century aliens had commanded the lion's share of fish imports, but by the close even this had shrunk to less than a quarter. Consequently, in their own town Ipswich merchants no longer had to fight for space for their cargoes, at the quayside and in the holds of ships, with rivals who had greater financial clout and better contacts.

TABLE 22: HANSEATIC AND ALIEN MERCHANTS' SHARE OF TOTAL IPSWICH HEADPORT TRADE 1491/2

	Exports (percentage)	*Imports (percentage)*
Hanseatic	15.2	32.9
Alien	3.7	10.4

(*Source:* PRO E 122/53/9)

The fragmentary 1483/4 particular account contains no reference to the importation of goods by any Ipswich merchants. Even in 1491/2 the value of their imports was little more than half that of exports, suggesting perhaps that they were still losing out in the battle to find merchandise to bring home. Nevertheless, they were beginning to flex their muscles abroad, as exemplified by the case of local hero Robert Cocoke. The Merchant Adventurers were seeking to exclude provincial members and keep them out of the Low Countries by charging an extortionate fee of ten pounds, which later doubled. In 1488 Cocoke was arrested at the Easter market in Bergen op Zoom by the treasurer of the Merchant Adventurers for refusing to pay this fee, causing a great furore and an outcry against their 'uncharitable and inordinate greed'. Ultimately, provincial merchants petitioned Parliament, which enacted that they should enjoy continuous free trade in the Low Countries and at its four great fairs in return for payment to the Merchant Adventurers of a membership fee of just ten marks.[58]

[58] Kerling (1954), pp. 155, 158; Webb (1962), p. 57; *Rot. Parl.*, vi, p. 513.

Although the Low Countries were by far the most important market for English merchants, there were others which Ipswich traders could now exploit with less competition from their own countrymen. At the end of April 1492, for instance, John Boldon set sail, accompanied by three other ships similarly laden, for an undisclosed destination. He was carrying, on behalf of Thomas Harford, a mixed cargo that included cloth, caps and honey, as well as goods that one would normally expect to see arriving, rather than leaving Ipswich, such as linen and osmond iron. More than four months passed before Boldon returned, in late August, with twelve last of dried fish and ten 'wad' of wadmole for Harford. This looks suspiciously like a round trip to Iceland.[59] The Icelandic people needed linen and iron and, lacking their own sophisticated textile industry, were ready customers for the cloth that was finished in Ipswich.[60] As Henry Gotkens' will illustrates, the Icelandic seas were a rich source of fish. The Icelanders also supplied the coarse woollen fabric known as wadmole.[61] Such products formed the basis of a mutually beneficial exchange. Thomas Waltrot was another who set out to make his fortune in Iceland, but did so in a less reputable manner. He agreed with Philip Balle, a London haberdasher, to travel with and supervise the latter's apprentice, John Tournar, as they both sailed north with Balle's goods aboard the *James of Ipswich*. It was, however, later alleged that, on arrival, rather than representing Balle's interests, Waltrott was guilty of maladministration by selling these goods on his own behalf.[62] The Icelandic trade continued to flourish in the hands of the next generation of Ipswich merchants, among them Henry Tooley.[63]

More peaceful conditions in western Europe at the close of the fifteenth century reduced the risk inherent in overseas trade. As we have seen, even Staplers continued to divide their wool among the various ships in a convoy, but they did so in the reasonable expectation that it would all reach Calais. For those Ipswich merchants who were far less able to absorb the loss of a valuable cargo to pirates or hostile navies, the seas were more inviting than they had been for many years.

New Designs of Ships

The peace dividend was also reflected in ship design. As the century closed, vessels became smaller once more, with Andrea Satler of Bruges commenting in 1478 that small ships had quite driven out the large.[64] In 1544 Ipswich shipping comprised

[59] Bolton notes that a mid-sixteenth-century expedition from Dunwich to Iceland took four months: (1980), p. 276.
[60] Power and Postan (1933), p. 175.
[61] Webb (1962), p. 83.
[62] PRO C 1/115/16; Webb (1962), p. 84.
[63] Webb (1962), pp. 71–88.
[64] Childs (1978), p. 160.

just one vessel of 150 tons or above, one of between 100 and 149 tons, five of between 40 and 99 tons and three of fewer than 40 tons.[65] As we have seen, an analysis of the recorded sizes of cargo carried by ships laden only with cloth shows that, between 1459 and 1466, the mean was just over sixty broadcloths or the equivalent, whereas in 1491/2 only one of the four vessels carried more than thirty. The petty court records from the closing years of the fifteenth century provide evaluations of certain vessels, and paint a similar picture of a harbour frequented by smaller craft. In 1488, for example, Robert Lye and William Dowe contested ownership of *The Christopher Dowe,* which was valued, with full rigging, at £25 10s.; and in 1498 Thomas Waltrot and Robert Brussele quarrelled over *The John of Ipswich* which, again with full rigging, was worth twenty-four pounds.[66] Several even less valuable craft also appear in these records. By way of comparison, at about the same time the Staplers Richard and George Cely bought in Brittany, for twenty-eight pounds, the *Margaret Cely*, which later sailed with a master, boatswain, cook and crew of sixteen hands.[67] These modest sums make it unlikely that any of the ships was particularly large.

The evolution of ship design during the fifteenth century and the need to build vessels which could survive the hostile waters of the North Sea led to 'a striking advance' in English shipbuilding.[68] Perhaps the most significant improvement was the 'skeleton built' carvel, in which each plank was separately fastened, edge to edge, to the ribs in turn, making the hull stronger and the deck watertight.[69] In 1481 Thomas Coke was commissioned by the king to take forty mariners to fight the Scots in *The Kervell of Ipswich.*[70] The carvel proved to be the flagship in the recovery of the English carrying trade, making a major contribution to the substantial increase, from the 1460s, in English sailings in and out of Ipswich and other east coast ports.[71]

The rude health of shipbuilding in Ipswich is reflected in references to ships 'of Ipswich'; the presence of ropers, such as those who were supplying Lord John Howard with rope and other rigging in the early 1480s; and the prosperity of shipwrights, such as Robert Peteman, who bequeathed nine silver spoons to his wife in 1488.[72]

In the context of generally gloomy surveys of English economic fortunes in the closing years of the fifteenth century, growth depended on lasting success in export markets.[73] The overseas trade of Ipswich had been buoyed up during the 1460s by

[65] Scammell (1961), p. 332.
[66] SROI C/2/10/3/1, f. 107 (a rare extant maritime court case); C/2/10/3/5, f. 117.
[67] Henry Elliott Malden (ed.) *The Cely Papers* (London: Longmans, Green and Co., 1900), pp. 176, 186.
[68] Power and Postan (1933), p. 159.
[69] C. Dyer (2002), p. 328; Meier (2006), p. 42.
[70] *CPR 1476–85*, p. 240; Crawford (1992), II, p 3.
[71] Kerling (1954), pp. 196–7; Scammell (1961), pp. 335–6.
[72] Malden (1900), p. xxxvi; Crawford (1992), II, pp. 66, 296; SROI R3/65.
[73] Britnell (1997), p. 238; (2004), pp. 321–2.

the presence of Hanseatic merchants, particularly those of Cologne. Their departure must have been a serious blow, undoubtedly compounded by the increasing dominance of key markets by the Merchant Adventurers of London. Almost certainly, the overall volume of the town's overseas trade in the 1490s was less than it had been in the 1460s. Exports of cloth were beginning to recover, but remained significantly below what they had been. The wool trade fluctuated, but the downward trend continued relentlessly. The preference for shipping cloth abroad in an unfinished state meant that imports of dyes and dyestuffs were depressed. The recovery of the French wine trade had only just begun in earnest and still remained well below its mid-century peak.

Nevertheless, in contrast to their peers in nearby Colchester, the leading burgesses of Ipswich appear to have responded to these challenges in a positive manner. They invested quite heavily in improving their port facilities. Moreover, Ipswich merchants returned to overseas trade in substantial numbers. In the 1490s this local recovery was largely export led, chiefly because they found it easier to source, buy and send domestic goods abroad, than to bring foreign goods home. What few sources survive suggest that their import trade was modest. Yet this situation was changing. The revival of the wine trade with Gascony presented new opportunities for those, such as Thomas Oake, who had sufficient nerve. Iceland also offered the prospect of mutually beneficial commerce to others, such as Thomas Harford, who were willing to risk their fortunes in the cold rough seas of the far north. Robert Cocoke left his mark on history, as a standard bearer of provincial merchants, by challenging, ultimately successfully, the Merchant Adventurers in the Low Countries. For each of them it was a matter of 'who dares, wins'.

The next chapter will examine the town's domestic trade and industry at this time. The rich borough archives allow a detailed analysis of how successful local merchants, tradesmen and craftsmen were in helping to boost Ipswich's economy after the difficult years of the mid-fifteenth century.

– 7 –

Recovery Begins

If the overseas trade of Ipswich gave some grounds for optimism in the closing years of the fifteenth century, how fared the home front? The mid-century slump in trade and industry and its impact on the town have already been considered. By the 1470s there were reasons to hope for recovery. In this decade Edward IV gradually restored the authority and finances of the Crown, and in the next Henry VII ushered in the Tudor Age and finally brought to an end the civil unrest that had plagued the country for so long. Political stability was not, however, in itself, sufficient to trigger economic growth. Manufacturers and tradesmen needed confidence that they could cover their costs and sell their products at a profit. In times of wage inflation, price deflation and population decline this is very difficult. The exploitation of new silver deposits in the Alps and in the Erzgebirge from the 1480s began to ease Europe's bullion famine.[1] This remedy was, however, slow working. The statistics suggest that, in the closing years of the fifteenth century, prices of both agricultural produce and manufactured goods generally remained depressed, while wages remained high.[2] An increase in the price of some grains and legumes in the 1480s was due more to a series of bad harvests than to long-term recovery.[3] Britnell is circumspect in his nationwide search for signs of economic growth, identifying 'only patchy and localised development'.[4] His pessimism is echoed by Hatcher who argues that 'the recovery in most regions remained patchy and partial, constituting more of a bounce back from extreme depression than the commencement of a strong upward trend'.[5]

Population trends at this time have been the subject of much historical debate. The growing consensus is that, before the end of the fifteenth century, even if England's population was no longer falling, it was almost certainly not yet increasing.[6] Hinde considers that 'England's population was, at best, stagnant during

[1] Spufford (2002), p. 361.
[2] Hatcher and Barker (1974), p. 276; Farmer (1991), pp. 523–4.
[3] Hatcher (1996), p. 271.
[4] Britnell (1997), pp. 236–8, 241.
[5] Hatcher (1996), p. 271.
[6] Britnell (1997), pp. 242–7.

the whole of the fifteenth century'.[7] Hatcher, Piper and Stone suggest that, in some places, the population may even have continued to fall.[8] Although Bailey generally shares this sombre assessment, he acknowledges that there may have been 'significant regional ... variations in demographic experience'.[9]

In the light of this discouraging national picture, we will now consider the fortunes of Ipswich in the closing years of the century and ask, if there was any upturn, why it happened, and who may have benefited. The prosperity of any town depended, to a large extent, on securing a share of the export growth that the country as a whole enjoyed, which, as we have seen, Ipswich appears to have done. The nature and vitality of its hinterland, and the ability of its residents to develop niche industries, were also important factors.[10] Since it now ranked as 'the most industrialised and urbanised' county in England, Suffolk appeared particularly vibrant at this time.[11] Britnell is cautious about the geographical extent and continuing success of the region's cloth industry.[12] Nevertheless, as noted in the introductory chapter, it has been generally assumed that Ipswich enjoyed the benefits of this economic buoyancy. Certainly, there is some reason to believe that it bucked the trend by experiencing population growth in the final quarter of the fifteenth century, partly due to the influx of refugees from the Low Countries. Whether or not this was indicative of genuine economic recovery will now be considered, first by looking at the extant sources, and then at substantive issues relating to the town's trading hinterland and networks, victualling trades and various other industries, particularly cloth, leather and metals.

As with the earlier chapters on domestic trade and industry, the principal sources used in the following pages are the records of the leet and petty courts, which are particularly rich for the closing years of the century. Although the series is not quite continuous, and there are no rolls for the 1490s, more leet court rolls survive from the 1470s and 1480s than for all preceding decades.[13] An isolated and incomplete set of petty court rolls is extant for the year 1478/9.[14] Composite court books have been consulted for the entire period from 1486 to 1500, and contain both petty court and general court records.[15] The petty court rolls provide inter-

[7] A. Hinde, *England's Population: A History since the Domesday Survey* (London: Hodder Arnold, 2003), p. 64.

[8] Hatcher (1977), p. 63; J. Hatcher, A.J. Piper and D. Stone, 'Monastic Mortality: Durham Priory, 1395–1529' *Econ. Hist. Rev.*, 2nd ser., 59 (2006), 667–687 (pp. 683–5).

[9] Bailey (1996), pp. 1, 18.

[10] Kermode (2000), p. 449; see also A. Dyer 'Urban Decline' (2000), p. 282.

[11] Bailey (2007), p. 8.

[12] Britnell (1986), pp. 190, 192. He is, however, more bullish in 'Woollen Textile Industry of Suffolk' (2003), p. 89.

[13] SROI C/2/8/1/13–22; C/2/10/1/7, mm. 4r–5v

[14] SROI C/2/10/1/7, 8.

[15] SROI C/2/10/3/1–5; Allen (2000), pp. 159–60, 188–190.

esting details of a limited number of cases. Conversely, the composite court books, running to nearly nine hundred folios by 1500, provide limited details of a large number of cases. Bearing 'all the characteristics of rough minute books', they list, with hardly any duplication, all the petty court cases that were heard in the borough.[16] While occasionally noting what the dispute was about or how it was concluded, their main value to the historian is in identifying the origins and occupations of a substantial number of litigants, and the amounts in contention. Sometimes this information alone provides clues as to the nature of the dispute. It has been used to create Tables 23, 25 and 26 which replicate similar Tables in chapters 4 and 6. Together, they allow a comparison between trade and industry in the opening, middle and closing years of the century.

Although its jurisdiction was curtailed, the general court continued to meet a few times each year. The extant register of its proceedings, including in particular admissions to the freedom of the borough, continues until 1483. Thereafter, with a short break, the record resumes in the composite court books. The entries recording these admissions sometimes state the occupation of the new freeman, but, even where they do not, many of the names can be cross-checked against the occupational descriptions in the petty court records. In this way, the information in the 'admissions' column of Tables 25 and 26 has been collected. Other sources for this period include wills, the assessment of aliens for the tax of 1483, and a variety of Chancery records.[17]

Broader Horizons

One measure of Ipswich's economic health and well being is the strength of its trading links with other towns and villages. In the mid-fifteenth century there is evidence that these links had been weakened by economic contraction and restrictive practices. In the closing years they were being restored, as two lawsuits illustrate. When John Depyng of Ipswich died in Calais in 1471, Alice, his widow and executrix, set about recovering what was owed to him. Seven years later she was still trying to extract payment for a consignment of wood ashes from John Berforth, who defended the claim on the grounds that he had previously settled Depyng's debts in Brandon Ferry, Peterborough and Stamford.[18] At the same time, another Alice, widow and executrix of John Gairstang, grocer of Ipswich, was facing the even more demanding task of collecting money due to him for 'grocerewares' and 'hustilments'. His debtors came from far and wide; Bury St Edmunds, Bishop's Lynn, Walsingham, Colchester, Needham Market, Brandon Ferry, Reedham,

[16] Allen (2000), p. 188.
[17] PRO E 179/180/111.
[18] SROI R2/258; C/2/10/1/7, m. 6v.

TABLE 23: ORIGINS OF NON-RESIDENT LITIGANTS IN THE PETTY COURT OF IPSWICH 1486–1500

Origin	*No. of litigants (all cases)*	*Percentage of litigants*	*Number of debt cases*	*Percentage of debt cases*	*Claimant less Defendant*	*Median value of claim*
< 6 miles	65	25.3	68	34.3	-26	£1 19s. 6d.
Hadleigh	6	2.3	5	2.5	-3	£3
Needham Market	10	3.9	5	2.5	1	£10
Woodbridge	11	4.3	8	4.0	2	£7 6s. 8d.
Other 6–10 miles	42	16.3	38	19.2	-16	£2 15s.
10–20 miles	42	16.3	21	10.6	2	£3 11s. 8d.
Bury St Edmunds	8	3.1	4	2.0	2	£6 10s.
London	25	9.7	15	7.6	7	£4 13s. 6½d.
East coast ports	7	2.7	6	3.0	-4	£6 13s.
Other > 20 miles	23	8.9	14	7.1	6	£4 16s. 8d.
Overseas	16	6.2	13	6.6	-13	16s.
Unidentifiable	2	0.8	1	0.5	-1	i.d.
	257	99.8	198	99.9		

Notes
Table 23 draws on the records of those petty court cases which mention litigants' parish of origin, and shows where they came from in Suffolk and North Essex (*Sources*: SROI C/2/10/3/1–5).
Only those litigants to whom a place of origin is specifically ascribed in the record are included in this table. In twenty-five cases both litigants were non-resident. In three cases there were two joint claimants who travelled different distances to Ipswich. In each of these cases both litigants/claimants have been counted under the heading of 'number of debt cases'.

Norwich, Ely, London, Kidderminster, Tower Street (presumably in London), Brandonbury in Devon (this may be a mis-translation), and Faversham in Kent.[19] These cases are indicative of a wider trend. Table 23 shows the origins of litigants in Ipswich's petty court in the final thirteen years of the century. It enables us to draw some tentative conclusions about the nature of Ipswich's trading links with, and the fortunes of, its neighbours, particularly when compared with the similar Table 8 for the opening years of the fifteenth century.

In some essential respects Tables 8 and 23 tell similar tales. The majority of cases involved litigants from close by, one-third from Ipswich's immediate environs, fewer than 6 miles away, and two-thirds from no more than 20 miles away. The places of origin of those living in Suffolk and north Essex are shown in Map 6. The median value of cases still generally rises with the distance travelled by litigants. Nevertheless, there are significant differences between the two tables, which

[19] *CCR 1476–85*, p. 126.

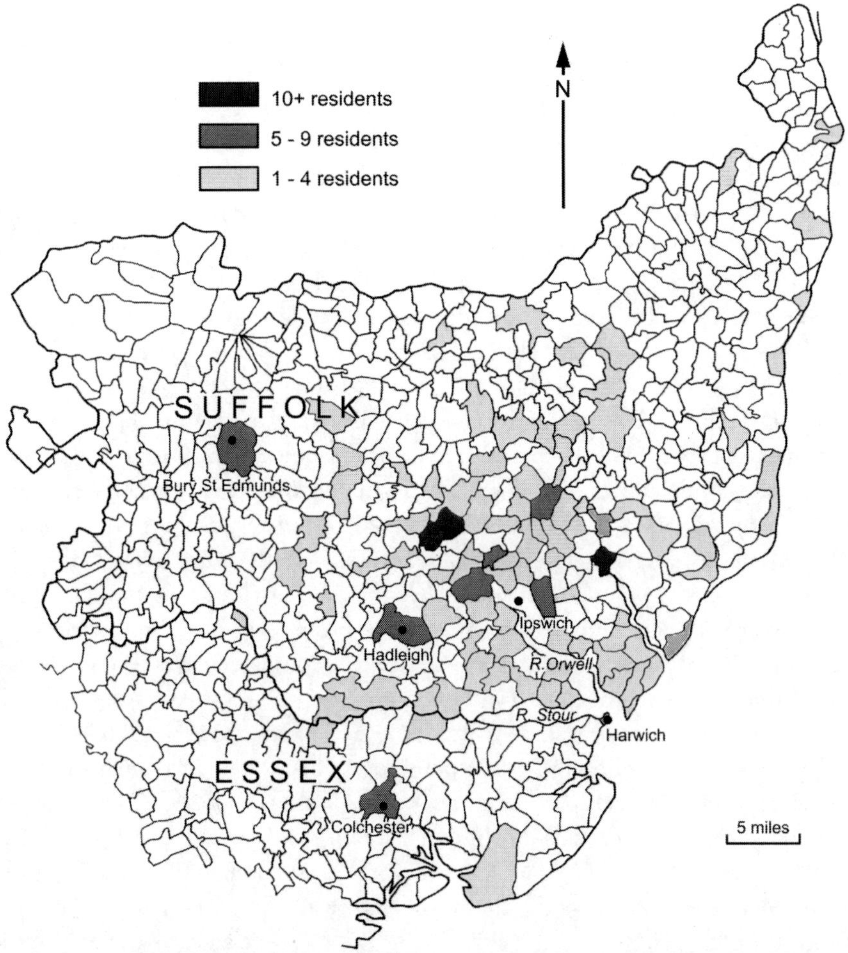

Map 6: *Residents of Suffolk and North Essex parished appearing before the Ipswich petty court 1486–1500*

illustrate changes in the nature of the town's trading network during the course of the fifteenth century. In the period 1400 to 1415 those litigants who had travelled the least distance tended to be claimants rather than defendants, suggesting perhaps that more of them were sellers of goods and services than buyers. In the period 1486 to 1500 they tended to be defendants and the median value of the cases in which they were involved had increased more than four-fold. Perhaps many of those now coming to the town were looking to buy manufactured goods, while the number of people supplying Ipswich with basic foodstuffs had fallen, and those who remained suppliers were dealing on a grander scale.

The fifteenth century witnessed the rise of 'active, dirty boot farmers', who stepped into the cleaner shoes of the often absentee lords of the manor who had governed Suffolk before the Black Death.[20] Gentlemen and yeomen, such as the Kebbyl family in Thorney, expanded their holdings by leasing demesne land, and by engrossment and enclosure, which often forced their more lowly neighbours into wage labour or off the land altogether.[21] This concentration of agricultural activity in fewer hands resulted in fewer, but higher value, transactions in grain and pastoral products.[22] Several petty court cases concern the unlawful detention of sizeable quantities of grain, almost exclusively wheat and barley. In 1486, for example, Thomas Benyt and William Gardyn disputed ownership of sixty quarters of wheat, and five years later James Patynmaker and Alan Cowpere quarreled over ten quarters of barley.[23] The high value of debt cases involving bakers, considered below, may be another sign of the same trend in favour of larger scale suppliers and consignments of grain. What happened in grain production was mirrored in the rearing of livestock, with affluent butcher graziers beginning to dominate the market.[24] John Bayly, a butcher of Colchester, was suing in 1486 for recovery of a five-pound debt.[25] Among the ten litigants from Needham Market were the butchers Matthew and Thomas Wode, of whom Matthew was defending a claim for ten pounds in 1491.[26]

Larger scale agriculturalists were using the profits they made from the sale of grain and meat to buy, in ever greater numbers, the consumer goods that were manufactured in Ipswich or flowed into the port from the Low Countries. Thomas Brantham, a yeomen of nearby Witnesham, was being pursued in 1486 for a debt of ten pounds by Nicholas Winter, a pewterer. William Walle, a yeoman of Otley, was indebted to another Ipswich pewterer, Giles Lackford, for 10s. 8d. in 1489 and a remarkable twenty pounds in 1492.[27] This 'consumer revolution' extended even further down the social ladder.[28] In 1487 the husbandman Thomas Tevell of Holbrook owed Simon Penell, a clothier of Harkstead, the not insubstantial sum of four pounds.[29] The evidence suggests that Ipswich's balance of trade with its immediate neighbours may well have shifted during the fifteenth century, so as to make the town a net supplier of goods and services, rather than a net receiver.

In the opening years of the century, Hadleigh had been the town's most important trading partner. Its residents were litigants in 9 per cent of all cases

[20] Bailey (2007), p. 210.
[21] Amor (2006), pp. 185–6, 194.
[22] Mate, *Trade and Economic Developments* (2006), p. 27.
[23] SROI C/2/10/3/1, ff. 5, 268.
[24] Swanson (1989), p. 170.
[25] SROI C/2/10/3/1, f. 5.
[26] SROI C/2/10/3/1, f. 269.
[27] SROI C/2/10/3/1, ff. 19, 166; C/2/10/3/2, f. 66.
[28] Britnell (1996), p. 194; Kowaleski (2006), pp. 239–41.
[29] SROI C/2/10/3/1, f. 79.

recorded in Table 8, and the value of those cases was significantly higher than that of lawsuits involving men and women from other nearby towns. This partnership rested on the cloth trade in which the two towns had a common interest. By the 1490s, however, Hadleigh had lost its pre-eminence and had been eclipsed by Woodbridge. Not all contact ceased. In 1500, for example, the Hadleigh clothier Simon Babyngton was suing the Ipswich merchant William Barbour for five pounds.[30] Such claims were, nevertheless, becoming unusual. Possibly Hadleigh's cloth industry was no longer the power it had been in 1400, although in the late 1460s the town still ranked as the second largest producer of cloth in the county. A more likely explanation for this decline in trade is that Hadleigh's clothiers were turning increasingly to Colchester and London for buyers.[31] In 1487 William Remyngtone, citizen and alderman of London, settled his differences with John Belcham, merchant of Hadleigh, in the Ipswich petty court.[32] Twelve years later the court ordered the seizure of two pokes of madder from John Thorp of Hadleigh in satisfaction of a debt due to Thomas Baldry, a prominent mercer of London.[33] Several of Hadleigh's leading clothiers, such as William and Robert Forthe, had strong connections with the capital.[34] Hadleigh was not the only Suffolk cloth town looking beyond Ipswich for custom. Indeed, excluding those from Bury St Edmunds, only six litigants appeared before the petty court from the eight other leading cloth towns: that is Lavenham, Bildeston, Melford, Nayland, Sudbury, the Waldingfields, Stowmarket and Boxford.[35] None of the six was described as a clothier or textile worker. If the cloth of these towns ever came near Ipswich, it was probably only as it was carried down the River Gipping for transshipment to London.[36]

Although there had been a small but distinct 'Woodbridge market' in Ipswich in 1345, by 1446–7 the rent from that market had fallen from £1 15s. to 10s.[37] No-one from Woodbridge appears in the early fifteenth-century petty court rolls from which Table 8 was compiled. Yet, by the end of the century, it had become Ipswich's single most important local trading partner, with eleven of its residents appearing as litigants, several engaged in high value transactions. The closeness of the tie between the two towns is underlined by the fact that five of the recorded nineteen foreign burgesses of Ipswich in the period after 1440 came from Woodbridge.[38] Bailey cites Woodbridge as a success story, since it was able to increase 'its wealth and importance in the later Middle Ages … [through] the bur-

[30] SROI C/2/10/3/5, f. 227.
[31] Amor (2004), p. 427.
[32] SROI C/2/10/3/1, f. 54.
[33] SROI C/2/10/3/5, f. 147.
[34] Sutton (2005), p. 222.
[35] Amor (2004), p. 419.
[36] Amor (2006), p. 190.
[37] *Annals*, p. 71; SROI C/3/3/1/1.
[38] BL, Ms Add. 30,158, ff. 12v, 26r, 27r; SROI C/2/10/3/1, f. 123.

geoning local trade in livestock, leather and dairy produce'.[39] The manufacture and trade in cloth also developed there, albeit late in the fifteenth century. No clothiers taxed in the alnage accounts of the late 1460s evidently came from Woodbridge, but several appeared before the Ipswich petty court in the 1480s and 1490s. Robert Lunt, who is called a clothier, was resisting a claim for £17 13s. in 1489, and Thomas Gernon, a mercer, sought to enforce his rights against a servant named John Powys in the following year.[40] Thomas Drayll took Robert Payn of Woodbridge as an apprentice in 1480 to train him as a mercer.[41] Thomas Alvard, yet another mercer, became one of Ipswich's leading merchants, serving as portman from 1492, bailiff in 1493/4, 1499/1500 and again in 1504/5, and MP in 1497. When he was first admitted to the freedom of the borough in 1488, it was as a foreign burgess living in Woodbridge, but he very soon became resident.[42] If, as previously suggested, the cloth industry in Ipswich itself was in decline by the 1460s, and if Suffolk's other leading cloth towns were no longer looking to Ipswich, then perhaps cloth making developed in Woodbridge to fill the vacuum. The clothiers of Woodbridge could not reach Colchester or London without passing through Ipswich. They may have created a captive market for the skilled cloth finishers who, as discussed below, thrived in Ipswich in the closing years of the century.

Needham Market was another nearby town that prospered at this time because of its position on the main northeast-southwest road through Suffolk, and also its cattle rearing and cloth making.[43] Although it was perhaps not quite as tightly locked into the orbit of Ipswich as Woodbridge, the mention of ten of its residents in the petty court records suggests that this connection was none the less significant. John Flegge the younger was a member of a prominent Needham Market family. He farmed the office of alnager after William Whelpdale, and made money both from his office and from cloth making, the latter on a scale that raised him to fortieth position among the county's top clothiers in the late 1460s. In 1498, shortly before he died, he sought recovery, in the Ipswich petty court, of forty pounds from William Reynolde of Coddenham.[44]

Further west, Bury St Edmunds lay well outside the orbit of Ipswich with a hinterland of its own. As we have seen, its cloth industry had for some years been more buoyant than that of Ipswich. Not surprisingly, therefore, several of those Bury residents who appeared before the Ipswich petty court were involved in the cloth trade. Two were mercers, a third was a clothier and a fourth, John Galeyt, was described

[39] Bailey (2007), p. 283.
[40] SROI C/2/10/3/1, ff. 161, 253.
[41] SROI C/2/3/6/4 m. 5r.
[42] SROI C/2/10/3/2, f. 90; C/2/10/3/1, ff. 123, 142; *Annals*, pp. 166, 170; Wedgewood and Holt (1938), p. 595.
[43] Bailey (2007), p. 142.
[44] Amor (2004), p. 415; SROI C/2/10/3/5, f. 117.

in more general terms as a merchant. He was quarrelling with William Hewet and his son John, clothiers of Stoke-by-Nayland, over a debt due to them of thirty pounds.[45] Another Bury merchant, William Spenser, settled in Ipswich and was admitted as a freeman in 1493.[46] Bury St Edmunds must have still looked to Ipswich for supplies of consumer goods and, despite the contraction of the trade in the late fifteenth century, for wine. William Kelynge, also of Bury, sued the Ipswich vintner John Martyn in 1490 for four pounds, perhaps because he had been unable to deliver on a pre-paid consignment.[47]

One of the key themes in the history of Ipswich's trade in the fifteenth century is its relationship with London.[48] Although Londoners now traded directly with the residents of the cloth towns of south Suffolk, and in doing so increasingly by-passed Ipswich, the town's dealings with London in other spheres of economic activity increased. In part, this reflects the growing relative importance of the London economy within England as a whole. The annulment by Parliament in 1487 of the anti-fair policy meant that London tradesmen were now free to travel to, and make retail sales in, the provinces.[49] This development may help to explain why the median value of individual debt disputes with Londoners was relatively modest. Six London litigants in the petty court are recorded during the opening years of the fifteenth century (Table 8), six during the middle years (Table 16) and twenty-five during the closing years (Table 23). Of these twenty-five, one was a brewer, two were drapers, five were fishmongers, four were grocers, two followed the leather trade, four were mercers, and three were simply described as merchants. For some of them Ipswich was, as it had always been, a port for the dispatch of wool or cloth to the Continent, offering an alternative route and spreading the risk inherent in international trade. London fishmongers were interested in purchasing marine fish which, as noted above, proved an increasingly popular dish and generated long distance trade. One of those Londoners travelling to Ipswich, to purchase catches arriving in the port, was William Copynger. In 1491, when he successfully sued William Tudenham, a burgess of Hull, for the sum of twelve pounds, the petty court enforced the judgment by seizing Tudenham's turbot.[50] Five years later another London fishmonger, Robert Eryke, contested the ownership of 400 large gill stockfish with John Robert.[51] At the same time, London grocers saw Ipswich as a market for the sale of the dyes that were so important to cloth making, and the

[45] SROI C/2/10/3/5, f. 148.
[46] SROI C/2/10/3/3, f. 9.
[47] SROI C/2/10/3/1, f. 246.
[48] Galloway suggests that 'for towns in south-east and midland England, the connection with London was usually much stronger than with any other place': (2003), p. 122.
[49] *Rot. Parl.*, vi, p. 402; Barron (2004), pp. 82–3.
[50] SROI C/2/10/3/1, f. 296.
[51] SROI C/2/10/3/3, f. 142.

spices that enlivened the dishes of wealthier residents. In 1492 one of them, John Smert, was seeking to recover debts due from two of Ipswich's leading dyers, Thomas Bunt and John Whetyngtone.[52]

Of the seven litigants from east coast towns, three came from nearby Dunwich, two from Lynn and two from Hull. Their disputes concerned sums of relatively high value. The two individuals from Lynn, being the clothier John Tigo and the merchant William Boteler, were quarrelling between themselves in 1488 over a debt of £9 19s. 4d., perhaps over the supply of cloth.[53] As we have seen, William Tudenham of Hull was almost certainly in the fish trade. East coast trade was not, however, solely dependent upon cloth and fish. Although no-one from Newcastle appeared before the petty court, Ipswich merchants were trading with the north-east at the beginning of the sixteenth century, just as they had at the beginning of the fifteenth. Between August 1508 and July 1511 nine ships arrived from Newcastle, all bringing coal to the town.[54] The scale of this trade with Ipswich was, however, significantly smaller than with many other east coast ports, such as Boston, Dunwich, Lynn and Yarmouth. Perhaps Ipswich was less busy as a port of coastal trade than they were, although, since all four had suffered a marked decline in the fifteenth century, this seems implausible. More likely, Ipswich had better access to firewood and was less dependent on coal.

The town's long distance overland trade appears to have grown since the opening years of the century. Excepting those from Bury St Edmunds and London, only four litigants had previously come further than twenty miles to appear in the petty court; now they numbered twenty-three. Six travelled from the far reaches of Suffolk, but one came from Coventry, three from Northampton, five from Norwich, and five from unlikely locations in the north-west, such as Flockton, Kendal, Under Skiddaw and Saltcoats. It is impossible to identify the occupations of more than a few of them. Richard Andeley from Coventry was a capper, following a trade that was expanding in late fifteenth century in Ipswich, as in his own town.[55] Two of the visitors from Northampton were pewterers.[56] One of those from Norwich, Robert Adams, was a cordwainer, as were Gerard Herrysone from Southwark and Herman Martynsone of Shoreditch, London, who, for unknown reasons, chose to settle their differences in Ipswich.[57] John Dokwra from Kendal was a chapman who clearly took his job as a travelling salesman seriously.[58] Some of the others hailing from the north-west may have brought livestock with them, as did the drover David of

[52] SROI C/2/10/3/2, f. 92.
[53] SROI C/2/10/3/1, f. 111.
[54] Fraser (1986), pp. 30, 33, 57, 102, 110, 170, 215, 235, 237.
[55] SROI C/2/10/3/5, f. 219; Britnell (1997), pp. 237–8.
[56] SROI C/2/10/3/1, f. 298.
[57] SROI C/2/10/3/1, ff. 138, 267.
[58] SROI C/2/10/3/1, f. 154.

Cenors, whose name suggests a Welsh origin.[59] Suffolk was becoming a favoured destination for long distance drovers, who could fatten their cattle in the county ready for sale in the urban markets of the south-east.[60]

This study of Ipswich's late fifteenth-century trading network prompts mixed conclusions. On the negative side, Ipswich appears to have been somewhat divorced from the major cloth making towns of Suffolk. Furthermore, the inland wine trade, that had once been such a good earner, showed little sign yet of revival. Nevertheless, the extent and diversity of the town's commercial network suggests that its economy may have begun to recover from the difficult middle years of the century. Consumer goods, in particular, were much in demand. The next step is to look more closely at how Ipswich's own tradesmen and artificers were faring, starting with an analysis of the victualling trades.

Beer and Bread become Big Business

The fortunes of these trades were assessed earlier through an analysis of the relevant entries in the leet court rolls, which identified some positive signs in the 1460s. Table 24 continues that analysis for the following two decades. It does not paint a particularly happy picture, but points to an apparent decline in activity in some of these trades. For example, the mean number of fines per leet court for brewing and selling ale, selling fish and meat, and innkeeping fell from the 1460s to the 1470s; and in the 1480s the mean number of fines for brewing and selling ale and selling fish declined yet again.

TABLE 24: MEAN NUMBER OF OFFENCES PRESENTED TO EACH LEET COURT 1465–88

	No. of courts	*Brewing ale*	*Selling ale*	*Brewing beer*	*Baking bread*	*Selling bread*
Late 1460s	12	12.8	17.83	0.75	1.91	3.33
1470s	20	11.5	15.1	0.85	2.20	3.85
1480s	24	6.33	14.08	1.08	2.04	4.17

	Selling fish	*Selling meat*	*Inn-keepers*	*Selling leather*	*Plus*	*Minus*	*Balance*
Late 1460s	4	3.17	5.4	2.75			
1470s	1.2	1.85	4.85	1.9	3	6	-3
1480s	0.83	3.08	5.71	1.54	4	5	-1

Sources: SROI C/2/10/1/2-6, C/2/8/1/13–22.

[59] SROI C/2/10/3/2, f. 114.

[60] Amor (2002), p. 135; Galloway (2003), p.125; Bailey (2007), p. 224.

In the 1460s Ipswich's overseas trade was bucking the national trend and doing rather well. Thereafter, much of this trade disappeared with the general exodus of the Hanseatic merchants (Figure 1). Their departure may well have dampened demand in the years that followed, particularly for board and lodging. Of all fines imposed on innkeepers, the proportion payable by those in east ward, nearest the docks, fell below a third in the 1470s and 1480s. Averages do not, of course, tell the whole story. Although it may simply reflect the greater number of extant court rolls, the actual number of recorded ale sellers, butchers and innkeepers continued to rise from the 1460s throughout the next twenty years, until they apparently became more numerous than ever before. The enhanced value of the meat trade is reflected in a sharp increase in the annual rental paid for the flesh market from £9 6s. 8d. in 1344/5 to eighteen pounds in 1486.[61] As Tables 9 and 25 show, both at the beginning and at the end of the fifteenth century, butchers appeared more frequently before the petty court than did those involved in any other victualling trade, defending rather than bringing claims, and forcing their suppliers to fight for their money. Robert Smyth alone was defending himself against a remarkable tally of at least sixteen debt claims in the 1490s.[62] Whether or not they played fair, some of them evidently prospered. In his will of 1494 John Broun mentioned not only his land in Westerfield and his bulls that grazed there, but also his valuable jewels.[63] It is perhaps not surprising that butchers were regarded with suspicion by so many of their contemporaries.[64]

Even more striking is the decline in the number of those selling fish in the 1470s, from twenty to fourteen, before a partial recovery in the 1480s to seventeen. Many of them were small-scale operators, such as John Cosyn, who broke the law by obtaining fresh fish from the baskets of other local fishermen in order to forestall the market.[65] This decline may reflect the concentration of the trade in the hands of wealthy fishmongers as a consequence of the growing taste for deep-sea marine fish. In Colchester the falling number of forestallers was a sign of greater opportunities for ordinary people, particularly women, rather than of recession.[66]

Undoubtedly, the brewing of beer and the baking and selling of bread show upward trends, whichever way one looks at the figures. The annual gathering of the good and the great in late fifteenth-century Ipswich took place at the feast of the Corpus Christi gild. While fiddlers played, a sumptuous meal was spread before the guests, with every possible variety of meat – mutton, lamb, veal, goose, pork, chicken and pigeon. In 1478 this carnivorous fare was washed down not with wine, which

[62] SROI C/2/10/3/2, f. 82; C/2/10/3/3, ff. 43, 72, 73, 88, 127, 167; C/2/10/3/3, f. 43; C/2/10/3/5, ff. 1, 14, 15, 26, 42, 59.

[63] NRO NCC, Reg. Typpes, ff. 89, 90.

[64] Swanson (1989), p. 25.

[65] SROI C/2/10/1/7, m. 5r (north ward).

[66] Britnell, *Britain and Ireland* (2004), p. 360.

TABLE 25: LITIGANTS IN THE PETTY COURT OF IPSWICH KNOWN TO HAVE BEEN ENGAGED IN VICTUALLING TRADES 1486–1500

Trade	*No.*	*Percentage of total*	*No. of debt cases*	*Percentage of total*	*Claimant less Defendant*	*Median value of claim*	*Admissions 1470–1500*
Baker	4	7.4	10	10.5	-6	£12 2s. 2d.	3
Brewer (inc. beer brewer)	13	24.1	14	14.7	-2	£1 8s. 8d.	1
Butcher	15	27.8	45	47.4	-33	18s.	2
Cook	2	3.7	0	0	0	n.d.	0
Fisherman/ fishmonger	7	13.0	7	7.4	-1	£11	1
Grocer	4	7.4	6	6.3	6	£4 9s. 10d.	0
Miller	6	11.1	7	7.4	-1	7s. 10d.	0
Spicer	1	1.9	1	1.1	-1	i.d.	0
Vintner	1	1.9	4	4.2	-4	£3 14s.	2
Waferer	1	1.9	1	1.1	-1	i.d.	0
Total	54	100.2	95	100.1			9

Notes
Cases are only recorded in Tables 25 and 26 if they describe the occupation of a party.
Five of the seven fishmongers and all four grocers came from London. They are counted as victuallers, but many of them had commercial interests that went well beyond food.
Source: BL Ms Add. 30,158; SROI C/2/10/3/1–5.

was hard to come by, nor just with traditional ale, but with beer.[67] It is a sign of official acceptance of the new drink, which had originally met with some suspicion as being fit only for Dutchmen. Five years later a tax was levied on aliens living within the realm. In London it recorded eight holders of beer houses.[68] In Ipswich five such individuals were taxed, and a further fourteen aliens were found to be working for them as brewers.[69] One of the five, Giles Johnesone, became the second beer brewer to be admitted as a freeman of the borough, subject to payment of a massive fee of ten pounds and examination by two local worthies.[70] Another, Henry Fulslo, left a barrel of beer to each of the town's houses of friars when he died in 1487.[71] In total eleven beer brewers were fined by the leet court in each of the

[67] *Annals*, p. 130; Account of William Sewale and John Portman as wardens of the Corpus Christi Gild, 14 June 1479: SROI C/2/10/1/7, m. 3v.
[68] Thrupp (1962), p. 50.
[69] PRO E 179/180/111.
[70] BL, Ms Add. 30,158, f. 41v; SROI C/2/10/3/1, f. 60.
[71] SROI R3/53.

decades of the 1470s and the 1480s. In the opening years of the century only one litigant before the Ipswich petty court had been described as a brewer. In the closing years, no fewer than eleven were designated as beer brewers, and several more bore names suggesting that they followed the same trade. Adding those named in the petty court to those named in the leet courts of the 1480s suggests that there were as many as nineteen different beer brewers in Ipswich at the end of the fifteenth century. In 1508 the borough authorities, recognising that 'the maintenance of this towne is much in malt', levied on alien maltsters a fine of 6s. 8d. for each quarter so malted.[72] All recorded brewing was carried on in the east ward, but beer was also being sold by retailers in the north and west wards.[73] The first named alehouses now begin to appear in the records, with John Baldwyn leasing *The Crown* in the parish of St Laurence in 1476, and John Depyng bequeathing his boots, doublet and hose to the master of *The Shippe*.[74] By 1577, twenty-two alehouses traded in Ipswich; and from the 1540s the borough authorities were taking steps, no doubt without much success, to keep the poor away from them.[75] Nowhere else in England had beer become so popular, so soon.[76]

At the same Corpus Christi gild feast in 1478 the wardens provided bread worth 7s. 1d. The record does not specify what type of bread was served, but in late fifteenth-century Ipswich there was plenty of choice. An assize of bread was held thirty times in a five-year period between 1486 and 1492 to test the quality and weight of the bread being sold in the town, and to fine any bakers not conforming to the requisite standard.[77] They record all-grain and wholemeal loaves at 1d. each, and simnel, temsyd, wastel and white loaves at ½d. Wholemeal and white loaves were by far the most popular. At least twenty-one different bakers were fined at the assizes, and at least six more appeared in a similar period before the leet court. Quite possibly, thirty or more bakers were carrying on business in Ipswich at this time. The apparent surge in their numbers since the 1460s may reflect population growth within the town, and an influx of poorer people who were largely dependent on a diet of cheap bread. It seems unlikely that their customers were limited to the town's boundaries, however. The median value of the transactions that they entered into was remarkably high, many of them very probably concerning bulk purchases of

[72] *Annals*, p. 180.
[73] SROI C/2/8/1/17–22.
[74] SROI C/2/10/1/7, m. 10v; R2/258. The reference to the master of 'the Shippe' in Depyng's will may possibly refer to the vessel that took him to Calais, but David Allen agrees that it is more likely to have meant *The Ship* inn, which was later sold in 1658 by the borough corporation to pay for improvements to the waterworks: 'The Public Water Supply of Ipswich before the Municipal Corporations Act of 1835' *PSIA*, 40 (2001) 31–54 (p. 44), and personal correspondence in November 2002.
[75] Clark (1983), pp. 42, 168–9.
[76] Bennett (1996), p. 81.
[77] SROI C/2/10/3/1.

grain from larger scale agriculturalists (Table 25). For example, Robert Hervy was the defendant in a series of substantial debt actions, in the late 1480s and 1490s, with a mean value of very nearly ten pounds.[78] In 1493 the Ipswich baker Thomas Philip sought to recover a debt of ten pounds from the London fishmonger John Milne, and two years later another debt of forty shillings from a London mercer.[79] Three Ipswich bakers were admitted to the freedom of the borough in the final thirty years of the century, more than the representatives of any other victualling trade: namely Robert Hervy, Thomas Philip and Gregory Soty.[80] Although Hervy served on the town council and as a collector of taxes in the parish of St Nicholas, none of them achieved high borough office.[81]

Having completed this survey of victualling trades, we now turn to other Ipswich trades and industries, concluding with a final look at cloth, leather and metal work.

New Energy and Surplus Wealth

The leet court rolls provide one set of indicators of the level of commercial activity in the town, the petty court records another more comprehensive one, taking into account not only the victualling trades, but the other industries discussed below. Some historians have identified a high or rising volume of debt litigation in a town's courts as a positive sign of its economic buoyancy. By the same token, a reverse trend may reflect urban decay. Figure 4 illustrates debt litigation in Ipswich in the fifteenth century, revealing a distinct peak of activity at the beginning of the century. The very modest value of the litigation at that time, as illustrated by a comparison of Tables 9 and 10 with Tables 25 and 26, is perhaps due to the fact that the petty court may have had a rather different function than it did by 1500. It is, therefore, debateable whether the level of economic, as opposed to simply legal, activity was higher in the opening years than the closing ones. What seems clear, though, judging from the jerky upward trend in the final decade of the fifteenth century, is that, at least by then, the local economy was recovering from its mid-century blues. How was this recovery achieved?

The wealth of Ipswich did not depend solely on beer, bread and trade with the wider world. Residents and visitors continued to follow a wide variety of other occupations (Table 26). The median value of the disputes in which these individuals were involved gives some idea of the scale of their operations. The number of practitioners of each trade or craft admitted to the freedom of the borough likewise provides some indication of the standing that each occupation enjoyed in the town.

[78] SROI C/2/10/3/1, ff. 20, 207; C/2/10/3/2, f. 80; C/2/10/3/3, ff. 25, 128, 132; C/2/10/3/5, ff. 39, 68, 144.

[79] SROI C/2/10/3/3, ff. 11, 73.

[80] BL, Ms Add. 30,158, f. 33r; SROI C/2/10/1/7, m. 15r; C/2/10/3/1, f. 141.

[81] SROI C/2/10/1/7, m. 17v; C/2/10/3/1, f. 93.

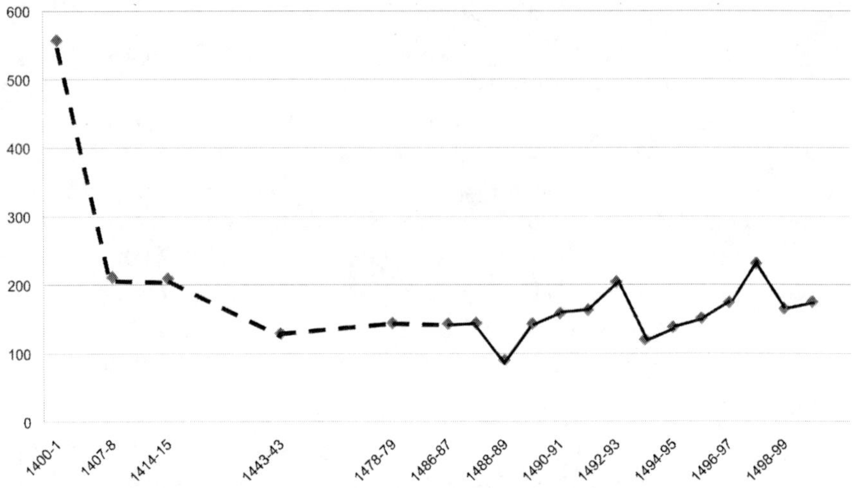

Figure 4: *Ipswich Petty Court Debt Claims in the Fifteenth Century*

At times in the fifteenth century, Ipswich, like many other late medieval towns, must have resembled one large construction site.[82] Every church was rebuilt in the 150-year period before 1551.[83] It was an age of new aisles and belfries.[84] Leading residents vied with each other in broadcasting their piety and prosperity through the generosity of their gifts towards the cost. Local wills track the progress of this work, and some of the more notable bequests deserve special mention. In 1472 Richard Machet left twenty shillings for lead on the roof of the tower of St Mary Quay.[85] A year later Alice Andrew bequeathed all her brass and latten towards a new middle bell for the same church.[86] In 1475 William Style provided half a fodder (9¾ cwt) of lead for roofing the church of St Nicholas, and soon afterwards money was left by Nicholas Bramston for the repair and plumbing of its south aisle.[87] Joan Terry contributed a small sum, in 1486, towards the purchase of a great bell for St Matthew's.[88] In the late 1490s Robert Blomfeld paid for the completion of the paving of the south aisle of St Mary Quay, and Cassandra Dameron donated four loads of

[82] In Norwich, in the late fifteenth century, good quality houses were built and parish churches such as St George Colegate and St Michael Coslany were expensively restored with the profits of the cloth industry: Dunn (2004), p. 217.
[83] Redstone (1969), p. 74; Webb (1962), p. 9.
[84] Schofield and Stell (2000), pp. 380–1.
[85] SROI R2/229.
[86] SROI R2/235.
[87] SROI R2/291, 300.
[88] SROI R3/38.

TABLE 26: LITIGANTS IN THE PETTY COURT OF IPSWICH AND THEIR OCCUPATIONS 1486–1500

Occupation	*No. of litigants*	*Percentage of litigants*	*No. of debt cases*	*Percentage of debt cases*	*Claimant less Defendant*	*Median value of debt claims*	*Admissions 1470–1500*	*Percentage of admissions*
Building	10	2.4	6	1.4	-4	12s. 8d.	1	1.3
Clothing	21	5.0	16	3.6	-4	19s. 10d.	3	3.8
Leather	32	7.6	22	5.0	-15	£4	8	10.1
Merchant or mariner	51	12.1	55	12.4	-21	£7	15	19.0
Metal	31	7.4	20	4.5	-12	£3 6s. 8d.	12	15.2
Other occupations	27	6.4	30	6.8	4	£1 1s. 4d.	12	15.2
Religious	109	26.0	136	30.8	12	£1	4	5.1
Servants/ labourers	34	8.1	7	1.6	-5	4s. 9d.	1	1.3
Textiles	34	8.1	35	7.9	3	£5	10	12.7
Transport	2	0.5	1	0.2	1	i.d.	1	1.3
Victuallers	54	12.9	95	21.5	-43	£1 17s. 9d.	9	11.4
Wood	14	3.3	19	4.3	-1	£1 17s. 4d.	3	3.8
Total	419	99.8	442	100			79	100.2

Notes
Some litigants followed more than one trade, in which case they have been classified by what appears to have been their principal trade. Some occupations, such as mercer and merchant, are almost indistinguishable, in which case the individual in question has been classified as a mercer.
Sources: BL Ms. Add. 30,158; SROI C/2/10/3/1–5.

bricks for the west doorway of St Mary Tower.[89] New building was not limited to churches. The borough authorities spent much of their time in meetings of the general court planning a variety of public works, involving the common quay, a new crane, the common conduit, the new mill, and a building to the south of the Moothall.[90] In 1487 they granted John Squyer land next to the Dominican Friary for the construction of a latrine for the grammar school boys.[91] In 1492 they admitted the tiler Peter Lamb as a freeman on condition that he provided tiles for the new chamber at one end of the house of pleas.[92] Archdeacon Pykenham built his new residence next to the church of St Mary Tower, of which the impressive

[89] SROI R3/208; NRO NCC, Reg. Muton, ff. 148, 149.
[90] *Annals*, pp.132–3, 139, 141–6, 153–5, 168–9.
[91] SROI C/2/10/3/1, f. 48.
[92] Redstone (1969), p. 68; SROI C/2/10/3/3, f. 9.

brick-fronted gatehouse survives today in Northgate Street (Plate 4).[93] Wealthier residents could afford grand private houses and were anxious to advertise their success. One such was Thomas Fastolf, who may well have erected what is now known as the Ancient House at this time.[94] Contemporary properties in Silent Street also survive (Plate 5).

Such building work is indicative of new energy and surplus wealth in the town, and in turn provided welcome opportunities for a variety of construction workers. Carvers, glaziers, masons, painters and tilers all appeared before the petty court. Glass was being imported into Ipswich in the late 1450s and again in the early 1490s, when William Keche and Thomas Alvard shipped respectively eight wey (perhaps 1120lbs) and three wey of it.[95] Although glass was certainly being made in England at this time, evidence of its production is hard to find.[96] Wherever its provenance, painted glass was being used in increasing quantities, at least in church windows, in the fifteenth century.[97] In 1499 William Mynott left instructions in his will for new panels in the windows of Lady Chapel ('Gracechurch') in the parish of St Matthew, requesting that there should be placed:

> In the east window of our lady of grace in glass an image of John Mynott, my grandfather, and William and Kathryn, my parents, and in the west window the images of myself and my wife.[98]

Possibly the work was carried out by Thomas Lopham, whose frequent appearances in the petty court mark him out as the town's foremost glazier. Although there is no record of his admission, he was probably a freeman by virtue of his family connection. In the previous generation John Lopham had been the leading Ipswich glazier and enjoyed a status unusual for his craft. He had been admitted as a burgess and simultaneously elected to Parliament by the town in 1463, and was described as a gentleman in a will of 1471. His eldest son Robert was probably educated, together with Thomas, son of Sir John Howard, to be a gentleman too.[99] Thomas Lopham, a younger son or perhaps some more distant relative of John, took over the family business. He served as a collector of taxes for the parish of St Matthew in 1488, but does not appear to have achieved any higher borough office.[100] In 1490 he contracted with Edmund Daundy and John Bedfeld for a payment of ten pounds to:

[93] K. Wilson, *Pykenham's Gatehouse, Ipswich* (Ipswich: The Ipswich Society for Ipswich Building Preservation Trust, 2006).
[94] Redstone (1969), p. 34.
[95] PRO E 122/52/42; E 122/53/9.
[96] Salzmann (1913), pp. 127–32.
[97] B. Howard, 'Stained glass', in *Suffolk Churches* ed. by Jean Corke, John Blatchly, John Fitch and Norman Scarfe (Woodbridge: Suffolk Historic Churches Trust, 1977) pp. 68–71 (p. 68).
[98] NRO NCC, Reg. Sayve, f. 10.
[99] BL, Ms Add. 30,158, f. 25r; SROI R2/257; Blatchly (2003), p. 19.
[100] SROI C/2/10/3/1, f. 122.

Plate 4: *Window of Pykenham's Gatehouse, Northgate Street*

Plate 6: *East window of the church of St Laurence*

Plate 5: *Properties in Silent Street*

> Make the glass for the east window of the church of St Laurence in Ipswich well, sufficiently, and with images and colours and other necessaries according to instructions from the said Edmund and John by next Christmas.[101]

This east window, sadly now lacking Lopham's glass, is shown in Plate 6. Four years later Lopham was being sued for £9 6s. 5d. by Thomas Drayll, one of the town's leading merchants and a member of one of its foremost families.[102] Perhaps Lopham had defaulted on the purchase of some glass, or on a commission for Drayll. The latter's family had its own oratory, probably within the same church, which was no doubt richly decorated.[103] Nevertheless, however skilled Thomas Lopham and his colleagues may have been, and however much we may admire their work centuries later, few building workers were entering into high value transactions, or earning big money.

Of workers in wood, in addition to the carvers who have already been mentioned, two carpenters, four coopers and two fletchers figure in the petty court records. The carpenters were a long-established craft, whose members were expected to contribute five shillings to the cost of the annual Corpus Christi procession, rather more than the average donation.[104] Their tools were of such importance to them that they are sometimes specifically mentioned in the records. Thomas Trowlop, who carried on the business of 'sawerscraft', hired Thomas Blakamore to work for him for three weeks and, when Trowlop defaulted on payment, Blakamore took his 'long saw'.[105] William Gravouse's assets in 1487 included two saws and a vice which, being valued in total at 8d., had probably seen better days.[106] In 1492 John Bradker and John Parker disputed ownership of a 'wood knife' worth a more respectable 3s. 4d.[107] Generally, wood workers were of modest status, but the coopers John and Robert Cukhook became freemen in 1479, and the carpenter William Guybon in 1490.[108]

Among those engaged in the making of clothes were cappers and tailors. The first constituted a relatively new trade. In the early 1470s Richard Capmaker had been fined four pence for washing caps in 'le Condich', and John Hatmaker for making poor quality hats.[109] The assessment of aliens of 1483 identifies three cappers and six hat makers in Ipswich.[110] One of them, Gerard Jacobson, was still working

[101] SROI C/2/10/3/1, f. 235.
[102] SROI C/2/10/3/3 f. 57.
[103] NRO NCC, Reg. Wolman, f. 9.
[104] SROI C/2/10/3/3, f. 85; Allen (2000), p. 189.
[105] SROI C/2/10/1/7, m. 11.
[106] SROI C/2/10/3/1, f. 47.
[107] SROI C/2/10/3/2, f. 59.
[108] BL, Ms Add. 30,158, f. 36v; SROI C/2/10/3/1, f. 236.
[109] SROI C/2/8/1/13 (north ward); C/2/8/1/14 (east ward).
[110] PRO E 179/180/111.

as such in 1498.[111] Before the end of the century at least four more local cappers had appeared before the petty court. They were responding to a growing demand for head wear which had previously been largely met from abroad with hoods of beaver, and kerchiefs of cotton and chrism-cloth.[112] Indeed, items that had once been imports were now becoming exports, as both lined and unlined caps were dispatched by the Ipswich merchant Thomas Harford, probably to Iceland, in 1492.[113] Caps were a relatively inexpensive alternative to foreign imports. In 1490 Derek Capper and John Sparhauk contested the ownership of five caps, the total value of which was just 3s. 6d.[114] Although caps were not yet sufficiently important possessions to appear in wills, cappers were, nevertheless, the pioneers of a knitting industry that was destined to prosper in the country's often cold and wet climate.[115]

Tailors had been established in Ipswich for centuries and had always ranked among the town's elite. Fine clothes were prized possessions of Ipswich townspeople and were mentioned more often in their wills than any other belongings. Gowns, of various colours, were the most frequent type of bequest, but references to coats, cloaks, doublets and hose, girdles, kirtles, shirts, stockings and tunics were also very common. No fewer than ten tailors are named in the assessment of aliens of 1483.[116] Of the fifteen who appeared before the petty court in the final fourteen years of the century, John Couper, John Luke and Robert Joury were sufficiently successful to be admitted as freemen.[117] Like Joury, they probably described themselves in polite company as drapers. John Luke was the most active, pursuing debts owed by nine customers, including William, rector of Copdock church, and Thomas Moor of Bramford.[118] With the exception of the claim against Moor, all these debts were for less than twenty shillings. Tailors acquired much of their raw material through merchants from overseas and the attendant transactions involved much larger sums. In 1498, for example, Robert Joury was being sued for forty pounds by Thomas Drayll and William Baker, which gives some idea of the remarkable scale of his operation.[119]

Men of the cloth figured prominently in the commercial life of Ipswich throughout the fifteenth century, but their presence grew as time went by. In the opening years of the century they had comprised less than a fifth of all those appearing before the petty court whose occupation was recorded, but by the end more than a quarter of all litigants were clergy, and nearly a third of all the debt

[111] SROI C/2/10/3/5, f. 68.
[112] See bequests in the wills of John Sudbury: NRO NCC, Reg. Jekkys, ff. 30, 31; and of Alice Andrew: SROI R2/235.
[113] PRO E 122/53/9.
[114] SROI C/2/10/3/1, f. 228.
[115] Britnell (1997), pp. 237–8.
[116] PRO E 179/180/111.
[117] BL, Ms Add. 30,158, f. 32r; SROI C/2/10/3/1, f. 236.
[118] SROI C/2/10/3/2, ff. 106, 108.
[119] SROI C/2/10/3/5, f. 72.

disputes involved them. These figures may overstate their importance, because their occupation was more likely to be noted than that of laymen. Nevertheless, they played a key role in the local economy. The majority of such litigants were clerks or chaplains, some of whom belonged to the unbeneficed clerical proletariat which flocked to towns in search of employment, but others were rich and influential. The prominent clerk, John Squyer, became a freeman and town treasurer in 1483. He was an executor of the will of the merchant Richard Felawe and master of the school that Felawe so endowed.[120] Squyer was involved in fifteen debt disputes in his own name, thirteen of them as a claimant, and a further four as Felawe's executor.[121] The priors of the Black Friars and the White Friars, and of Holy Trinity and St Peter and St Paul, all appeared frequently before the court. John York, the prior of St Peter and St Paul, who was also a freeman, is named as claimant in eight debt disputes.[122] The incumbents of at least a dozen parishes within ten miles of Ipswich pursued commercial activities there, in consequence of which they either sued or were sued. Many such cases related to agricultural produce since the clergy's glebe lands and their right to tithes generated crops, animals and poultry, surplus to the requirements of their own households, which could be marketed.[123] Thus, for example, in the autumn of 1492 Thomas Frost, rector of the church of Stoke, brought separate claims against a butcher, a miller and a tanner.[124]

A comparison between Tables 10 and 26 provides some evidence as to the changing fortunes of various trades and industries between the opening and closing years of the fifteenth century. The proportion of litigants working in building, leather and wood, or as servants/labourers remained broadly similar. Notaries and attorneys made good money and held prominent positions within the town. Among the lawyers who served Ipswich as bailiff in the fifteenth century, William Baker, Benedict Caldwell, and John Walworth were prominent in the closing years. The growing number of attorneys in the county became a source of Parliamentary disquiet. In 1455 the Commons had reported that they caused 'great and intolerable injury, manifold vexation and trouble', and had petitioned the king, ultimately without success, to limit their number to six.[125] The retailing of clothing had become more important, reflecting perhaps higher standards of living and levels of dis-

[120] BL, Ms Add. 30,158, f. 41v; Blatchly (2003) pp. 15–26.

[121] SROI C/2/10/3/1, ff. 9, 12, 17, 42, 98, 99, 126, 127, 196, 217, 224, 284, 292; C/2/10/3/2, f. 41; C/2/10/3/3, f. 137; C/2/10/3/5, ff. 126, 185.

[122] BL, Ms Add. 30,158, f. 35v; SROI C/2/10/3/1, ff. 72, 172, 281; C/2/10/3/2, f. 79; C/2/10/3/3, ff. 25, 63, 139, 140.

[123] D. Dymond, 'The Parson's Glebe', in *East Anglia's History: Studies in Honour of Norman Scarfe* ed. by C. Harper-Bill, C. Rawcliffe and R.G Wilson (Woodbridge: Boydell for the Centre of East Anglian Studies, University of East Anglia, 2002) pp. 73–91 (pp. 75–7).

[124] SROI C/2/10/3/2, ff. 83, 84.

[125] *Rot. Parl.*, v, pp. 326–7.

posable income in the town and surrounding countryside.[126] Metal workers were slightly more numerous, and the possible reasons for this development are considered below. Conversely, the victualling trades appear to have become relatively less important, perhaps because business was now concentrated in fewer hands, and because of the dramatic decline of the wine trade. On the other hand, this trend may simply lend support to the general economic rule that wealthier people spend a smaller proportion of their income on food and drink and a higher proportion on property and other consumables. It was, however, the number of litigants involved in textiles that experienced the sharpest fall. Earlier, they had comprised nearly a fifth of all those appearing before the Ipswich petty court, but by the end of the century this proportion had fallen significantly, to below one-tenth. Moreover, fifteen of the thirty-four named individuals came from out of town. The troubles of Ipswich's cloth industry in the middle years of the century have already been considered, and its fortunes in the closing years are discussed next.

The Art of Finishing Cloth

In 1495 practitioners of the various Ipswich trades and crafts were called upon to contribute to the cost of the Corpus Christi procession.[127] Out of the £2 12s. raised in this way from those specifically named, textile workers gave 18s., or just over a third of the total. Weavers donated 3s., fullers 5s., dyers 3s. 4d., and mercers 6s. 8d. On first appearances, we are presented with a picture of a healthy industry pulling its weight in support of the town's most important annual festival. It is, however, a somewhat misleading picture that was out of date by the time it was painted. There had already by then been a marked shift away from cloth production. Earlier in the century, at least four litigants before the petty court had described themselves as weavers, and seven as fullers.[128] By the end only William Vyne answered as a fuller and only John Game as a weaver.[129] By contrast, at this time, the weavers of Bury St Edmunds were sufficiently powerful to obtain, from the sacristan of the abbey, a new set of ordinances to govern their craft.[130] A few other weavers were still carrying on business in Ipswich. One of them, John Clerk, enjoyed the confidence of both Thomas Lodbrook, who appointed him as his executor in 1470, and of the borough, which he served as valuer and juror on the petty court later in the decade.[131] Marion Forest made provision in her will, in 1476, for the weaver John Broun to go on pil-

[126] C. Dyer (1989), pp. 175–7, 205–7.
[127] Allen (2000), p. 189; SROI C/2/10/3/3, f. 85.
[128] SROI C/2/3/1/34–37, 41, 48.
[129] SROI C/2/10/3/3, f. 141; C/2/10/3/1, f. 3.
[130] Unwin (1907), II, p. 256.
[131] SROI R2/200; C/2/10/1/7 mm. 13r, 14r.

grimage on her behalf to Walsingham in Norfolk.[132] He was probably grateful for the money, because in his own will, in 1479, he left only one modest bequest of 12d. to his parish church of St Laurence.[133] Thomas Deye and William Mynott, he of the glass window, were evidently doing rather better when they died in the late 1490s. Deye left two woollen looms to his son Thomas, and a third to 'young' John, who was possibly his apprentice.[134] Mynott bequeathed to his son John all his equipment and 'stuff of weaving'. He was, even so, a newcomer to Ipswich from Dedham, with which he clearly maintained a close connection. His arrival in Ipswich was, indeed, so recent that he was still awaiting full payment for the substantial property that he had just sold in Dedham.[135]

In truth, by the end of the century, the Ipswich cloth industry was dominated by two different groups, namely shearmen and dyers, who finished the woven cloth, and mercers, who were primarily concerned with the trade in unfinished cloth. Although, as we have seen, much cloth making migrated to the countryside in the late Middle Ages, townspeople often kept control of the finishing processes.[136] Munro offers various explanations for this phenomenon, observing that urban textile workers were better trained and more highly skilled, worked full time at their craft, and were generally more professional.[137] Even if errors had been made by rural weavers earlier on in the process, slight flaws and irregularities could be expertly disguised.[138] Urban magistrates were, moreover, better equipped to police the quality of the work. Clothiers in towns also had easier access to credit, and were in a stronger position to market and export their wares. Nevertheless, for reasons outlined earlier, many English clothiers preferred to ship their merchandise abroad unfinished. Not surprisingly, as the fifteenth century drew to a close, friction developed between English cloth finishers and the mercers, who they felt were depriving them of work.[139] As noted above, the clothiers of many of Suffolk's leading cloth towns bypassed Ipswich altogether, and sent their wares direct to London. Ipswich's cloth finishers must, out of necessity, have looked increasingly for their supplies to nearby towns such as Woodbridge, where the cloth industry itself, and the trading networks of local clothiers, were less well established.

Dyers had long enjoyed high status in the town, as elsewhere. The dyeing of woollen cloth was such a highly prized skill that in 1478 John Sele engaged David Brewer to teach him the art for an agreed tuition fee of two pounds. Brewer duly

[132] SROI R2/323.
[133] SROI R2/356.
[134] NRO NCC, Reg. Typpes, f. 99.
[135] NRO NCC, Reg. Sayve, f. 10.
[136] Cloth finishing was important in fifteenth-century London: Baron (2004) p. 65. Among larger towns, Bury St Edmunds, Norwich and Salisbury were exceptions in retaining cloth making.
[137] Munro (2003), p. 275.
[138] Walton (1991), p. 351.
[139] Sutton (2005), pp. 318, 335–6.

delivered his crash course, alleging that he 'well and faithfully taught, serviced and informed Sele so that he learned all things relating to the art', but his pupil nevertheless failed to pay up.[140] It was not just woollen cloth that provided dyers with their work, but also linen. In 1479 John Furbushour reneged on his promise to John Fyshman to dye four linen bed sheets in various colours with a pattern of roses and flowers. At the request of the petty court, in the same year, the dyer John Halle valued various pieces of linen cloth that had been seized from Robert Monktone.[141]

In the closing years of the century Halle was the most prominent Ipswich dyer. He called himself a 'woddyer' and, as we have seen, in the dye trade woad was big business.[142] Halle first appears in the historical record in 1477 when he became a freeman. Thereafter, his progression through the ranks saw him become chamberlain in 1479/80, a councillor in 1480, portman in 1488 and bailiff in 1489/90 and 1495/6.[143] Henry Tenyrsham allegedly broke into his house in 1479 and stole fifty yards of woollen cloth worth £2 13s. 4d. Halle appeared several times before the petty court, but only ever as claimant. In 1486, for example, he sought to recover £9 16s. 10d. from the tailor John Lunt, and, in 1493, £4 6s. 8d. from Robert Hall, a shearman.[144] Two of Halle's contemporaries, Thomas Bunt and John Whetyngtone, were also dyers and freemen.[145] Their dealings with London grocers have already been touched upon, and they may have been in partnership together. In 1489 they borrowed, jointly with the shearman, George Pate, the sum of six pounds from Clementine Walworth, one of the town's wealthy widows.[146] Perhaps the partnership was not as successful as they had hoped. In the final months of 1491 they faced a series of petty court claims by some leading local merchants, Thomas Harford, William Style and Richard Gosse, probably for payment for dyestuffs.[147] No high value claims by Ipswich dyers against merchants are recorded, reinforcing the view that less coloured cloth was being sold for export.

As noted above, the job of the shearman was to produce a smooth finish to the cloth with his shears. Such shears continue to figure in the records as valued possessions. Thomas Deye's shears were worth no less than ten shillings.[148] Edmund Dameron bequeathed at least two pairs to his widow Cassandra, who, in turn, passed them on to her son John and servant Harry.[149] Robert Fuller is described as a shear grinder, and it was he who made and kept these precious tools in good repair.

[140] SROI C/2/10/1/7, m. 11r.
[141] SROI C/2/10/1/7, m. 19r.
[142] NRO NCC, Reg. Popy, f. 275.
[143] BL, Ms Add. 30,158, ff. 34r, 37r; *Annals*, pp. 142, 157, 159, 169.
[144] SROI C/2/10/3/1, f. 5; C/2/10/3/2, f. 138.
[145] BL, Ms Add. 30,158, f. 33r; SROI C/2/10/3/1, f. 295.
[146] SROI C/2/10/3/1, f. 163.
[147] SROI C/2/10/3/1, f. 299; C/2/10/3/2, ff. 14, 24.
[148] SROI C/2/10/3/3, f. 146.
[149] SROI R3/197; NRO NCC, Reg. Muton, ff. 148, 149.

His admission as a freeman in 1483 reflects the value of the service that he provided.[150] Shearmen were now more numerous than any other textile workers in Ipswich, with nine appearing before the petty court, and, in the 1490s, up to three becoming freemen.[151] Their ubiquity, if not their wealth, is reflected in the legal records, as we can see from the example of George Pate, who brought a string of ten debt claims over five years in the late 1480s and early 1490s, albeit only one of them for more than twenty shillings.[152] Several of the legal disputes in which shearmen became embroiled were fought with the town's leading merchants, almost certainly over cloth. Pate himself settled a claim in 1490 for four pounds brought against him by the executors of Richard Felawe;[153] and at the end of the decade another shearman Robert Smyth was indebted for fourteen shillings to the merchant William Harlewyn.[154]

Of the twelve mercers who were so described in the petty court in the closing years of the century, only five resided in Ipswich, while two came from Bury St Edmunds, four from London and one from Woodbridge. Thomas Baldry and William Style were among the town's foremost mercers, although they ventured well beyond the comparatively narrow commercial horizons of Ipswich, since both had been apprenticed in London and admitted to the Mercers' Company there.[155] Baldry, the more impressive of the two, became a freeman of Ipswich in 1480, and went on to serve as bailiff nine times before dying in 1525.[156] His brother, of the same name, actually became mayor of London.[157] He was predictably engaged in high value litigation in the petty court, pursuing debts together worth over eighty-one pounds.[158] A single sum of fifty pounds was owed jointly to Baldry and Thomas Sampson by Robert Tyler, a merchant of Harwich. These bare details mark out Baldry as a man of ambition, who was primarily interested in big business. William Style's career followed a less spectacular trajectory. He worked his way steadily up the Ipswich borough hierarchy, although there is no record of his becoming a freeman, probably because he was admitted by virtue of his patrimony. Another William Style, almost certainly his father, had been a mercer and prominent Ipswich burgess, holding office as bailiff in 1467/8, and again briefly in 1472.[159] By 1487 the son had served as chamberlain, an assessor of tax in the parish of St Nicholas and a warden of the

150 BL, Ms Add. 30,158, f. 41r.

151 SROI C/2/10/3/1, f. 236; C/2/10/3/2, f. 116.

152 SROI C/2/10/3/1, ff. 97, 113, 138, 208, 269, 286, 287; C/2/10/3/2, ff. 9, 10, 79.

153 SROI C/2/10/3/1, f. 217.

154 SROI C/2/10/3/5, f. 185.

155 Sutton (2005), pp. 221–2.

156 BL, Ms Add. 30,158, f. 37r; *Annals*, pp. 150, 158, 166, 172, 179, 186, 191, 197; PCC Bodfelde (PROB 11/21).

157 Sutton (2005), p. 222.

158 SROI C/2/10/3/1, ff. 199, 273; C/2/10/3/2, f. 83; C/2/10/3/3, f. 128.

159 SROI R2/291; *Annals*, pp. 126, 132.

Corpus Christi gild.[160] He was claviger for two years between 1491 and 1493, and coroner for another three between 1493 and 1496, and, by 1497, he was well established as a member of the town council, although not as a portman.[161] If not for his untimely death in 1500, he might have become bailiff, but one suspects reluctance on his part, or perhaps his contemporaries in general, to assume such high office.[162] William Style pursued twenty-three separate debt claims in the Ipswich petty court between 1486 and 1493. A few were for substantial sums, such as the thirty-two pounds due from Thomas Stub, and the twenty-four pounds owed by Richard Lathered of Debenham.[163] However, eight were for less than twenty shillings and, all together, these claims had a median value of well below two pounds. This suggests that much of his trade was of a relatively small-scale, local nature, being conducted with the residents of villages such as Harkstead, whose rector owed him two pounds.[164]

Coloured cloth, probably finished by Ipswich dyers and shearmen, is mentioned in the late fifteenth-century records. In 1477 Cornelius Wynnour bought from Adam Clerk four pieces of narrow strait cloth, coloured red, crimson, violet and green, for two pounds; and in the following year Clerk allegedly failed to deliver a yard of red cloth to John Gravener.[165] In 1488 the petty court seized a modest quantity of blue cloth worth 8s. belonging to John Nynge, and, three years later, confiscated 22½ yards of more sombre russet from William Dowe.[166] Occasional references to the unfininished cloth, both broad and narrow, in which the mercers dealt, are also recorded. In 1479 the petty court seized 2½ white broad cloths worth £3 3s. from John Alvard, and in 1490 another worth one pound from Thomas Yong.[167] In 1489 Richard Stone and William Vyne were disputing ownership of a white strait valued at 15s.[168]

The combined activities of the dyers, shearmen and mercers confirm that, after merchants and victuallers, those working with or selling woollen cloth remained the largest trade group in Ipswich. The median value of their transactions, at five pounds, was second only to those of the merchants. It is, moreover, significant that at least ten of them became freemen. Despite the gloomy prognosis pronounced upon the late medieval urban woollen cloth trade in this and so many other studies, money was still to be made by entrepreneurial or highly skilled individuals.

[160] SROI C/2/10/3/1, ff. 30, 48, 123.
[161] *Annals*, pp. 163, 165–7, 169; SROI C/2/10/3/4, f. 15.
[162] NRO NCC, Reg. Cage, f. 32.
[163] SROI C/2/10/3/1, f. 73; C/2/10/3/2. f. 94.
[164] SROI C/2/10/3/1, f. 11.
[165] SROI C/2/10/1/8, m. 7v; C/2/10/1/7, m. 13v.
[166] SROI C/2/10/3/1, f. 119; C/2/10/3/2, f. 21.
[167] SROI C/2/10/1/7, m. 14r; C/2/10/3/1, f. 216.
[168] SROI C/2/10/3/1, f. 173.

Making Leather Shoes

Leather goods remained much in demand in late fifteenth-century Ipswich. Consumers wanted a variety of products, but above all shoes. The wealthiest bought those made of cordwain leather. At the beginning of the century cordwainers had been powerful figures in the town, but by the end none of the three mentioned in the petty court records was resident.[169] Most shoes were of a fairly basic quality and did not necessarily cost much or last very long.[170] In 1478 John Baldewyn had twenty-four pairs of shoes and four pairs of thigh boots in stock worth a total of just £1 5s. 4d.[171] Some years later the petty court seized ten pairs of shoes belonging to Philip Peerson worth a mere 2s., and thirty-one pairs belonging to James Johnesone valued at just 7s.[172] Higher standards of living meant that people could replace their shoes more often, which in turn generated a strong and steady flow of work for those who made them.[173] Shoemakers were, therefore, numerous in Ipswich. Fourteen appeared before the petty court between 1486 and 1500, among them Henry Man, who was the only one ever recorded as becoming a freeman of the medieval borough and was sufficiently prosperous to acquire property to let.[174] He relied on the services of curriers, such as Henry Grove, who ensured that rough, dried leather attained the thickness, softness and flexibility necessary for foot ware, and who sued him for a debt of four pounds in 1500.[175] The alien assessment of 1483 discloses the names of twelve shoemakers and nine cobblers living in Ipswich, of whom Jurgoll Bolton of Flanders made the greatest impact on the town.[176] He was already a householder with four servants, all fellow countrymen, working for him in his business, and in 1490 he sued another servant, John Guybone, for an infringement of the Statute of Labourers. Although there is no extant record that he ever became a freemen, Bolton was clearly a man of substance and doing sufficiently well, in 1488, to be listed among those required to contribute twelve pence towards the upkeep of four valets in the service of the king – one of Henry VII's more imaginative forms of taxation.[177]

If few shoemakers enjoyed high status in the town in the closing years of the century, several of the tanners, who manufactured and supplied their leather, certainly did. Their sense of mutual solidarity is apparent from the fine example of William Knatte. He served as executor to the widow of Edmund Gigehoo tanner in

[169] SROI C/2/10/3/1 ff. 138,267.
[170] Swanson (1989), pp. 145–6.
[171] SROI C/2/10/1/7, m. 10v.
[172] SROI C/2/10/3/1, ff. 116, 208
[173] Bailey (2007), p. 204.
[174] SROI C/2/10/3/2, f. 67; R5/112.
[175] SROI C/2/10/3/5, f. 216.
[176] PRO E 179/180/111.
[177] SROI C/2/10/3/1, f. 1.

1472, and, in the same capacity, to his fellow tanner Thomas Puntyng five years later, before, when he died in 1488, instructing a chantry priest to pray for those belonging to his craft.[178] Six tanners, including William's son John, were made freemen during this period.[179] Both John Forgon and William Ropkyn became members of the town council, before going on to serve as chamberlain and, in the early sixteenth-century, as bailiff.[180] Before he died in 1525 Forgon had become one of the wealthiest men in Ipswich.[181] He brought nine debt claims in the petty court and faced two more between 1486 and 1493, thereby enabling us to establish his chain of supply, as well as the names of some of his customers. For example, John Broun, presumably the butcher of that name, who provided hides, was suing him for £1 13s. 4d.[182] Three of Forgon's debtors, to whom he had evidently sold leather, bore the surname 'Shoemaker' and owed him sums of up to twenty shillings.[183] He owned a tenement on the Cornhill, by the flesh stalls, perhaps to store the carcasses that he bought there.[184]

Other leather trades appear to have made only a limited impression on the late fifteenth-century town. The skinner Thomas Byrd became a freeman in 1479 and later served as warden of the Corpus Christi gild in 1482, an assessor of tax in the parish of St Margaret in 1488 and as chamberlain in 1490/1, before finally achieving the status of portman in 1501.[185] Four other skinners are named in the petty court records, but only two, Peter Nycholson and Richard Spek, came from Ipswich. William Rippingale of Colchester probably operated on a grander scale than any of them, since he was pursuing two Ipswich customers in 1499 for substantial debts of £10 and £6 13s. 4d.[186] As discussed above, the demand for furs had fallen sharply since the beginning of the century, and with it the business for skinners. Some of their remaining trade had been appropriated by the increasingly successful tailors. Ipswich wills still occasionally mention fur. Alice Langcroft remembered John Winter in 1486 with a bequest of a russet gown trimmed with fur of polecat, the chaplain Thomas Denby left a hood of squirrel fur to his friend Father Edmund Cook when he died in 1488, and Roger Tymperley bequeathed two tawny gowns furred with white lamb to John Pyte in 1499.[187] Such references were, however, becoming fewer and further between as fashions changed.

[178] SROI R2/327, R3/54; NRO NCC, Reg. Hubert, f. 10.
[179] BL, Ms Add. 30,158, ff. 31v, 35r, 37r; SROI C/2/10/3/1, ff. 127, 152.
[180] SROI C/2/10/3/4, ff. 9, 15; *Annals*, pp. 148, 150, 156, 175, 179, 181, 187, 193.
[181] SROI C/1/9/1/1.
[182] SROI C/2/10/3/1, f. 292.
[183] SROI C/2/10/3/1, ff. 226, 288; C/2/10/3/2, f. 89.
[184] PCC Bodfelde ff. 307r–308r (PROB 11/21).
[185] BL, Ms Add. 30,158, f. 40r; SROI C/2/10/1/7, m. 19r; C/2/10/3/1, f. 122; C/2/10/3/5 f. 329; *Annals*, p. 161.
[186] SROI C/2/10/3/5, ff. 131, 188.
[187] NRO NCC, Reg. Aubry, f. 104; Wolman, f. 9; Sayve, ff. 11, 12.

Those concerned with the light leather trades, such as tawyers and glovers, comprised a small minority among the leather workers in Ipswich. Despite the discovery in Italy of new deposits, no imports of the alum that was essential to their work are recorded in the particular accounts for 1483/4 or 1491/2. Jurgoll Bolton employed a tawyer to assist with shoe making, presumably for his wealthier customers. The glover William Lowder died in 1471, apparently without issue, and no-one subsequently appears to have taken up his trade.[188] Various petty court cases were concerned with the ownership of leather purses and, probably more important, the money in them.[189] In an age before bank notes, some of these purses must have been quite a size, one allegedly containing seven pounds in cash.

In the opening years of the century skinners and pelterers had formed the largest group from the leather industry to appear before the petty court, with one solitary tanner being then cited in the petty court. By the end of the century it was tanners and makers of shoes who were predominant. While, for most, shoemaking remained a fairly humble craft, tanning was big business. Whether they manufactured leather in the town, or more likely at a discreet distance, tanners were important men in the Ipswich community.

A Craze for Pewter

There can be no doubt about the success of metal working in Ipswich in the closing years of the century. Pewter was a 'rare if welcome growth point' in 'an age of urban decline', while the late fifteenth century stands out as 'a period of unprecedented expansion of provincial pewtering'. In the 1490s, when the price of industrial products was generally falling, the enormous demand for pewter made its price rise sharply.[190]

Pewter is an alloy of tin hardened by small quantities of other metals such as copper, lead or antimony. Pewterers worked with two kinds of metal. Fine metal, comprising tin and copper, was used in the production of flatware, such as plates; while lay metal, comprising tin and lead, made round ware, such as tankards.[191] It was ordained that, in order to avoid poisoning, the lead content should not exceed 20 per cent.[192] Pewter was widely used for ecclesiastical vessels in the fourteenth century, but it was only in the fifteenth that it became popular on the tables of laymen in provincial England. Pewter was not indestructible and had to be recycled from time to time, but in normal domestic use it was hard wearing and attractively

[188] SROI R2/208.
[189] SROI C/2/10/3/1, ff. 32, 34; C/2/10/3/2, ff. 49, 89.
[190] Hatcher and Barker (1974), pp. 63, 75, 80, 276.
[191] Hatcher and Barker (1974), pp. 59–60; Swanson (1989), p. 76; Homer (1991), p. 73.
[192] Hatcher and Barker (1974), p. 18.

similar in appearance to silver.[193] An Italian visitor of the time commended English pewterers on making 'vessels as brilliant as if they were of fine silver'.[194]

Pewter was apparently first mentioned in an Ipswich will of 1458, in which the spinster Joan Freborne left all 'my vessels of pewter and brass' to Agnes Sargent.[195] The new fashion caught on relatively slowly, with just three more testators referring to pewter before 1470. Among John Drayll's bequests in 1465 were several pint and quarter pots and half a garnish of pewter, a garnish comprising one dozen each of plates, dishes and saucers.[196] When, in the same year, John Peperwyght burgled Robert Buxton's house, he robbed him of six pieces of pewter worth two pounds.[197] From 1470 pewter is mentioned with increasing frequency, bequeathed by ten Ipswich testators in the closing years of the century. Most of these gifts took the form of flatware, but there is an occasional reference to round ware. John Goldwyn, for example, left his son two pots of pewter in 1488, of which one contained half a gallon and the other a quart.[198] Sir John Howard took an early and enduring interest in the metal. In 1467, following their election to Parliament as knights of the shire, he and Thomas Brewse spent 19s. 4d., out of a total budget of £40 17s. 8d., on the hire of pewter for a celebratory feast in Ipswich.[199] Later he bought significant quantities of pewter from the Ipswich pewterer, William Revet. In two deliveries, on 23 December 1482 and 6 January 1483, Revet sold Howard flatware weighing in total 131 pounds. When Revet made his second delivery, he also took away Howard's worn pewter in part exchange.[200] A taste for pewter extended further down the social scale. The tailor Robert Cowpere owed six pounds to the same William Revet in 1494; and the tanner John Knatte left half a garnish to his daughter Margaret five years later.[201] When the petty court seized the goods of John Robsone in 1492, his creditor must have been sorely disappointed. Their total value was no more than 13s. ½d. and most of the haul was junk, although it at least contained six plates of new pewter worth 3s. 7½d.[202]

Pewter being big business, some pewterers ran extensive businesses, employed relatively large workforces, and held substantial stocks.[203] Edmund Winter had turned his interests to pewter by 1453 and practised the craft for the next twenty

[193] Homer (1991), p. 78; Glyn James, 'Suffolk Pewterers' *PSIA*, 41 (2005), 63–78 (p. 63); Dyer (2005), p. 141.

[194] Hatcher and Barker (1974), p. 66.

[195] SROI R2/5.

[196] SROI R2/5; R2/113; R2/124; C/2/10/1/2, m. 14r–v.

[197] SROI C/2/10/1/2, m. 8r.

[198] SROI R3/58.

[199] Hatcher and Barker (1974), p. 52.

[200] Crawford (1992), II, pp. 331, 340.

[201] SROI C/2/10/3/3, f. 42; NRO NCC, Reg. Sayve, f. 11.

[202] SROI C/2/10/3/2, f. 44.

[203] For instance, in London: Thrupp (1962), p. 9; and York: Swanson (1989), p. 2.

years. His brother William Winter was working with pewter in the same period.[204] Two, perhaps three, generations of the family were to make a major contribution to the civic and commercial life of the town in the closing years of the century. They appear to have been operating not just as manufacturers and retailers, but as wholesalers. In the early 1470s Edmund Winter pursued John Keggyll of Bildeston, another pewterer, for a debt of £3 2s. 10d. which suggests such activity.[205] His son Nicholas remembered, in his will of 1488, churches in London, Hounslow and Burton Lazars, Leicestershire, indicating perhaps the extraordinary geographical spread of his trading interests. He also made cash bequests to each of his three apprentices, and divided three hundredweight of fine and three hundredweight of lay metal, together with all the utensils of his craft, including moulds and tools, among his sons.[206] In his will of 1476 William Winter bequeathed a hundredweight of new wrought ware and a hundredweight of old lay metal to each of his apprentices.[207] Like the Winters, Giles Lackford kept a well stocked workshop. In July 1478 William Large broke in and allegedly stole his stock of '200 pounds of newly forged tin, that is pewter vessel'. Whether this was its true weight must be judged against statements made about Lackford three months later. In the public market place, John Petit accused him of using false weights to double his return.[208] Such accusations clearly did little harm to Lackford's business. Between 1489 and 1492 he sought recovery in the petty court of eight debts with a median value of twenty shillings owed by different customers.[209]

The market in Ipswich was brisk enough to keep a growing number of pewterers busy. Eleven pewterers appeared before the petty court between 1486 and 1500, including two from Northampton, and nine who were probably all resident in Ipswich itself. Of these, William Creyk and William Revet were the most litigious, and probably most successful, businessmen. If Revet numbered the duke of Norfolk among his customers, then Creyk, coming from a well established Ipswich family, used his connections to supply John Walworth, who is tellingly described in one case as John 'Rycheman'.[210]

Pewterers were not only earning money, but also enjoying corresponding status in the town. Although merchants maintained pre-eminence in borough government, in the final thirty years of the century eight pewterers were admitted as freemen, more than any other manufacturing occupation, and many achieved high office.[211] The

204 James (2005), p. 65.
205 *CPR 1467–77*, p. 382.
206 PCC 11 Milles, f. 254v (PROB 11/8).
207 SROI R2/293.
208 SROI C/2/10/1/7, m. 10r.
209 SROI C/2/10/3/1, ff. 166, 226, 262; C/2/10/3/2, ff. 42, 53, 65, 66, 97.
210 SROI C/2/10/3/2, f. 60.
211 BL, Ms Add. 30,158, ff. 29v, 36r, 37r, 37v; SROI C/2/10/3/1, f. 125; C/2/10/3/5, f. 167.

Winters were the first and foremost of the pewterer families in Ipswich, becoming an administrative as well as a commercial dynasty. Among the elder generation, Edmund was the most successful, being admitted in 1446, becoming chamberlain in 1452, portman by 1453 and MP in 1453/4, and serving as bailiff six times between 1456 and 1477.[212] William never achieved the office of bailiff, but occupied an impressive series of subordinate administrative positions. He was appointed treasurer in 1449 and again in the following year, a collector of subsidy in 1455 and 1459, chamberlain in 1465, surveyor of the fish market in 1467, coroner in 1471 and claviger on several occasions in the late 1460s and early 1470s.[213] Nicholas was the most prominent of the next generation, becoming a portman, and serving as chamberlain in 1477/8 and bailiff in 1485/6.[214] Edmund's youngest son, or perhaps his grandson, John, was another pewterer who became member of the town council and served as chamberlain in 1493/4.[215] One of William's apprentices, the above-mentioned William Revet, benefited from the connection to become a member of the town council, chamberlain in 1490/1 and bailiff in 1501/2.[216] Outside this charmed Winter circle, only the controversial Giles Lackford achieved office, as chamberlain in 1492/3.[217]

Gold and silver had long been prized, indeed hoarded, by wealthier Ipswich residents. The discovery of new deposits in Europe made silver available to a broader spectrum of society, if only in the relatively modest form of a mazer, a cup, or a few spoons. Items of precious metal were bequeathed in significantly more wills than was pewter; before 1450 by eight known testators, in the period from 1450 to 1469 by sixteen, and in the period from 1470 to 1499 by twenty-four. This reflects a rise in disposable income and a desire for its ostentatious display. Similar objects are recorded in the inventories of goods seized from debtors by the petty court, and were, not surprisingly, the subject of ownership disputes. If gold is mentioned it is usually in the form of rings or similar objects. William Winter left two gold rings each, including one with a diamond, to his niece Isabelle Spryngot and her daughter Alice.[218] Anne Holm was the fortunate recipient of a gold brooch left by her sister Alice Kempe.[219] Roger Tymperley made Amice Style the ultimate beneficiary of a gold crucifix.[220] The local taste in silverware was more inventive. In 1487 an esquire

[212] BL, Ms Add. 30,158, f. 10r; J.C. Wedgewood and A. Holt, *History of Parliament 1439–1509 Register* (London: HMSO, 1938), p. 205; *Annals*, pp. 115, 117, 120, 126, 129, 139.

[213] BL, Ms Add. 30,158, ff. 18v, 22v, 28r; *Annals*, pp. 107, 125, 128–30, 137.

[214] BL, Ms Add. 30,158, f. 37v; *Annals*, pp. 140, 152.

[215] SROI R2/293; PCC 11 Milles, f. 254v (PROB 11/8); SROI C/2/10/3/1 ff. 83, 126; C/2/10/3/4, f. 9; *Annals*, p. 166.

[216] SROI C/2/10/3/4, f. 9; *Annals*, pp. 161, 174.

[217] *Annals*, p. 165.

[218] SROI R2/293.

[219] NRO NCC, Reg. A. Caston, f. 219.

[220] NRO NCC, Reg. Sayve, ff. 11, 12.

named John Penley was forced to deliver up to the petty court, perhaps in order to pay legal fees outstanding to the notary William Baker, a gilt cup with a cover depicting an eagle, two salt cellars with a cover partly of gilt, twelve spoons bearing the image of a maiden's head, and a cup of silver plate weighing fourteen ounces.[221] The silver was valued at between thirty-seven and forty-four pence an ounce, giving a total of £17 11s. 2d., which was still not quite enough to cover the bill.[222]

Two of the three goldsmiths who engaged in petty court litigation at this time appear to have been aliens, of whom John Rotterdam was the most visible. In the summer of 1491 he was besieged on all sides, with eight claimants seeking restitution from him. John Thurlow, prior of the Carmelites, sought to recover a debt of £1 6s. 8d. The merchant Thomas Alvard was pressing for delivery of sixteen ounces of silver worth £2 13s. 4d, while four others were demanding the smaller quantities of precious metal that they had bought.[223] Rotterdam clearly survived this onslaught with his reputation intact, because in the following year he valued items seized by the court from another unhappy debtor.[224]

Among other workers in metal, the more prosperous smiths have been discussed in a previous chapter. The appearance before the courts of a gunner, two ironmongers, two locksmiths, two plumbers, a maker of spoons, and two spurriers or makers of spurs attests to the breadth of services available in the town.

The major change in the composition of the metal industries between the closing and opening years of the century was the rise of the pewterers. They had demonstrated no visible presence in the town in 1400, but by 1500 they were by far the most important of the metal workers and, after the merchants, the most prominent men in town. Their rise is symptomatic of the growing wealth and influence of the middle classes, and of the capacity of late medieval economy to generate consumer demand for new products.[225]

We have now completed our survey of the trade and industry of Ipswich in the closing years of the fifteenth century, and have looked specifically at some of its more important trading partners, trades and industries. As is invariably the case with any study of urban life in this period, the picture is not entirely clear and the evidence sends mixed messages. In part, this is the inevitable consequence of the fragmentary nature of the surviving records. It is, however, also a reflection of the economic climate of the period. Some recovery from the mid-fifteenth-century slump had been achieved, but it was patchy and concentrated in specific sectors.

221 So called 'maidenhead' spoons, symbolic of the Virgin, were popular, as were Apostle spoons of the kind that belonged to the tanner John Forgon: PCC Bodfelde ff. 307r–308r (PROB 11/21); Goldberg (2008), p. 134.

222 SROI C/2/10/3/1, f. 55.

223 SROI C/2/10/3/1, ff. 281, 282, 287, 288.

224 SROI C/2/10/3/2, f. 33.

225 Hatcher and Barker (1974), pp. 52–4.

In the early fifteenth century Ipswich had benefited directly from the growth of the Suffolk cloth industry, but by the end it was concentrating on the finishing of such cloth. The proportion of petty court litigants working in the cloth trade had fallen dramatically. This development is further illustrated by the declining presence in the petty court of suitors from Hadleigh, and the growing number of those from Woodbridge. The widely accepted view that the town enjoyed a late medieval boom on the strength of the buoyant cloth industry in the towns of south Suffolk has been challenged. On the contrary, Ipswich's links with these towns appear to have been weak. Nevertheless, the wealth that was generated there was available for visitors to spend on the produce of Ipswich's more successful trades and industries. In this way Ipswich may have indirectly benefited from an increase in aggregate demand for goods within the county.

Some other long established trades were also experiencing difficulties. In 1500 wine was only just beginning to flow again, in any volume, into the country from Gascony. The supply networks that had previously made the fortunes of Ipswich vintners remained to be rebuilt. Skinners, pelterers and cordwainers were not doing well. The victualling trades remained vital to the wellbeing of the town, but were slowly being concentrated into fewer hands. It was far more difficult for the ale-wife or fish-wife, operating on a modest scale, to compete with more commercial beer brewers and fishmongers. Their businesses were larger and better organised for regular trade. They enjoyed economies of scale and benefited from the growing demand for higher quality produce. This may not have mattered so much in 1500, when the demographic tide had yet to turn, but the loss of income from such activities would be felt much more by the growing ranks of the urban poor fifty years later.

On a more positive note, many Ipswich residents prospered. Some sectors of the construction trade, particularly in ecclesiastical and high quality domestic building work, were kept very busy. The produce of beer brewers, bakers, butchers, dyers, shearmen, tanners, pewterers, tailors and, to a lesser extent, cappers, hat makers and shoemakers, was in demand, not just in Ipswich, but within a hinterland that probably stretched a little further than it had done in 1400. Many craftsmen were becoming increasingly specialised and thus more highly skilled. They were building relationships with expanding towns, such as Woodbridge, and making the most of their pre-existing links with London. They were responding to greater consumer demand for better quality food and drink, clothes, shoes and household goods which could be manufactured locally, rather than in the Low Countries. The pewterers are perhaps the outstanding example of craftsmen who had made no impact at the beginning of the century, but who were enjoying a boom by the end. They were meeting demand from a burgeoning middle class, who wanted greater comfort and style in their homes, not only in Ipswich, but in a hinterland which included the wealthy cloth towns. In the borough hierarchy, they were not quite equal to those Ipswich merchants who made, and lost, fortunes in international trade, but many of them became freemen, achieved respectability and played their part in running the town.

The enduring effect of the difficult years of the mid-fifteenth century was to re-orientate the economy of Ipswich. Old patterns had been severely disrupted and many smaller traders had been pushed out of business. This almost Darwinian process had created openings for enterprising individuals to operate on a grander scale and to profit from demand for new and better quality products.

– 8 –

Inventiveness and Enterprise

The fortunes of many late medieval towns were blighted by 'the Great Slump' of the middle years of the fifteenth century. Ipswich appears to have fared rather better than many comparable towns, such as the east coast ports of Hull, Lynn and Yarmouth, or, even closer to home, Colchester. Its population in 1524/5 was very similar to what it had been in 1377. The borough continued to attract immigrants, including political and economic refugees from the Low Countries, who introduced new industries and helped to keep the local economy buoyant. Nevertheless, the burgesses of Ipswich, like all their contemporaries, worked under constraints, particularly weak demand, a paucity of silver coin, an absence of large commercial organisations and a lack of investment and innovation. Furthermore, they were not immune from the problems of the wider world.

International relations at the beginning of the fifteenth century were conducive to Ipswich's trade. The town was situated close to the Low Countries with whom commercial contacts were, and would remain, very close. They were the town's most important overseas market, and even the wool that was shipped to Calais eventually ended up in the workshops of Flemish clothiers. The town's merchants were also active in the trade with Gascony and Spain, exchanging woollen cloth for wine, dyes and dysestuffs, and had begun to penetrate the Baltic, where their cloth was much in demand. The good times were not to last, however. The middle decades of the century were punctuated by a series of wars with the rulers of all these trading partners, made worse by intermittent embargoes and bullion policies that undermined the vital network of international credit. By the closing years of the century there were, none the less, some promising signs of recovery. Although excluded from the Baltic, Ipswich merchants were re-establishing themselves in the Low Countries and Gascony, and the more adventurous were conducting a lucrative trade with Iceland.

Wool and cloth remained throughout the most important exports from Ipswich, with the value of cloth overtaking that of wool certainly by the 1460s. Butter and cheese became other notable commodities laded from the town's quays, reflecting the development of dairy farming in eastern Suffolk. Wine, dyes and dyestuffs comprised most of the imports arriving at the end of the fourteenth century; but the flow of wine was severely disrupted by the loss of Gascony in 1453, while the volume of dyes and dyestuffs dwindled as imports were increasingly channelled through London and overseas demand for finished cloth contracted. Instead, ever increasing quantities of linen, furniture, household utensils and other luxuries arrived from the more technologically advanced Low Countries, all helping to create what might be termed our first consumer revolution. Protectionist measures, enacted by Yorkist kings to encourage home manufacture, were partially successful in stemming the flow of some of these luxury items by the end of the century.

Merchants travelled considerable distances to ship their goods from Ipswich. Members of the great London livery companies, fishmongers, grocers and mercers, despatched their wool to Calais, as did prominent residents of Norwich and various East Midland towns. In the middle years of the century merchants of the Hanseatic League, particularly those from Cologne, dominated the town's overseas trade, all but monopolising commerce in cloth and a variety of other commodities. At times other aliens, from Holland and Zeeland, won significant shares in the export of hides and the import of beer and later of fish. In the 1450s and 1460s, local merchants struggled to maintain a share of overseas trade. Nevertheless, some, such as John Deken and Richard Felawe, clung tenaciously to their overseas markets. After the Cologners left, their efforts helped to cushion the town from the potentially crippling loss of Hanseatic commerce. In the 1390s Ipswich merchants had enjoyed a substantial share of the cloth and wine trade, and they did so again in the 1490s.

Ship design underwent significant change during the fifteenth century. The cog, which appears on Ipswich's medieval seal, gave way to the carvel. Some change was necessary to equip vessels for the cold rough seas of the far north. The exigencies of war were, however, even more critical. Small ships, many of them skippered by adventurous Dutch masters, such as Andrew Johnessone, dominated the seaways in the 1390s. They enjoyed many advantages, but were easier to attack. Consequently, by the middle years of the century, when the seas were at their most dangerous, some craft grew to an unprecedented size, before shrinking again in the more peaceful period that followed. These trends are evident in the records of ships visiting Ipswich.

Of course, Ipswich served important markets at home, as well as those abroad. The history of its fifteenth-century domestic trade illustrates the growing importance of London, whose merchants, including mercers, grocers and members of other City companies, appear with increasing frequency in the borough records. Nevertheless, like most towns of its size, Ipswich's core trading hinterland was largely concentrated within a radius of twenty miles. In the borough's petty court three-quarters of all non-resident litigants at the beginning of the fifteenth century, and two-thirds at the end, came from within this catchment area. Although the geographical range of the town's basic trade may have altered little, its structure underwent some important changes. Rather than relying for its food supply on a large number of peasant agriculturalists, Ipswich turned increasingly to fewer producers of grain and meat operating on a much larger scale. The distribution network for wine disintegrated when supplies from Gascony dried up in the period around 1450, but it was replaced by another delivering pewter and other consumer goods to the countryside. Hadleigh was the town's key local trading partner in 1400, but was later eclipsed by Woodbridge and Needham Market, symbolising Ipswich's separation from the main production centres of the Suffolk cloth industry.

The fortunes of trade and industry within Ipswich itself reached a nadir in the middle years of the century. Harvest failure in the 1430s caused civil unrest. Inland trade networks were disrupted. A shortage of silver coin affected all businesses, but was particularly painful for the petty trader. The military engagements between Lancaster and York did not directly touch the town, but the more general breakdown in law and order certainly did. The presence of alien merchants and mariners may have kept demand for board and lodging reasonably buoyant, but small-time brewers and regrators of bread were being squeezed out of the victualling trades. Other sectors were also clearly suffering. The growth of the Suffolk cloth industry had largely bypassed Ipswich, partly perhaps because of the restrictive practices that the borough authorities had applied to protect its own residents. Skinners and cordwainers, who had been doing so well in 1400, had lost much of their business, as fashions changed and supplies of squirrel from eastern Europe dwindled. In their place, tanners, such as the father and son who both bore the name William Keche, and later John Forgon, emerged as successful local businessmen. Ipswich's economy adapted through the growth of brewing beer and making bricks and tiles, products previously imported from the Low Countries. In the metal trades, smiths prospered in producing arms, while Edmund Winter started to foster a demand for pewter among his neighbours.

Ipswich emerged from the challenges of the Great Slump rather more strongly than many towns. While in 1500 the economy of much of the country was still stagnant, the records point to healthy recovery in Ipswich. The contrast with Colchester, the nearest comparable town, is marked. There, the relatively small number of suits presented to its petty court, together with the apparent failure of its merchants to engage in overseas trade, suggest that Colchester was still in the doldrums. In the case of Ipswich, trading networks had been re-established and appear to have extended rather further than they had done in the early fifteenth century, with the appearance of long-distance travellers from places such as Kendal and Under Skiddaw. Building work on parish churches, the common quay and domestic properties provided employment for craftsmen, such as the glazier Thomas Lopham. As well as the above-mentioned beer, bricks and tanned leather, locally made clothes, hats and shoes were much in demand. Pewter is mentioned in an increasing number of wills and made the fortunes of several members of the

Winter family. Even in the textile industry, the skills of dyers and shearmen were still needed to finish the cloth produced elsewhere. They are all indicative of growing specialisation and sophistication of consumer demand in an increasingly wealthy and industrialised area of England. Many of Ipswich's residents would have regarded these years as a time of affluence.

Late medieval Ipswich does not fit neatly into the general debate over urban fortunes as either a town in crisis or one that clearly bucked the trend. The town's fifteenth-century experience was in a very real sense unique. Residents seized opportunities and faced setbacks. They took risks, and sometimes struck lucky, but often suffered the consequences. Many adapted well to the shifting and difficult market conditions of the fifteenth century. Some were born well, or succeeded against the odds, and so left their mark on the records. Others are only remembered by reason of their financial embarrassment. The wheel of fortune, to which they were all subject, was a popular contemporary image.

There is, however, a more general lesson to be learnt from this conclusion which needs to be factored into future debate. It is the sheer resilience of the Ipswich economy. Notwithstanding the constraints already identified, and the body blows sustained to key trades and industries – cloth, wine and wool – the town emerged from the Great Slump with renewed vigour. Such resilience is reflected in the willingness of townsfolk to risk life and livelihood in overseas trade; an ability to absorb immigrants, particularly the Dutch, into the community and to utilise their talents and energies; and a spirit of inventiveness and enterprise in seizing the opportunities offered by new industries. They were not mere pawns in a world over which they had no control. This lesson, that individual initiative matters, and that blind economic forces are not the sole determinant of human fortunes, may help guide future studies of medieval towns.

– Appendix 1 –

Timeline

1396	Truce with France Seizure of English shipping in Danzig
1397	Bullion ordinance
1399	Richard II deposed by Henry IV Bullion ordinance revoked
1404	Petition to Parliament saves Ipswich's wool trade
1407	Commercial treaty with Duke John of Burgundy
1410	Defeat of Teutonic Knights by Poles at Tannenburg
1412	Arrest of London trade mission in Italy
1413	Henry V succeeds Henry IV
1419	Philip the Good succeeds John as duke of Burgundy Alliance with Duke Philip the Good of Burgundy
1422	Henry VI succeeds Henry V
1428–31	English cloth imports into Holland and Zeeland banned
1429–30	Calais Staple partition and bullion ordinances
1431	Requirement to export all cheese and butter via Calais relaxed
1434	English cloth imports into Holland and Zeeland and Hanseatic lands banned
1436	War with Burgundy
1437	'Vorrath' treaty with the Hanse grants reciprocity to English merchants
1439	Commercial treaty with Burgundy ends war and opens markets
1442	Calais Staple ordinances relaxed
1445	Calais Staple ordinances revived

1447–52	English cloth imports into Burgundy banned
1448	War with France resumes
1449	Capture of the Bay Fleet of the Hanse
1450	Loss of Normandy
1451–52	Denmark closes Baltic to English cloth exports
1453	Loss of Gascony
1455	French tax ('*tournois*') on export of wine Battle of St Albans begins the Wars of the Roses
1456	Truce with the Hanse
1458	Capture of Lubeck fleet of the Hanse
1461	Henry VI deposed by Edward IV
1462	Import of wine from Gascony forbidden
1463	Statutes encourage use of English shipping and prohibit imports of certain manufactured goods Calais Staple ordinances revived Truce with France
1465	English cloth imports into Burgundy banned
1465–66	English currency devalued
1466–67	Treaty with Castile
1467	Charles the Bold succeeds Philip the Good as duke of Burgundy Commercial treaty with Burgundy
1468	Capture of English ships and naval war with the Hanse Statute prohibits export of unfinished cloth
1470	Treaty with Castile repudiated Edward IV deposed and Henry VI restored
1471	Edward IV restored
1473	Calais Staple ordinances revoked
1474	Treaty of Utrecht with the Hanse Alliance with Burgundy
1475	Treaty of Picquigny with France

1482	Death of Duchess Mary of Burgundy triggers civil war in the Low Countries
1483	Richard III succeeds Edward IV after deposing Edward V
1484	Statute prohibits imports of certain manufactured goods
1485	Battle of Bosworth Field, Richard III killed and deposed by Henry VII Statute prohibits imports of certain manufactured goods
1487	Annulment of anti-fair policy by Parliament Statute prohibits export of unfinished cloth
1489	Statute encourages use of English shipping Treaty of Medina del Campo with Castile
1490	Treaty with king of Denmark allows free trade in Iceland
1494	Order to ship all cloth through Calais
1496	Intercursus Magnus with Burgundy
1497	Provincial merchants allowed continuous free trade in Low Countries in return for payment of a subscription fee to Merchant Adventurers of 10 marks

– Appendix 2 –

Fifteenth-Century Bailiffs of Ipswich

Name	*No. of times*	*First*	*Last*	*Occupation*	*Parish of residence/burial*	*MP*	*Will*
Alvard Thomas	3	1493-94	1504-05	Mercer/Merchant	St Stephen	MP	
Andrew Thomas	3	1405-06	1412-13				
Astley Thomas	4	1422-23	1425-26	Esquire		MP	
Baker William	4	1486-87	1506-07	Lawyer/Merchant	St Mary Tower		W
Baldry Thomas	9	1484-85	1422-23	Mercer/Merchant	St Mary Tower	MP	W
Baldry William	1	1455-56	1455-56	Merchant			
Bayly Richard	3	1488-89	1501-02			MP	
Bernard John	2	1396-97	1401-02	Merchant		MP	
Bickleswade Robert	1	1430-31	1430-31				
Blomfeld Robert	2	1481-82	1487-88	Vintner/Lawyer	St Mary Tower		W
Caldwell Benedict	4	1473-74	1482-83	Lawyer	St Peter		W
Caldwell John	8	1426-27	1458-59	Merchant	St Laurence	MP	W
Cherche Richard	1	1401-02	1401-02			MP	
Creyk John	1	1471-72	1471-72	Lawyer	St Mary Tower		W
Daundy Edmund	3	1498-99	1510-11	Merchant	St Laurence	MP	W
Debenham John	1	1414-15	1414-15				
Debenham William I	6	1402-03	1417-20	Vintner/Merchant		MP	
Debenham William II	4	1429-30	1444-45	Vintner	St Mary Tower (?)	MP	
Deken John	10	1422-23	1445-46	Mercer/Merchant	St Mary Quay	MP	W
Denys Thomas	9	1433-34	1463-64	Lawyer	St Margaret	MP	W
Drayll John	2	1449-50	1457-58	Mercer/Merchant	St Mary Tower		W
Drayll Thomas	7	1478-79	1508-09	Mercer/Merchant	St Mary Tower	MP	W
Drye Robert	3	1429-30	1436-37		St Mary Tower		W
Fastolfe Thomas	1	1451-52	1451-52	Lawyer	St Laurence	MP	W
Felaw John	1	1439-40	1439-40	Tanner/Merchant			
Felaw Richard	8	1448-49	1474-75	Merchant	St Mary Quay	MP	W
Geete John	2	1450-51	1453-54	Merchant			
Gosse John	5	1466-67	1484-85	Merchant	St Matthew		W
Hall Robert	3	1463-64	1470-71	Merchant	St Peter		W
Halle John	2	1489-90	1495-96	Dyer	St Margaret		W
Harlewin William I	1	1438-39	1438-39				
Harlewin William II	2	1490-91	1495-96	Merchant	St Clement		W

Name	*No. of times*	*First*	*Last*	*Occupation*	*Parish of residence/burial*	*MP*	*Will*
Hastings John	4	1473-74	1489-90	Chandler/Merchant			
Haxwade Richard	4	1480-81	1497-98	Merchant	St Laurence		W
Hoo Hugh	2	1414-15	1416-17				
Horkslee John	8	1400-01	1415-16	Cordwainer/Merchant			
Joye John	4	1420-21	1430-31	Vintner/Merchant	St Mary Tower (?)	MP	
Ketche William I	1	1437-38	1437-38	Tanner	St Stephen		
Ketche William II	1	1453-54	1453-54	Tanner/Merchant			
Knepping John	7	1407-8	1421-22	Skinner/Merchant		MP	
Langtoft John	1	1462-63	1462-63				
Lluellin John	2	1399-1400	1400-01				
Lucas Robert	9	1404-05	1419-20	Clothier/Gentleman		MP	
Parker John	1	1399-1400	1399-1400	Merchant	St Peter		W
Rever John	2	1475-76	1478-79	Mercer/Merchant		MP	
Ridout William	3	1460-61	1468-69			MP	
Rous John	2	1408-09	1409-10	Merchant		MP	
Sewall William	3	1483-84	1497-98		St Mary Tower		W
Smith Robert	2	1447-48	1452-53	Vintner			
Stannard Roger	3	1461-62	1472-73				
Starling John	4	1404-05	1416-17	Butcher		MP	
Style William	2	1467-68	1472	Mercer/Merchant	St Nicholas		W
Terry Peter	2	1440-41	1444-45	Merchant			
Tymperley Roger I	1	1438-39	1438-39				
Tymperley Roger II	3	1485-86	1494-95	Gentleman (?)	St Mary Tower		W
Walworth John	9	1456-57	1486-87	Lawyer (?)	St Mary Tower		W
Walworth William	2	1436-37	1447-48	Merchant			
Wethereld William	6	1427-28	1450-51	Merchant		MP	
Winter Edmund	6	1456-57	1476-77	Pewterer	St Peter	MP	
Winter Nicholas	1	1485-86	1485-86	Pewterer	St Peter		W
Wode Robert	5	1434-35	1446-47	Merchant			
Wymbyll Robert	1	1469-70	1469-70	Lawyer	St Mary Tower	MP	

Notes

(?) means that the information is probably correct, but some doubt remains.

Unless otherwise expressly stated, it has been assumed that the parish of residence of each bailiff corresponded to the church in which he was buried.

'MP' means that a bailiff served, at least once, as the town's MP.

'W' means that a bailiff has left an extant Will.

– Appendix 3 –

Fifteenth-Century Ipswich People Mentioned in the Text

Alvard, Thomas; born 1460 (?), Woodbridge; father Thomas; married Anne, daughter and heir of John Rever; eight children, including son Thomas who was MP in 1529 and a prominent servant of cardinal Wolsey; died 1504; buried, St Stephen; mercer; overseas trade, exported dairy, grain, tanned leather, woollen cloth, imported glass, salt and wine 1491/2; apprentice Edmund Dameron 1500; freeman 1488; portman 1492, 1497; bailiff 1493/4, 1499/1500, 1504/5; other borough office, tax assessor 1490, claviger 1494–97; JP 1493–95, 1496–1500; MP 1497, 1504; interests in borough land, grant of foreshore rights in St Clement 1499. Other information; litigant in the petty court 1490–98; pressed John Rotterdam for delivery of sixteen ounces of silver worth £2 13s. 4d. 1491, with Edmund Daundy sued William Dewe for £6 13s. 4d. 1495, sued executors of the baker Thomas Philip for £26 13s. 4d. 1498.

Andrew, Alice; Dame (?); married Thomas; no children recorded; will proved 1473; parish of residence at death, St Mary Quay; buried Franciscan friary; property bequests, house in Harwich, in respect of which Richard Felawe was granted right of first refusal; other notable bequests, all brass and latten for middle bell of St Mary Quay, contents of wardrobe to the poor nuns of Bruisyard who have most need, contents of bedchamber and kitchen, mazer and silver spoons, gilt cup to Richard Felawe. Other information; sued for debt by executors of Robert Broke.

Andrew, John; parents, James and Alice; sibling, Thomas; married Elizabeth; two daughters; died c.1472; parish of residence in Ipswich, St Mary Tower (?); buried Baylham (?); lawyer, entered Lincoln's Inn in 1433 (?); freeman, foreign burgess 1470; JP various times; MP 1442, 1449 (Feb.); served on various royal commissions, including one on smuggling 1449. Other information; a villain of the Paston letters, quarrelled with Sir John Fastolf 1450s.

Andrew, William; fuller, indebted to the Ipswich miller John George under various contracts, and also to John Deen of Melton, 1400; borough office, juror in the petty court 1415. Other information, assaulted by Thomas Smyth (the dyer?) 1407.

Arnold, John; born Blaxhall (?); merchant in overseas trade, exported cheese 1386, later wool and woollen cloth to Low Countries 1386/7, imported wine 1386/7, 1397; bailiff 1391/2, 1397/8; MP 1388, 1394, 1397, 1399; customs official, collector of customs and subsidies, betrayed John Bernard, charged with embezzlement; alnager and serjeant at arms; interests in borough land, grant with others of land by river to build two water mills 1391, declared unlawful by the Crown 1399, but still leasing the land 1415. Other information; moved to Ipswich c.1386, with John Knepping acquired a quay, shops and crane 1396, witnessed settlement on Sir John Howard of a manor at Broke in Suffolk 1397, sold John Bernard five shops in St Mildred for £240 and sued for payment 1399, assisted in the delivery of supplies for a convoy sailing to Scotland in support of Henry IV's army of invasion 1400.

Baker, William; married first Katherine, then Joan; children Harry, Thomas, William, Agnes; will made 1503, proved 1509; buried St Mary Tower, before the tomb of John (?) Walworth; property bequests, various tenements in Ipswich, including one in St Mary Quay occupied by Thomas Harford, lands in Rushmere, Whitton; other notable bequests, bedding, plate, brass, pewter; executors, wife, Edmund Daundy, supervised by John Wyngfield; notary, merchant (?). Other occupation; innkeeper in west ward 1484–88; freeman 1479 (?), admission fee used to pay for repairs to the mills and fishmarket; portman 1480, 1501; bailiff 1486/7, 1491/2, 1496/7, 1506/7; other borough office, tax assessor 1487; JP 1487–90, 1491–93; interests in borough land, grant at Colehill 1483, grant of three stalls in fish market 1486, grant outside St Laurence churchyard gate 1492, lease in St Laurence 1498, grant in St Mary Tower 1499. Other information; took a lease from prior of Rochester 1479, granted to the borough the profits of Stoke Mill 1486, fined for public health offences in west ward 1482–87, litigant in the petty court 1487–99, court seized various items of gilt and silver from John Penley esquire in payment of a debt of £18 1487, claimed £4 from William Benyt 1491, £13 6s. 8d. from Nicholas Jeffrey 1492, £2 7s. 6d. from Robert Hervy 1499.

Baldry (alias Baldrey), Thomas; born Stowmarket; father, Thomas; siblings Thomas, who became mayor of London; married first Alice, then Christine; no children recorded; nephews, George and Thomas; will made 1520, proved 1525; buried, St Mary Tower, where his two memorial brasses survive; property bequests, dwelling place called Dryys with Dyers and Mongomerys, land in Middleton, Fortley, Stowe; other notable bequests, to each church, friary and priory in Ipswich twenty shillings, to wife a hundred marks worth of each of money, plate and book debts and forty pounds per annum in rent, to other relatives and friends, gowns, silver goblet and gold rings; executors, wife, brother Thomas, James Hall, Thomas Mansar; appointed as executor by William Wymbyll 1485, Robert Blomfeld 1497, John Halle 1503; appointed as supervisor of will by Nicholas Winter 1488, Cassandra Dameron 1498 (?); received bequests under the will of Thomas Drayll; mercer, admitted following his apprenticeship as a member of the mercers' company in London; freeman 1480; portman 1497, 1501; bailiff 1484/5, 1488/9, 1493/4, 1498/9, 1502/3, 1507/8, 1513/14, 1518/19, 1522/3; other borough office, auditor 1486, 1488, tax assessor 1487, treasurer 1487, claviger 1502/3; JP 1485–88, 1501/2, 1506/7, 1509/10; MP 1504, 1512, 1515; customs official, controller 1484, weigher 1510–death. Other information; litigant in the petty court 1489–96, sued William Padnale for £7 10s. 1489, with Thomas Sampson sued Robert Tyler, a merchant of Harwich, for £50 1496, donated a complete set of armour to the king 1491, property valued at 1000 marks 1524.

Baldry (alias Baldrey), William; born 1420 (?); married Joan; son, Thomas; died c.1484; executor, wife; merchant; overseas trade, chartered a Dutch ship, in Prussia, to carry merchandise back to England, which was intercepted by French and Breton ships and escaped, only to be captured on landfall by the inhabitants of Spurn Head in the East Riding of Yorkshire 1450, laded a cargo of wine on five ships in Bordeaux but was forced by the '*submaire*' of the town to pay further duties before being allowed on his way 1467; shipowner, owned a share in *le Margarete* of Ipswich 1462; freeman; portman 1448; bailiff 1455/6; JP 1453/4, 1455/6, 1457–59; MP 1460, 1461, paid two shillings a day in 1461; customs official, tronager of Ipswich 1452, 1465, also held office in London as searcher of ships; interests in borough land, leases in St Mary Quay 1445, 1446. Other information; spent his later years in London, described as draper of London 1458, enjoyed the favour of Edward IV and had business dealings with Sir John Howard.

Baldwyn (alias Baldewyn, Baldwyne), John; married Joan; no children recorded; will made 1488, proved 1488; buried St Laurence, where three carvings, including one of his draper's shears, and a black-letter inscription in flint flushwork, still commemorate him; notable bequest of £6 13s. 4d. for building work on the Carmelite friary; executors, wife, John Hastyngs, William Sewale; clothier, six straits 1466, twelve broadcloths 1468; draper; other occupation brewed ale in south ward 1466–88; freeman 1458; councillor 1479; other borough office, chamberlain 1466–68, chief pledge in the leet court of south ward 1471/2, tax assessor 1481, 1487/8 in St Laurence, auditor of tax collectors' accounts 1482. Other information; authorized to use burgesses' admission fines for repair of common quay and crane 1476, leasing *The Crown* in St Laurence 1476.

Balley, Geoffrey; kinsman, John; butcher. Other occupations; brewed and sold ale in south ward 1419–37. Other information; bought corn from John Corton, and pigs and sheep from Thomas Brid 1400/1, sued by the merchant John Clerk for £28 13s. 11d. 1401, sued by the prior of St Peter 1410, submitted a dispute with Richard Elmham to arbitration by John Symond and Richard Belcham 1401, dumped the entrails of slain beasts in the river at Friars Bridge and thereby obstructed the flow of water to the mill 1419.

Barbour, Robert; married Isabel; son, Thomas; will made 1447, proved 1447; buried St Nicholas; notable bequests, a quarter of barley to the church of Butley; executors, wife, son and John Tiler; occupation, sold ale in south ward 1437; borough office, juror in the petty court 1415. Other information; leased a house from Geoffrey Pipho, sued by John Wolfard for payment for the balance due for 3 pipes (1½ tuns) of wine, 1415.

Basse, Henry; son, Robert (?); parish of residence St Matthew (?); smith; freeman 1457; apprentices Robert Basse 1477, Edmund Bladsmyth 1482; borough offices, collector of funds raised for borough litigation in St Matthew 1455, chamberlain 1466/7; interests in borough land, lease of meadow plot lying beside Hanford Bridge 1463/4. Other information; fined for public health offences in west ward 1467/8.

Basse, Robert; father, Henry (?); parish of residence St Matthew (?); smith; freeman 1477, following an apprenticeship with Henry Basse; borough offices, assessor and collector of funds raised for expenses of new charter 1488, tax assessor 1488, both in St Matthew. Other information; litigant in the petty court 1487–1500, sued the cooper Thomas Barker for £1 15s. 6d 1488, sued by Edmund Daundy for £4 1500, fined for a public health offence in west ward 1488, submitted a dispute with Roger Newport to arbitration 1489.

Bernard, John; born Akenham; married Juliana; son, John; died c.1421; merchant; overseas trade exported cloth and grain, imported herring and iron 1397/8. Other occupation; brewed ale in north ward 1415 (?); bailiff 1396/7, 1401/2. Other borough offices, coroner 1397–1401, 1404–10, 1413/14, 1416–20; JP for Suffolk 1397; MP 1397, 1407, 1411; customs official, searcher of ships 1392–97, customer 1395–1401 (discontinuously). Other information; leased Bigod's quay from the countess of Norfolk 1390s, bought, for £240, a parade of shops from John Arnold in 1399 and later defaulted on payment, convicted of embezzlement in his role as customer and ordered to repay £120, his share of the ill-gotten gains, and fined a further £10 in 1401.

Bishop (alias Bushop, Bustop, Bysshop), Thomas; appointed as executor by Katherine Tyndale 1442, William Haken 1444, Robert Forthe 1447, Margery Wode, Alice Grenehood 1448; appointed as supervisor of will by Joan Wellyng 1458; occupation, practised as an attorney in the petty court mid 1460s. Other occupation; brewed ale in north ward 1472; freeman 1439, admitted in return for a buck deer, two sheep and six flagons of wine for Guildhall feast. Borough offices; common clerk (recorder) 1439–64, received an annual fee of £2 and a clothing allowance for coloured woollen cloth of 12s. 10d., 1446/7, in the same year rode to London to assist in obtaining the new charter from King Henry VI, claviger 1455/6. Other information; granted a pension for his service of all the common rent 1464, ordered to deliver up town records and give account of rents 1472.

Blake (alias Blak), William; will made 1476, proved 1477; married Jane; sons, William, admitted 1485 (?), Edmund, John and Nicholas; buried St Peter; property bequests, house in Ipswich, property in Chelmondiston; other notable bequests, book debts due from Mrs Gilbert Nicoll and William Wattys; executor, wife; merchant; overseas trade, imported wine 1459. Other occupations; brewed ale 1466–75, sold bread 1466–75, all in south ward; borough office, porter 1471. Other information; allowed his pigs to wander 1472–74.

Blankpayn, John; daughter, Margaret; occupations barber, brewed and sold ale 1434–38, sold ale 1455, all in north ward; apprentices William Chaffeld 1438, John Baset 1459; freeman 1422; 'of the better sort' 1445, worthy burgess 1452–59. Borough offices; treasurer 1432/3, one of those entrusted with an extension to the Guildhall 1435, chief pledge in the leet court of north ward 1436–38, claviger 1439–41, 1442–63, attended court general 1449–54, auditor of chamberlains' accounts 1452, tax assessor 1453, chamberlain 1456–59; interests in borough land, lease in St Nicholas 1437. Other information; ordered to account for his time as treasurer 1433, allegedly joint leader, with William Taliser, of a food riot 1438, acted as surety in various petty court cases 1443, and for John Thweyt 1448.

Blast, Roger; married Isabel; died 1407 (?); executors, wife, William Russell; merchant; overseas trade, imported two consignments of wine, one vintage and one reek, worth in total £50 in 1397/8. Other information; claimed compensation for defamation from Adam Skelton 1400, executors sought to recover a loan made in 1386 to Thomas Game of £4 11s. 8d., recovered only 33s. 4d. 1407.

Blomfeld (alias Blomvyle, Blomvile (?)), Robert; married Margery; son, Thomas; will made 1497, proved 1497; buried St Mary Tower; property bequests, one tenement; other notable bequests, for paving of the southern aisle of St Mary Tower; executors, son Thomas, Thomas Baldry; appointed as executor by John Creyk 1472; lawyer (?), clerk of the peace 1468–70, 1473–79; vintner, sold wine in north ward 1466–88. Other occupations, innkeeper in north ward 1465–88; apprentice, Thomas 1482; freeman 1460; councillor 1479/80; portman 1480; bailiff 1481/2, 1487/8. Other borough offices, chief pledge in the leet court of north ward 1464–79, chamberlain 1470/1, claviger 1478–80, 1488/91, warden of Corpus Christi gild 1480; JP 1487; interests in borough land, grant next to Handford Bridge in St Matthew 1475.

Bolle, Henry; father John (?); sister Isabelle married William Style; married, no wife or children recorded in will; will made 1479, proved 1479; parish of residence at death, St Mary Quay (?); buried Franciscan Friary; notable bequests, contents of bedchamber and wardrobe; executors, sister and nephew John Style; merchant, selling grain to a Spaniard 1474; freeman (?).

Bolle (alias Bole), John; married Joan (?); died 1434 (?); tanner. Other occupations; innkeeper, brewed and sold ale in east, north and west ward 1415–34 (?). Borough offices, juror in the petty court 1415, tithingman 1423, chief pledge 1424–34, both in leet court of east ward. Other information; brawl in his inn involved Thomas Medewe, John Sutton and John Godston 1415, sold wine for £3 7s. to the merchant Robert Crome 1415.

Bolton, Jurgoll (alias Jugyll); born Flanders; shoemaker 1483. Other occupation, sold ale from 1474 in north ward and then from 1479-87 in west ward; servants Richard Lucas,

Henry Johnson, Gerard Hermanne, all shoemakers of Flanders, John, a tawyer of Flanders, all 1483, John Guybone absconded (?) in breach of Statute of Labourers 1490. Other information; fined by the petty court for public health offences in north ward 1471/2, and then west ward 1475–88, litigant in the petty court 1479–91, householder 1483, donated 12d. for the upkeep of four young men in the service of the king 1486.

Boteler, William; parish of residence, St Mary Tower; armourer, worked for Sir John Howard for twenty days for 6s. 1464, pledged his stock to Thomas Wath as security for arrears of rent which included ten swords, fifty-nine pieces of armour, a shield, a grindstone and roller for burnishing armour, five dagger blades, a throat protector and a poleaxe 1466.

Bottold (Boteld, Botild), John; died 1431; parish of residence, St Laurence; remembered as '*primus inceptor*' (founder) on a commemorative stone that once stood in the parish church; merchant; overseas trade, exported woollen cloth and hides in the *Botolf* 1397. Other information; litigant in the petty court 1414, sued Edmund Rede and William Towres.

Boulge, Gilbert; died 1400 (?); merchant; overseas trade, exported wool 1377, imported 44 tuns of wine in *The Trinity* 1396; vintner, supplied wine to Margaret Marshall, countess of Norfolk 1385, and to merchants of Bury St Edmunds, Sudbury and Norwich 1393/4; freeman; bailiff 1392/3, 1394/5; customs official, collector 1393–95; interests in borough land, grant comprising a quay in St Mary Quay 1390, grant with others of land by river to build two water mills 1391, declared unlawful by the Crown 1399, but still leasing the land 1415, grant comprising a causeway from 'Portbregge' to 'Stokebregge' 1394.

Bramston (alias Bramstone), Nicholas; married Joan; sons, John, Thomas who became a freeman in 1474 and chamberlain in 1478/9; will made 1475, proved 1477; buried St Nicholas; property bequests, various including tenement next to Colehill in St Nicholas; other notable bequests, two pounds for the repair and plumbing of the south aisle of St Nicholas church; executors, wife and sons; appointed as executor by Thomas Lodbrook 1470; plumber (?). Other occupation, brewed ale in south ward 1466–74; freeman (?). Other information; took a lead weight as security for a debt of 8s. 8d. due from John Pratte 1465.

Brewys, John; shearman, sued by Thomas Smyth for 3s. in respect of dyed cloth that he had bought from him 1414, took from John Brewer madder and two narrow dozen woollen cloths as security for a debt 1414; and/or tawyer, sued Nicholas Smyth for payment for his services in tawing the pelts of fox cubs 1415; borough office, juror in the petty court 1407 and 1415. Other information; assaulted by Thomas Smyth 1415 (?).

Brook, Edmund; merchant; overseas trade, exported woollen cloth 1396; shipowner of the *Laurence*. Other information, sued by William de Burton of Hull in the court of Common Pleas 1403, involved in a protracted dispute, before the court of Admiralty, with a number of Hull merchants and awarded £1466 13s. 4d, including general damages of £1000 1408.

Broun (alias Brown), John I; married Alice; no children recorded; will made 1479, proved 1479; buried St Laurence; only bequest, 12d. to the high altar of St Laurence; executors, wife, John Feer of Brokeshalle; appointed as executor by Marion Forest, who made provision for him to go on pilgrimage on her behalf to Walsingham in Norfolk 1476; weaver; clothier, eight broadcloths 1468 (?). Other occupation, sold ale in south ward 1465.

Broun (alias Brown), John II; married Margaret; two sons, including John, who were admitted to the freedom with him, and Agnes, who had her own daughters when he died; will made 1494, proved 1495; buried St Margaret; property bequests, land in Westerfield; other notable bequests, candles to three Ipswich churches, money to gilds of Corpus Christi and of St Katherine and St Mary in the church of St Margaret, money for the road from Ipswich to Westerfield, all the bulls in his fields, silver and jewels; executors, daughter, Gosenold of Otley; appointed as executor by Robert Heed 1465; butcher in east ward 1465–88, leased the butchery from the borough for £20 per annum 1463/4. Other occupations, sold ale 1468–84, brewed ale 1472; freeman 1461 or 1463 (?); councillor 1479/80; interests in borough land, grant, on condition that he build a stone wall next to the town ditch, 1467, grant 1473. Other information; assaulted John Henbury 1467, allowed pigs to wander in east ward 1472, acted as surety for Richard Barbour tanner 1479, litigant in the petty court 1487–90.

Bunt, Thomas; married Margaret; no children recorded; will made 1513, proved 1513; parish of residence at death, St Margaret; buried St Margaret; executor, wife; dyer, in partnership with John Whetyngtone (?); freeman 1475. Borough offices, attended court general 1479, juror in the petty court 1479, tax collector 1480, 1487 in St Mary Tower. Other information; pledge for Roger Newport 1489, litigant in the petty court 1489–93, William Bylys the elder claimed from him a gown of blood red 1489, with Whetyngtone sued by Thomas Harford for £2, by William Style for £2 9s. 10d., by Richard Gosse for £4, all 1491, defended claims for significant sums by the London grocer John Smert 1492/3.

Burre, William; born Great/Little Leighs, Essex; siblings, John (?); married Margaret; son, John (?); grocer/chapman; freeman 1455, admitted by virtue of his apprenticeship for seven years to the grocer John Wytton for which an indenture dated 1446 survives. Other information; defended claims brought for payment under two letters of obligation by a London mercer John Wendey in the total sum of just under £10 1465, the petty court took his goods, including woollen cloth, as security for payment of a debt of just over 41s. to a London grocer John Gairstang 1465, party to a deed transferring the extensive property holdings of John Wytton (deceased) in St Laurence to John Kyng, grocer of London, and others 1466.

Buxton (alias Buxston), Robert; Gentleman; married Alice; daughter, Elizabeth, who married Helyot Sorby, merchant of Bordeaux; will made 1490, proved 1490; parish of residence at death, St Nicholas (?); buried, 'wheresoever God decides'; property bequests, lands and tenements Ipswich, Monewden, Sproughton, Stoke; other notable bequests, £6 13s. 4d. to the church of St Nicholas for a pair of organs, a gilt bowl, and all charters, letters and muniments; executors, daughter, Gregory Adgor; merchant (?); overseas trade (?). Other occupation, sold ale in south ward 1481–87. Other information; John Peperwyght burgled his house and robbed him of six pieces of pewter worth £2 1465, sued William Pykeryng for payment of balance of account 1478, Pykeryng argued that the royal courts had declared that no debt was due, kept pigs 1487.

Byrd, Thomas; skinner; other occupation, brewed ale in north ward 1479–84; freeman 1479; portman 1501; other borough offices, warden of the Corpus Christi gild 1482, tax assessor 1487, tax assessor in St Margaret 1488, chamberlain 1490/1; JP 1501/2. Other information; fined for public health offences in north ward 1481–88, litigant in the petty court 1490–92, with William Revet sued John Manser for £2 1491 and £6 3s. 4d. 1492, donated a horse for the service of the king 1491.

Caldwell, Benedict (alias Benet); born 1435 (?); father John; siblings Edmund, Robert and Thomas; married Elizabeth; children, John, Richard, Anne, Elizabeth, Margaret

(Bulverstone); will proved 1487; buried church of St Peter; property bequests, in Ipswich and manors and closes in Ashbocking, Ashfield with Thorp, Debenham, Earl Soham, Helmingham, Kenton, Stutton in Suffolk and Hempnall and Pulham Market in Norfolk; other notable bequests, cash gifts to variety of churches and religious houses; executors, wife, son John; appointed as executor by his father John 1461, John Byles 1472; lawyer, clerk of the peace 1470–73; arbitrated a dispute between Thomas Yooll and John Broun 1479; freeman 1450; bailiff 1473/4, 1476/7, 1479/80, 1482/3. Other borough offices, auditor of chamberlains' accounts 1470, claviger 1476/7, 1479–85, auditor of tax collectors' accounts 1482; JP 1477–79, 1480–82, 1483–85; MP 1484; under-sheriff of Norfolk and Suffolk 1463/4. Other information; claimed payment of £11 3s. 4d. arrears of rent from William Folkard for four enclosed pastures 1462, jointly with Edmund Winter took a letter of obligation for £100 from William Cakebread yeoman 1476, disenfranchised for various offences, including encroachment on borough land 1485, acquired valuable lands in East Bergholt, Reydon and Ipswich from Sir Gilbert Debenham 1486.

Caldwell (alias Caldewell), Edmund; father John; siblings Benedict, Robert, Thomas; appointed as executor by his father John 1461; merchant; overseas trade, imported fish, soap and bow staffs 1459; freeman. Other information; in Ipswich gaol 1460, father bequeathed money for his release, inherited his father's place at the quay.

Caldwell (alias Caldewell), John; married first Cecily, then Margaret and then Joan; sons, Benedict, Edmund, Robert and Thomas; will made 1460, proved 1461; buried, St Laurence by unnamed wife's grave; property bequests, his dwelling at *waldiches* with garden and stables, place at the quay, land in Monk Soham; other notable bequests, money to secure release of son Edmund from Ipswich gaol, £3 to John Drayll; executors, Benedict and Edmund Caldwell, supervised by John Drayll; merchant; overseas trade, sent his apprentice Thomas Bradde to trade on his behalf in Danzig, where Bradde fell into debt with local merchants including one Hans Stendell and was ultimately imprisoned in Ipswich gaol mid 1440s, sued William Baldry for the goods that Baldry had exchanged in Prussia for £200 worth of his cloth, no later than 1456; shipowner, jointly owned the ship *le Trinete* 1436. Other occupations, brewed ale 1423/4, innkeeper 1424, in north ward; apprentices Thomas Bradde, John Geserd 1435; freeman; portman 1420, 1429; bailiff 1426/7, 1431/2, 1435/6, 1442/3, 1448/9, 1451/2, 1454/5 and 1458/9; other borough office, claviger 1443–47, 1448–58, alderman of the merchant gild of Corpus Christi and responsible for pageant 1445/6, auditor 1449; JP 1449–60; MP 1427; interests in borough land, leases lately part of town wall, St Mary Quay, 1434 and 1439, lease in St Nicholas 1437, another lease in St Mary Quay 1439, lease Shirehouse Hill 1454, grant common marsh 1459. Other information; involved in various building projects, including Stoke bridge 1435, new building next to the hall of pleas 1448, erection of new gaol near the west gate 1449.

Caldwell (alias Caldewell), Thomas; father, John; siblings, Benedict, Edmund, Robert; merchant; with others chartered from Lord John Howard *The Barbara* which set sail to Bordeaux 1481; clothier, four broad cloths 1466. Other occupation, sold wine to the borough 1463/4, sold wine at an exorbitant price in north ward 1466; freeman 1455 (?); served on royal commission on smuggling 1449. Other information; sued the Ipswich dyer John Deye for payment under an account of £3 10s. 1465, created a cesspit next to his barn 1465, fined for other public health offences 1465–67.

Catfield, John; married Joan (?); son, John (?); kinsman and business partner Thomas; parish of residence at death, St Stephen; waterman, used the boat of William Austyn without consent, and damaged goods while unloading them from the boat of John Stampes, 1401. Other occupations, sold ale 1415–24, sold fish 1416–24, forestalling mackerel, herring and oysters 1424, sold bread 1423, in various wards; borough office, juror in the petty court 1408, tithingman in leet court of east ward 1423. Other information; convicted of assault 1423, court entries suggest that he moved between various wards during his life.

Clerk, John; mariner, master of the *Marye* of Ipswich; overseas trade, with south-west Europe, exported woollen cloth on the *Kogg John* of John Michell 1397/8; lost a share of a cargo of wool on *le Christofre* of Ipswich when the ship burnt in dock 1413. Other information; sold wine worth £1 6s. 8d. to Robert Crume 1401.

Cocoke (alias Cukhook), Robert; merchant, arrested at the Easter market in Bergen by the treasurer of the Merchant Adventurers for refusing to pay membership fee of £10, causing a great furore and an outcry against their 'uncharitable and inordinate greed' 1488; overseas trade, exported beef, beer, dairy, lead 1491; freeman (?). Other information; fined for public health offence 1483, fined for dumping waste from his oyster catch on the river bank 1484, in both cases in east ward, litigant in the petty court 1486–98, sued by Robert Halle, citizen and grocer of London, for £20 1498.

Cok, William; butcher, bought sheep and bulls at market from John Pronale for £3 3s. 4d. 1415, dumped the entrails of slain beasts in the river at Friars Bridge and thereby obstructed the flow of water to the mill 1419; borough office, juror in the petty court 1414.

Coke (alias Cok), Thomas; mariner, commissioned by the king to take forty mariners to fight the Scots in *The Kervell of Ipswich* 1481; overseas trade (?). Other occupation, sold ale in east ward 1481–84; borough office, porter 1474, juror in the petty court 1478–80, assessor of funds raised for expenses of new charter 1488, tax collector 1488, both in St Stephen. Other information; litigant in the petty court 1488/9.

Cosyn, John; fisherman 1472–82, broke the law by obtaining fresh fish from the baskets of other local fishermen in order to forestall the market 1479. Other occupations; brewed ale 1472, sold bread 1475, sold ale 1479–87, innkeeper, 1481–87, first in north ward and then from 1481 in east ward. Other information, sued by Robert Kyrkehous 1479, moved his operations from north to east ward between 1479 and 1481.

Cowman, Thomas; born Colchester; father, John; draper, sold six yards of blue woollen cloth to John Rede for 7s. 6d. 1443. Other occupations, brewed and sold ale 1421–55, innkeeper 1455, in west ward; freeman 1416, following apprenticeship with William Markes; attended court general in 1440s and 1450s; borough office, tithingman in leet court of west ward 1421–24, chief pledge in leet court of north ward (?) 1455, treasurer 1439/40, 1451/2; interests in borough land, lease in St Mary Quay 1439, lease with others of common marsh 1443. Other information; John Tyler broke into his house 1443, claimed compensation from Elizabeth Eed for defamation when she accused him of theft 1443, granted a recognisance of debt to Peter Terry, a merchant of Ipswich, for £11 10s. 1452.

Creyk (alias Creyck, Creyke), John; married Margery; children, Nicholas, Roger, William, Elizabeth, Helen, Margaret; will made 1461, proved 1472; buried St Mary Tower; property bequests, tenement called 'Smythes' in St Stephen, other tenements St Margaret and St Nicholas, garden and pasture next to the ramparts, six acres and a rood of land next to Malyneswode; other notable bequests, to wife goods in his shops; executors, wife, John Walworth, Robert Blomfeld; appointed as executor by John Feltwell 1461; appointed as supervisor of will by John Sudbury 1466; lawyer, clerk of the peace 1455–68, attorney in the petty court 1464–67; freeman 1448; councillor 1448; bailiff 1471/2; other borough office, chief pledge in north ward (?) 1455, claviger 1454–68, 1471/2, coroner 1460–66, auditor 1470. Other information; acquired (with others) two cottages in St Peter 1452, fined for public health offence by the leet court of north ward 1466.

Creyk, William; parents, John, bailiff 1471/2, Margery; siblings Nicholas, Roger, Elizabeth, Helen, Margaret; married Katherine; pewterer; freeman 1480. Other information; litigant in the petty court 1487–92, sued Geoffrey Sharrowe for £4 1491, in dispute with John ('Rycheman') Walworth 1492.

Dalton, William; tailor, owed William Recher a Bury draper £13 13s. 4d. 1443. Other occupation brewed ale in east ward 1436/7; freeman 1432; attended court general 1440–54.

Dameron, Cassandra; married Edmund; sons, John, Robert; will made 1498, proved 1498; parish of residence at death, St Mary Tower; buried St Mary Tower; property bequests, house in St Mary Tower; other notable bequests, four loads of bricks for the west door of St Mary Tower, shearman's shears to son John and servant Harry, contents of bedchamber, kitchen, wardrobe and washroom, silver spoons; executors, son Robert, Mr and Mrs Thomas (?) Baldry; servants, Harry, John 1498.

Daundy (Dandy, Dawndy), Edmund; a man 'of great substance'; parents, Thomas and Mary; siblings Richard and Joan, mother of Cardinal Wolsey to whom he was patron (?); married first Anne, then Margaret; children, John and Joan (both under twenty years of age at date of will), Robert, William (eldest), Agnes Adgore; will made 1515, proved 1515; parish of residence at death, St Laurence; buried St Laurence; property bequests, Creeting St Peter, Cretingham, Great Ashfield, Harwich, Holbrook, Monk Soham, Rushmere, Sproughton, Stoke, Stutton, house in St Laurence, place called *The Toune* in St Peter; other notable bequests, £200 to wife, other substantial cash gifts to children, £13 6s. 8d. to the repair of Borne bridge, stuff and merchandise and furniture in shops and warehouses, plate of silver and gilt, endowments to support his alms houses and St Thomas chantry, wall hangings, clothes to Henry Stannard; executor William Stysted; appointed as executor by William Baker 1509; merchant, overseas trade; freeman, as apprentice to John Wodeward, 1482; councillor by 1497; portman 1501; bailiff 1498/9, 1503/4, 1510/11, bought exemption from holding office as bailiff for six years in return for a payment of £33 and a consignment of brick and lime so that 20,000 bricks could be laid upon the common quay 1509. Other borough offices; tax collector 1487, assessor of funds raised for expenses of new charter 1488, both in St Laurence, warden of Corpus Christi gild 1489, 1490, chamberlain 1489/90, claviger 1491–1510; MP 1512, 1515. Other information, sworn into a tithing in south ward 1479, litigant in petty court 1486–1500, with John Bedfeld (as church wardens?) engaged Thomas Lopham to make stained glass for the east window of the church of St Laurence 1490, donated a horse for the service of the king 1491, acting as an arbitrator in petty court 1491, in joint business ventures with Thomas Alvard 1500, acquired lands in Sproughton and Stoke from Sir John Audley 1503, paid for the town's first market cross, obtained a licence to found a chantry in church of St Laurence for benefit of souls (among others) of Thomas Wolsey's parents 1510.

Debenham, Gilbert; Esquire; parents, Gilbert and Joan (?); married first Elizabeth, then Margaret and then Agnes; children, Gilbert, admitted as a freeman 1455, and two others; will no longer extant; died c.1481; buried, Lady Chapel in the Carmelite friary at Ipswich; property bequests, property in Ipswich, Harwich and various manors elsewhere; other notable bequests, collection of plate worth some £126; executors, his son Sir Gilbert, Benedict Caldwell and John Moss; merchant; traded with Prussia, where he employed Thomas Cadon as his factor and whose imprisonment he procured on his return to England;

shipowner of *le George* which he used for smuggling, caught in transit by the earl of Oxford 'with a large quantity of wool packed in a suspicious manner' in the early 1450s; freeman (?); MP 1427, 1432, 1437, 1442, 1449 (Feb.); sheriff of Norfolk and Suffolk 1427/8; JP many times; interests in borough land, lease 1446/7. Other information, one of the most lawless gentry of East Anglia, intermittently a retainer of the Mowbray dukes of Norfolk, and also of the de la Pole faction, embroiled in disputes with the Paston family, brought at least five claims in the petty court, between 1443 and 1478, for payment under letters of obligation and acquired a reputation for specialising 'in fraudulent actions over these obligations'.

Debenham, William I[1]; born Wenham (?); sons, John, William (?); merchant; overseas trade, exported woollen cloth, imported wine and salt in three different vessels 1397/8, exported woollen cloth and candles, imported wine 1413/14; clothier, forty straits 1396/7; freeman; bailiff 1402–04, 1414/15, 1417–20; MP 1397; customs official, deputy butler, tronager, 1420/1. Other information; his servant deposited garden waste in Carle Street, north ward 1415, fined for public health offences in north ward 1415, left timber in king's highway in Clement Street, east ward 1416.

Debenham, William II; father, William; parish of residence, St Mary Tower (?); vintner, sold 80 gallons of red wine at the exorbitant price of 8d. per gallon in west ward 1424; apprentices Robert Smyth and Thomas Kemp 1420, Edmund Blake and Richard Melys 1434; freeman; attended court general 1418, councillor 1424 (?), portman 1440; bailiff 1429/30, 1433/4, 1441/2, 1444/5; MP 1414 (Nov.), 1417, 1419, 1421 (May), 1437; JP 1433–40; interests in borough land, lease in St Nicholas 1437, lease in St Mary Quay 1439. Other information; fined for public health offences in west ward 1415–23, made threats of violence against John Shipley 1420, claimed payment under an account with William Wrighte, and payment of two years' arrears of rent from Richard Gowty 1443.

Deken, John; born Ipswich; father, Thomas; married Eleanor; no children recorded; will made 1448, proved 1449; parish of residence at death, St Mary Quay; buried Dominican friary; property bequests, house in Brook Street, lands elsewhere; other notable bequests, items of silver; executors, Father John Bromleygh, rector of St Stephen's, John Burdyvaunt; mercer; overseas trade, exported grain 1427/8, woollen cloth 1447, and carried pilgrims to Santiago de Compostella 1433, 1445; unsuccessfully resisted the appointment of the London mercer, John Warren, as permanent governor of the Merchant Adventurers in the Low Countries 1421; shipowner of *Cristofre* 1436; other occupation, brewed ale in north ward 1415–21; apprentices, Thomas Patewey 1420, John Drayll 1432, who remembered Deken in his will, John Smyth 1449, four others remembered in Deken's will; portman 1420, 1429; bailiff 1422–26, 1427–29, 1431/2, 1434/5, 1441/2, 1444/5. Other borough office, coroner 1430/1, 1438/9, claviger 1430–35, 1440/1, 1445–death; JP 1424–49; MP 1425, 1427; interests in borough land, leases in St Margaret 1415 and 1419, grant near the houses of the office at the quay 1433, lease lately part of town wall, St Mary Quay, 1434, lease in St Nicholas 1437. Other information, first mentioned in the records late 1300s or early 1400s, convicted of assault against Henry Barbour 1415, accused of robbery and surrendered to the Marshalsea prison in London, but acquitted, 1423, appointed to oversee extension to Guildhall 1435, on his death owed a Bury St Edmunds baker, John Joynour, the sum of £16 16s. 1450.

Denys (alias Denis), Thomas; married first Joan, then Ellen, then Margery; children Thomas, William (both under age at date of will), William (illegitimate), Elizabeth; died

[1] It is not always easy to differentiate in the records between the two William Debenhams, father and son.

1464, while in office as bailiff; will proved 1464; buried St Margaret; property bequests, tenements in St Laurence, St Mary Quay, St Mary Tower; other notable bequests, cash gift to Campsey Priory; executors, Richard Felawe, John Drayll; appointed as executor by John Felawe c.1450; appointed as supervisor of her will by Alice Pipho 1462; lawyer, represented the borough as its 'attorney at common law' from 1443, received (with Roger Stannard) a fee of 26s. 8d. for having the town's charter enrolled in court 1446/7, received a fee of 20s. to go to London on behalf of the borough in its suit with the king 1459, agreed an annual retainer with the borough for a fee of 20s. per annum 1459, appeared before the court of common pleas for William de la Pole and others, and before the court of King's Bench; other occupation, sold ale in north ward 1423; freeman; portman 1429; bailiff 1433/4, 1439/40, 1442/3, 1445/6, 1449/50, 1454/5, 1457/8, 1460/1, 1463/4; other borough office, treasurer 1431/2, claviger 1433/4, auditor of borough accounts; JP 1428–40, 1448–58, 1460–64; MP 1431, 1432, 1435, 1442; served on various royal commissions, including one on smuggling 1449; interests in borough land, lease in St Nicholas 1421, grant in St Clement 'next to the salt water' 1435, grant in St Mary Elms 1437, leases in St Mary Quay 1439 and 1453, grant at Shire house 1451. Other information; stood bail for John Deken when charged with robbery 1423, and subsequently for William Keche for a similar offence, brought several claims on his own behalf in the court of common pleas 1450.

Depyng, John; married Alice; children, John plus others (?); will made 1471, witnessed by Master Walter, Ralph Jerald merchant, John Parker; proved 1471; parish of residence at death, St Nicholas, Calais; buried St Nicholas, Calais; notable bequests, book debts to widow which she was still trying to recover seven years later, clothes including doublet, hose and boots to the master of 'the Ship' (boat or inn?); executor, wife supervised by John Gosse; merchant; clothier, twelve straits 1467. Other occupations, innkeeper 1465–68, fishmonger 1465–68, brewed ale 1466/7, sold wine 1467, sold ale 1468, all in east ward; freeman 1463; borough office, porter 1471. Other information; widow tried to extract payment for a consignment of wood ashes from John Berforth, who defended the claim on the grounds that he had previously settled Depyng's debts in Brandon Ferry, Peterborough and Stamford 1478.

Deve, John; butcher 1415–23, slaughtered sheep in the flesh market 1415, dumped the entrails of slain beasts in the river at Friars Bridge and thereby obstructed the flow of water to the mill 1419. Other occupations (?), brewed ale 1434–38, innkeeper 1434–38, in south ward; freeman 1418, in return for collecting butchers' tolls for seven years; borough office, juror in the petty court 1414, chief pledge in leet court of south ward 1434–38. Other information; with William Grene acquired twenty-nine sheep from Walter Reynburgh for £5, but William Debenham claimed that nineteen of the animals belonged to him 1415.

Deye, John; kinsman Robert (?); dyer, sued by the wool carder/shearman Thomas Wysman for payment for woollen cloth including two kerseys, a dozen and flock, and by John Munnyng of Hadleigh and Thomas Caldwell for payment of balance of account, and by Richard Lee and Stephen Burgess, both grocers of London, for payment under a letter of obligation, all 1465; clothier, two broadcloths 1466; other occupation, sold ale in east ward 1465/6; freeman 1463; borough office, served as a valuer in petty court 1465, juror in the petty court 1478–80, tax collector in St Nicholas 1481. Other information, assaulted John Omund and John Tough 1465.

Deye, Robert; son, Thomas; kinsman John (?); clothier, one broadcloth 1466; other occupations innkeeper 1465–72, sold ale 1466–71, in east ward; freeman 1464; interests in borough land, lease of Horsewade mill for annual rent of £10 1463/4.

Deye, Thomas; married Christina; sons, John, Thomas; will made 1490, proved 1495; parish of residence at death, St Nicholas; buried St Nicholas; property bequests, dwelling house; other notable bequests, two woollen looms to son Thomas, one to 'young John'; executors, wife, John Luke; weaver; apprentices, 'young John' (?). Other information; fined for assault by leet court of south ward 1472.

Disse (alias Dysse), Richard; married Margaret, who took over his business as brewster and innkeeper after he died; a son and daughter (?); will made 1437, proved 1438; parish of residence at death, St Mary Tower, neighbours John Caldwell, Robert Deye, William Walworth; buried St Mary Tower; property bequests, part of a shop with two upper rooms next door to his house; other notable bequests, silver basin and two ampullae to church of St Mary Tower, £10 for an honest chaplain to go on his behalf on pilgrimage to Rome, gift to the poor in the greatest deprivation; executors, son, Nicholas Wymbysh clerk, Walter Disse clerk, Robert Stone notary public. Occupations, brewed ale 1415–37, innkeeper 1416–37, in north ward; borough office, tithingman in leet court of north ward 1421–24.

Drayll (alias Drayle), John; siblings, brother a priest, sister Amy Benet; married Margaret; sons, John (chaplain) and Thomas; will made 1464, proved 1465; parish of residence at death, St Mary Tower; buried Carmelite friary, next to the tomb of William Debenham; property bequests, in five different parishes in the town, including a shop in the parish of St Mary Elms; other notable bequests, gifts to the poor, salary to servant Margaret Copping, to be determined by executors, contents of bedchamber and wardrobe, including a gown of scarlet, Prussian chest, silver and gold plate, pewter, funds for erection of a plaque with his name in the church of St Mary Tower, whereby he can be remembered by parishioners, £70 to Carmelite friars to pray for himself and others including William Debenham and John Deken; executors, wife, son Thomas and Robert Wymbyll notary; appointed as executor by Edmund Blake 1444, Thomas Kempe 1460, Thomas Denys 1464; mercer. Other occupation, brewed ale in south ward 1437; freeman 1432, by virtue of his apprenticeship to John Deken; portman 1445; bailiff 1449/50, 1457/8; other borough office, coroner 1443–45, chamberlain 1447/8 (?), claviger 1449/50, 1457–59, auditor 1457; JP 1448–62; interests in borough land, lease in St Mary Quay 1439, lease common marsh 1445, 1455, lease of a small parcel of land next to his home 1446/7, grant 1454. Other information; sued Rumbald Herryessone for payment of £18 under a letter of obligation 1443.

Drayll (alias Drayle), Thomas; parents, John and Margaret; sibling John; married Margaret, then Agnes, then Joan; daughter, Anne Hert; will made 1512, proved 1512; parish of residence at death, and buried St Mary Tower, where his memorial brass survives, in north aisle chapel of St Katharine's chapel which he had endowed during his lifetime; property bequests, various properties in Ipswich including the 'Stylyard' in St Mary Quay, and Debenhams and Joyes in St Mary Tower; other notable bequests, £16 to Hantforth Bridge and £20 to Bourne Bridge, a grave stone of marble 'with an image thereon after my person', £140 (?) to the borough on condition that 'strangers' and 'foreigners' should be helped and eased from tolls and charges on transporting merchandise to and from the town, on carrying on trade and on opening a shop, best gown and best standing cup of silver to Thomas Baldry; executors, son-in-law William Hert of Norwich, Sir William Barowne priest; appointed as executor by his father John 1465, William Wymbyll 1485; appointed as supervisor of will by William Sewall 1501; merchant/mercer; overseas trade, exported lead 1492; apprentice Robert Payne, for whom an indenture dated 1480 survives; freeman; portman 1477, 1501; bailiff 1478/9, 1482/3, 1487/8, 1491/2, 1496/7, 1503/4, 1508/9; other borough office, chamberlain 1470, claviger 1474–79, auditor 1482, 1487; JP 1479–81, 1483/4, 1485–87, 1488–91, 1492–96, 1498–1510; MP 1489/90; interests in borough land, joint grant of three stalls in the fish market. Other information; fined for public health offences by leet court of west ward 1483–88, litigant in the petty court 1490–98, sued the glazier Thomas Lopham for £9 6s. 5d. 1492, with William Baker, a notary and fellow merchant, sued the shearman Richard Faryngton for £40 1498.

Drye (alias Dreye), Robert; married Matilda; son, John; will made 1449, proved 1450; parish of residence at death and buried St Mary Tower; property bequests, tenement in the old fish market next to St Mary Tower; other notable bequests, a pyx with a gilt incense boat, two covered silver bowls ornamented respectively with vines and an upright eagle, great cupboard, to the Corpus Christi gild 10s. and a gold ring; executors, William Harleston esquire of Denham, William Gosselyn. Other occupation, brewed ale in north ward 1434–38; freeman; portman 1440; bailiff 1429/30, 1432/3, 1436/7; other borough office, treasurer 1431/2; JP Ipswich and Suffolk 1433.

Fadinor, Robert; married Joan (?); parish of residence at death, St Stephen (?); merchant and fisherman; overseas trade, exported 60 wey of cheese 1389 (?); other occupations, dealt in horses, William Snow did not pay for a horse and Robert Burghard stole one 1408, sold fish 1416–23, including porpoise, turbot and conger eel 1416, sold dairy products 1419, sold ale 1419–24, mainly in east ward; servant Agnes Bemytoo left his service prematurely after about a month 1407. Other information, brothel keeper 1416.

Fastolf, Margaret; brother, Nicholas Kent of London; married, no husband mentioned; no children recorded; will made 1452, proved 1452; buried St Laurence; notable bequests, gifts to houses of friars in London, contents of bedchamber, kitchen and wardrobe including gowns of scarlet, crimson and murrey lined with the fur of pole cat, and a book with engraved binding; executors, John Braham of Wetheringsett, Father Robert Bramford.

Fastolf, Thomas;[2] Esquire; born Cowhaugh/Nacton 1430 (?); son of John, and ward and heir of Sir John Fastolf (?); son, John (?); parish of residence, St Laurence, probably built the Ancient House, described as 'of Pondes next to Ipswich' 1497; merchant; overseas trade (?); freeman 1446 (?); bailiff 1451-52 (?). Other borough office, treasurer 1448/9; JP 1449/50; MP, on half the wages established by ancient custom, i.e., 12d. per day 1487; interests in borough land, grant adjoining the quay 1482, leases in St Margaret 1482 and 1484. Other information; mentioned in the Paston letters as preparing to claim Caister by force, probably on behalf of the duke of Norfolk 1467, donated 12d. to the upkeep of four young men in the service of the king 1486, litigant in petty court 1486–97, including claim for £200 against John Newport and Geoffrey Wynt 1486, donated a set of body armour and a standard of mail to the king 1491, gave recognisances to the king 1501.

Felaw, John; born Harwich (?); died 1450 (?); son, Richard; executors, son Richard, Thomas Denys; merchant, trading with men of Hadleigh, Lowestoft and Yarmouth before 1450. Other occupations, brewed ale 1416–38, tanner 1416–21, all in east ward, fined 12d. for soaking leather in the town ditch in east ward and making pits there 1419; freeman; bailiff 1439/40; other borough office tithingman 1419–21, chief pledge 1423–34, both in leet court of east ward, claviger 1439/40. Other information; witnessed a transfer of land in St Mary Quay 1427, was granted all income of the office of chamberlain for twelve years 1439, although there is no evidence that he held such office.

[2] As Colin Richmond recognised, Thomas Fastolf is an elusive figure and, having regard to the apparent longevity of his career, the biographical details given here may well relate to more than one man of that name.

Felawe, Richard; born Harwich 1421 (?); father, John; married Agnes; daughter, Agnes; will made 1482; buried St Mary Quay; property bequests, provision of a school house and endowment for Ipswich school and for almshouses, appointed John Squyer as master of school and prescribed regulations for its future governance; executors, James Hobard and John Squyer; appointed as executor by Thomas Denys 1464; merchant, overseas trade, exported woollen cloth, grain 1452, carried pilgrims to Santiago de Compostella 1445; shipowner, in partnership with Sir William Rider, jointly owning the *Gyles* of Hull, until Rider complained about the lack of profit from his investment; clothier, one broadcloth 1466; portman 1479; bailiff 1448/9, 1452/3, 1455/6, 1458/9, 1461/2, 1465/6, 1469/70, 1474/5. Other borough office; tax assessor 1453, claviger 1452/3, 1455/6, 1469/70; JP 1449–death; MP 1449 (Feb.), 1460, 1461 and 1470; customs official, various offices including collector and controller; various royal commissions, including one on smuggling 1449; interests in borough land, grant of foreshore rights in St Clement 1446, grant at Shirehouse Hill 1451, leases in St Mary Quay 1453 and 1462, various leases including the new mill for £10 pa 1461–64, grant 1462, grant between Mert ditch and Chestains close, St Clement, 1479. Other information; moved to Ipswich mid 1440s, went to London on behalf of the borough in its suit with the king 1459, commercial agent for Sir John Howard, later duke of Norfolk.

Fen, William atte; kinsman Hugh; merchant/vintner; overseas trade, jointly with William Thorp imported 34 tuns of wine 1398, sold 5 tuns of Gascon and 6 of Rochelle wine from his own tavern, and unlawfully sold wine without gauge to merchants of Bury St Edmunds, Sudbury and Norwich 1393/4. Other occupations, brewed and sold ale in west ward 1415; freeman; bailiff 1386/7, 1392/3, 1394/5; JP for Suffolk 1397; member of a royal commission ordered to assemble and man all ships, barges and boats for the purpose of attacking, arresting and committing to prison, pirates who lie in wait for merchants and have pursued them from port to port, wounding, killing, robbing and imprisoning until ransom made 1398. Other information; pardoned from outlawry in respect of a debt to the executors of the will of William Crouges of London 1387, witnessed the grant of land comprising a quay in St Mary Quay 1390.

Forgon, John; married, wife not named; sons, John and Thomas, step sons John and William Sewell (all minors at date will made); will made 1525, proved 1525; buried St Clement, before the pew where wife sits; property bequests include lime pit yard, tenement on the Cornhill by the flesh stalls; other notable bequests, leather tanned and untanned, bark, gilt goblets, silver apostle spoons, gown furred with fox, tawny *gawberdyne* lined with say; supervisor of his will William Hall; appointed as executor by Robert Peteman 1488; tanner in east ward from 1481; apprentices, five servants and three apprentices c.1520; freeman 1480; councillor 1501; portman 1508; bailiff 1509/10, 1514/15, 1519/20; other borough office, tax collector 1481, 1487 in St Clement, warden of the Corpus Christi guild 1489, 1490, tax assessor 1490, 1491; interests in borough land, two grants in St Mary Quay 1499. Other information; fined for public health offences by leet court of east ward 1481–88, active as claimant in the petty court from 1487, taxed on land worth £5 per annum and goods and chattels worth £100 c.1520.

Freborne, Joan; siblings John, Nicholas (?) who sold ale 1437/8, Anne; spinster (?); no children recorded; will made 1458, proved 1459; buried St Laurence; notable bequests, contents of bedchamber, kitchen and wardrobe, including earliest extant Ipswich testamentary reference to pewter, a mazer lined with silver, gowns lined with the fur of winter squirrel; executors, John Sergeant, Thomas Gylis, Margaret Wethereld.

Fulslo (alias Foslowe), Henry; alien, born Zeeland; married Isabelle; no children recorded; will made 1487, proved 1487; buried St Mary Quay; notable bequests, a barrel of beer to each order of friars in Ipswich; executor wife, supervised by John Squyer and Robert Wentworth; beer brewer 1484–87; servants Root Johnson, Gerard of Deventor, Gerard Dyrykson, all of Zeeland, 1483, John Newys, absconded (?) in breach of Statute of Labourers 1487. Other information; described in the alien subsidy as a householder and master of a brew house 1483, litigant in petty court, sued the Dutchman Denis Wyman 1486/7, fined for keeping pigs on the common quay 1487.

Fyshman, John; parents, Robert and Margaret; siblings John, Robert, Thomas; married Matilda; appointed as executor by Robert Fyshman 1469; occupations, regrator 1437, sold ale 1438, both in south ward. Other information, with his knowledge his wife allegedly broke into the house of William Style and stole 52lbs of woollen yarn and brought it to him 1464, assaulted by John Herd who stole eighty rabbit skins worth 24d. 1479, engaged John Furbushour to dye four linen bed sheets in various colours with a pattern of roses and flowers 1479.

Gairstang (alias Gairstange, Garstangyr), John; father, Robert (?); married Alice; described as of London in the petty court 1465 and in the calendar of patent rolls 1469, as of Ipswich in the calendar of close rolls 1478; died before 1477; executor, wife; grocer, widow collecting debts due to him for 'grocerewares' and 'hustilments' from debtors in Bury St Edmunds, Bishop's Lynn, Walsingham, Colchester, Needham Market, Brandon Ferry, Reedham, Norwich, Ely, London, Kidderminster, Tower Street (presumably also in London), Brandonbury in Devon (this may be a mis-translation), and Faversham in Kent 1477. Other information; took security over woollen cloth from William Burre as security for a debt of £2 1s. 2d. 1465, sued the two administrators of Gaudeberus Makenham (both from Ipswich) and Herman Williamson lately of Ipswich beer-brewer for £12 10s. 1469.

Garne, Peter; alien; married Isabel, beer-brewer in east ward 1466/7 (?); merchant, overseas trade, imported fish, furniture, hops, linen, litmus (dye), madder, stone, stoneware, timber 1459. Other information, acted as a pledge before the Ipswich maritime court for his kinsman Gerard Garne, in the latter's dispute with another merchant-mariner, sued in the petty court for payment of an account by the clerk Ralph Belaby, 1464.

Gigehoo (alias Gygoo), Edmund; kinsman, John another tanner; married Joan, who continued tanning business 1436–38, and died 1473; children, John, Alice, Joan and Rose; tanner in north ward 1416–34, soaked leather in common water 1421; freeman 1433; borough office, juror in the petty court 1415.

Goldwyn, John; married Matilda; son, Thomas; will made 1488, proved 1488; notable bequests, contents of bedchamber, kitchen, wardrobe and washroom, brooch with diamond stones, silver and pewter, to servant Richard blue gown and 40s. if he is true and faithful; executor, wife; other information, admitted to a tithing in east ward 1483, wife sold bread, ale and fish in east ward 1488.

Gosenold (alias Gosewold), Roger; merchant; overseas trade, exported woollen cloth in the *Kogg John* of John Michell 1398. Other information; acquired from the Crown 100 acres of land, 8 acres of meadow, 12 acres of pasture, 2 acres of wood and 10s. of rent in Brandeston 1373, pardoned from outlawry in respect of a debt to the executors of the will of William Crouges of London 1387, witnessed the grant of land comprising a quay in St Mary Quay 1390, sold a consignment of iron, wine and salt to Robert Waleys for £31 13s. 4d. 1401. His descendants built Otley Hall, Suffolk, and also named Martha's Vinyard in Massachusetts and founded Jamestown in the state of Virginia.

Gosse (alias Goss), John; father, Robert; brother, Thomas; married Agnes; children, none recorded; will made 1497, proved 1498; buried St Matthew; property bequests, Ramsey, Essex; executors, wife and William Winter; merchant; overseas trade, exported cloth 1465; clothier, five broad cloths 1466, twenty straits 1467; apprentice, William Sprunt 1462; freeman 1443, by patrimony; councillor 1448; portman 1474–89; bailiff 1466/7, 1472/3, 1475/6, 1479/80, 1484/5. Other borough office, tax assessor 1453, chamberlain 1454–56, auditor 1470, claviger 1475/6, 1484/5; JP 1466–68, 1474–78, 1479–81, 1483–86; interests in borough land, grants 1454, 1463, lease in St Mary Quay 1466. Other information, granted liberty of quay 1453, litigant in the petty court 1486–90.

Gosse, Richard; merchant; overseas trade, imported fish 1481; other occupations, sold ale 1484, innkeeper 1484–88, both in east ward; freeman 1472. Borough office, warden of the Corpus Christi gild 1487/8, assessor of funds raised for expenses of new charter 1488, and tax assessor 1488, both for St Mary Quay, chamberlain 1488/9. Other information; litigant in petty court 1489–93, sued John Whetyngton and Thomas Bunt for £4 1491, sued William Harlewyn for £11 1493, donated a horse to the king 1491.

Gouty (alias Goutee, Gowty), Richard; married Joan; nochildren recorded; will made 1448, proved 1448; parish of residence at death, and buried St Mary Quay; property bequests, tenement and garden; other notable bequests, quoin stone for the new church of St Mary Quay; executor, wife; merchant, master of the ship *Nicholas* of Ipswich, embroiled in a dispute with William Johanson of Newcastle-upon Tyne in 1424. Other occupations, sold ale 1416–38, brewed ale 1421-24, in east ward. Borough office, tithingman in leet court of east ward 1419–24; interests in borough land, lease in St Mary Quay 1446.

Grene (alias Greyne), John; born Fleet, Lincolnshire (?); chapman or merchant; other occupation, innkeeper 1421 in north ward. Other information; claiming payment under an account with Andrew Coke a dealer in woad 1407, pardoned for not defending debt claims in the court of King's Bench by John Colbroke, a citizen and tailor of London, for £20, and by John Chirche, a citizen and mercer of London, for £17.13s. 4d. 1425.

Grenehood, Alice; married Richard (Wethermerth) and William; daughter, Margery a nun of Campsey; will made 1448, proved 1449; buried St Laurence; property bequests, extensive holdings in Ipswich and elsewhere in Suffolk; other notable bequests, bell for the belfry of St Laurence (the bell survives and has recently been reinstated), provision for pilgrimages to Walsingham and other local shrines, white loaves for poor and feast for all tenants, contents of bedchamber, kitchen and wardrobe; executors, Thomas Bishop, Walter Fulborn, William Jerald, John Neve and (Norwich will) Gilbert Stonham.

Guybone (alias Gibbon, Gybon), William[3]; kinsman William Guybon (?), carpenter; chandler, stocked 'cloth indies' 1498. Other occupations, sold ale and bread 1487/8, baked bread 1487, in south ward; freeman; councillor 1497. Other borough office, tax assessor 1487/8, collector of funds raised for expenses of new charter 1488, all in St Nicholas, chamberlain 1495/6. Other information, fined for public health offences in south ward 1484–88.

Hall, Robert; sons, Stephen, John and William; spicer. Other occupation, sold ale 1436–38, in west and then north ward; servant Henry 1436; freeman 1435; attended court general 1440; borough office, treasurer 1449/50, chamberlain 1452/3 (?), coroner 1458/9.

[3] William Guybone had a contemporary of the same name who was a carpenter, and was admitted as a freeman in 1490. They were probably related as they both acknowledged a debt to Robert Fox 1498.

Halle (alias Hall), John; married Katherine; son, William who also became bailiff; will made 1503, proved 1503; buried St Margaret, in front of the crucifix; property bequests, to son a house called a 'woodehows'; other notable bequests, five marks to church of Bildeston; life time gift for the building of the clerestory of St Margaret's church, where his merchant mark appears; executors, wife, Thomas Baldry, William Ropkyn; 'woodyer' (dyer/woad merchant), constructed a dye pit called 'Adam' in the town ditch in north ward 1466/7; freeman 1477; councillor 1480; portman 1488, 1496; bailiff 1489/90, 1495/6; other borough office, chamberlain 1479/80, after leaving office paid 13s. 4d. for exoneration from his account, tax collector in St Margaret 1481, claviger 1486–88, 1495/6, treasurer 1487/8; JP 1490/1, 1496/7; interests in borough land, lease in St Margaret 1480. Other information; litigant in the petty court 1479–99, sued Henry Tenyrsham for breaking into his premises and stealing 50 yards of woollen cloth worth £2 13s. 4d. 1479, John Lunt tailor for £9 16s. 10d. 1486, Robert Hall shearman for £4 6s. 8d. 1493, Robert Hervy baker for £10 17s. 8d. 1496, Thomas Wode butcher of Needham Market for £4 1498, valued various pieces of linen cloth that had been seized from Robert Monktone 1479, fined for public health offence in north ward 1484, donated a set of body armour to the king 1491.

Hammond (alias Hamond), Thomas; brother, Richard; married Joan; daughter, Alice; will made 1455, proved 1455; parish of residence at death, and buried St Peter; property bequests, various properties in Ipswich, including chief tenement in St Peter and two gardens; other notable bequests, cash to servants; executors, wife and brother; tanner; servants Thomas Yol, Margery Wrighte; freeman 1438.

Hamond, John; died not before 1493; tanner in south ward 1460–82; other occupation brewed ale in south ward 1467; freeman 1460, threatened with disenfranchisement 1493; borough office, juror in the petty court 1478/9, attended court general 1479. Other information; assaulted Thomas the servant of Edmund Winter 1465, assaulted by John Gravener 1466 and by John White 1475, pledged as security for a debt an iron tool with silver decoration 1467, permitted his pigs to wander 1468, 1488.

Harford (alias Herford), Thomas; merchant and mariner, traded with Iceland; overseas trade, exported woollen cloth, beer, onions 1483, exported caps, gloves, honey, iron, linen cloth, malt, woollen cloth, imported fish, wadmole etc. 1492; freeman (?); borough office, tax collector in St Mary Quay 1488, tax assessor 1490; interests in borough land, grant of foreshore rights on partly developed land in St Mary Quay 1499. Other information; dumped muck on the common quay 1488, litigant in petty court 1487–97, in joint business venture with Nicholas Porchet 1489, and with Robert Brusone 1493, refused to deliver up stockfish 1491, pursued the dyers Thomas Bunt and John Whetyngtone for recovery of a debt 1491, granting recognisances for large debts 1489/90.

Harlewyn (alias Harlewin), William; father, William (?); married Margaret; son, William; will made 1506, proved 1506; buried St Clement; property bequests, property in Petham, Kent (?), house in Ipswich; other notable bequests, £20 for the highways in Petham; executors, wife, John Felgate of Stonham Aspal; merchant; overseas trade, exported dairy 1483, exported dairy, linen, imported dyes, fish, haberdashery, iron, linen, oil, stone etc. 1491/2. Other occupation, sold ale in east ward 1474/5; apprentices Reginald Rous 1491, Robert Doobyll 1496; freeman 1472; portman 1488, 1497; bailiff 1490/1, 1495/6; other borough office, chamberlain 1483–85, tax assessor in St Clement 1488; JP 1491/2, 1494/5, 1496/7, 1501/2; interests in borough land, grant of foreshore rights in St Clement 1499. Other information; accused of passing off the goods of alien merchants as if they were his own 1477, litigant in petty court 1487–99, in joint business ventures with Sir Henry Wyngfeld 1487, and with Thomas Cole and William Hewet 1489/90, donated a complete set of armour to the king 1491.

Hastyngs (alias Hastyng), John; married Joan; children, William and Agnes (?); appointed as executor by John Baldwyn 1488; chandler, 'sub-owned' from John Drayll a shop with garden in St Mary Elms 1464, sold candles for excessive profit in south ward 1468. Other occupations, brewed ale 1466–71, innkeeper 1471, in south ward; apprentice John Crosse 1498 (?); freeman 1457, portman 1470–74; bailiff 1473/4, 1477/8, 1481/2, 1489/90. Other borough offices, collected funds for borough litigation 1458, chamberlain 1463/4, for which office his account survives, chief pledge south ward 1466–68, coroner 1466–71, joint trustee of common marsh and Portmans' meadow 1469, auditor 1472–88, claviger 1485/6, 1489/90. tax assessor 1487; JP 1473/4, 1477/8, 1481–83, 1489–91; interests in borough land, grant 1463, grant at the new mill dam 1470. Other information; donated a complete set of armour to the king 1491.

Haxwade (alias Hakeswade, Haukiswade, Hawkyswade), Richard; sister, Clare; married Agnes; sons, Robert and Thomas, both apprentices, William admitted 1500; will made 1499, proved 1500; buried St Laurence; property bequests, house, three tenements in St Mary Quay; other notable bequests, wool in the solar of house, silver plate, bedding; executor, wife supervised by Benjamin Dygby; appointed as executor by Helen Haynys 1496; appointed as supervisor of will by John Heynys 1495; merchant; overseas trade, exported woollen cloth 1483/4. Other occupations, sold ale 1474/5, innkeeper 1475–88, sold fish 1488, all in east ward; apprentice, John Saxsyndam 1498; freeman 1475; portman 1477, 1479; bailiff 1480/1, 1483/4, 1492/3, 1497/8. Other borough office, claviger 1492/3; JP 1481/2, 1484/5, 1493/4, 1498/9; customs official, collector 1467 (?). Other information; litigant in petty court 1478–95, in joint business ventures with William Sewale 1487 (?), after death his wife sold property called Berthclotestent, with half a quay called Berthlotiscay, in St Peter 1500.

Heede, William; miller; freeman 1445; councillor 1448; borough office, treasurer 1451/2, tax assessor 1453. Other information, in partnership with William Ridout (?), threatened with disenfranchisement for suing John Caldwell in the court of Chancery 1455, with William Ridout resisted paying rent to borough for lease of Horsewade Mill 1455/6.

Herreyssone (alias Henrykson), Rumbald; alien, born Arneburgh in Saxony; kinsmen, Henry and Peter; merchant, overseas trade, imported grain, wood ash; shipowner of *le Cogship* which was captured by pirates 1440; other occupation, brewed and sold beer in east ward 1434–38, sold beer to Katherine Monke for Twelfth Night celebrations 1443, fined 10s. for brewing ale 1437. Other information; took oath of fealty to the Crown 1436, assaulted Henry Booth and John Cobbe 1437, owned pigs who fouled the quay 1438, taxed as an alien householder 1440, prominent litigant in petty court both as claimant and defendant, in cases involving the sale of beer, and the grant to John Drayll of a letter of obligation for the sum of £18, which he later dishonoured and, in consequence, spent a few days in Ipswich gaol 1443, traded with Simon Rankyn a merchant of Cambridge 1445.

Hervy, Robert; baker in south ward 1479–99, sold all-grain, simnel, temsyd, white and wholemeal bread; other occupation, sold ale in south ward 1487; servant, John Crowe, absconded (?) in breach of Statute of Labourers 1494; freeman 1475; councillor 1479; borough office, collector of funds raised for expenses of new charter, in St Nicholas 1488. Other information; litigant in petty court 1486–99, defended a series of relatively high value claims brought by leading burgesses including Nicholas Porchet for £2, William Style for £2 13s., executors of Isabelle Style for £20, John Squyer for £13 6s. 8d., John Halle for £10 17s. 8d., Robert Smyth for 10s., Roger Tymperley for £30, prior of Holy Trinity for £2 13s. 4d., William Baker for £2 7s. 6d.

Hewett, John; father, John (?); merchant; overseas trade, exported fish, tallow, woollen cloth, imported dyes, linen cloth, wine etc. 1492. Other information; litigant in the petty court 1489–91, in dispute with John Hapet over three butts of romeney wine 1489, sued John Martyn for delivery of goods worth £25 1491

Horkslee, John; married Isabel; daughters, Margaret and Elizabeth; died 1416 in office as bailiff; cordwainer; other occupation, merchant; overseas trade, imported salt on the *Trinity* of Robert Templeman 1398, exported woollen cloth 1414; freeman; bailiff 1400/1, 1402–04, 1406/7, 1410–12, 1413/14, 1415/16; customs official, collector 1406/7. Other information; member of a royal commission ordered to assemble and man all ships, barges and boats for the purpose of attacking, arresting and committing to prison, pirates who lie in wait for merchants and have pursued them from port to port, wounding, killing, robbing and imprisoning until ransom made 1398.

Johnesone (alias Johnsone), Giles; born Low Countries/Cologne (?); sons, Gerard and Giles; executor Hans Rook, lately of London; merchant. Other occupations, beer brewer 1479–88, innkeeper 1488, in east ward; servants Edward Lybardson, Simon Petirson both of Cologne, 1483; freeman 1483, admitted notwithstanding his alien status in return for a payment of £10, and after examination by Thomas Fastolf and John Tymperley. Other information; sworn into a tithing 1479, described in the alien subsidy as a merchant, householder and master of a brew house 1483, fined for keeping pigs on the common quay 1487/8.

Johnessone, Andrew; born Low Countries; master of *Godbered* and later *Holyghost;* overseas trade, exported woollen cloth, imported dyes 1397/8. Other information; most active master recorded in John Bernard's account, made fifteen short-haul voyages in and out of Ipswich and Harwich 1396–98, carried wool in *Godbered* 1401/2, dispute with John Rous in the petty court successfully arbitrated 1407, subsequently carried wool on behalf of Rous.

Joury, Robert; kinsman, Richard (?); tailor/draper; freeman 1490; borough office, attended court general 1497, councillor 1501; interests in borough land, grant in St Mary Tower 1499. Other information; litigant in the petty court 1491–99, sued the alien merchant Robert Johnesone for £2 5s. 1491, sued by Sir William Carewe for 50s. 1497, and by Thomas Drayll and William Baker (as bailiffs?) for £40 1498.

Joye, John; kinsmen, John (mariner), Peter, Richard, Robert and Simon (?); married Joan; no children recorded; died mid 1430s (?); parish of residence, St Mary Tower (?); executors, William Gosselyn, clerk, Richard Doget and William Wethereld; baker/merchant/vintner; overseas trade, exported woollen cloth, hides and timber from Manningtree 1398 (?), exported woollen cloth, cheese and hides, imported wine 1413/14. Other occupations, brewed ale 1415/16, innkeeper 1416, in north ward; apprentices, Thomas Cobald 1420, Richard Walle 1434; portman 1418, 1429; bailiff 1420–22, 1426/7, 1430/1. Other borough office, coroner 1423/4, 1425/6, claviger 1430–32; JP for Ipswich 1424, 1428; MP 1425; customs official, customer and collector 1421–25; interests in borough land, lease in St Peter on the water front 1415, grants of foreshore rights in St Peter 1416, 1424. Other information; implicated in piracy against merchants of Hamburg 1405, guest of Lady Alice de Bryene of Acton Hall 1412/13, partner of London grocer John Aylesham 1415, described as citizen of London and a member of the Company of Fishmongers 1419.

Joye, Richard; kinsmen John, Richard, Robert, Simon (?); married Gudren; no children recorded; died in or before 1421; parish of residence at death, St Peter (?); miller/baker in west ward 1415. Other occupations, brewed and sold ale 1415 in west ward; apprentices William Torrell, Thomas Bast 1415, Thomas Periell 1420; freeman; worthy burgess 1417; borough office, juror in the petty court 1415. Other information; attested parliamentary elections in the borough 1411, 1413, 1414.

Keche (aka Ketch), William I; kinsmen, Laurence, Robert another tanner; son, William (also became bailiff); parish of residence, St Stephen (?); tanner, soaked leather in common water 1421, incurred more than half of the larger fines of 12d. or more imposed on tanners by leet court of north ward, and twice paid the unusually high penalty of 3s. 4d. 1415–38. Other occupations, sold ale 1415–21, brewed ale 1434, in north ward; freeman; portman 1440; bailiff 1437/8; other borough office, chief pledge 1415/16, tithingman 1421–23, both in leet court of north ward. Other information; charged with robbery for which Thomas Denys stood bail, damaged Roper Lane with his cart 1434.

Keche, William II; father, William (also became bailiff); son, John (?); died intestate 1464; administrator John Hyll, who unsuccessfully defended a petty court claim by Gilbert Debenham esquire for payment of £14 1s. 8d. under a letter of obligation; appointed as executor by William Markes 1454; tanner and merchant; overseas trade, in buying salt had to put on the line all his lands and tenements, rents and services, and goods and chattels in Ipswich, by entering into a recognisance of debt with the shippers Burghard Wydoot and Hans Prise to pay them £100 within fifteen days of the ship's arrival 1457, imported glass, iron, madder, stone, timber, wax, twelve tuns of Gascon wine 1459; freeman 1443; councillor 1448; bailiff 1453–54; other borough office, claviger 1453–55; JP 1453–55; interests in borough land, grant 1454. Other information; avoided his creditors by obtaining royal immunity from prosecution in return for service in Calais 1463.

Knatte (alias Gnate, Gnatte), John; parents, William and Margaret; married Agnes; daughter Margaret; will made 1498, proved 1499; parish of residence at death, and buried St Margaret; property bequests, Brachet Hill, Shallys Land and two acres at Chekerhall; other notable bequests, contents of bedchamber, kitchen and wardrobe, pewter, silver spoons; executors, John Portman, William Ropkyn; appointed as executor by his father William 1488, Richard Bery 1489; tanner; freeman 1488; borough office, tax collector 1490, elected as a warden of the Corpus Christi pageant 1491; interests in borough land, lease of land and ditches in St Margaret 1482. Other information; donated 12d. for the upkeep of four young men in the service of the king 1486.

Knatte (alias Gnatte), William; married Margaret; son, John; will made 1486, proved 1488; parish of residence at death, and buried St Margaret; property bequests, house and adjoining land, five acres of land at Shrybbe and two acres at Chekerhall; executors, wife and son; appointed as executor by Margaret Sylvester 1472, Joan Gigehoo 1473, Thomas Puntyng tanner 1477; tanner, dug pits in the highway from which the waste of his tanning flowed into the water supply 1455, kept noxious pits called 'Barkputes' in north ward 1471. Other occupation, brewed ale in north ward 1455(?)–84; freeman 1458; councillor 1479/80; other borough office, chamberlain 1472/3, chief pledge in leet court of north ward 1479–87, tax assessor in St Margaret 1481, 1487.

Knepping (alias Knapping), John; merchant; overseas trade, exported woollen cloth 1414; clothier, thirty narrow dozens 1396/7 (?); dealer in skins. Other occupation, vintner, sold 80 gallons of red wine at the exorbitant price of 8d. per gallon in west ward 1424; apprentice, Robert Parker 1416; freeman; councillor (?) 1424; portman 1429; bailiff 1407/8, 1410–12, 1413/14, 1415/16, 1420–22. Other borough office, coroner 1404–07, 1427/8; MP 1420; customs official, tronager 1393–99. Other information; with others acquired rights to a quay with shops and a crane 1396, acquired property in St Matthew, St Peter, St Laurence and St Nicholas 1394–1417.

Kyrkehous, Robert; dead by 1488; married Matilda; son, Christopher; executors, wife, James Hobard, son Christopher; fishmonger in east ward 1465–82; clothier, six straits 1466.

Other occupations sold ale and in some years beer 1466–87, innkeeper 1467/8, brewed ale 1483, sold bread 1484, all in east ward; freeman 1462; councillor 1479/80. Other borough office, chamberlain 1485/6; interests in borough land, grant in St Stephen 1483, grant of messuage to the north of the palace of the archdeacon of Suffolk 1485. Other information; allegedly took delivery from Richard Cowpere, to hold in safe custody, but failed to return, a crimson belt, a silk harness with silver and gilt, and a pair of gold rings 1459, disenfranchised 1463, involved in a brawl with John Kent 1465, witnessed a deed produced in the petty court 1466, let property in St Laurence to Thomas Fraunceys who was in arrears of rent 1467, kept an unlicensed stall 1483–87, traded with John Dokwra, a chapman of Kendal in Westmoreland, before 1488.

Lackford, Giles; yeoman; father, John (?); siblings, one brother, two sisters (?); parish of residence, St Matthew (?); pewterer, accused of using false measure for pewter 1478. Other occupations, fishmonger 1466, brewed ale in west ward 1471–88; servant, Thomas Lackford 1478; freeman 1480; borough office, tax assessor in St Matthew 1488, chamberlain 1492/3. Other information; granted protection from claims while serving Ralph Wolseley the official victualler of Calais 1466, burgled and robbed of pewter vessels by William Large 1478, litigant in the petty court 1487–92, sued a yeoman of Otley for £20 1492.

Lackford (alias Lakford), John; married Margery; children, John, Thomas, Agnes, Joan 1457, none mentioned in his will; will made 1477, proved 1477; parish of residence at death, St Matthew, where he owned a shop; buried St Matthew; property bequests, home in St Matthew, two tenements leased from Holy Trinity priory; other notable bequests, contents of shop to John Osberne; executors, wife, William Jeffreyes, supervised by Benedict Caldwell; appointed as executor by Thomas Vyncent 1470; cordwainer; freeman, on condition that he took lease for seven years of Horsewade Mill at a rent of £20 per annum, 1457; councillor 1470. Other borough office, affeerer in the leet court of west ward 1468; interests in borough land, Horsewade Mill. Other information; he and Ralph Recher sued each other each for breaking into the home of the other 1443, caught cheating at games called 'Whistilds, Prelleds, and Quarter spells', fined 26s. 8d. by the court general and threatened with the pillory if he did the same again 1448.

Ladyesman, John; married Alice; three sons, including John; will made 1445, proved 1445; buried St Mary Tower; property bequests in Great and Little Finborough; other notable bequests, gifts of malt to churches of Great and Little Finborough, and to the poor of Buxhall, Hitcham and Great Finborough, tools of his trade to his apprentice; executors, not recorded; appointed as executor by William Haken 1444; miller; his will made arrangements for his apprentice to complete his training with a colleague.

Lamb, Peter; married Anne (?); daughter, Johanne (?); tiler; freeman, on condition that he tiled the house of pleas 1493; tiler (?); interests in borough land, grant in Clay Street 1499/1500, grant in St Matthew. Other information; fined for various public health offences in west ward 1487, litigant in petty court 1487–96, in dispute with Edward Gawge, sued by the prior of St Peter.

Lopham, Thomas; father, John (?); brother, Robert (?); glazier, contracted with Edmund Daundy and John Bedfeld for a payment of £10 to 'make the glass for the east window of the church of St Laurence in Ipswich well, sufficiently, and with images and colours and other necessaries according to instructions from the said Edmund and John by next Christmas' 1490; freeman (?); borough office, juror in petty court 1478–80, tax collector in St Matthew 1488. Other information; litigant in petty court 1478–94, sued the Dutchman Nicholas Jamys for £3 16s. 8d. 1488, sued by Thomas Drayll for £9 6s. 5d. 1494, arbitrated a dispute between Thomas Bunt and Robert Basse 1489.

Luke, John; appointed as executor by Thomas Deye weaver 1495; tailor; freeman 1490; borough office, tax collector in St Margaret 1488, elected for gild of St John as warden of the Corpus Christi pageant 1491. Other information; fined for public health offences in north ward 1487/8, litigant in the petty court 1487–1500, including claim and counterclaim with the goldsmith John Rotyrdam, 1491, claim against prior of Carmelite friary 1497.

Machet (alias Maiet), Richard; mother, Margaret; siblings Stephen, Thomas, Agnes, Margaret; married Margaret; children, Thomas, Agnes, Katherine (all under age at date of will); will made 1472, proved 1472; buried St Mary Quay; property bequests, lands and tenements acquired from Richard Felawe; other notable bequests, one pound for leading the roof of St Mary Quay, cash and silver cup and silver spoons bearing his mark; executors, wife and brother Stephen; mercer. Other occupations, sold ale 1465–71, sold wine 1465, innkeeper 1465–71, sold fish 1465–71, all in east ward; freeman (?); borough office, served as a valuer for the petty court 1465, chamberlain 1470–72, chief pledge in east and south wards 1471. Other information, acquired property from Richard Felawe shortly before death.

Man, Henry; married Beatrice; sons, Richard, William; will made 1509, proved 1509; buried St Mary Tower; property bequests, two houses in which William Taylour and John Vyncent capper live; executor wife, supervised by William With; shoemaker; freeman 1492. Other information; petty court litigant 1491–1500, sued by Roger Tymperley and Richard Bayly for £5 1496, sued Henry Grove, currier of Ipswich, for £4 1500.

Manser, John; sons, Thomas and William; parish of residence St Mary Tower (?) before 1465; appointed as executor by John Mascall 1471; butcher in west ward 1468–88, still active as a butcher in the petty court in the early 1490s, sued by John and William Tymperley for £10 1491, granted a stall in the flesh market for life 1495; freeman 1446; tax collector in St Mary Elms 1481. Other information; ordered to repair a way made by him to the ditch of the town well 1450, assaulted William Clerk 1467, assaulted by John Tylere 1468, fined for public health offences by leet court of west ward 1472.

Marteyn, John; parents, Robert and Matilda; married, widower (?); children, Thomas and Margaret; will made 1472, proved 1472; buried St Mary Tower; notable bequests, contents of bedchamber and wardrobe, two silk belts, gown and doublet to each apprentice; executors, parents; occupation, cutler; apprentices Robert and William 1472.

Martyn, John; merchant; overseas trade, took delivery of six rolls of beaver skins 1478, with others chartered from Lord John Howard *The Barbara* which set sail to Bordeaux 1481, sought recovery from Andrew Cornelye of 6½lbs of pepper and two pieces of sugar 1487, brought a claim against Juan, the master of a Spanish ship which had docked at the town's quay 1488, exported cloth 1491. Other occupation, vintner, sold wine at exorbitant price in east ward 1487/8; freeman 1477. Other information; litigant in the petty court 1487–91, sued by William Kelynge of Bury St Edmunds for £4 1490, and by John Hewett for delivery of goods worth £25 1491.

Medewe, Thomas; married Agnes; children, John, a canon of Butley priory, Thomas, Alice, Margaret, Margery; will made 1479, proved 1486; buried St Margaret; property bequests, house and other property in Ipswich; executors, wife, John Portman, Robert Smyth; baker in north ward 1455–death, selling all-grain, simnel, white and wholemeal bread 1487. Other occupation brewed ale 1465–75; freeman 1459; borough office, affeerer in the leet court of north ward 1466, exempted from the office of chamberlain and all other offices of the town in perpetuity in return for five marks payable towards the repair of the quay 1472.

Motte, John; parents, John and Agnes; brother Richard; married Joanne; no children recorded; will made 1473, proved 1473; residence at death, London; buried St Michael besides Crokislane; notable bequests, substantial sums for upkeep of roads, including that from Bildeston to Ipswich, remembered his spinners, fullers and weavers in Suffolk; executors, wife and John Fynkell; merchant; overseas trade with Spain, and between Ireland and Gascony, maintained a factor in the Andalusian ports; stockfishmonger of London; clothier, second leading clothier of Suffolk 1465–69, based in Bildeston; apprentices, Robert Coldaker, Robert Sergeant, John Dryver 1473; freeman 1435, foreign burgess. Other information, claimed payment under an account with Ipswich innkeeper John Myddlyton in the sum of 30s. 1466.

Myddlyton, John; vintner, sold two gallons of wine to the borough 1463/4, sold wine at an exorbitant price in north ward 1466. Other occupations, baked bread 1465, innkeeper 1465–67, in north ward, renting property from Thomas Wath, to whom he pledged his assets, which included eleven feather beds, in arrears of rent 1467. Other information; indebted to John Motte in sum of 30s. 1466, audited account between Roger Tymperley and John Buktone, 1477.

Mynott, William; parents, William and Kathryn; married Margaret; children, John, Thomas, William, Margaret (?); will made 1499, proved 1499; buried Lady Chapel in parish of St Matthew; property bequests, reference to proceeds of sale of property in Dedham; other notable bequests, funding for a stained glass window in the Lady Chapel, wool, corn and cloth, £1 10s. to son Thomas to be a canon of Holy Trinity, weaving equipment to son John, two gowns; executors, William Dawes, William Myldnale of Dedham. Other information, litigant in the petty court 1490–92, moved from Dedham shortly before he died (?).

Oake (alias Oak), Thomas; married Maud; children, Richard and Margery; will made 1488, proved 1489; buried, 'where God disposes me to die'; property bequests, in Ipswich and Stoke, including in St Mary Quay; other notable bequests, debt due from John Moor as proceeds of sale of property in Haughley; executor, wife; merchant; overseas trade, will made in anticipation of a voyage to Bordeaux. Other occupations, sold ale 1471–79, brewed ale 1487/8, in east ward; freeman (?); borough office, juror in the petty court 1478–80, tax assessor in St Clement 1488.

Osberne, John; married Agnes (?); parish of residence at death, St Clement (?); smith; other occupation, brewed ale in east ward 1466–75; apprentice Robert Lynkolne 1481; freeman 1458; councillor 1470. Other borough office, tax collector in St Clement 1455, chief pledge in leet court of east ward 1467–75; interests in borough land, grant 1454, grant Shirehouse Hill 1477. Other information; party to a deed transferring land in St Clement 1468.

Parker, Henry; merchant; other occupation, sold ale in north ward 1438; servant Geoffrey Middleton, who delivered forty dozens of undyed woollen cloth and 3000 pounds of tallow to Richard Walle for which he did not pay c.1443. Other information; involved in petty court litigation 1443, sued by John Baker and John Woodhouse both of Dedham for £18 under a letter of obligation, and by John Wode and Peter Terry for £40, made two claims against Richard Walle, one for payment for goods delivered, and the other for repayment of a loan of 20s., and a third against John Van Wynter, summoned by general court to answer charges and at risk of disenfranchisement 1444, sued in court of common pleas by a London fishmonger Stephen Wolf 1450.

Parker, John; born Coggeshall (?); parents, John and Rose; married Margery; no children recorded; will made 1401, proved 1401; buried St Peter; property bequests, lands in Ipswich, Coggeshall and Colne; other notable bequests, silver goblets, contents of wardrobe; executors,

John Swyft clerk, John Brygge chaplain, Simon Sygor; freeman; merchant; overseas trade, exported woollen cloth, imported wine and salt, in each case in the *Trinity*, probably to and from south-west Europe, 1397/8; apprentice Robert Bech 1401; bailiff 1399/1400. Other information; granted, by the Crown, income from lands in Kent 1389.

Parmasay (alias Parmafey), Robert; married Alice; one daughter; will made 1452, proved 1453; parish of residence at death, and buried St Nicholas; property bequests, tenement in St Nicholas; other notable bequests, several gifts of malt; executors, wife, John Randolf; appointed as executor by John Priour 1437, John Asselott 1439; tanner, dumped the filth of his trade in the river next to Friars Bridge 1419. Other occupations, sold ale 1419–38, brewed ale 1437/8, in south ward; apprentice Thomas Petyte 1433; freeman; attended court general 1440; borough office, chief pledge in leet court of south ward 1421–38, treasurer 1432/3, chamberlain 1444–46; interests in borough land, two leases in St Nicholas 1417, further leases in St Nicholas 1437 and 1443, grant abutting on his garden 1443, lease 1446/7. Other information; ordered to account, as treasurer (?) 1433.

Peteman, Robert; married; daughters, Joan and Katherine; will made 1488, proved 1488; buried St Clement, 'before the seat where I used to sit'; property bequests, in Ipswich including a close at the cliff and land by the water, tenement called 'the Cok'; other notable bequests, mazer, nine silver spoons to wife, cows to daughters; executors, John Forgon, Geoffrey Osberne, supervised by Richard Gosse; shipwright. Other information, litigant in the petty court, sued Thomas Stubbe for payment of £4 6s. 8d. 1487.

Philip (alias Phylip, Phylypp), Thomas; married Elizabeth; no children recorded; dead by 1498; executors, wife, Thomas Baron; baker in east ward (?) 1487-95, sold simnel, white and wholemeal bread; freeman 1488; councillor 1496. Other information; litigant in petty court 1491–95, brought relatively high value claims against John Milne, a London fish-monger for £10, and a London mercer for £2, executors defended a claim by Thomas Alvard for £26 13s. 4d. 1498.

Pratt (formerly Rolf), Alice; married John Rolf and, after his death, Thomas Pratt who were both fishmongers; no children recorded; will made 1447, proved 1448; buried St Laurence; property bequests, tenement; other notable bequests, eight silver spoons and two silk belts with silver ornamentation to church of St Laurence, belts and linen kerchiefs to friends; executors, husband and John Wytton; occupations sold ale 1421–38, sold fish 1436–38, in south and then north wards.

Priour (alias Pryowr, Prior), John; married Joan; sons John and William; will made 1437, proved 1437; buried St Mary Tower; property bequests in parishes of St Mary Tower and St Margaret, properties next to Typtoft Cross, and Horsewade Mill, and tenement in Brook Street called Goldyng; executors, wife, William Wethereld, Robert Parmesay, Robert Havell of Needham; merchant; overseas trade, exported woollen cloth 1414; unsuccessfully resisted the appointment of the London mercer, John Warren, as permanent governor of the Merchant Adventurers in the Low Countries 1421. Other occupations, brewed and sold ale 1415–36, innkeeper 1424, in west ward; borough office, juror in the petty court 1415. Other information; arbitrated a dispute between Thomas Felde and Simon Butler 1414.

Puntyng, Thomas; brother Simond; married Aveline; children, William, who became a freeman after serving an apprenticeship with Robert Rydout 1477, Alice, Jane, Margaret; will made 1477, proved 1477; parish of residence at death, St Mary Elms (?); buried Carmelite friary; property bequests, house, tenement in St Nicholas; other notable bequests, bark vats to wife; executors, wife, William Knatte, supervised by his brother

Simond Puntyng; appointed as executor by Joan Sharpe 1470; tanner in south ward 1466–77 (?); interests in borough land, lease in St Mary Elms. Other occupation, brewed ale in south ward 1466–75; servants John Valyaunt, John Sudbury, who benefited under his will 1477; freeman 1463; borough office, chief pledge in leet court of south ward. Other information, built a weir 1472.

Rever (alias Rivers), John; children, Augustine, Anne; appointed as executor by John Wellyng 1456; mercer; overseas trade, imported alum, bow staffs, fish, iron, kitchenware, madder, oil, soap, wax 1459; clothier, two straits 1465/6; freeman 1446; councillor 1448; portman 1474; bailiff 1475/6, 1478/9; other borough office, tax collector 1452, tax assessor 1453, chamberlain 1453–55, coroner 1460–66, 1471/2, chief pledge in the leet court of south ward 1466–71, claviger 1470–72; JP 1479/80; interests in borough land, grant near St George's church 1467, grant of garden called 'Bonbrokes garden' 1471.

Revet (alias Rivet), William; father, William; appointed as executor by Robert Baldwyn 1490; pewterer, sold Sir John Howard flatware weighing in total 131 pounds, and took away his worn pewter in part exchange, 1482/3; freeman 1478, following apprenticeship with William Winter; councillor 1496, 1497; excused office of portman 1509 on grounds of ill health; bailiff 1501/2; other borough office, assessor of funds raised for expenses of new charter 1488, tax collector in St Mary Tower 1488, chamberlain 1490/1, elected for gild of St George as warden of the Corpus Christi pageant 1491, claviger 1498/9. Other information, fined for public health offences in south and west wards 1479–88, donated twelve pence for the upkeep of four young men in the service of the king 1486, and a horse to the king 1491, petty court litigant 1486–94, sued the tailor Robert Cowpere for £6 1494.

Ridout (alias Rydout), William; born 1415 (?); father, William (?); son, John; appointed as executor by John Pypere 1443, John Wade 1456; freeman; councillor 1448; portman 1454–79; bailiff 1460/1, 1464/5, 1468/9. Other borough office, treasurer 1439/40, coroner 1443–53, alderman of the merchant gild of Corpus Christi 1446, claviger 1461–63, 1464–66; JP 1460–62, 1465–67, 1468/9; MP 1447; interests in borough land, lease in St Nicholas 1437, lease lately part of town wall, in St Mary Quay, 1439, lease with others of the common marsh 1443, lease of Horsewade Mill 1447, with William Heede resisted paying rent for lease of Horsewade Mill 1455/6. Other information, threatened with disenfranchisement for suing John Caldwell in the court of Chancery 1455.

Roberd, John; son Thomas (?); merchant/mariner; overseas trade, with south-west Europe, exported woollen cloth, imported forty tuns of wine, salt and fish all on the *Kogg John* of John Michell 1397/8; clothier, twenty-two narrow dozens 1396/7. Other information, a dozen of his chaldrons of sea coal were taken as security for the payment of a debt 1400.

Roberd (alias Robard), Thomas; woad dealer, polluted the common well in Brook Street by washing his dyed cloth 1424; other occupations, brewed ale 1416–21, sold ale 1415–24, in north ward; apprentices, John Bowyer 1433; freeman; borough office, juror in the petty court 1415, tithingman in leet court of north ward 1421–24.

Ropkyn (alias Ropkin), William; married Johanne; children, Richard, Sir William, a priest, Anne, Joanne, Margery, Margaret; will made 1512, proved 1512; buried St Margaret where his altar tomb still stands; property bequests, principal dwelling house, the corner house at the lane's end called Bertys, and two adjoining houses, also Westys House in St Helen, Whytlokke House, Pottrye with land; executors, wife, two sons, assisted by William Halle; appointed as executor by Robert Whyttloke 1494, John Knatte 1499, John Halle 1503; tanner in north ward 1479/80; freeman 1480; councillor 1497; portman 1501; bailiff 1502/3, 1507/8.

Other borough office, tax collector in St Margaret 1481, chamberlain 1487-88, chief pledge in the leet court of north ward 1488, appointed by borough to value ten horses for service of king 1489, tax assessor 1490; interests in borough land, grant in St Margaret 1499. Other information, erected an unlicensed 'hoggys kote' on land next to his tenement in north ward 1483, donated a horse to the king 1491, petty court litigant 1492.

Rous, John; married Joan; died 1419 (?); Merchant of the Staple; overseas trade, exported wool 1400–02, 1407/8; bailiff 1408–10; MP 1410, 1414; customs official, collector 1404–12. Other information, with Richard Whittington and four other merchants, lent the king £4000 1407, dispute with the Dutch master Andrew Johnessone in the petty court successfully arbitrated 1407, purchased with Robert Andrew two shops in St Mary Quay (?) and also 'La Condythous' 1408, friend of John Lardener for whom he acted as arbitrator 1410, and whom he accompanied on his appointment as captain of Oye in the marches of Calais 1413, allegedly contracted with William Bowes of York for sale of wool in Bruges 1412, with his wife acquired more property in Ipswich 1414, robbed of letters of obligation and debentures from his house in Ipswich 1414, embarked from Southampton for France as victualler in the retinue of Sir Edward Holand 1418.

Sextayn, John; married Agnes; appointed as executor by Robert Forthe 1447; 'husbandman' 1443, barber 1448, 1465; other occupation, sold ale in east ward 1436–38, and in south ward 1466; apprentices, John Frere for whom an indenture dated 1448 survives, John Wapone 1477; borough office, tax collector in St Laurence 1455. Other information, ordered to make payment of £10 to Stephen Wetheryngsete and Robert Forde, and £20 to Gilbert Debenham, under letters of obligation, committed to Ipswich gaol because unable to pay debts 1443, sold property in St Mary Tower and St Laurence to John Caldwell and John Drayll 1445, sued John Clerk for payment of balance of account, and instructed John Frensh as his attorney 1465.

Sharp, John: married Joan; son, John; will made 1463, proved 1463; buried St Mary Elms; property bequests, various tenements occupied by third parties, including two in St Nicholas, various closes; other notable bequests, book debts due from William Ridout; executors, wife, Roger Aspolime, William Manser; glover; freeman 1454; borough office, collector of funds for litigation with the prior of Ely 1459; interests in borough land, grant in St Mary Elms 1455/6.

Smyth, John; died between 1488 and 1493; married Margery; merchant, overseas trade, imported madder and soap 1463; clothier, eleven straits 1466. Other occupations, vintner (?), sold to the borough a tun of red wine for £4 13s. 4d. to present as a gift to the duke of Suffolk 1451, brewed and sold ale in east ward 1467–84; freeman, as apprentice to John Deken, 1449; customs official, collector 1463 (?).

Smyth, Nicholas; son, John; skinner, sold pelts to John Deye 1401 and '*ruskyn*' (poorer quality summer squirrel skins) to Walter Drayll 1407, bought rabbit skins from John Brewys and hired him to sew various fur pelts for hoods 1415, leased a store room from Thomas Page 1407, his creditors seized furs and a hood of '*poleynwork*' (red or black Polish squirrel skins) as security for the payment of his debts 1415. Other occupation, sold ale in west ward 1421–23; borough office, tithingman in leet court of west ward 1421–23.

Smyth (alias Taylour), Remkyn; tailor. Other occupations, innkeeper 1466–68, sold ale 1466–68, in east ward; other information, within his house held and used a weigh-beam with which he weighed various merchandise which should have been weighed on the common weigh-beam of the town of Ipswich 1466.

Smyth (alias Smith), Thomas I; son, Thomas; dyer, sued John Brewys (a shearman ?) for 3s. in respect of cloth that he had dyed and sold to him 1414, convicted of assaulting him 1415, polluted the common well in Brook Street by washing his dyed cloth 1424. Other occupations, owned a guest house 1416 (?), brewed and sold ale 1416–38, in north ward; apprentice, John Rolf 1433; freeman 1422; borough office, juror in the petty court 1414, tithingman in leet court of north ward 1423 (?). Other information, assaulted William Andrew 1407 (?), assaulted by John Wisbech 1443.

Smyth, Thomas II; father Thomas (?); brother Robert; married Maud; son John, and at least two daughters; will made 1470, proved 1470; buried St Matthew; property bequests, two houses; other notable bequests, the stuff in his shop and his beam; executor, wife; dyer; freeman 1454; borough office, tax collector in St Matthew 1455.

Soty, John; son, Thomas (?); baker in south ward 1419–21, sold white, wholemeal and horse bread to Thomas Drury 1414. Other occupation sold ale in south ward 1421; borough office, juror in the petty court 1407, 1414, tithingman in leet court of south ward 1419.

Soty, Thomas; father, John (?); married Joan; son, Gregory; will made 1468, proved 1469; parish of residence at death, St Nicholas (?); buried in church of the Carmelite friars; property bequests, tenement with garden; other notable bequests, two shillings to the church of St Nicholas for making a window in the vestry; executor, wife; appointed as executor by Elisabeth Roberts 1446, John Artour 1460; baker in south ward 1434–68, bought three quarters and seven bushels of wheat from John Sewall of Rushmere for £2 4d. 1443, paid 12d. for the right to sell without toll or custom within the borough 1446/7. Other occupation, sold ale in south ward 1468; interests in borough land, grant 1455, lease outside his gate and as far as the wall of John Campyon for an annual rent of 1d. 1467. Other information, hired a horse to Henry Gerard for a year for £1 6s. 8d. 1443, witnessed a deed produced to court general 1449.

Squyer, John; father, Alexander (?); appointed as executor by Richard Felawe 1482; appointed as supervisor of will by Henry Fulslo 1487; chaplain/clerk in holy orders. Other occupation, master of Ipswich school, appointed by the will of Richard Felawe 1482; servant James Hyll, admitted as a burgess 1487; freeman 1483; borough office, treasurer 1483, as such received £11 1s. 10d. from William Baker; interests in borough land, for the building of a latrine for the school 1487, grants of two gardens and land in St Mary Quay 1499, grant of foreshore rights in two quays in St Mary Quay 1499. Other information, granted the customs on all mill stones, quernstones, dogstones and 'grynstones' coming to the town of Ipswich or the port of Orwell, both for repair and for sale, in return for paying for an honest priest to serve the gild of Corpus Christi 1479, frequent litigator in petty court 1486–99, granted with others farm of the profits of the stone trade 1489.

Starling, John; father, Geoffrey (?); married Margaret; son, Thomas (?); butcher; freeman; bailiff 1404/5, 1407/8, 1412/13, 1416/17; MP 1402, 1406, 1411, 1413 (May); customs official, collector 1399–1415, deputy butler 1407/8, clerk of the king's ships 1409–11 (?). Other information, with wife Margaret acquired a tenement in Ipswich 1403, acquired a shop in St Mary 1405, acquired through Margaret an interest in manor of 'Bokkyng' in Crowfield as well as lands in Coddenham, Stonham Aspal and Creeting, held property at Holbrook, so became freeman of Colchester 1407, in arrears of rent for lease from Nicholas Smyth 1415.

Style (alias Stile, Stiles), William I; married Isabelle; children, John, William, Anneys; will made 1463, proved 1475; buried St Nicholas, where his memorial brass and monogram survive; property bequests, house, tenement called Sprottys; other notable bequests, half a fodder (9¾ cwt) of lead for roofing the church of St Nicholas, £20 to daughter for her marriage if she behaved herself to the satisfaction of her mother and her friends, 10s. to servant Isabelle Dowe if she remained in his service until his death 1463; executor, wife; appointed as executor by William Tynmer 1456; appointed as supervisor of will by John Artour 1460; mercer; clothier one broadcloth, eight straits 1466, sixty straits 1467. Other occupation, brewed ale in south ward 1466–74, paid a fine of 3s. 4d. 1468; freeman; councillor 1448, 1454; bailiff 1467/8, 1472 (following death of John Creyk). Other borough office, tax assessor 1453, tax collector in St Peter 1455, chamberlain 1459–61, auditor of the chamberlains' account 1466; JP 1472/3. Other information, a William atte Style provided security for various defendants in the petty court 1443, sued John and Isabelle Owting for assault and theft of 120 pounds of woollen yarn worth £4 1465.

Style (alias Stile), William II; parents, William and Isabelle; siblings John, Anneys; married Margery; children, John, William, and others (under 24 years of age at his death); will made 1500, proved 1500; buried St Nicholas, where his memorial brass survives; property bequests, lands and tenements in Ipswich and Suffolk; no other notable bequests; executors, wife, Robert Couper his priest; appointed as executor by his mother 1491, Roger Tymperley 1499; mercer, admitted following his apprenticeship as a member of the mercers' company in London 1479. Other occupation, brewed ale in south ward 1487/8; freeman; councillor 1497; other borough office, chamberlain 1486/7, warden of the Corpus Christi gild 1487, tax assessor 1487/8, assessor of funds raised for expenses of new charter 1488, both St Nicholas, claviger 1491–93, coroner 1493–96. Other information, frequent litigant in the petty court 1486–93, sued Thomas Stub for £32 1487, and Richard Lathered of Debenham for £24 1492, beneficiary of the will of his mother 1491, and of Roger Tymperley 1499.

Sudbury, John; father, John; kinsmen (not described as immediate family) John and his son John, William, Margaret; will made 1463, proved 1466; buried St Peter; property bequests, tenement called 'le Sonne' in St Margaret bought from Alexander Watkyn; other notable bequests, book debts due from Robert Deye, to each of the friaries a hood of beaver; executor, William Wattys, supervised by John Creyk; appointed as executor by Henry Black 1432, Geoffrey Shryd 1455; appointed as supervisor of will by Robert Fennyng 1458; butcher in west ward 1421. Other occupations sold ale 1424–38, innkeeper 1438, in west and then east ward; servant Margaret, remembered in his will; freeman, disenfranchised for failing to obey the ordnances and customs of the town 1459; borough office, tithingman in leet court of west ward 1423, chief pledge in the leet court of east ward 1438, chamberlain 1439/40, coroner in 1440/1, 1442/3, 1453/4. Other information, assaulted by Thomas Sparhauk 1424.

Taliser, William; barber. Other occupation brewed and sold ale 1415–36, sold ale 1424, in west ward; borough office, juror in the petty court 1414, tithingman and affeerer in leet court of west ward 1423, chief pledge 1424, 1436, claviger 1439–41, 1442–46. Other information, allegedly joint leader, with John Blankpayn, of a food riot 1438.

Terry, Peter; died 1457 (?); executor Geoffrey prior of the church of St Peter; appointed as executor by John Fennyng 1437, John Wall 1443; merchant, together with John Wode, sued Henry Parker for £40 1443. Other occupation, sold ale in south ward 1419; apprentices, William Skynner 1436, Geoffrey Terry 1445; freeman 1421; portman 1440; bailiff 1440/1, 1444/5; JP 1438, 1440; interests in borough land, leases lately part of town wall, St Mary Quay, 1434, 1439, lease Portman meadow for seven years 1443, lease next to the river. Other information, penalised by leet court of north ward as a common night walker 1423, ordered to pay £5 arrears of rent on town mill and also arrears on Portman meadow 1448, executor produced various title deeds to petty court 1466.

Tholy, Thomas; owned a tile kiln in east ward 1424; other occupation, brewer in north ward 1421–24; servant, Robert Cotoun who had lived in Ipswich for many years without being admitted to a tithing; borough office, juror in the petty court 1415, tithingman in leet court of north ward 1421–23.

Trotte, John; father, Bartholomew (?); sibling Bartholomew (?); married Alice (?); appointed as executor by Nicholas Swan 1472; baker in east ward 1466–87, selling simnel bread 1487; other occupations, innkeeper 1471, brewed ale 1472–83, in east ward; freeman 1459; borough office, tax collector in St Stephen 1481, exempted from the office of chamberlain in return for £4 payable towards the repair of the quay 1476.

Turner (alias Turnour), John; children, John and Margery; dyer, dug a ditch and perilous (dyeing?) pits in the road at the church of St George 1424, had unlicensed (dyeing?) pits in the town ditch 1438. Other occupations, sold ale 1421–36, brewed ale 1423–38, baked bread 1423–38, in west ward until 1436, then in north ward, innkeeper 1424; freeman 1431; attended court general 1448/9, tax collector 1451; councillor 1454 (?). Other information, assaulted John Omund 1436.[4]

Tymperley (alias Timperley), Roger; father, Roger (?); married Agnes; children, Margaret and Roger; will made 1498, proved 1499; parish of residence at death, St Mary Tower (?); buried St Mary Tower, next to son Roger, bequest for marble tomb stone; property bequests various, including *dosshouse close*, herb garden and stables; other notable bequests, rich clothes, pewter, two silver salt cellars, other silver, gilt and gold and two swans; executors, wife, William Style; freeman 1471; councillor 1479/80; portman 1496; bailiff 1485/6, 1490/1 and 1494/5. Other borough office, coroner 1472–75, claviger 1475–84, 1485/6, 1490/1, auditor 1482; JP 1487–89, 1491/2, 1493/4, 1495/6; interests in borough land, grant next to the wall ditch opposite 'le Deyery lane' in St Mary Tower 1479, grant of part of town ditch in St Mary Tower 1482, grant south of his garden 1485. Other information, fined for public health offence by leet court of north ward 1472, acted as arbitrator in civil dispute 1488.

Vyne, William; fuller. Other occupation, sold ale in south ward 1475–81; servant, Reginald absconded (?) in breach of Statute of Labourers 1490; borough office, juror in the petty court 1479, appointed by the petty court as a valuer 1489, 1495, elected as a warden of the Corpus Christi pageant 1491; interests in borough land, grant south of the new mill for the construction of a 'trutorum' (tenter-yard or trout lake?) 1478. Other information, litigant in the petty court 1479–96, disputed with Richard Stone ownership of a white strait valued at fifteen shillings 1489, sued by the former chamberlains for £40 1496.

Wade, Thomas; married Alice (?), who sold unfinished cloth to Henry van Colen 1415; son, John, who produced his father's sword and petitioned to be admitted to the freedom 1419; mariner and merchant; overseas trade (?); freeman (?). Other information, sought to avoid his creditors by obtaining royal immunity from prosecution in return for service in Ireland, but failed because he was shortly after detained in Newgate prison 'for divers debts to divers of the king's lieges' 1404.

Waleys (alias Walleis), Robert; born Hadleigh/Kersey; merchant; overseas trade, with

[4] John Turner is a difficult figure to pin down as he put his hand to so many different occupations. He may sometimes be confused with a John Turner who also baked bread and was described as a baker. It is assumed that the dyer achieved the freedom of the borough and became a leading burgess because his craft was of higher status than that of baker.

ports of Low Countries, Baltic and possibly Gascony dealing in grain, vetch, cheese, skins, cloth and iron and possibly wine; clothier, twenty-seven broad dozens 1396/7; other occupation, attorney for Crown in suits before local courts; freeman; bailiff 1375/6, 1377/8, 1384–86, 1387–90; MP 1386, 1388; customs official collector, customer and deputy butler. Other information, acquired land at Thurleston, on outskirts of Ipswich, 1365, acquired shops in St Mary and St Leonard, 1368, later added forty acres in Stoke, tenements in St Laurence and St Nicholas, with Geoffrey Starling the Elder sued by Henry Lakford of Bury St Edmunds for £252 1381, brought several claims in the court of Common Pleas 1370, goods and merchandise seized in Prussia 1385, sued William Malyn in Guildhall in London over supply of wool 1385, in Fleet prison as a result of legal action by the Exchequer for recovery of £23 10s. collected as customs revenue 1400, later released and cleared, given (with others) the keeping of 'Fissheres' in St Laurence, formerly of Henry Dekeman, which had been escheated to the king 1400, bought a consignment of iron, wine and salt from Roger Gosenold for £31 13s. 4d. 1401.

Wall, Henry; kinsman Hugh; merchant; overseas trade, exported grain and cloth 1388; MP 1394; interests in borough land, grant with others of land by river to build two water mills 1391, declared unlawful by the Crown 1399, but still leasing the land 1415. Other information, owed Thomas Dobbys of Sudbury £37 1395, witnessed settlement on Sir John Howard of a manor at Broke in Suffolk 1397.

Waltrot, Thomas; married Margaret; merchant; overseas trade Iceland, agreed with Philip Balle, a London haberdasher, to travel with and supervise the latter's apprentice, John Tournar, as they both sailed north with the goods of Philip Balle, a London haberdasher, aboard the *James of Ipswich,* but was later accused of maladministration by selling these goods on his own behalf; shipowner, disputed, with Robert Brussele, ownership of *The John of Ipswich* which, with full rigging, was worth £24 1498; other information, litigant in petty court 1497–99, sued by William Walter for £37 1497.

Walworth (alias Wallworth), John; Gentleman; father, William (?), bailiff 1436/7, 1447/8; married Clementine; children, John, MP, borough clerk of the peace 1483–96, Alice, Elizabeth, Margaret; will made 1488, proved 1488; buried St Mary Tower; property bequests, lands and tenements in Suffolk; other notable bequests, payment to a chantry priest to pray for Thomas Fastolf, Elizabeth Rewge and himself for three years, gilt and silver plate to son; executor wife; appointed as executor by Thomas Fastolf 1452, John Creyk 1472, Matilda Scalpy 1476, John Smyth 1486; lawyer (?), acted as arbiter in a land dispute 1472; freeman 1448; portman 1479; bailiff 1456/7, 1459/60, April 1464/5, 1468/9, 1471/2, 1474/5, 1477/8, 1480/1, 1486/7; other borough office, coroner 1454–56, auditor 1470, 1473, 1474; JP 1458–70, 1471/2, 1473–88; MP 1472–75 (?); customs official, collector 1475; interests in borough land, granted a stretch 250 feet long of the town ditch and embankment for a pigsty 1467. Other information, allowed his pigs to wander in west ward 1474, litigant in the petty court 1486/7, sued James Kene, a tanner, of Ipswich for £6 13s. 4d. 1487.

Wath, Thomas; Esquire; born Norwich (?); married Margery; living in east ward by 1465; merchant, held in store in Ipswich twenty timbrels of grey squirrel, thirty timbrels of ermine, twenty timbrels of Baltic furs and six timbrels of marten 1442; overseas trade (?); servant George Graband; freeman 1466. Other information, owned property in St Mary Tower which he let to William Boteler 1466, and to John Myddlyton 1467.

Wattys (alias Watts), William; appointed as executor by John Sudbury 1466; occupations, sold wine 1465–67, sold ale 1468, in east ward; freeman 1458, paid only twenty shillings for admission; councillor 1479/80; other borough office, affeerer 1465/6, then chief pledge in the leet court of east ward 1466–81, coroner 1466–82, tax assessor in St Mary Quay 1481.

Wentworth, Roger; Gentleman; born 1465, Codham Hall, Essex (?); parents, Sir Henry and Elizabeth; married Anne Tyrell; children, John, Henry, Lora and Margaret; died before 1500; executors, Christopher Wentworth and William Lovesone; merchant; overseas trade, exported dairy, fish, wheat, stone, woollen cloth 1491/2, executors sued the Breton Grunondus Guyseney for £35 3s. 4d. 1500; freeman 1482; MP 1483 (June), 1489/90; customs official, collector 1484/5. Other information, cousin of Howard dukes of Norfolk, sheriff of Essex and Hertforshire, litigant in the petty court 1487–93.

Wethereld (alias Weathereld, Whethereld, Witherell), William; married Margaret (?); appointed as executor by John Joye mid 1430s, John Priour 1437, John Asselott 1439, Joan Peryman 1447; merchant; unsuccessfully resisted the appointment of the London mercer, John Warren, as permanent governor of the Merchant Adventurers in the Low Countries 1421. Other occupation, brewed ale 1415–24, innkeeper 1424, in east ward; apprentice Robert Roger 1433; freeman; attended court general from 1418; portman 1429; bailiff 1427/8 (?), 1432/3, 1435/6, 1443/4, 1446/7, 1450/1; other borough office, coroner 1421–23, 1430/1, 1438/9, claviger 1432/3, appointed to oversee extension to guildhall 1435; JP 1448–53; MP 1421 (Dec.), 1429, 1445; interests in borough land, grant of foreshore rights in St Peter 1424, lease lately part of town wall, St Mary Quay, 1434, lease in St Nicholas 1437, lease 1446/7; other information, commissioned to collect subsidies in the county of Suffolk, acting as host to Herman Rollesthorp, a Dutchman, 1427/8 (?), defended claims in petty court as executor of John Joye 1443, faced a claim in the court of common pleas for £40 jointly with others of Otley and Ashbocking 1450.

Whetyngtone, John; dyer, in partnership with Thomas Bunt (?). Other occupation, sold ale in south ward 1481–87; freeman 1491. Other information, litigant in the petty court 1487–93, with Bunt sued by Thomas Harford for £2, William Style for £2 9s. 10d., Richard Gosse for £4, all 1491.

Winter (alias Wynter), Edmund; born 1421 (?); died 1476 (?); brother William; sons, Geoffrey (eldest), John (youngest), Nicholas, Robert; buried St Peter; pewterer, mentioned in the records of the London Pewterers' Company 1453–73, sued John Keggyll late of Bildeston, pewterer in the royal courts for 62s. 10d. 1473. Other occupations, ironmonger, sold to the borough for 20s. a brace for the grain mill 1446/7, brewed ale in south ward 1466–68; apprentice, son Nicholas 1471, servant Thomas 1465; freeman 1446; councillor 1448; portman 1453; bailiff 1456/7, 1459/60, 1462/3, 1466/7, 1470/1, 1476/7; other borough office, chamberlain 1452/3, claviger 1456/7, 1459/60, 1462/3, 1466/7; JP 1441, 1462–67, 1470–72; MP 1453/4; interests in borough land, grant next to the river 1457, grant in St Nicholas 1465. Other information, fined for public health offences in south ward 1466–71, allowed pigs to wander 1471/2, leased to Thomas Denys a tenement in St Nicholas at a rent of 6s. per annum which he failed to pay 1473, together with Benedict Caldwell took a letter of obligation for £100 from William Cakebread yeoman 1476.

Winter (alias Wynter), Nicholas; father, Edmund; siblings, Geoffrey, John, Robert; married Agnes, who later married John Walworth; children, Edmund, John, Nicholas, Alice, Elizabeth; will made 1488, proved 1488; buried St Peter; notable bequests, to the Corpus Christi gild half a garnish of best made pewter vessel and a pewter charger, to sons all utensils of craft of pewterer, that is moulds and tools, and to each a hundredweight of fine metal and a hundredweight of lay metal, to each apprentice 3s. 4d., cash gifts to churches in London, Hounslow and Burton Lazars, Leicestershire; supervisor of his will,

Thomas Baldry; appointed as executor by William Winter 1476; pewterer; apprentices, Robert Hogon, William Black, Thomas Newman 1488; freeman, as apprentice to his father, 1471; councillor, portman 1480; bailiff 1485/6. Other borough office, chief pledge in leet court of south ward 1472–79, chamberlain 1477/8; interests in borough land, lease in St Peter 1473, grant in St Peter 1474, grant 1486. Other information, fined for public health offence by leet court of south ward 1472.

Winter (alias Wynter), William; brother Edmund; married Katherine; children, none recorded; will made 1476, proved 1476; buried St Mary Tower; property bequests, house, garden adjacent to the barn of St Peter's priory, house at Colehill, close between Ipswich and St Albright's chapel, close at St George; other notable bequests, purses, mazers, jewellery and precious metal, contents of bedchamber and wardrobe, to each apprentice a hundredweight of new wrought ware and a hundredweight of old lay metal; executors, William Sewale, Nicholas Winter; pewterer, mentioned in the records of the London Pewterers' Company 1445-72; apprentices Peter Broun and William Revet 1478; freeman; borough office, treasurer 1449-51, tax collector in St Peter 1455, collector again 1459, chamberlain 1464/5, surveyor of the fish market 1467, chief pledge in leet court of west ward 1467–75, claviger 1468–72, 1474/5, coroner 1471/2; interests in borough land, grant next to salt water 1452, grants of foreshore rights in St Peter 1452 and 1463, grant for the purpose of a quay 1462, 1463, grant of 'Dikehole' 1472. Other information, transferred a tenement with buildings, curtilages and gardens in St Peter 1445.

Wode, John; son, Robert (?); merchant/vintner; overseas trade, jointly with John Parker imported fifty-two tuns of vintage wine 1397, brought claims in the court of Common Pleas 1410, imported wine 1414, sold fortified wine worth £1 to John Catfield 1401, sold 600 gallons of red wine at exorbitant price of 8d. a gallon 1424. Other occupations, brewed and sold ale, baked bread 1415–37, innkeeper 1415–37, in east, north and west wards; apprentices William Barker 1420; freeman; portman 1418, 1429; other borough office, coroner 1420/1, 1427/8; MP 1420; customs official, tronage and pesage of wools, hides and wool-fells 1410.

Wode, Robert; married Margery; merchant, licensed to ship Norfolk barley from Yarmouth to Ipswich 1440; portman 1429; bailiff 1434/5, 1437/8, 1440/1, 1443/4, 1446/7; other borough office, appointed to oversee extension to Guildhall 1435, claviger 1439–41, 1442–44.

Wulcy (alias Wolsey), Robert; born 1438 (?); married Joan; son, Thomas, later Cardinal Wolsey; will made 1496, proved 1496; parish of residence at death, St Nicholas; buried St Mary Elms (?); property bequests, in Ipswich and Stoke; other notable bequests, £6 13s. 4d. to his son Thomas, if he became a priest and sang for his soul for a year, painting of the archangel to the church of St Nicholas; executors, wife, son, Thomas Cady, Richard Ferryngton; butcher in west and then south ward 1467–88. Other occupations brewed ale 1467–88, innkeeper 1467–88, kept an unruly house 1468, 1483–87, moved from west to south ward 1473, and thenceforward lived in St Nicholas Street; servant Robert 1468; freeman (?). Other information, occupied borough land next to the church of St George without licence and grazed his beasts on the town embankment 1468, donated 12d. towards payment of £4 by the borough for the upkeep of four young men in the service of the king 1486, unlawfully retained Robert Kebyll's horse with bridle and saddle worth £1 12s. 1491, sued John Rotyrdam for recovery of three ounces of silver worth 9s. 1492.

Wursop (alias Worsop), William; Esquire; born 1430 (?) in Nottingham; father, Richard of Nottingham; vintner, supplied white wine, red French and red Gascon wine to Sir John Howard, and made at least two separate sales to the borough, including one of sweet wine,

1463/4. Other occupations, practised as an attorney in the petty court 1470s; freeman 1457; councillor 1479/80; other borough office, coroner and clerk of the peace 1479–83; MP 1459, 1463–65, 1472–75. Other information, retainer of John Mowbray, fourth duke of Norfolk, fined for public health offence in east ward 1475.

Wymbyll (alias Wimbill, Wymbill), Robert; married Alice (?); children, four sons and five daughters including John, William, and Elizabeth; buried, St Mary Tower, where his two memorial brasses survive; appointed as executor by Richard Mongomery 1462, John Drayll 1465; lawyer, notary to John Drayll; clothier, eight straits 1467; freeman 1460; bailiff 1469/70; other borough office, claviger 1471/2, 1475/6, 1477/8; JP 1470–78; MP 1470. Other information, party to a quitclaim of land formerly belonging to Hugh Liew 1453, pursued payment of £100 under a recognisance from William Gilberd clerk, John Thweyt, John Hayle and William James dyer 1457, fined for public health offence by leet court of north ward 1466–75, created an unlawful path over the town ramparts next to 'Morellyspond' 1468, arbitrated a land dispute 1472, sued the prior of Holy Trinity c.1473, produced a deed of release made by John Kent executor of the will of Henry Trevylyan lately archdeacon of Suffolk 1478, litigant in the petty court 1479.

Wysman, Thomas; married Alice (?); sons, John, Thomas (?); died 1437 (?); executors, Richard Curteby clerk, Ede Burnham clerk and John Wysman; lead worker, also sold woollen cloth to Henry van Colen 1415. Other occupation, brewed ale in east ward 1416–37; apprentice John Boyton 1437; freeman; borough office, chief pledge in leet court of east ward 1416–36; interests in borough land, lease in St Nicholas 1421. Other information, acted as surety for John Peyton 1418.

Wytton (alias Witton), John; dead by 1466 (?); appointed as executor by Alice Pratt 1448, John Free 1449; grocer; other occupation, sold ale in west ward 1423/4 (?); apprentice, William Burre for whom an indenture dated 1446 survives; freeman; borough office, claviger 1434/5, coroner 1435–38, 1439–41; interests in borough land, grant to the east of the wall of the Carmelite friars 1435, grant of foreshore rights in St Clement 1446, lease behind the wall of the Carmelite friary in St Stephen 1446–48. Other information, owned premises including shops in St Laurence which were sold by William and Margaret Burre and others to John Kyng, citizen and grocer, of London and others 1466.

Notes

(?) means that the information is probably correct, but some doubt remains.
A reference to a saint means (as the context requires) either the church or the parish bearing that saint's name.
References to parishes, churches, priories and friaries are, unless otherwise stated, to those in Ipswich.
Dates given for an occupation are normally those in the earliest and latest extant records, and do not necessarily represent the full extent of a person's career in that occupation, nor mean that the person was following that occupation throughout the period stated.
Dates given for being a freeman are those of actual admission.
Dates given for being a councillor or portman are those of the earliest records in which the person is so described, not necessarily the dates on which they were elected to office.
Fuller biographies of those men who served as MP, often giving more details of their activities outside the town, are set out in volumes of *HoP*, in the notes on Ipswich MPs.

– Appendix 4 –

Surviving Memorials to Medieval Ipswich Burgesses

Name	*Church*	*Nature of memorial*
John and Joan Baldwyn[1]	St Laurence[5]	Flint flushwork
John Bryd[2]	St Margaret	Initials
John and Katherine Halle[2]	St Margaret	Merchant's mark, initials
William Ropkyn[2]	St Margaret	Altar tomb
Henry and Isabel Tylmaker[2]	St Margaret	Initials and monogram 'TILER'
Thomas Baldry[3]	St Mary Tower	Two brasses
Thomas Drayll[3]	St Mary Tower	Brass
Robert Wymbyll[3]	St Mary Tower	Two brasses
William Style I	St Nicholas	Brass and monogram
William Style II	St Nicholas	Brass
Thomas Alvard[4]	St Stephen	Slab with matrices of missing brasses

Notes:

1. John Blatchly and Peter Northeast, *Decoding Flint Flushwork on Suffolk and Norfolk Churches* (Ipswich: Suffolk Institute of Archaeology and History, 2005), p. 49.

2. John Blatchly and Peter Northeast, 'Discoveries in the Clerestory and Roof Structure of St Margaret's Church Ipswich' *PSIA* 38 (1996), 387–407; Birkin Haward, *Suffolk Medieval Church Roof Carvings* (Ipswich: Suffolk Institute of Archaeology and History, 1999), pp. 110–11.

3. John Blatchly and Peter Northeast, 'Seven Figures for Four Departed: Multiple Memorials at St Mary le Tower, Ipswich' *Transactions of the Monumental Brass Society* 14 (1989), 257–267.

4. Diarmaid MacCulloch and John Blatchly, 'Recent Discoveries at St Stephen's Church, Ipswich: The Wimbill Chancel and the Rush-Alvard Chapel' *PSIA*, 36 (1986), 101–114.

5. A commemoratory stone inscription for John Bottold in the church of St Laurence, recorded in John Weever *Antient Funeral Monuments* (London: Thomas Harper, 1631; repr. London: William Tooke, 1767), p. 486, has now disappeared.

I am indebted to Dr John Blatchly for the information and references in this Appendix.

– Appendix 5 –

Merchants Shipping Wool from Ipswich, 1396–1413

Merchant	*Residence*	*Occupation*	*1396/7*[1]	*1397/8*[2]	*1399/1400*[3]
Thomas Ashbourne					
Robert Baker			42.33	41.31	
William Bedford		Merchant[4]			71.34
John Brasyngburgh					
Geoffrey Brook	London	Grocer[5]		107.3	229.20
John Broun					
Thomas Broun	London	Grocer[6]	27.25	72.11	
William Broun		Merchant			
John Burton	Bristol	Merchant[7]			
Thomas Chacomube			20.41		
John Channdeler					
John Chirche	London	Mercer[8]			
John Clerk	Ipswich	Mariner[9]			
John Clirsham					
Roger Cupper	Yarmouth				
John Dalton			32.9	4.13½	
Thomas Derby					
John Devill					
Walter Eton	Norwich	Lawyer[10]		4.13½	
John Fielding		Merchant			
Gere Flore	Oakham, Rutland[11]				
Roger Galden					
Geoffrey G[alfe]					
Thomas Garton	London	Mercer[12]			
Thomas Godewen	Ipswich	Draper[13]			
John Godstone	London/Colchester	Mercer[14]	53.16	179.2	31.37
John Goldsmyth					
William Hanwode					
Thomas Harleston					
Thomas Harpesfeld	Coventry	Mercer[15]			
John Horkslee	Ipswich	Merchant			53.51
John Lardener	London	Mercer[16]	122.12 [F]		
William Lesyngham	Carlby, Lincs	Merchant[17]			
William Lewys		Merchant			
Robert Loksmyth					
John Loudham	Northampton	Merchant[18]			
William Lytill					
Hugh Martyn		Merchant			
William Matchisson					

Merchant	*Residence*	*Occupation*	*1396/7*[1]	*1397/8*[2]	*1399/1400*[3]
Paul Meliane	Alien				
William Nese					
Thomas Neweman	London[19]			56.23	
Simon Noke	London	Woolman[20]			60.8 [F]
John Olney	London	Grocer or Mercer[21]			
John Osberne	London[22]	Stockfishmonger[23]		48.25	
William Penythorne		Merchant[24]			
Nicholas Persey					
Geoffrey Peterssone	Alien				
Ralph Prat					
William Prudhome		Merchant			
John Pykwell	Leicester	Merchant[25]			
William Pylton	Northampton	Merchant[26]			
Richard Reynold	London	Tailor/Vintner[27]		26.35	
William Reynold	London	Vintner[28]			
John Rous	Ipswich	Merchant[29]			
John Salston				8.6	
John Sapcote		Merchant			
Richard de Seyntyvee					
John Simond	Herbergh		51.2		
Thomas Simond	London	Draper[30]			
John Skot	Scarborough	Merchant[31]			
William Spencer	Leicester and/ or Northampton	Merchant[32]			
Nicholas Squyer		Merchant			
John Stoodle					
Richard Thorp	Lynn	Merchant[33]			
John White	Alien/Rome	Mercer[34]			
Robert Wodecombe		Merchant			
John Woodcock	London	Mercer[35]			
Nicholas Wotton	London	Draper/Woolman[36]			
Thomas Wyntringham	Northants	Merchant[37]			

Merchant	*1400/1*[38]	*1401/2*[39]	*1403/4*[40]	*1406/7*[41]	*1407/8*[42]	*1410/11*[43]	*1412/13*[44]
Thomas Ashbourne				17.0			
Robert Baker							
William Bedford	58.41	108.3					
John Brasyngburgh						7.4[F]	
Geoffrey Brook		49.8					
John Broun				12.49			
Thomas Broun	33.7	48.44					
William Broun							n.d.
John Burton				16.11			
Thomas Chacomube							
John Channdeler					8.1		
John Chirche		58.14		6.29			
John Clerk							n.d.
John Clirsham				6.28			

Merchant	*1400/1*[38]	*1401/2*[39]	*1403/4*[40]	*1406/7*[41]	*1407/8*[42]	*1410/11*[43]	*1412/13*[44]
Roger Cupper						50.39	
John Dalton							
Thomas Derby				23.1			
John Devill							
Walter Eton							
John Fielding	31.21	62.25			4.3	42.45	n.d.
Gere Flore		24.48+					
Roger Galden					6.11		
Geoffrey G[alfe]					10.11		
Thomas Garton				3.38			
Thomas Godewen						8.39[F]	
John Godstone							
William Hanwode		30.20[F]					
Thomas Harleston				12.13			
Thomas Harpesfeld						43.8	
John Horkslee	55.30	45[F]					
John Larden							
William Lesyngham					1.46		n.d.
William Lewys				17.5			n.d.
Robert Loksmyth					8.8		
John Loudham	18.42	45.20					
William Lytill					2.2	13.26	
Hugh Martyn							n.d.
William Matchisson					3.50		
Paul Meliane						53.12	
William Nese				6.25[F]			
Thomas Neweman							
Simon Noke							
John Olney	45.11	38.10					
John Osberne							
William Penythorne						43.13	
Nicholas Persey			2.4[F]				
Geoffrey Peterssone			1.26[F]				
Ralph Prat		47.46					
William Prudhome					8.24	72.0	n.d.
John Pykwell							n.d.
William Pylton						70.33[F]	
Richard Reynold							
William Reynold	25.3	27.25[F]				28.10[F]	
John Rous	126.4[F]	71.3[F]			7.26		
John Salston							
John Sapcote		43.27+[F]		27.30			n.d.
Richard de Seyntyvee		30.44[F]					
John Simond		4.35[F]					
Thomas Simond		73.16[F]					
John Skot					3.23		
William Spencer						20.13	
Nicholas Squyer							n.d.
John Stoodle	12.13[F]						

Merchant	*1400/1*[38]	*1401/2*[39]	*1403/4*[40]	*1406/7*[41]	*1407/8*[42]	*1410/11*[43]	*1412/13*[44]
Richard Thorp				2.6			
John White			2.0				
Robert Wodecombe							n.d.
John Woodcock					8.2		
Nicholas Wotton	12.38	41.19+					
Thomas Wyntringham			(21.1)[1]		8.5	81.35 F	
Richard Wyssenden				4.13			

Notes
See notes to Table 6.
Figures are given in sacks (364lbs) and cloves (7lbs).
F means includes woolfells.
n.d means no data available.
( ) means figures are sarplers and pokes – a sarpler contained about two sacks.
+ means that there were additional cloves, but the figures are illegible.
All merchants are assumed to have had an equal share in joint ventures.
A reference given at the head of a column means that it applies to all data in that column.
A footnote reference to one of the printed calendars of Chancery records normally relates to an individual's first appearance.

Notes to Appendix 5

1 PRO E 122/193/33.
2 PRO E 122/193/33.
3 PRO E 122/51/2.
4 *CCR 1396–99,* p. 46.
5 *CPR 1401–05,* p. 147; Lloyd (1976), p. 253.
6 *CCR 1419–22,* p. 110.
7 *CPR 1399–1401,* p. 215; J. Roskell and L.S. Woodger, 'John Burton', in *HoP*, II, pp. 437–9.
8 PRO CP40/655, Michaelmas Term, rot. 379.
9 SROI C/2/3/1/34–37 (several references).
10 *CPR 1408–13,* p. 187; L.S. Woodger, 'Walter Eton', in *HoP*, III, pp. 2–3.
11 *CPR 1401–05,* pp. 416-17.
12 Sutton (2005), p. 151.
13 SROI C/2/3/1/48 (31 Jan. 1415).
14 *CPR 1399–1401,* p. 443.
15 *CCR 1405–09,* p. 101.
16 *CCR 1409–13,* p. 85; Sutton (2005), p. 153n.
17 *CPR 1416–22,* p. 223.
18 *CPR 1401–05,* p. 411; C. Rawcliffe, 'John Loudham', in *HoP*, III, pp. 628–9.
19 *CCR 1396–99,* p. 228.
20 *CCR 1396–99,* pp. 62-4.
21 *CCR 1409–13,* pp. 334, 348, 350; Lloyd (1977), p. 253; Sutton (2005), pp. 145n, 221. There were at least two, perhaps as many as four, related John Olneys in different parts of the country. While John Olney of London is described once as a mercer, he appears more often as a grocer.
22 PRO E 122/193/33.
23 *CCR 1402–05,* p. 307.
24 *CCR 1413–19,* p. 416.
25 C. Kightly, 'John Pykwell', in *HoP*, IV, p. 151.
26 *CCR 1402–05,* pp. 308-9; C. Rawcliffe, 'John Loudham', in *HoP*, III, pp. 628–9.
27 Lloyd (1976), p. 253.
28 *CPR 1408-13,* p. 334.
29 K.N. Houghton, 'John Rous', in *HoP*, III, pp. 238–9.
30 *CPR 1405–08,* p. 403.
31 *CPR 1399–1401,* p. 545.
32 *CPR 1399–1401,* p. 355; *CPR 1416–22,* p. 164.
33 *CPR 1416–22,* p. 3.
34 Sutton (2005), p. 227.
35 C. Rawcliffe, 'John Woodcock', in *HoP*, IV, pp. 896–9; Sutton (2005), pp. 113, 125.
36 *CCR 1413–19,* p. 74; Lloyd (1976), p. 253; C. Rawcliffe, 'Nicholas Wotton', in *HoP*, IV, pp. 905–7.
37 *CCR 1402–05,* p. 332.
38 PRO E 122/51/2.
39 PRO E 122/51/2.
40 PRO E 122/51/10.
41 PRO E 122/50/41.
42 PRO E 122/50/41.
43 PRO E 122/51/28.
44 *CPR 1413–16,* p. 127.

– Appendix 6 –

Exports and Imports by Ipswich Merchants, 1396–98

EXPORTS

Merchant	*Wool*	*Woollen cloth*	*Hides*	*Cheese*	*Other*
John Arnold					
John Belcham					
John Bernard		£2 10s.			
Roger Blast					
John Bottold		£5 2s.	£3 5s. 4d.		
Gilbert Boulge					
Edmund Brook		£5			
Thomas Canntebregge					
John Cattiwade					
John Chapman		£2 6s. 8d.	5s.		
John Clerk		£12 14s. 2d.			
Thomas Croucheman		£19 1s. 8d.			
William Debenham		£31 18s. 8d.			
Thomas Edone		£1			
William Fen					
Roger Gosenold		£1 10s.			
Richard Gouty		£3			
John Horkslee					
Thomas Lestyman		£2			
Henry Lomenour		£86			
John Long					
Alexander Louf					
John Ludham					
Robert Mersh		£2			
John Michell		£25 15s.			
John Monk					
Thomas Oston					
John Parker		£61			
John Roberd		£28 4s. 2d.			
Thomas Scot		£15 4s.			
Robert Templeman					
John Toyt		£3			
Richard Wagestaf		£3 10s.			
John Wode					
Ipswich total	0	£310 16s. 4d.	£3 10s. 4d.	0	0
% of total exports by all merchants from Ipswich	0	75.8	9.3	0	0

IMPORTS

Merchant	*Wine*	*Dyes*	*Iron*	*Salt*	*Grain*	*Fish*	*Beer*	*Stone*	*Tiles*	*Timber*	*Other*
John Arnold	£60										
John Belcham											£1 13s. 4d.
John Bernard						6s.8d.					
Roger Blast	£50										
John Bottold											
Gilbert Boulge	£220										
Edmund Brook											
Thomas Canntebregge	£67 10s.										£4
John Cattiwade											
John Chapman		£1 6s. 8d.					£1 16s.				£1 10s.
John Clerk											13s. 4d.
Thomas Croucheman		£3									
William Debenham	£110			£8 6s. 8d.							
Thomas Edone	£30							£1 10s.			
William Fen	£85										
Roger Gosenold											
Richard Gouty	£17 10s.			£4 6s. 8d.	£5 6s. 8d.	13s. 4d.					
John Horkslee				£5							
Thomas Lestyman											
Henry Lomenour											
John Long											£2 8s.
Alexander Louf								£3			
John Ludham	£150										
Robert Mersh											

Merchant	*Wine*	*Dyes*	*Iron*	*Salt*	*Grain*	*Fish*	*Beer*	*Stone*	*Tiles*	*Timber*	*Other*
John Michell		£3									
John Monk											11s. 8d.
Thomas Oston		£45									
John Parker	£380			£5							
John Roberd	£200			£15 15s.		£1					
Thomas Scot	£30			£4							£10
Robert Templeman	£60										
John Toyt											
Richard Wagestaf											
John Wode	£130										
Ipswich total	£1590	£52 6s. 8d.	0	£42 8s. 4d.	£5 6s. 8d.	£2	£1 16s.	£4 10s.	0	0	£20 16s. 4d.
% of total imports by all merchants in to Ipswich	39.8	31.1	0	53.0	17.8	6.9	8.2	23.7	0	0	20.7

Notes

All merchants are assumed to have had an equal share in joint ventures.

Source: PRO E 122/193/33.

– Appendix 7 –

Denizen Merchants Active in Overseas Trade from Ipswich, 1459–66

Merchant	*Residence*	*Occupation*
Thomas Alvard[1]	Woodbridge	
John Bailly[2]	Bristol	Merchant
John Baker[3]	London	Stockfishmonger
John Bardalf		
William Blake	Ipswich	
Richard Browne		
John Bull		
Richard Buntyng		
William Buntyng[4]	Bury St Edmunds	Clothier
Edmund Caldwell	Ipswich	
John Clerk[5]	London	Grocer
Robert Coke[6]	Stowmarket	Clothier
Roger Crytote[7]	Lavenham	Clothier
John Dexter		
John Drake		
Stephen Dryver[8]		Master
John Durday		
William Edon		
Thomas Estmond		
Robert Fen[9]		Master
John Gosse[10]	Ipswich	Clothier
John Gunne		
John Hamond[11]	Nayland, Suffolk	Clothier
John Hawe		
Richard Helperby[12]	Calais	Stapler
Thomas Hempstede[13]	Norwich	Merchant
Richard Hoste		
John Howard	Stoke-by-Nayland, Suffolk	Knight
Robert Hunte		
William Keche[14]	Ipswich	Merchant/Tanner
Thomas Kempe		
John Kyng[15]	London	Grocer
Roger London		
William London		
Peter Loveday		

Merchant	*Residence*	*Occupation*
John Makeer		
John Mareot		
John Martin[16]	Melford, Suffolk	Mercer
Richard Parker[17]	Colchester	Clothier
William Parker[18]		Master
John Peek[19]	London	Ironmonger
Thomas Pygot[20]		Stapler
John Rever[21]	Ipswich	Mercer
William Roos[22]	Calais	Stapler
Thomas Slowby		
John Smyth[23]	Ipswich	Merchant
Cuthbert Stekenham		
John Stokker[24]	London	Draper
Robert Strangman[25]	Debenham, Suffolk	
Robert Toke[26]	London	Ironmonger
William Trafford[27]	Boston	Stapler
John Webster		
John Whitesote		
John Wigston		Stapler
Roger Wigston		Stapler
James Wright[28]	London	Stockfishmonger

Source: PRO E 122/52/42–8

Notes to Appendix 7

[1] Probably the father of Thomas Alvard who was a leading Ipswich burgess at the end of the fifteenth century.
[2] *CPR 1452–61*, p. 649; Childs (1978), p. 96.
[3] *CCR 1461–68*, p. 183.
[4] PRO E 101/343/4–5.
[5] *CPR 1461–67*, p. 417; Nightingale (1995), pp. 422, 520.
[6] PRO E 101/342/25; E 101/343/2–4.
[7] PRO E 101/343/5.
[8] *CPR 1467–77*, p. 318.
[9] *CPR 1461–67*, p. 232.
[10] PRO E 101/342/25; E 101/343/2.
[11] PRO E 101/342/25; E 101/343/2–4.
[12] *CPR 1467–77*, pp. 212–13 among other references.
[13] *CPR 1467–77*, p. 579.
[14] *CPR 1461–67*, p. 262.
[15] Nightingale (1995), pp. 510, 515, 529n, 535. Kyng appears in various Ipswich records, see above pp. 124, 148, 170, 241, 268, 277.
[16] Sutton (2005), pp. 222, 295, 528n, 529.
[17] Britnell (1986), p. 211n.
[18] *CPR 1467–77*, p. 355.
[19] *CCR 1461–68*, p. 257.
[20] *CPR 1446–52*, pp. 314–15; *CPR 1452–61*, pp. 210–11.
[21] *CPR 1461–67*, p. 418.
[22] Lloyd (1991), p. 209.
[23] SROI C/2/10/1/4, 6 (east ward); C/2/8/1/13 (east ward).
[24] *CPR 1452–61*, p. 314.
[25] BL, Ms Add. 30,158, f. 24r.
[26] *CPR 1461–67*, pp. 229, 297.
[27] *CCR 1454–61*, p. 263; *CPR 1452–61*, pp. 210–11, 226.
[28] *CCR 1461–68*, p. 183; *CCR 1468–76*, p. 27.

Bibliography

Manuscript Sources

British Library (London)

Ipswich General Court Register	Ms Add. 30,158
Medieval seal of the bailiffs of Ipswich	Seal LXXI.117
Henry VIII's Survey of the Coast, Yarmouth to Orwell	Cotton Augustus I.i.58

The National Archives (Public Record Office, London)

Chancery:

Miscellaneous Chancery Records	C 1/16/427, C 1/16/469, C 1/73/162, C 1/115/16, C1/1500/3

Records of the Court of Common Pleas and other courts:

Plea Rolls, Court of Common Pleas	CP 40/402, 437, 556, 571, 596, 636, 655, 676, 756

Exchequer, Records of King's Remembrancer:

Alnage accounts	E 101/342/10, E 101/342/25, E 101/343/2, E 101/343/4, E 101/343/5
Particular accounts	E 122/50/30, E 122/51/28, E 122/51/39, E 122/52/42, E 122/52/43, E 122/52/45, E 122/52/46, E 122/52/47, E 122/52/48, E 122/52/56, E 122/53/1, E 122/53/9, E 122/193/28, E 122/193/33
Cocket certificates	E 122/50/41, E 122/51/2, E 122/51/10
Miscellaneous Exchequer Records	E 159/230, E 210/625
Assessment of aliens for tax 1440 and 1483	E 179/180/92, E 179/180/111

Registers of Wills and Letters of Administration of Prerogative Court of Canterbury:

PCC Wills	PROB 11

Suffolk Record Office (Ipswich)

Lay subsidy	C/1/9/1
Rental	C/2/1/1/3
Petty court rolls	C/2/3/1/34–37, 41, 48 and 51
Extracts of Proceedings	C/2/3/6/4
Maritime court certificate	C/2/5/2
Admiralty jurisdiction	C/2/6/2–3
Leet court rolls	C/2/8/1/1–22
Composite enrolments (including general court, petty court and leet court)	C/2/10/1/1–8
Composite court books	C/2/10/3/1–5
Chamberlains' compotus rolls	C/3/3/1/1–2
Grants of common soil	C/3/8/5/2, C/3/8/6/3–4, C/3/8/7/1
Ipswich Domesdays	C/4/1/2, 4
Apprenticeship indenture 1448	C/6/11/1

Tax assessments for Ipswich 1689–94	HA247/5/2
John Speed's map 1610	MC5/50
Monson's map of Ipswich 1848	HD477/10
Wills	Registers: R1–3

Suffolk Record Office (Bury St Edmunds)

Wills	Register Hervye

Norwich Record Office

Norwich Consistory Court, Wills	Registers: Aleyn, Aubry, Betyns, Brosyard, Cage, A. Caston, Doke, Gelour, Hubert, Jekkys, Multon, Neve, Sayve, Surflete, Typpes, Wight, Wolman and Wylbey

Joseph Regenstein Library, University of Chicago

Ixworth Priory Court Book 1467–83	Bacon MS 912

Printed Primary Sources

Allen, David (ed.) *Ipswich Borough Archives 1255–1835* (Woodbridge: Boydell for SRS, 43, 2000)

Bacon, Nathaniel *The Annals of Ipswiche … by Nathaniel Bacon serving as Recorder and Town Clerk … 1654* ed. by W.H. Richardson (Ipswich: Cowell, 1884)

Bailey, Mark (ed.) *The Bailiffs' Minute Book of Dunwich, 1404–1430* (Woodbridge: Boydell for SRS, 34, 1992)

Bolton, J.L. (ed.) *Alien Communities in London in the Fifteenth Century: The Subsidy Rolls of 1440 and 1483–4* (Stamford: Paul Watkins for the Richard III and Yorkist History Trust, 1998)

Bracton, Henry *Bracton on the Laws and Customs of England* ed. by S.E. Thorne (Cambridge, Mass: Belknap, 1977)

Breen, Anthony M. and John Ridgard 'The Ipswich Tallage Rolls 1227' The Suffolk Review, New Series, 54 (Spring 2010)

Calendar of the Charter Rolls, 1226–1517, 6 volumes (London: HMSO, 1903–27)

Calendar of Close Rolls, 1272–1509, 47 volumes (London: HMSO, 1892–1963)

Calendar of Fine Rolls, 1272–1509, 22 volumes (London: HMSO, 1911–62)

Calendar of Inquisitions Miscellaneous, 1219–1485, 8 volumes (Chancery), (London: HMSO, 1916–2003)

Calendars of Patent Rolls, 1232–1509, 52 volumes (London: HMSO, 1891–1916)

Childs, Wendy R. (ed.) *The Customs Accounts of Hull 1453–90* (Leeds: The Yorkshire Archaeological Society, 144, 1986)

Crawford, Anne (ed.) *The Household Books of John Howard, Duke of Norfolk* (Stroud: Sutton Publishing, 1992)

Domesday Book ed. by Ann Williams and G.H. Martin (London: Penguin Books, 2002)

Dymond, D.P. (ed.) *The Register of Thetford Priory* (Oxford: Oxford University Press for NRS, 59 and 60, 1994 and 1995/6)

Farrow, M.A. (ed.), *Index of Wills Proved at Norwich 1370–1550* (NRS, 16, 1942–44)

Fortescue, Sir John *De Laudibus Legum Anglia* ed. by S.B. Chrimes (Cambridge: Cambridge University Press, 1942)

Fraser, C.M. (ed.) *The Accounts of the Chamberlains of Newcastle-upon-Tyne 1508–11* (Newcastle: Society of Antiquaries of Newcastle-upon-Tyne, 38, 1986)

Grimwade, M.E. (comp.), *Index of the Probate Records of the Court of the Archdeacon of Suffolk 1444–1700* (London: British Record Soc., 90 and 91, 1979 and 1980)

Harris, M. D. (ed.) *The Coventry Leet Book* III and IV (London: Kegan Paul, Trench and Trubner for The Early English Text Society, 138, 1913; repr. Cambridge: D.S. Brewer, 2006)

Hervey, S.H.A. (ed.) *Suffolk in 1524, Suffolk Green Books X* (Woodbridge: Booth, 1910)

Jay, A. (ed.) *Oxford Dictionary of Political Quotations* (Oxford: Oxford University Press, 3rd edition 2006)
Hudson, William (ed.) *Leet Jurisdiction in the City of Norwich* (London: Bernard Quaritch for The Seldon Society, 5, 1892)
Luders, A. and others (eds.) *The Statutes of the Realm (1101–1713),* 11 vols. (London: Rec. Comm., 1810–28)
Malden, Henry Elliott (ed.) *The Cely Papers* (London: Longmans, Green and Co., 1900)
Millea, Nick (ed.) *The Gough Map: The Earliest Road Map of Great Britain* (Oxford: The Bodleian Library, 2007)
Northeast, Peter (ed.) *Wills of the Archdeaconry of Sudbury, 1439–1474, Part I* (Woodbridge: Boydell for SRS, 44, 2001)
Oswald-Hicks, T.W. (ed.), *A Calendar of Wills relating to the County of Suffolk proved in the Prerogative Court of Canterbury* (London: Poole and Pemberton, 1913)
Redstone, V.B. (ed.) *The Household Book of Dame Alice de Bryene of Acton Hall, Suffolk, September 1412 to September 1413* (Ipswich: Suffolk Institute of Archaeology and Natural History, 1931)
Ridgard, John (ed.) *Medieval Framlingham* (Woodbridge: Boydell for SRS, 27, 1985)
Rigby, S.H. (ed.) *The Overseas Trade of Boston in the Reign of Richard II* (Woodbridge: Boydell for the Lincoln Record Society, 93, 2005)
Strachey, J. and others (eds.) *Rotuli Parliamentorum ut et Petiones et Placita in Parliamento,* 6 vols. (Rec. Com., London, 1767–77)
Twiss, Sir Thomas (ed.) *The Black Book of the Admiralty, Appendix, Part II, Volume II,* 4 volumes (London: Rolls Series, 55, 1873)
Warner, Sir George (ed.) *The Libelle of Englyshe Polycye* (Oxford: Clarendon Press, 1926)
Webb, John (ed.) *The Town Finances of Elizabethan Ipswich* (Woodbridge: Boydell for the Suffolk Records Society, 38, 1996)

Printed Secondary Sources

Allen, David 'The Public Water Supply of Ipswich before the Municipal Corporations Act of 1835' *PSIA,* 40 (2001), 31–54
Allen, Martin 'The Volume of the English Currency, 1158–1470' *Econ. Hist. Rev.*, 2nd ser. 54 (2001), 595–611
Allen, Martin 'Silver Production and the Money Supply in England and Wales, 1086–c.1500' *Econ. Hist. Rev.*, 2nd ser., 64 (2011), 114–31
Allen, Robert C. 'The Industrial Revolution in Miniature: the Spinning Jenny in Britain, France and India' Oxford University, Department of Economics Working Paper, 375 (2007)
Amor, Nicholas R. 'Riding out Recession: Ixworth and Woolpit in the Late Middle Ages' *PSIA*, 40 (2002), 127–44
Amor, Nicholas R. 'Merchant Adventurer or Jack of All Trades: The Suffolk Clothier in the 1460s' *PSIA*, 40 (2004), 414–36
Amor, Nicholas R. 'Late Medieval Enclosure – A Study of Thorney, near Stowmarket, Suffolk' *PSIA*, 41 (2006), 175–97
Bailey, M. *A Marginal Economy? East-Anglian Breckland in the Later Middle Ages* (Cambridge: Cambridge University Press, 1989)
Bailey, Mark 'Demographic Decline in Late Medieval England: Some Thoughts on Recent Research' *Econ. Hist. Rev.*, 2nd ser., 49 (1996), 1–19
Bailey, Mark *The English Manor* (Manchester: Manchester University Press, 2002)
Bailey, Mark *Medieval Suffolk: An Economic and Social History* (Woodbridge: Boydell, 2007)
Bailey, Mark 'Technology and the Growth of Textile Manufacture in Medieval Suffolk' *PSIA*, 42 (2009) 13–20
Barraclough, Geoffrey (ed.) *The Times Atlas of World History* (London: Times Books, 1979)
Barron, Caroline M. 'Introduction: England and the Low Countries 1327–1477', in *England and the Low Countries in the Late Middle Ages* ed. by C. Barron and N. Saul (Stroud: Alan Sutton Publishing, 1995), pp. 1–28

Barron, Caroline M. 'London 1300–1540', in *The Cambridge Urban History of Britain: 600–1540* ed. by D.M. Palliser, 3 vols. (Cambridge: Cambridge University Press, 2000), I, pp. 395–440

Barron, Caroline M. *London in the Later Middle Ages: Government and People 1200–1500* (Oxford: Oxford University Press, 2004)

Barron, Caroline M. 'The Child in Medieval London: The Legal Evidence', in *Essays on Medieval Childhood* ed. by Joel T. Rosenthal (Donnington: Shaun Tyas, 2007), pp. 40–53

Bean, J.M.W. 'Plague, Population and Economic Decline in England in the later Middle Ages' *Econ. Hist. Rev.*, 2nd ser., 15 (1963), pp. 423–37

Bennett, Judith M. *Ale, Beer and Brewsters in England* (Oxford: Oxford University Press, 1996)

Betterton, Alec and David Dymond *Lavenham Industrial Town* (Lavenham: Terence Dalton, 1989).

Bindoff, S.T. (ed.) *The History of Parliament: The House of Commons 1509–1558*, 3 vols. (London: Secker & Warburg, 1982)

Blair, Claude and John Blair 'Copper Alloys', in *English Medieval Industries* ed. by J. Blair and N. Ramsay (London: Hambledon Press, 1991), pp. 81–106

Blatchly, John 'Preface' in *Ipswich Borough Archives 1255–1835* ed. by David Allen, (Woodbridge: Boydell for The Suffolk Records Society, 43, 2000), p. xi

Blatchly, John *A Famous Antient Seed-Plot of Learning: A History of Ipswich School* (Ipswich: Ipswich School, 2003)

Blatchly, John and Peter Northeast 'Seven Figures for Four Departed: Multiple Memorials at St Mary le Tower, Ipswich' *Transactions of the Monumental Brass Society* 14 (1989), 257–67

Blatchly, John and Peter Northeast 'Discoveries in the Clerestory and Roof Structure of St Margaret's Church Ipswich' *PSIA*, 38 (1996) 387–407

Blatchly, John and Peter Northeast *Decoding Flint Flushwork on Suffolk and Norfolk Churches* (Ipswich: Suffolk Institute of Archaeology and History, 2005)

Bolton, J.L. *The Medieval English Economy 1150–1500* (London: Dent, 1980)

Bolton, James L. 'What is Money', in *Medieval Money Matters* ed. by Diana Wood (Oxford: Oxbow Books, 2004), pp. 1–15

Bolton, J.L. and Francesco Guidi Bruscoli 'When did Antwerp Replace Bruges as the Commercial and Financial Centre of North-Western Europe? The Evidence of the Borromei Ledger for 1438' *Econ. Hist. Rev.*, 2nd ser., 61 (2008), 360–79

Bridbury, A.R. *Economic Growth: England in the Later Middle Ages* (London: Allen and Unwin, 1962; repr. Brighton: Harvester Press, 1975)

Bridbury, A.R. *Medieval Clothmaking: An Economic Survey* (London: Heinemann, 1982).

Briggs, Asa *A Social History of England* (London: Weidenfeld & Nicolson, 1983; repr. London: Penguin Books, 1987)

Britnell, R.H. *Growth and Decline in Colchester, 1300–1525* (Cambridge: Cambridge University Press, 1986)

Britnell, R.H. 'Farming Practice and Techniques: Eastern England', in *The Agrarian History of England and Wales: 1348–1500* ed. by E. Miller, 8 vols. (Cambridge: Cambridge University Press, 1991), III, pp. 194–209

Britnell, Richard H. *The Commercialisation of English Society* (Cambridge: Cambridge University Press, 1993; repr. Manchester: Manchester University Press, 1996)

Britnell, Richard *The Closing of the Middle Ages? England 1471–1529* (Oxford: Blackwell, 1997)

Britnell, Richard 'The Economy of British Towns 1300–1540', in *The Cambridge Urban History of Britain: 600–1540* ed. by D.M. Palliser, 3 vols. (Cambridge: Cambridge University Press, 2000), I, pp. 313–333

Britnell, Richard H. 'England: Towns, Trade and Industry' in *A Companion to Britain in the Later Middle Ages* ed. by S.H. Rigby (Oxford: Blackwell, 2003), pp. 47–64

Britnell, Richard 'The Woollen Textile Industry of Suffolk in the Later Middle Ages' *The Ricardian* 13 (2003), 86–99

Britnell, Richard *Britain and Ireland 1050–1530* (Oxford: Oxford University Press, 2004).

Britnell, Richard 'Uses of Money in Medieval England' in *Medieval Money Matters* ed. by Diana Wood (Oxford: Oxbow Books, 2004), pp. 16–30.

Britnell, Richard 'Town Life', in *A Social History of England 1200–1500* ed. by R. Horrox and W.M. Ormrod (Cambridge: Cambridge University Press, 2006), pp. 134–78.

Campbell, Bruce M.S. *English Seigniorial Agriculture* (Cambridge, Cambridge University Press, 2000)

Campbell, Marion 'Gold, Silver and Precious Stones', in *English Medieval Industries* ed. by J. Blair and N. Ramsay (London: Hambledon Press, 1991), pp. 107–66

Carlin, Martha 'Fast Food and Urban Living Standards in Medieval England' in *Food and Eating in Medieval Europe* ed. by Martha Carlin and Joel T. Rosenthal (London: Hambledon Press, 1998) pp. 27–51

Carus-Wilson, E.M. *Medieval Merchant Venturers* (London, 1954; repr. London: Methuen, 1967)

Carus-Wilson, E.M. and Olive Coleman *England's Export Trade, 1275–1547* (Oxford: Clarendon Press, 1963)

Castor, Helen *Blood and Roses: The Paston Family in the Fifteenth Century* (London: Faber and Faber, 2004)

Chapman, Colin R. *How Heavy, How Much and How Long: Weights, Money and other Measures used by our Ancestors* (Dursley: Lochlin Publishing, 1995)

Chaucer, Geoffrey *The Canterbury Tales*, ed. by Jill Mann (London: Penguin Books, 2005)

Cherry, John 'Pottery and Tile', in *English Medieval Industries* ed. by J. Blair and N. Ramsay (London: Hambledon Press, 1991), pp. 189–209

Cherry, John 'Leather', in *English Medieval Industries* ed. by J. Blair and N. Ramsay (London: Hambledon Press, 1991), pp. 295–318

Childs, Wendy R. *Anglo-Castilian Trade in the Later Middle Ages* (Manchester: Manchester University Press, 1978)

Childs, Wendy R. '"To oure losse and hindraunce": English Credit to Alien Merchants in the Mid-Fifteenth Century', in *Enterprise and Individuals in Fifteenth-Century England* ed. by Jennifer Kermode (Stroud: Alan Sutton, 1991), pp. 68–88

Childs, Wendy R. 'Moving Around', in *A Social History of England 1200–1500* ed. by R. Horrox and W.M. Ormrod (Cambridge: Cambridge University Press, 2006), pp. 260–75

Clark, Peter *The English Alehouse: A Social History* (London: Longman, 1983)

Clarke, G.R. *The History and Description of the Town of Ipswich* (London: Piper, 1830)

Copinger, W.A. *Manors of Suffolk*, 7 vols. (Manchester: Taylor, Garnett, Evans, 1905–11), II (1908)

Coss, Peter 'An Age of Deference', in *A Social History of England 1200–1500* ed. by R. Horrox and W.M. Ormrod (Cambridge: Cambridge University Press, 2006), pp. 31–73

Crawford, Anne *A History of the Vintners' Company* (London: Constable, 1977)

Davis, James 'Baking for the Common Good: A Reassessment of the Assize of Bread in Medieval England' *Econ. Hist. Rev.*, 2nd ser., 57 (2004), 465–502

Dobson, Barrie 'General Survey 1300–1540', in *The Cambridge Urban History of Britain: 600–1540* ed. by D.M. Palliser, 3 vols. (Cambridge: Cambridge University Press, 2000), I, pp. 273–90

Dunn, Penelope 'Trade', in *Medieval Norwich* ed. by Carole Rawcliffe and Richard Wilson (London: Hambledon, 2004), pp. 213–234

Dyer, Alan *Decline and Growth in English Towns 1400–1640* (Basingstoke: Macmillan, 1991; repr. Cambridge: Cambridge University Press, 1995)

Dyer, Alan '"Urban Decline" in England', in *Towns in Decline AD 100–1600*, ed. by T.R. Slater (Aldershot: Ashgate, 2000), pp. 266–88

Dyer, Alan 'Appendix: Ranking Lists of English Medieval Towns', in *The Cambridge Urban*

History of Britain: 600–1540 ed. by D.M. Palliser, 3 vols. (Cambridge: Cambridge University Press, 2000), I, pp. 747–770

Dyer, Christopher, *Standards of Living in the Later Middle Ages: Social Change in England c.1200–1520* (Cambridge: Cambridge University Press, 1989)

Dyer, Christopher 'Small Towns 1270–1540', in *The Cambridge Urban History of Britain: 600–1540* ed. by D.M. Palliser, 3 vols. (Cambridge: Cambridge University Press, 2000), pp. 505–37 (pp. 513–14).

Dyer, Christopher *Making a Living in the Middle Ages* (London: Yale University Press, 2002)

Dyer, Christopher *An Age of Transition? Economy and Society in England in the Later Middle Ages* (Oxford: Oxford University Press, 2005)

Dymond, David 'The Parson's Glebe', in *East Anglia's History: Studies in Honour of Norman Scarfe* ed. by C. Harper-Bill, C. Rawcliffe and R.G. Wilson (Woodbridge: Boydell for the Centre of East Anglian Studies, University of East Anglia, 2002) pp. 73–91

Dymond, David and Peter Northeast *A History of Suffolk* (Chichester: Phillimore, 1985; repr. 1995)

Dymond, David and Roger Virgoe 'The Reduced Population and Wealth of Early Fifteenth-Century Suffolk' *PSIA*, 36 (1986), 73–100

Eleyn, White Rev C.H. 'The Ipswich Domesday Books' *PSIA*, 6 (1888) 195–219

Farmer, David L. 'Prices and Wages, 1350–1500', in *The Agrarian History of England and Wales: 1348–1500* ed. by E. Miller, 8 vols. (Cambridge: Cambridge University Press, 1991), III, pp. 431–525

Finch, Jonathan, 'The Churches' in *Medieval Norwich* ed. by Carole Rawcliffe and Richard Wilson (London: Hambledon Press, 2004) pp. 49–72

Ford, C.J. 'Piracy or Policy. The Crisis in the Channel, 1400–1403' *TRHS*, 5th ser., 29 (1979), 63-78

Galloway, James A. 'Urban Hinterlands in Later Medieval England', in *Town and Country in the Middle Ages: Contrasts, Contacts and Interconnections 1100–1500* ed. by Kate Giles and Christopher Dyer (Leeds: Maney, 2003), pp. 111–30

Geddes, Jane 'Iron', in *English Medieval Industries* ed. by J. Blair and N. Ramsay (London: Hambledon Press, 1991), pp. 167–88

Goldberg, P.J.P. 'The Fashioning of Bourgeois Domesticity in Later Medieval England: A Material Culture Perspective' in *Medieval Domesticity. Home, Housing and Household in Medieval England* ed. by Maryanne Kowaleski and P.J.P. Goldberg (Cambridge: Cambridge University Press, 2008) pp. 124–44

Greenberg, Janelle 'Bacon, Nathaniel', in *The Oxford Dictionary of National Biography* ed. by H.C.G. Matthew and B. Harrison, 60 vols. (Oxford: Oxford University Press, 2004), III, pp. 162–3

Haggar, Arthur L. and Leonard F. Miller *Suffolk Clocks and Clockmakers* (Wadhurst: The Antiquarian Horological Society, 1974)

Hammond, P.W. *Food and Feast in Medieval England* (Stroud: Alan Sutton, 1993; repr 1995)

Harding, Vanessa 'Cross-channel Trade and Cultural Contacts: London and the Low Countries in the Later Fourteenth Century', in *England and the Low Countries in the Late Middle Ages* ed. by C. Barron and N. Saul (Stroud: Alan Sutton Publishing, 1995), pp. 151–168

Hare, J.N. 'Growth and Recession in the Fifteenth-Century Economy: The Wiltshire Textile Industry and the Countryside' *Econ. Hist. Rev.*, 2nd ser. 13 (1999), 1–26

Hatcher, John *Plague, Population and the English Economy, 1348–1530* (London: Macmillan, 1977)

Hatcher, John 'The Great Slump of the Mid-Fifteenth Century', in *Progress and Problems in Medieval England: Essays in Honour of Edward Miller* ed. by Richard Britnell and John Hatcher (Cambridge: Cambridge University Press, 1996), pp. 237–272

Hatcher, John and Mark Bailey *Modelling the Middle Ages: The History and Theory of England's Economic Development* (Oxford: Oxford University Press, 2001)

Hatcher, John and T.C. Barker *A History of British Pewter* (London: Longman for the Master Wardens and Commonalty of the Mystery of Pewterers of the City of London, 1974)

Hatcher, John, A.J. Piper and David Stone 'Monastic Mortality: Durham Priory, 1395–1529' *Econ. Hist. Rev.*, 2nd ser., 59 (2006), 667–87

Haward, Birkin 'Stained glass', in *Suffolk Churches* ed. by Jean Corke, John Blatchly, John Fitch and Norman Scarfe (Woodbridge: Suffolk Historic Churches Trust, 1977), pp. 68–71

Haward, Birkin *Suffolk Medieval Church Roof Carvings* (Ipswich: Suffolk Institute of Archaeology and History, 1999)

Haward, W. 'Gilbert Debenham: A Medieval Rascal in Real Life' *History*, n.s. 13 (1928–9), 300–14

Hilton, Rodney, 'Introduction', in *The Transition from Feudalism to Capitalism* ed. by Rodney Hilton (London: Verso, 1978), pp. 9–30

Hinde, Andrew *England's Population: A History since the Domesday Survey* (London: Hodder Arnold, 2003)

Hodges, Richard *The Anglo Saxon Achievement* (London: Gerald Duckworth, 1989) Homer, Ronald F. 'Tin, Lead and Pewter', in *English Medieval Industries* ed. by J. Blair and N. Ramsay (London: Hambledon Press, 1991), pp. 55–80

Hornsey, Ian S. *A History of Beer and Brewing* (Cambridge: The Royal Society of Chemistry, 2003)

Hoskins, W.G. *Local History in England* (Harlow: Longman, 1984)

Hutton, Ronald *The Rise and Fall of Merry England* (Oxford: Oxford University Press, 1994).

Hybel, Nils 'The Grain Trade in Northern Europe before 1350' *Econ. Hist. Rev.*, 2nd ser. 55 (2002), 219–47

James, Glyn 'Suffolk Pewterers' *PSIA*, 41 (2005), 63–78

James, Margery Kirkbride *Studies in the Medieval Wine Trade,* ed. by Elspeth M. Veale (Oxford: Clarendon Press, 1971)

Keene, Derek 'Changes in London's Economic Hinterland as Indicated by Debt Cases in the Court of Common Pleas' in *Trade, Urban Hinterlands and Market Integration* ed. by James A. Galloway (London: Centre for Metropolitan History, Institute of Historical Research, University of London, 2000), pp. 59–81

Kerling, Nelly Johanna Martina *Commercial Relations of Holland and Zeeland with England from the Late 13th Century to the Close of the Middle Ages* (Leiden: E.J. Brill, 1954)

Kermode, Jennifer 'The Greater Towns 1300–1540', in *The Cambridge Urban History of Britain: 600–1540* ed. by D.M. Palliser, 3 vols. (Cambridge: Cambridge University Press, 2000), I, pp. 441–465

Kirby, John *The Suffolk Traveller (1732–34)* (Woodbridge: Smith & Jarrold, 1800)

Kowaleski, Maryanne *Local Markets and Regional Trade in Medieval Exeter* (Cambridge: Cambridge University Press, 1995)

Kowaleski, Maryanne 'Port Towns: England and Wales 1300–1540', in *The Cambridge Urban History of Britain: 600–1540* ed. by D.M. Palliser, 3 vols. (Cambridge: Cambridge University Press, 2000), I, pp. 467–494

Kowaleski, Maryanne 'A Consumer Economy' in *A Social History of England 1200–1500* ed. by R. Horrox and W.M. Ormrod (Cambridge: Cambridge University Press, 2006), pp. 238–59

Kowaleski, Maryanne 'Warfare, Shipping and Crown Patronage', in *Money, Markets and Trade in Late Medieval Europe: Essays in Honour of John H. A. Munro* ed. by Lawrin Armstrong, Ivana Elbl and Martin M. Elbl (Leiden: Brill, 2007), pp. 233–54

Langdon, John *Mills in the Medieval Economy* (Oxford: Oxford University Press, 2004)

Le Patourel, H.E.J. 'Rural Buildings in England and Wales', in *The Agrarian History of England and Wales: 1348–1500* ed. by E. Miller, 8 vols. (Cambridge: Cambridge University Press, 1991), III, pp. 820–919

Lilley, Keith D. 'Decline or Decay? Urban Landscapes in Late-Medieval England', in *Towns in Decline AD 100–1600* ed. by T.R. Slater (Aldershot: Ashgate, 2000), pp. 233–265

Lloyd, T.H. *The English Wool Trade in the Middle Ages* (Cambridge: Cambridge University Press, 1977)

Lloyd, T.H. *England and the German Hanse 1157–1611* (Cambridge: Cambridge University Press, 1991)

MacCulloch, Diarmaid and John Blatchly 'Recent Discoveries at St Stephen's Church, Ipswich: The Wimbill Chancel and the Rush-Alvard Chapel' *PSIA*, 36 (1986), 101–114

Maddern, Philippa 'Order and Disorder', in *Medieval Norwich* ed. by Carole Rawcliffe and Richard Wilson (London: Hambledon, 2004), pp. 189–212

Malster, Robert *A History of Ipswich* (Chichester: Phillimore, 2000)

Marten, Lucy 'The Rebellion of 1075 and its Impact in East Anglia', in *Medieval East Anglia* ed. by Christopher Harper-Bill (Woodbridge: Boydell, 2005), pp. 168–182

Martin, Geoffrey 'Shipments of Wool from Ipswich to Calais' *The Journal of Transport History*, 2 (1956), 177–181

Martin, Geoffrey 'The Governance of Ipswich: From its Origins to c.1550', in *Ipswich Borough Archives 1255–1835* ed. by David Allen, (Woodbridge: Boydell for The Suffolk Records Society, 43, 2000), pp. xvii–xxix

Masschaele, James *Peasants, Merchants, and Markets* (Basingstoke: Macmillan, 1997)

Masschaele, James 'Toll and Trade in Medieval England', in *Money, Markets and Trade in Late Medieval Europe: Essays in Honour of John H. A. Munro* ed. by Lawrin Armstrong, Ivana Elbl and Martin M. Elbl (Leiden: Brill, 2007), pp. 146–183

Mate, Mavis 'Agrarian Economy after the Black Death: The Manors of Canterbury Cathedral Priory, 1348–91' *Econ. Hist. Rev.*, 2nd ser., 37 (1984), 341–54

Mate, Mavis E. *Trade and Economic Developments, 1450–1550; The Experience of Kent, Surrey and Sussex* (Woodbridge: Boydell, 2006)

Mate, Mavis E. 'Work and Leisure', in *A Social History of England 1200–1500* ed. by R. Horrox and W.M. Ormrod (Cambridge: Cambridge University Press, 2006), pp. 276–92

Matthias, P. *The First Industrial Nation: An Economic History of England* (London: Methuen, 1969; repr. 1983)

Mayhew, N.J. 'Coinage and Money in England, 1086–c.1500', in *Medieval Money Matters* ed. by Diana Wood (Oxford: Oxbow Books, 2004), pp. 72–86

Meier, Dirk (translated by A. McGeoch) *Seafarers, Merchants and Pirates in the Middle Ages* (Woodbridge: Boydell, 2006)

Moore, Nicholas J. 'Brick', in *English Medieval Industries* ed. by J. Blair and N. Ramsay (London: Hambledon Press, 1991), pp. 211–36

Munro, John H. 'Medieval Woollens: Textiles, Textile Technology and Industrial Organisation' and 'Medieval Woollens: The Western European Woollen Industries and their Struggle for International Markets', in *The Cambridge History of Western Textiles*, ed. by D. Jenkins, 2 vols. (Cambridge: Cambridge University Press, 2003), I, pp. 181–324

Munro, John 'Spanish Merino Wools and the *nouvelles draperies*: An Industrial Transformation in the Late Medieval Low Countries' *Econ. Hist. Rev.*, 2nd ser., 58 (2005), 431–84

Newman, J. 'Boss Hall' *Current Archaeology*, 130 (1992), 424–25

Nightingale, Pamela *A Medieval Mercantile Community: The Grocer's Company and the Politics and Trade of London 1000–1485* (London: Yale University Press, 1995)

Nightingale, Pamela 'Money and Credit in the Economy of Late Medieval England', in *Medieval Money Matters* ed. by Diana Wood (Oxford: Oxbow Books, 2004), pp. 51–71

Nightingale, Pamela 'Gold, Credit, and Mortality: Distinguishing Deflationary Pressures on the Late Medieval English Economy' *Econ. Hist. Rev.*, 2nd ser., 63 (2010), 1081–1104

Oppenheim, M. 'Maritime History' in *Victoria County History, Suffolk*, ed. by William Page, 2 volumes (London: Archibald Constable, 1907), II, pp. 199–246

Owles, Elizabeth 'The West Gate of Ipswich' *PSIA*, 32 (1971), 164–7

Palliser, D.M. *Tudor York* (Oxford: Oxford University Press, 1979)

Pankhurst, Charles 'The Brick Making Industry', in *An Historical Atlas of Suffolk* ed. by David

Dymond and Edward Martin (Ipswich: Suffolk County Council, 1988; repr. 1989 and 1999), pp. 146–7

Parker, Kate 'A Little Local Difficulty', in *Medieval East Anglia* ed. by Christopher Harper-Bill (Woodbridge: Boydell, 2005), pp. 115–29

Phythian-Adams, Charles *Desolation of a City: Coventry and the Urban Crisis of the Late Middle Ages* (Cambridge: Cambridge University Press, 1979)

Platt, Colin *Medieval Southampton: The Port and Trading Community, AD 1000–1600* (London: Routledge and Kegan Paul, 1973)

Pollard, A.J. *The Wars of the Roses* (Basingstoke: Palgrave, 2001)

Postan, Michael 'The Trade of Medieval Europe: The North', in *The Cambridge Economic History of Europe, Volume II, Trade and Industry in the Middle Ages* ed. by M. Postan and J. Habbakuk, 4 vols. (Cambridge: Cambridge University Press 1952), II, pp. 119–256

Postan, M. *Medieval Trade and Finance* (Cambridge; Cambridge University Press, 1973).

Powell, E. *A Suffolk Rising 1381* (Cambridge: Cambridge University Press, 1895)

Powell, E. 'The Taxation of Ipswich for the Welsh War in 1282' *PSIA*, 12 (1906), 137–57

Power, Eileen and M.M. Postan (eds) *Studies in English Trade in the Fifteenth Century* (London: Routledge, 1933)

Pryour, Francis *Britain in the Middle Ages – An Archaeological History* (London: Harper Collins, 2006)

Rackham, Oliver *The History of the Countryside* (London: Dent, 1986)

Ramsay, N. 'Introduction', in *English Medieval Industries* ed. by J. Blair and N. Ramsay (London: Hambledon Press, 1991), pp. xv–xxxiv

Rawcliffe, C. '"That Kindliness Should be Cherished More, and Discord Driven Out": the Settlement of Commercial Disputes by Arbitration in Later Medieval England', in *Enterprise and Individuals in Fifteenth-Century England* ed. Jennifer Kermode (Stroud: Sutton, 1991), pp. 99–117

Rawcliffe, C. and Richard Wilson (eds), *Medieval Norwich* (London: Hambledon Press, 2004)

Redstone, Lilian J. *Ipswich through the Ages* (Ipswich: East Anglian Magazine, 1948; repr., 1969)

Redstone, Vincent B. 'Early Suffolk Wills' *PSIA*, 15 (1918), 291–304.

Reynolds, Susan *An Introduction to the History of English Towns* (Oxford: Clarendon Press, 1977)

Richmond, C. *John Hopton: A Fifteenth-Century Suffolk Gentleman* (Cambridge: Cambridge University Press, 1981)

Richmond, Colin 'East Anglian Politics and Society in the Fifteenth Century: Reflections 1956–2003', in *Medieval East Anglia* ed. by Christopher Harper-Bill (Woodbridge: Boydell, 2005), pp. 183–208

Rigby, S.H. *Medieval Grimsby: Growth and Decline* (Hull: University of Hull Press, 1993)

Rigby, S.H. 'Introduction', in *A Social History of England 1200–1500* ed. by R. Horrox and W.M. Ormrod (Cambridge: Cambridge University Press, 2006), pp. 1–30

Rigby, Stephen H. 'Urban Population in Late Medieval England' *Econ. Hist. Rev.*, 2nd ser., 63 (2010), 391–417

Roskell, J.S., Linda Clark and Carole Rawcliffe (eds) *The History of Parliament: The House of Commons 1386–1421*, 4 vols. (Stroud: Sutton, 1992/3)

Salzmann, L.F. *English Industries of the Middle Ages* (London: Constable, 1913)

Scammell, G.V., 'English Mercantile Shipping at the End of the Middle Ages: Some East Coast Evidence' *Econ. Hist. Rev.*, 2nd ser., 36 (1961), 327–41

Scammell, G.V. 'Shipowning in England c. 1450–1550' *TRHS*, 5th ser., 12 (1962), 105–22

Scarfe, Norman 'Medieval and Later Markets', in *An Historical Atlas of Suffolk* ed. by David Dymond and Edward Martin (Ipswich: Suffolk County Council, 1988; repr. 1989 and 1999), pp. 76–7

Schofield, John and Geoffrey Stell 'The Built Environment 1300–1450', in *The Cambridge Urban History of Britain: 600–1540* ed. by D.M. Palliser, 3 vols. (Cambridge: Cambridge University Press, 2000), I, pp. 371–93

Sherlock, David *Suffolk Church Chests* (Stowmarket: Mike Durrant for the Suffolk Institute of Archaeology and History, 2008)
Spufford, Peter *Power and Profit: The Merchant in Medieval Europe* (London: Thames and Hudson, 2002)
Sutton, Anne F. *The Mercery of London: Trade, Goods and People, 1130–1578* (Aldershot: Ashgate Publishing, 2005)
Sutton, Anne F. 'London Mercers from Suffolk c.1200–1570: Benefactors, Pirates and Merchant Adventurers' *PSIA*, 42 (2009), 1–12
Swanson, Heather *Medieval Artisans* (Oxford: Basil Blackwell, 1989)
Tait, James *Medieval English Boroughs* (Manchester: Manchester University Press, 1936; repr. 1968)
Thrupp, Sylvia L. *The Merchant Class of Medieval London* (Chicago, 1948; repr. Ann Arbor: University of Michigan Press, 1962)
Unger, Richard W. 'Market Integration', in *Money, Markets and Trade in Late Medieval Europe: Essays in Honour of John H. A. Munro,* ed. by Lawrin Armstrong, Ivana Elbl and Martin M. Elbl (Leiden: Brill, 2007), pp. 349–80
Unwin, George 'Woollen Cloth – The Old Draperies' in *Victoria County History, Suffolk*, ed. by William Page, 2 volumes (London: Archibald Constable, 1907), II, pp. 254–66
Veale, Elspeth M. *The English Fur Trade in the Later Middle Ages* (Oxford: Oxford University Press, 1966; repr. London: London Record Society, 38, 2003)
Wade, Keith 'Anglo-Saxon and Medieval Ipswich', in *An Historical Atlas of Suffolk* ed. by David Dymond and Edward Martin (Ipswich: Suffolk County Council, 1988; repr. 1989 and 1999), pp. 158–9
Walton, Penelope 'Textiles', in *English Medieval Industries* ed. by J. Blair and N. Ramsay (London: Hambledon Press, 1991), pp. 319–54
Ward, Robin *The World of the Medieval Shipmaster: Law, Business and the Sea, c.1350–1450* (Woodbridge: Boydell, 2009)
Warner, Peter *The Origins of Suffolk* (Manchester: Manchester University Press, 1996)
Webb, John *Great Tooley of Ipswich: Portrait of an Early Tudor Merchant* (Ipswich: Cowdell, 1962)
Wedgewood, J.C. and A. Holt *History of Parliament 1439–1509 Register* (London: HMSO, 1938)
Weever, John *Antient Funeral Monuments* (London: Thomas Harper, 1631; repr. London: William Tooke, 1767)
Wilson, K. *Pykenham's Gatehouse, Ipswich* (Ipswich: The Ipswich Society for Ipswich Building Preservation Trust, 2006)
Wodderspoon, J. *Memorials of the Ancient Town of Ipswich* (Ipswich: Pawsey/Longman, Brown, Green and Longmans, 1850)

Unpublished papers and dissertations

Dunn, Penny 'After the Black Death: Society and Economy in Late Fourteenth-Century Norwich' (PhD thesis, University of East Anglia, 2003)
Martin, Geoffrey 'The Borough and the Merchant Community of Ipswich, 1317–1422' (DPhil. thesis, University of Oxford, 1955)
Saul, A. 'Great Yarmouth in the Fourteenth Century: A Study in Trade, Politics and Society' (DPhil. thesis, University of Oxford, 1975)

Index

Illustrations are indicated by bold type.